M000300609

John Mackenzie

JOHN MACKENZIE

SOUTH AFRICAN MISSIONARY AND STATESMAN. ❧ BY W. DOUGLAS MACKENZIE, M.A. PROFESSOR OF SYSTEMATIC THEOLOGY IN THE CHICAGO THEOLOGICAL SEMINARY ❧

NEGRO UNIVERSITIES PRESS
NEW YORK

Originally published in 1902
by A. C. Armstrong & Son, New York

Reprinted 1969 by
Negro Universities Press
A DIVISION OF GREENWOOD PUBLISHING CORP.
NEW YORK

SBN 8371-2443-3

PRINTED IN UNITED STATES OF AMERICA

To

THE DIRECTORS AND OFFICERS

OF THE

LONDON MISSIONARY SOCIETY

WHO SHOWED SO WISE A SYMPATHY
FOR HIM IN HIS MOST
BURDENED YEARS

THIS BIOGRAPHY

OF ONE WHO REGARDED THEM
WITH A MOST LOYAL LOVE

IS GRATEFULLY DEDICATED

PREFACE

MANY dangers confront the son who writes the biography of his father. It is easy to err in every direction, now by withholding what the reader ought to know if the biography is to be written at all, and again, by touching on aspects of character and life which the sensitive stranger shrinks from gazing upon too closely. In the following pages I have tried to be natural ; neither to hide nor to obtrude admiration for my father's character ; neither to suppress nor to defend sympathy with most of his political doctrines. Nor has it been thought best to avoid all reference to those tender and sacred sides of his personality, which it may be hard to describe fittingly, but without which no life, and therefore no life's record, can either have or convey any real grace and inspiration.

The task of compression has been found perplexing. Since the manuscript was completed many incidents and documents continue to thrust themselves forward, reproachfully asking why they were omitted. And no good reason can be given, except the general one, which appeases no particular complainant, that it had been resolved to make the biography brief at all costs. It would have been much easier to make it much longer.

A word or two must be said on the political side of

my father's lifework. He was drawn into it gradually, irresistibly, for the sake of his mission work. His was the kind of nature which cannot think of religion and religious work, except in relation to the whole round of human interests and activities. For such men, it is hard, nay impossible, to see the Kingdom of God suffering from the very forces which it ought to control, without loud protest and active resistance. It has been no pleasant task to study closely the records of my father's efforts to persuade the British Government, between the years 1882 and 1891, to adopt a South African policy which would have prevented the horrors of this great war. He failed, not for lack of earnest and powerful supporters of his policy throughout the country, but because the Government was persuaded to adopt a form of Imperialism which may not, for long years to come, be applicable in South Africa—however excellent its results may have been in Canada and Australasia.

The Confederation of South Africa is a dream which Lord Carnarvon tried to hurry in one direction, with disaster to Sir Bartle Frere. It is a dream which the Africander Bond has tried to hurry in another direction, with disaster to the two Republics. The difficulty of confederation in South Africa lies ultimately, not in the mere rivalry of the two European races, but in the existence of the great and ever growing native population. I believe that the deepest and wisest words on that difficulty and on the way to meet it are to be found in my father's writings ; and

I trust that readers of the biography may obtain enough light upon it to wish for more. Unhappy the Government that tries to solve the permanently portentous problem of South Africa, while treating the native aspect of that problem, incidentally or superficially ! It has always been and is very close to the heart of the whole matter, a responsibility that has already worked its own terrific revenges, a challenge to the nobleness of Great Britain that no mockery can ever silence.

It remains to record my gratitude to various kind helpers in this undertaking. My father's dear and long tried friends the Rev. James Ross of Glasgow, Mɪ Charles G. Oates of Meanwoodside, Leeds, and Mr Henry Beard of Cape Town, furnished me with letters from my father, and with valuable memoranda of their own. Principal A. W. W. Dale, of University College, Liverpool, sent a bundle of letters addressed to his father, the late Dr R. W. Dale of Birmingham, and Mr W. T. Stead let me have a number of equally important letters addressed to himself. The Right Honourable Lord Knutsford sent several letters of the year 1891, with an explanatory note of his own ; and Mr Arthur H. Loring who, with Mr H. O. Arnold Forster, worked most faithfully for the South African Committee, when that Committee laboured to promote my father's views, gave me useful information and some documents. Lieut.-General Sir Charles Warren, K.C.M.G., took much interest in the proposed memorial of his old friend and fellow-worker, but was prevented by his appointment to active service from carrying out his intention of rendering further aid. I have also to thank the Rev. R. Wardlaw Thompson, Foreign Secretary of the London Missionary Society, and the Directors, for permission to search the files of their South African Correspondence.

It is perhaps right to add that the appearance of this book has been delayed by two illnesses, which overtook the author at periods when he had expected comparative freedom from other duties.

Much and special gratitude is due to the Rev. James Ross of Glasgow, for undertaking the task of reading the proof sheets.   W. D. M.

CONTENTS

CHAPTER VI

CHAPTER VII

CHAPTER VIII

CHAPTER IX

CHAPTER X

CHAPTER XI

CONTENTS

CHAPTER XIX

CHAPTER XX

CHAPTER XXI

CHAPTER I

FROM KNOCKANDO TO BEDFORD (1835-1855)

IN the remote valley of Knockando, in Morayshire, a certain family of Mackenzies was to be found far from the true home of their clan in Ross-shire. Their presence there seems to have been accounted for by supposing that an unknown ancestor had found it necessary to flee into hiding after one of the several futile rebellions of the 18th century. Knockando is a bleak district lying behind a low range of hills on the left bank of the river Spey ; which used to be described in the school geographies as " the swiftest river in Scotland."

Throughout life this " solemn rolling Spey," as he called it, was ever mentioned by Mackenzie with a certain tenderness of personal affection. The scenery of the river valley for some miles up and down is peculiarly beautiful, and at several points, as at Craigellachie, it even reaches a certain grandeur. It is easy to see how the music of the rushing waters, the broad and deep pools where it flows in silent stretches under the gloom of overhanging crags, must have left indelible and romantic impressions upon the mind of a sensitive young Celt. Long years afterwards he wrote out of the desert heart of South Africa to his eldest son, who was about to spend a holiday season in Morayshire : " Tell me if you heard again the noise of the Spey ; the one solemn sound in the still and lovely summer evening. It is worth hearing ; and you will never need to try to remember it."

The soil of Knockando indeed is bare and ungenerous ; but its scattered little farms have been the homes of warm hearts. In one of these humble homes John Mackenzie, the youngest of six children, was born on August 30th, 1835 ; and there he lived till he was nine years of age.

The only record of his earliest years which he has preserved is brief and reads thus :—

"The first verse and prayer which my mother taught me was as follows :—

"This nicht whan I lie down tae sleep
I gie my soul tae Christ tae keep.
An' wauk' I noo, an' wauk' I never
I gie my soul tae Christ forever."

His parents were unable to give him more than the primary education of the parish school ; but circumstances made it possible for the little lad to be received into the Anderson Institution in the beautiful and ancient city of Elgin. Thither he went in his tenth year, making the whole journey of sixteen miles, which he was to repeat so often in the next few years, on foot. The Anderson Institution was founded and endowed by a General Anderson, whose life-story had been from beginning to end of strangely mingled pathos and brilliance. The purpose of the Institution was said to be "the support of old age and the education of youth." When John Mackenzie entered the school its head master was one John Eddie, a licentiate of the Church of Scotland, a man of some learning and a most kind heart ; of great patience and carefulness as a teacher. Intelligent pupils received a very thorough foundation under his tuition. His school did not aim at keeping children beyond the age, about thirteen or fourteen years, when they could become apprenticed to some trade ; but it followed them right through their apprenticeship with substantial aid and almost parental interest. For Mr Eddie, Mackenzie felt a life-long gratitude and affection, named his second son after him, and sought in various ways to maintain a friendly connection with him until he died in the year 1887, at the age of eighty-seven. And Mackenzie appears, on the other hand, to have excited the special interest of his master, who followed his career, even in the days of his apprenticeship, with an attentive sympathy.

On October 23rd, 1848, the young boy left the school which had become almost a home to him, and was apprenticed to Mr Alexander Russell, the proprietor and printer, editor and publisher of the local newspaper named *The Elgin Courant*. The " indenture " bound him to serve this master faithfully and diligently for seven long years, during which the master was bound " to teach him or cause him to be taught " every branch of the printing trade. The hours were irregular but seem to have averaged ten hours a day, and at times late work had to be done on the newspaper. Leisure could be therefore found for reading and study only by those who had strong inclinations in that direction.

Although so young, John Mackenzie had to live in lodgings, virtually master of his own time and habits at fourteen years of age! How significant and pathetic are the words which he wrote in his diary at a certain crisis when he was almost twenty years of age : " It is now ten years since I have asked parental advice. During that period, when not under the eye of a teacher or of an employer, I have been entirely my own adviser, and my own master. Instead of giving, both parents ask advice from me, so that I am not acting in any way undutifully towards my parents, but simply in that way which circumstances at first produced, which after events continued, which our different dispositions and feelings fostered, and which is now acted as duty by me, and expected by them." At first he appears to have lived the happy life of a boy, without great or strenuous self-exertion.   He was not particularly fond of reading, as yet, but threw himself heartily into boyish fun and games.   He used to recall in later years the fact that he played cricket on Elgin Green, the game which he liked most.   One remembers a scene in South Central Africa when some English travellers met at a mission station and a game at cricket was improvised out of primitive materials, and Mackenzie was one of the most eager and happy players.

For several years, as he afterwards stated at his ordination, he found himself surrounded by the thoughtless, the foolish, and the vicious, and his religious feelings were stifled.   He gave up going to church, never opened his Bible, and only read " silly or sinful publications."   His intellectual life was suddenly and effectually awakened by an incident which he owed to the influence of his younger fellow apprentice, James Ross (now the Rev. James Ross of Eglinton Street Congregational Church, Glasgow), the dear friend with whom he maintained affectionate correspondence for the rest of his life.   This friend had been led to join the Bishopmill Literary Association, which met in a hired room in the village of Bishopmill, across the river Lossie.   Mackenzie was amazed to see young men and younger lads, most of whom he knew, discussing a matter of intellectual interest with intense earnestness and freedom.   It was a new and fascinating world.   He himself became quickly absorbed in the subject of debate and in the arguments offered on each side ; so absorbed indeed that before the meeting closed he had found himself on his own feet and delivered his first public speech !

The rousing of the intellectual life led gradually to that religious quickening from which his whole character ever after drew its most distinctive qualities. Although brought up as a son of the Church of Scot-

land, Mackenzie was led, mainly by his intimacy with
James Ross, to attend what was called the Independent
Chapel, to which Ross's family belonged. The aged
minister, Rev. Niel M'Niel, was now unequal to pulpit
work, but took much interest in several branches of
pastoral duty. There came to preach one summer,
1853, a student from the Theological Academy of the
Congregational Churches of Scotland, by name Alexander Williamson, afterwards so widely known as a
missionary in China. This young man, tall and
powerful of build, forceful in manner and speech,
was aflame with religious zeal and, above all, with
enthusiasm for that missionary career to which he had
dedicated his life. He exercised upon Mackenzie an
influence of peculiar strength. In his personal jottings
in June, 1854, the latter says, " I could not tell the
exact time either of my conversion or of my first
desiring to become a minister." But he also says that
both events had happened, the one about a year and
the other more than a year before. This would
indicate that it was under the summer ministry of
Alexander Williamson that the full light broke upon
his young soul, and then that he made the inward
resolution, from which there was henceforth no swerv-
ing, to become a preacher of the gospel in the heathen
world.

Somewhere in this early period of his spiritual
history Mackenzie began to write a diary. The
earliest portion which has been preserved is not the
first. It is dated " 1854, May 19, Friday." The
heading is, " Jottings of My Life—Continued." With
some intermissions, this habit of writing almost daily
memoranda and meditations was maintained until the
first voyage to Cape Town was ended. These jottings
were entered almost always on little boardless booklets,
evidently made by the writer himself from sheets of
unruled paper, folded and stitched together. In them

the young man pours out his soul day by day with the utmost simplicity and with an earnestness amounting sometimes to real passion. If it be remembered that the extracts which are given from that diary were begun by a young lad yet in his 'teens, who had left school at thirteen to fight his life's battles without the shelter and comfort of home life, they will most probably strike every reader as indicating the possession of unusual powers, as well as of a full measure of that divine grace which we sometimes call religious genius.

On June 5th, 1854, he sat down for the first " communion season." It was the custom at Elgin, as, happily, in many Congregational Churches in Scotland, to celebrate the Lord's Supper every Sunday morning, at the close of the ordinary public service. Thus did he express the feelings which that solemn event stirred in his heart :—

June 4, 1854—*Morning.*—How sweet is the Sabbath morn, how calm, how placid, how solemn ! To the believer the Sabbath is a day of delight and holy pleasure. It is the Lord's day—that day on which Jesus burst the gates of the tomb and rose triumphant. It is the day on which the apostles and first believers came together to " break bread " —to do so in remembrance of Jesus. Oh, how pleasing the day and its associations and duties ! I look forward this day that I shall, by God's great mercy and grace, be enabled to observe this Lord's day as did the Christians of old. At the table of the Lord I, by His grace, will be a guest ; and, oh ! grant, Lord, that I may go there with, and while I am there may I feel, true love to Jesus ; and may the remembrance of His atonement, His death for me and for sinners everywhere, come to my soul at that table with peculiar force ! Oh, how sweet a thing is Christianity, with its trust in Jesus, its love to Him and to our fellow-Christians ! The world knoweth it not, and yet this happiness is but imperfect here, although it *shall* be perfect *yonder* !

Afternoon.—By the grace of God, I have been a guest at His table, and have done according to His commands and in remembrance of Him, and I don't think I ever felt so happy on earth. Oh, the *nearness* of such a place to God !

How solemn it therefore is! God is near us always, but in
the associations and circumstances of this holy ordinance our
weak faith is made sufficient to perceive and to discern Him
with greater vividness and clearness.   I will always, I think,
remember the peculiar feeling I possessed.   It was one of
rest, repose, and peace created by sweet *leaning* on Jesus.
Satan was busy, however, as he always is, to prevent me from
either enjoying or realising my position ; but grace prevailed,
and I was enabled to overcome, to a certain extent, at any
rate.

It is characteristic of Mackenzie's life-long interest
in organisation, in the way of doing things, that on
this very day he makes the following remarks upon
the conduct of a business meeting of the members of
the Church, which he that day attended for the first
time.

Both resolutions, after deliberation, were agreed to, and
the meeting was a harmonious one.   But I think I could
suggest improvements in the management of this Church,
instead of being so much benefited by surveying its working.
The Church has no secretary or clerk, and I am told their
business meetings are sometimes without a preses or chairman.   It was not so, however, in the meeting to-day.   I
have unshaken belief in the simplicity and the divinity of the
system, although its working here, as far as I have seen and
heard of it, has not gone altogether to foster this notion.

The daily " jottings " are at this earlier period much
occupied with the obstacles which seemed to lie between
him and the mission field.   The chief difficulty arose
from the determination which he had formed to go *at
once* to some school of training for the ministry.   In
order to do that he must obtain permission from
Alexander Russell, " my master " as he always calls
him, to break his apprenticeship.   And there lay the
occasion of many troubled days.   Further, his friends
were divided in their counsel as to whether he should
apply at once to the London Missionary Society and
attend their training school at Bedford, or first go
through the course of the " Glasgow Theological

Academy" (later known as the Congregational Theological Hall). Now, any form of advice which seemed to hasten his arrival on the mission field was for that very reason preferred by Mackenzie. The motto which he at this period chose for himself is referred to in a most interesting letter written to James Ross after he had begun his studies at Bedford.

For many months previous to my leaving the *Courant* office, my daily, almost *hourly*, breathing to God was, "Make my feet like hinds' feet : make me to walk in mine high places."[1]   The burden of this is, *compress*, as it were, mine experience : teach me *much* in a *short time* : and deliver me from, yea make me triumph over mine enemies.

It was in this spirit of intense eagerness that he entered into correspondence with the London Missionary Society, believing that if the Directors were to accept his application all other difficulties would speedily disappear.   At the same time he went on with his studies in his leisure hours, though he confesses several times that his correspondence and anxieties occasionally made Latin rudiments uncongenial and close study impossible.   Throughout the uncertainties of those months he kept his own counsel, pouring out his fullest confidences and the reflection of his daily thoughts and various emotions, in the pages of his diary—and, as those pages abundantly prove, in frequent and prolonged prayer.   Once a week he met several other young men at the house of a companion named James Mackintosh, who died two or three years later, for prayer : and his diary frequently refers gratefully to this intimate communion of friends. Once a week also he had a special season of private prayer for the spread of the kingdom of God, in which his daily pleadings were elaborated.

It was in June, 1854, that after considerable hesitation, caused by the divergent opinions of the friends

[1] Habakkuk iii. 19.

whom he consulted, Mackenzie applied directly to the London Missionary Society for appointment as one of its agents in the foreign field. Of course, it was understood that if they accepted him he would have to spend some time in preparative study. Unfortunately for his peace of mind no answer to his application was received until October 6th, and then it was declined. The reasons given by the Society's Directors was that he was too young, alike in years and as a member of the Christian Church : it was also felt that he must carry his education further ere he could be accepted. At the same time he was encouraged to renew his application nine or twelve months later. The disappointment was met with courage and unabated hope.

About this time Mackenzie, who had a good singing voice, received, after the usual public competition, the appointment of precentor at the Parish Church of New Spynie, on a salary of £5 per annum. From Dr Kyd, the minister, he received much kindness and encouragement. Long years after he used to recall with intense amusement the dread day of his trial singing, and how the friend who coached him got him into a field behind a hedge on their way to church for one more rehearsal. The following paragraph occurs in a letter to his boys written more than twenty years afterwards :—

The five pounds per annum which I earned as precentor of New Spynie Parish Church were of very great service to me at that particular time of my life. My income was on one occasion almost too much for me; I shall explain how. Dr Kyd and I had always a grand counting of the pennies and bawbees which were put into the *brod*, and out of which my salary was paid, whenever the happy day came round for me to receive my money. This was scene the first. The second is a moving one, in which you behold the youthful precentor toiling along through the beautiful fir-wood, and through Bishopmill too, and up the Lossie Wynd, sadly oppressed

with his burden of bawbees and pennies, which the laddie
carried in a handkerchief twisted at the corners.   Frequently
changing hands he reached Winchester, the grocer's, where
he very readily got "small change" for his copper.   But on
one occasion the second scene was not the last.   He had
rounded the corner into High Street, had descended the one
step into Winchester's shop, when the material of the handkerchief could hold out, or rather hold in, no longer, and
away went the offerings of the decent people of New Spynie
all over the grocer's shop floor!   It was inside and not outside the shop—which made a great difference in Elgin, and
no doubt would do so anywhere.

The following extracts from his Diary for the
month of September, 1854, while he was waiting for
the answer of the Directors, will probably do much to
reveal the spirit of this young man, as he tried to
walk with God.

Sept. 6.—O that I were removed from my present *secular*
and, in my circumstances, useless employment, and employed
busily in the preparations necessary to my carrying the
Gospel far, far away to those who have never heard it.

Sept. 7.—But let me *wait*—yes, *wait*, for God will surely
help me as I need! How cheering the thought! How
faithless my heart!

Sept. 9.—I promised to Mr Kyd last Sabbath to drink
tea with him this afternoon in Quarrywood.   I hope to
enjoy, at all events, much pleasure from the natural
scenes with which I will be surrounded on this lovely
afternoon.

I would here note my present state of mind.   The *war*
is going on incessantly; only God is gracious and aids me
and upholds me.   I have an increasing desire to work for
God, and I am only happy at present in the office from the
prospect of my soon leaving it.   My faith in God is sometimes such as to give me joy even when surrounded by
difficulties; but I distrust Him much—I confess I do—
although nothing is more ungrateful.   I am, I humbly trust,
advancing heavenward; following on to know the Lord;
although I am not at all what I ought to be.   Oh, no! I
have not attained to anything at which I can sit down and
content myself.   Perfection—that is the goal; eternity is its

period of enjoyment ; *life* is the period of trial—of struggles. But the goal, the goal is at the end ; and by God's help I am confident I shall reach it.

Sept. 11.—I got confused a little when visiting a prominent citizen on business ; I cannot meet such a one.   What must I do to get more *brass* in my face ?

Sept. 11, *Monday.*—I am more and more convinced that *pride* is a scrambling weed within me and that God is wisely chastising me by *maiming* me in my love of applause and distinction.   O that I may be enabled to pray very earnestly against this most heinous of sins !

Sept. 12.—O that I may grow in every Christian grace. I am now convinced that I am very vain and proud ; and I want with God's help to crucify these remaining weeds. I pray for *lowliness* of heart, to be made, in short, like my blessed Saviour.   O, who was ever like Him !

Sept. 13.—I continue to pray in an especial manner for humility ; and I indeed find that I have very much need. How deceitful is my own heart !   I have just lighted, as it were, on a nook containing contraband goods—which had no right to be there, but which I in my blindness overlooked. The heart is indeed deceitful above all things.   O may the Holy Spirit aid and help me to continue to carry on a successful warfare with everything that defileth the heart— every evil which may be lurking unperceived.   How silly and vain is this feeling which is so strong within me.   Sometimes I am tempted thus by Satan : " Now look at so and so. He is a Christian like you and yet every one knows he is prouder and vainer than you are.   You are good enough. Take it easy.   See what a fearful amount of labour you will have before you overcome these propensities.   Be contented with your position.   You are better than many and as good as a great number of Christians.   Don't bestir yourself. Just look at that high difficult mountain.   When would you reach its summit ?   You are best where you are."   So whispers the Devil ; but God be glorified and praised, I can say, " Get thee behind me, Satan."   I am not striving to be like *other men*.   Man is not the model or pattern which I am striving to imitate—guilty fallen man.   No ; I look to a perfect model.   I take a pattern from perfection.   I must therefore reach forward and not look on what I may have attained, but daily strive to become more and more *like Jesus*.   I trust I shall continue more and more to per-

ceive and realize the true beauty and blessedness of that
character which Jesus possessed, and still possesses.

Sept. 16.—Passed the afternoon with my father, and afterwards began to read the report of the L. M. S., which really
gave delight to my heart. Think of sixty native young men
in one of the South Sea Islands, in course of being trained as
ministers of the Gospel. Glory be to God! O the future!
the future! when the earth shall be full of the knowledge of
the Lord.

Held my weekly prayer in the midst of a clump of trees
to-night in darkness and solitude. I had some freedom and
some sense of the presence of God.

Sept. 17, *Sunday.*—At the communion table to-day I felt
more overcome than ever before. What a glorious feeling!
Dear Jesus! He was not there hidden as He often is to my
darkened mind. Heaven seemed very near, life very short;
and to spend my life as a missionary of the Gospel appeared
a glorious work indeed. O, I felt eager to engage in it!
Surely God, when He thinks proper, will open a door for
me.

Sept. 19.—Felt some strange doubts sweep into my mind
this afternoon. I cannot account for their coming, nor for
their strength, but I know they are of such a nature as to
undermine the whole matter of religion altogether in my soul.
They strike at the very root.

But when I think of the matter, I am led to wonder why
I would trifle with such things. Religion subject to a
doubt? Get thee behind me, Satan. Thou alone couldst
say so. Away with all doubt. I cannot look on religion in
any way but it convinces me of its truth. I would as soon
deny my own existence as deny the truth of religion. God
help this darkened, blinded, stumbling, but trusting and
confiding soul! For Jesus' sake!

The immortality of the soul is what the tempter would
have me discredit, and of course denying it I deny all
religion. God forbid!

Sept. 20.—Before retiring to rest last night I had a sweet
outpouring of my soul to God in prayer. I felt as if I could
suffer all things to be taken away if God Himself remain. I
felt that He was the only Being in the universe whom I
could depend upon, love or seek after; and in the language
of the Psalmist I cried, "Whom have I in heaven but Thee,
and there is none in all the earth that my soul desireth

beside Thee." Then indeed did God seem precious and
to be all in all, *sine qua non*, in the estimation of my
soul.

This morning I find my mind is at comparative rest; and
I enjoy this rest more when I shut my eyes to *everything*
and let my soul commune with God. 'Tis then I know
there must be a God, and if a God then the God of the
Bible; and if a God of the Bible—then the Bible with all
its doctrines is the Word of God.

I read a paper on "The Past and Present of Christianity,"
the leading idea in which is that arguing on plain fact, there
is nothing clearer than that the religion of Jesus of Nazareth
will soon become the religion of the world—excluding for
the time the question whether or not it is divine or true.

I have been reading the report of the L. M. S. and considering what country I would like to go to. I would prefer
India, China, or Africa to all others. Wide, glorious, fields
there. O that I were there; speaking to them the saving
truths of the Gospel in the people's language. O God!—Do
not delay my beginning to devote myself entirely to preparation for Thy own work.

Sabbath, 24th Sept.—I repeated my address [an address
intended for a Sunday evening meeting] this morning in
about twenty-five minutes, and I am pleased with it. I
think it will do. I hope God will bless me and give me
much of His Spirit, so that I may preach boldly and also
simply, clearly, truthfully, meekly from the heart. Preaching is a gift. I pray God earnestly for it. . . . Spoke to
Mr M'Laren, Treasurer to the Congregational Union, who
was in town and sat down with the church at the Lord's
Table to-day.

Sunday, 30th September.—In the afternoon I was singularly dealt with. My confusion and reddening of face
came on me: and I became miserable, for I know it was
my own desperate wicked heart that was to blame. After I
came home I found liberty to pray earnestly to God against
pride and vain glory.

Friday, 6th October.—This morning I read the decisive
answer by the Directors of the L. M. S. on my application.
I am rejected. I am too young—have not been long
enough member of a church—and it would be too expensive to educate me at the Society's expense. These are
their *reasons* for not accepting me. . . . After reading this

letter I found my way to God's Throne and then poured out
my thanks to Him as the God of Providence for giving me
this new token that He is looking over my affairs and guiding
my footsteps.   I shall call on Messrs M'Niel and Guthrie in
the evening or through the day.   I have to work at two
o'clock.   How many feelings crowd upon me !   Pride rises
at the disappointment : but I trust God will enable me in
humility and true meekness to conduct myself.

October 29.—From this Sabbath forward I will, O God
—trusting in Thee—struggle and cry like one drowning,
and I will hold on to the anchor of safety, even Jesus ; and
I will give Thee no rest until Thou hast blessed me with
Thine own blessing, O God, imperfect guilty wretch that I
am.   I love Thee ; I delight in Thee ; I long for Thy fellowship more and more.   Fan the flame O God of Hosts, and
fit me for a residence in heaven.

Thursday, 2d November.—I am rather afraid there is
something going on decidedly evil with respect to my health.
I am afraid of colds and consumption.

The ensuing winter proved to be a very trying one.
The intense energy of the young man, his absorption
in the pursuit of the spiritual life, and his unsated
yearning to be definitely at work in the Master's ex-
clusive service, told upon his health.   When spring
time came he had good reason to be anxious about
his cough and his sense of weakness.   His state of
perplexity and his spiritual struggles led him to draw
up several papers dealing with his religious life and
character.   The longest of these, as it reveals the
depth of his religious convictions and contains one or
two passages of intense pathos, should be read here in
full.   It is entitled :—

A Solemn Covenant and Confession, made on account
of a recent temptation and in view of my present critical
circumstances.   Dated February 16, 1855.

My Father and God,—In the name of Jesus I approach
Thy throne, adoring Thy glorious Majesty and supreme
dominion.   I am the clay ; Thou art the Potter ; what I
am, I am through Thy favour and help alone.   I joy most
of all that I can behold in Thee a Friend, in whom I once

only saw an angry judge; and that I can address Thee in the language of a child of Thine, and call Thee *Father*. I thank Thee for the infinitely lovely scheme of redemption— for my interest in it and for all the precious solacing promises, counsels, and warnings given in Thy Revealed Will. At this time, it is my desire reverently to seek Thy presence and throne of grace that I may pour out my whole heart in Thy sight — lay all my griefs before Thee, and make my supplications and prayers known unto Thee. I desire to do so in a solemn, godly, confiding spirit; that so my soul may be strengthened and mine eyes opened and my steps directed and confirmed by Thee, in my present circumstances.

O Lord, Thou knowest that my heart is vile, corrupt, and bespotted with the impurities of corruption. Thou hast seen how it has gone awhoring after what is not allowable; how it has caused me to sin even in Thine own courts; how my heart has been alienated from Thee, and drawn away after the desires of the flesh and of the eye. Satan, to hinder my prayers, has wounded me—caused me to stumble; but oh, I thank Thee I have not fallen. Though with a divided heart, still, Lord, Thou knowest how I struggled. Hear, O God, my confession of sin; listen when I seek Thy pardoning mercy; grant me Thy Spirit's healing, restoring, reviving influences. May I see where my hope is. May I have always before me where my weakness lies; and may I watch and pray that I enter not into temptation. Lord, save me from my carnal heart; O free me from seeking greedily the applause of men; deliver me, I implore Thee, from mingling the things of sense and worldly beauty with Thy service and sanctuary and its spiritual, undivided heart- worship. I confess my bent to fall into such sins; and Lord, I know that Thou alone canst help me. Therefore, O Lord, I call upon Thee to save me from my besetting sins— especially as Thou hast set before me the prospect of taking the leading part in the services of Thy House on a portion of Thy Holy day. O may I have then, and at all times, a single eye to Thy glory; may time sink to its true position, and Eternity assume its place in my mind's eye; may I have Jesus' spirit inwrought in my heart; may I breathe the breath of heavenly benevolence over my fellow-creatures; may I wrestle mightily for their souls, in public and in private; and may I have eloquence to persuade and entice them to follow Thee, and leave the unsatisfying employments of time and of this world.

O my God, I desire also to remember before Thee my position. Since Thou knowest the inmost workings of my heart, I can confidently appeal to Thee. Every day, Lord, from Monday morning till Friday, I am engaged as a printer. I cannot then think on Thee, or if I do I cannot think on my work ; I cannot learn languages, or study sermons, or meditate on Thy Word in order to work Thy work ; no, I am tied to the earth. Then I have on an average seven hours work after publication, when Thy Sabbath steals upon me in all its loveliness. Father, while I admire Thine infinite wisdom and providential foresight, I joy and glory in Thee when I remember that Thou art pleased to call some not only to repentance and faith, but also to the holy work of the service of the Gospel. Father, I feel in my heart that I am called by Thee for this service ; all Thy dealings with my soul testify to this ; and above all Thou hast been pleased, most gracious Lord, even in my present situation, to allow me to conduct the public worship of Thy sanctuary, and on various occasions publicly to proclaim Thy great Salvation. Seeing that Thou, most blessed Father, hast been so leading me and honouring me with regard to the work of the ministry, I come with trembling boldness and request Thee to separate me to the work. Give me over to the Saviour ; liberate me from worldly engagements ; grant that my time may be the property of Jesus ; and that henceforth my whole life may be spent in His service. Father, I have much to learn, in language and other knowledge, before I could take upon me Thy work and its mighty responsibility ; and alas ! Thou knowest how very little I am able to do in this way in my present situation. O take me away, then, dear Father. O let those who have no higher aspirations—alas that there should be such !—occupy my present worldly situation, and give me, O give me, to Thy work and Thy ministry all my lifetime. Thou knowest my heart and Thou knowest all things. My God, I *complain* to Thee because I am so far away from the true end and object of my being. My heart is far away ; my calling is far away ; verily, O God, I am at a distance from Thee. But O, draw Thou near to me, and give me power to draw near to Thee both in heart and in occupation ; and as the work of the ministry is the nearest to Thee that I could engage in, I desire that my heart and my time, my intellect, my all, may be given to Thee, that so I may be united and become in some measure like to those holy beings who never feel a distracting thought, and are never at a distance from Thee, but are always serving Thee and doing Thy will. O God, come and rescue me. Come, I plead—I beseech—and make no tarrying. Father, I ask that Thou wouldst place me where I will be *all*, time, heart, talent, *all* the property of my dear Jesus. O, is He not worthy? And though my sins may be as mountains, O can they endure before the purifying influences of Jesus' glorious and all efficacious atonement? Is not Thy Spirit able to work in me, both to will and to do of Thy good pleasure? Is He not able to give me the Spirit of the holy calling to which I aspire? And hast Thou not said that those who seek Thee early shall find Thee? My God! my God! I appeal to Thee. O, for the sake of Jesus, who is infinitely worthy—for the sake of the world, which is the object of Thy boundless pity, and for Thy Name's sake and Thy glory's sake—form this heart of mine into conformity to Thy will, and separate me to the work of the service of Thy Gospel. Do not delay—make no tarrying — come and do unto me above my request.

O guide my steps, Lord ; O take me to Thyself ; O permit me not to go astray or aside, but to go right onwards unto perfection. Bless this day's exercises ; bless this writing ; O God, may my soul be strengthened mightily with strength from on high, and may every day of my life and every hour here be given to Thee, and every volition of my will and every affection of my heart.

And unto Thee, the King eternal, immortal, and invisible, the only wise God, be all the glory now, henceforth, and evermore. Amen.

In March there comes a paper entitled " A Prayer while in a Dilemma," to which are added observations on the same subject for the week following. It was a small incident which had aroused his conscience and his liveliest emotions, because it seemed to have a bearing on his release from the printer's desk. But that is followed by a " Resolution, dated May 2, 1855," which shows very clearly that his unnatural state of

excitement had brought on and was now aggravated
by serious ill-health.

Resolution, dated May 2, 1855.

Seeing I have been for some time suffering from a
nervous complaint or disorder, which prevents my preserving equanimity or calmness of mind, especially when exposed
to the observation of others, and which also produces effects
on my external frame quite out of keeping with that mild
and dignified serenity which ought to characterise a child of
God, I resolve, for the glory of God and the honour of my
Saviour's name, to take such steps as are most likely to
succeed in overcoming this seated weakness in my constitution. For this purpose I note the underneath resolves, which
are all embodied in the one idea—to be like Christ :—

1. Labour to preserve *calmness* in all places and on all
occasions—in imitation of my Saviour.

2. Avoid being angry. Where there is cause for displea.
sure, preserve mildness and composure.

3. In my manner, seek after *true politeness*, and banish
all clownish *awkwardness*, which of itself produces confusion
of mind. No ostentation.

4. As it is *an idea* which causes the disorder in my system,
harbour it as little as possible. Leave myself in my thoughts.
Ask not what I shall eat, etc., or how I shall ever progress.
Is He not able? Am I not His? If I seek Him with my
whole heart—if I pour out the plaint of a downcast, sobbing,
sighing soul—O will not JESUS hear it? Will He not lead
me on? Are my talents—is my whole life on earth—to be
lost for good because of *one idea* lodging in my mind? When
encouraged to seek the Lord's work and the Lord's glory, is
it my duty to sit down and *cherish* an *idea* that I shall never
be enabled to do anything in that work to which God is
calling me and fitting me? Ought I not to banish that idea?
Ought I not to lean upon God in confidence of soul? If I
had *full confidence* I would have the victory. O it is hard—
and yet it is pleasant—it is painfully sweet to be afflicted !

But I pray God that, at all events, His glory may be
wrought out in me and by me—according to His own good
will and pleasure—that *my feet may be made like hinds' feet.*

5. I may add to my *resolutions* to take and grasp in my
mind *the truth* about all things. Treat God as God, Jesus
as my own Jesus, distinguished men with becoming respect,

but with no sheepish dread.   Treat men as men, always with
respect as possessors of souls that shall last for ever ; never
with disdain or pride.

6. On all occasions do my utmost for Jesus Christ,
depending on His aid and support.

Very shortly after this Mackenzie was allowed, on
the ground of ill-health, to leave the printer's office.
He went to his native air of Knockando, where he
engaged in study and found opportunities for preaching.   Into both he threw his energies very heartily.
His diary, as well as his letters to James Ross, reflect
the zest and zeal with which he prepared and delivered
his earnest gospel addresses.   Health returned steadily
though slowly, as he walked over that portion of
Strathspey, musing and praying, visiting and preaching.
All this time his mind was fixed on his high aspirations and the career he longed for.   He enjoyed many
" trances of thought and mountings of the mind."

As he now believed that he was finally cut off from
his Elgin life, and would soon be permanently removed
from his former associations, a strong desire took hold
of him to address the young men of that royal burgh,
to deliver one last, earnest message in the name of his
Master.   He knew the risks, but determined to face
them.   His friends, not without trepidation, helped
him, James Ross rendering special aid as to the
advertising of the event.   The Independent Chapel
was lent for the occasion on Sunday evening, September 2nd.   Mr Ross still remembers the scene, and
his memory tallies wonderfully with the " Jottings "
which Mackenzie made at the time.   " What crowds !
Passages, vestry, stairs, even the lane near the door,
were occupied, and many went away."   " An old man
remarked regarding the attendance of young men,
that he did not believe there were so many in Elgin."
The young preacher delivering his soul to his compeers
was nervous and excited ; but he had chosen for his

address that theme of which his own heart was ever
full—"Christ is all and in all" (Col. iii. 11)—and
his intense passion made its own impression on his
audience.

In the previous July Mackenzie had renewed his
application to the London Missionary Society, and
it so happened that three days after the delivery of
this farewell address to the young men of Elgin he
received a letter summoning him to London to meet
with the Committee of the Directors on September
10th. After a forty minutes' examination before
the venerable directors and officials the young candidate, to his overflowing delight, was informed that
he had been accepted "on probation," and would be
now sent to the Society's Seminary at Bedford to
undergo what training and education might be found
necessary to fit him for active service in the mission
field. It was characteristic of his whole spirit at
this period that during the few days of sight-seeing
which he could spend in London he found time to
look up one or two young men from the North,
whom he wished to bring to the faith of Christ.

CHAPTER II

THE London Missionary Society had some difficulty in its earliest years with regard to the education of its missionaries. While some came before the Directors whose education for the ministry was complete, many, if not most, of the candidates were young men whose advantages had been limited, and who needed assistance to obtain an adequate training. To meet this need the Society from time to time established Seminaries at various places, generally under the care of some minister whose scholarship and fervour fitted him to do the best for the young men. One of these seminaries was for a long while conducted by the Rev. J. Jukes, Congregational minister at Bedford, who had as his colleague-instructor, the Rev. W. Alliott. The students, whose numbers varied between three or four and eight or ten, usually boarded with Mr Jukes. They worked at New Testament Greek, a little Hebrew, Christian Evidences and Systematic Theology, Logic and Mathematics. Much attention was given to the writing and delivery of sermons. The students were also sent out every Sunday to preach in the neighbouring villages, and were encouraged and expected to engage in other forms of Christian work.

Here, then, Mackenzie lived and studied, prayed and preached from September 1855 till December 1857. At the latter date he went to Edinburgh for some months of further study in medicine and theology. His Diary bears constant witness to the eager joy with which he cast himself into the task

of direct and rapid preparation for his life's calling.
Perplexities and difficulties were by no means all at
once dispersed. He was on "probation" for a full
year, and he found that the course even of a theological student can present its own peculiar obstacles,
temptations, and sorrows. One fact, however, stands
out above all others in the written mirror of his daily
life, that, in spite of the rush of work which came
upon him, in spite of domestic distractions, he steadily
and almost invariably gave much time every day to
intense and humble prayer. For Mackenzie, it might
be said that, to pray was to live. The experiences
of his soul in prayer were as fascinating, varied, and
momentous, as any events in his outward life. He
records often and often that his prayer-hour was
free or restrained, that he wrestled or was calm
and restful, that God was near and His voice clear,
or far off and unattainable, that he "overcame God"
and won an answer from Him, or rose unsatisfied,
but determined to trust, and trust forever.

It may be said here once for all, that this full life
of prayer was maintained by Mackenzie to the end.
Though he did not continue to record his experiences
in a diary, and was ever reticent about his personal
life, it was known in his home that he prayed about
everything. Intercessory prayer was always a most
real and sacred obligation and joy to him ; and what
may be called consultative prayer, in which he went
over his duties and practical problems before God,
seeking light and the assurance of his Master's
approval, was as necessary to him as food and drink.
The present writer remembers as a boy coming into
his father's room and finding him leaning on the post
of his bed. When he raised his head a deep red
mark on the forehead made by the pressure of the
knuckles of his hand, and the dimmed look of his
eyes, bespoke at once the length and intensity of his

prayer.   When childishly asked what was the matter, he said he had been praying about some point connected with his book, his first book, on which he was at the time busily engaged.   It may be confidently said that he never entered upon any important undertaking without real consultative prayer.   On the other hand, the extent to which he believed in the power of the prayers of others for him was often revealed in his letters urging his correspondents to pray.   As a young man he wrote to James Ross to say, " Do not forget me, Jamie, you yourself know where.   At work you may forget me ; but oh ! ' mind' me *there !*"

Among the students who were at Bedford in 1855 there may be named two for whom Mackenzie retained a permanent affection.   One of these was James Duthie, afterwards a well-known missionary in South India.   Of him he writes to James Ross saying, " We made ourselves brothers, although he belongs to Aberdeen."   The other was Arthur Hall, brother of the already famous Rev. Newman Hall, who was preparing for his entrance upon the full course of study at New College, London, and who became an honoured Congregational minister.   In the person of a third student, who was a Eurasian, and with whom he was thrown into close and very friendly association, the young Scottish student was brought face to face with that problem of the mixture of races which in after years put him into many a perplexing situation, and gave him food for endless, painful, and inconclusive reflection.   He came on one occasion unexpectedly upon this fellow-student, and found him absorbed in a kind of agony over the life-long bitterness of his lot, looking at his hands, apostrophising them, and asking his Maker why this colour, which made him the scorn and dislike of so many, had been bestowed upon him.   Mackenzie never forgot that scene ; it made him, when mixed marriages were proposed or discussed, think always and first not of those who in choosing each other deliberately chose their social lot, but of the children who would inherit it with its burdens and sorrows.

His evangelic zeal was so real and sincere that he did not allow the pursuit of his studies or even the discharge of mission duties at Bedford to absolve him from similar responsibilities elsewhere. During this winter he corresponded with former Elgin friends, and with his own family relatives regarding their spiritual interests. About one friend he writes in his diary, "Oh! how I long for that young man's conversion. It is my *constant* prayer to God, that mercy may be extended to him." The following extracts from the diary and other personal memoranda of the year 1855-6 will throw light upon the strenuous life of this young missionary student in his twenty-first year :—

Saturday, Nov. 3, 1855.—In spiritual things, I have received this idea very powerfully into my mind—that all my afflictions, distresses and alarms, are the produce of sin within me. If I weep because of heavy afflictions or dis-quietude—sin has procured it for me—yea, *mine own sin.* Let me remember this : I never felt it so deeply before. If I weep at all let it be, not because of the heavy affliction or distress, but let me turn to the producing cause and weep over my sins with a penitent heart, and let my prayer be, not principally as before, that God would remove His afflictive hand and give me health and soundness—but that he would be pleased to qualify me for the receipt of that blessing—that He would sanctify my heart so as to take away the strength from the sin which is there indwelling—and having done so, extend me the blessings I have so long pleaded for. O may I be taught of God ! O may He be ever very near me ! I have had some seasons of deeply earnest prayer—may they be multiplied in strength and number !

Thursday, Nov. 8.—To-night I had a season of prayer such as I have not enjoyed on any previous occasion, both as regards intensity of feeling and the enlightenment which pervaded my mind. I was alone in my study : my light I had extinguished : the flickering of some fire from the grate cast a dim light over the room. I communed with God—felt His presence — spoke to Him — wrestled with Him—for about an hour. I went to bed a happy, victorious man : there was a smile on my lips and calmness in my countenance ; and oh my heart was full—glowing with emotion : for I lay down that night with the *assurance* that I would be specially honoured—specially favoured—specially endowed by God ; and that my life would be made *more* than even I could imagine. I felt the calmness which follows assurance ; and I shall consider this night one of the great eras of my life.

Sunday, 11 *Nov.*—Preached in the evening at Cardington. Tea at Mr Bodgers'. Thank God for my present state and feelings and ideas ; but I am not at all *what I shall be*. I preached more rousingly than I have yet done in England. And, strange to say, it was almost extempore ; although I had notes, somehow I did not stick to them. I must guard against this. It encourages *looseness* in preaching.

Saturday, 16*th Nov.*—To-night I have devoted my time after supper for meditation and reflection on my state before God ; and I shall begin by *noting* my past week's history, at least what bears on the matter before me. As a whole the past week has been one of considerable spiritual earnestness : prayers for progress—for a special outpouring of God's Spirit—for strength to advance and make life henceforth a great and noble thing—have been daily uttered. I have also had much sweet communion with my God : and having been engaged during a part of most of the days of the week in writing on " The Prodigal's Resolution," I felt my mind much benefited thereby, and my spirit led out to regard my God as a merciful Father. I am much afraid, however, of spiritual pride or rather—a desire for the applause of men. This is a most disgusting feature in my character. Let me come forth from it entirely ; and regard no expressions of applause as to me, but to the grace of God in me. Let men say of me what they will—I will come to my dear Jesus and say, " It is all Thine." I am studying in the same room with a lad who is rather rude in his manners, and I would wish his influence were removed ; for one cannot help being to some extent thus affected by association. One thought has come prominently into my mind this week : it has been its lesson, its leading idea, viz.: that association with God and deep meditation—holy communion and earnest prayer—are the only means which will effectually develop a noble mind—a great spirit within me. At the same time it is of the utmost importance that the other associations of my mind be of a healthy description. I must say that I feel a great want here—for although all the young men here are excellent persons yet their company has not that effect which I could wish: their conversation is not what I would desire. I yearn to read (since I can't *speak* with such) the thought and lives of the truly great. May the Lord guide me! I must keep hold of this idea: it is of great importance. For I must not stand still: no, by every means I must go forward. I shall see if I can't get some biography for half an hour each day. And I shall take up one of the Apostles, follow out all that is recorded of him, and endeavour to follow him as he followed Christ, and derive also suitable lessons from his whole life.

Mr Jukes has passed high encomiums upon me; and to-day he praised very much my sermon on the Prodigal Son. O if I deserved this praise! O if I strained every *nerve* for Christ! I must do this. I will do it in the strength of the Lord.

Have obtained much consolation and strength and encouragement from the thought that the Lord will help the *resolved* man. I have resolved to rise. But now I must record somewhat regarding my habits as a student during the past week. They have been very irregular—not what they must be. Everything except Greek had to be thrown aside to complete my sermon, and after all I had barely time for it. I have not had more than 7 hours sleep, nor less than 6 during past week. I am really quite lazy: it requires effort to rise on a freezing morning while your companion is soundly sleeping. I have a watch now—a very fine one; and I must be regular in this matter now. Next week I shall always be in bed by 11 and up at 5—for a trial. I shall encourage meditation and soul communion with God in the house and by the way, so I shall be moulded. I have done nothing besides Greek this week, and that sermon. It was too long.

In health I am improving. But palpitation at the heart has not abated. It is not troublesome, however—although I do wish it were away. I think I may record increased strength of nerve and energy in public.

Wednesday, 20th Nov.—My *breath* is towards heaven. My heart yearns, longs for the mighty God, my deliverer. But I am *sure* of one thing—that as the power of the living God is unquestionable with me I must prevail.   But, oh, it is speed I long for !   *Now* I would arise.   And alas ! alas ! I feel all wrong.   I will look to God for the blessing *now*.   I feel crushed at the thought of life.   Great God ! in mercy visit a poor worm and lift him up and enable him to carry out the resolutions which I am persuaded are begotten within me by Thy good Spirit.   I feel certain I am on the right track : what a mercy !   If I do not succeed, by the grace of God I will die with the wish.

Saturday, 24th Nov.—On a retrospective view of the past week, I have much cause for thankfulness, principally because I am still kept in an earnest praying frame.   I have, as it were, assaulted the Divine throne, and I do believe God will do great things for me.   I feel more resolute.   But, oh, how easily I am cast down !   Prayer, however, as I trust, will conquer.

Prayer becomes sweeter and more pleasant and also *nobler* than formerly.   I am enabled to realize the Divine Presence more and Jesus never appeared so lovely—so dear to my soul—as He does now.   I love Him and He loves me. *Who shall separate us ?*   And if He wills me to rise and do His will, and if I will the same, who can thwart the glorious movement ?

I resolved and vowed before God (in dependence entirely on His grace) to be resolute and decided in the path of duty ; to crucify every habit which stands in the way of my developing my character and working my work ; to exert *all my energies* to do thoroughly whatever lies before me ; to realise and assume the dignity and bearing belonging to my position.   All these resolutions have reference to *one practical idea*—a life of devoted missionary labour.   That is my aim ; to that I will in the strength of God press forward ; for that, I will continually seek qualification and strength from on high—and especially FAITH to lay hold on the rich treasures of all needed gifts which are *within* my *reach* and to which I have a *claim*, which are in fact *mine* but for my want of faith to lay hold on and appropriate them.   This is an *era*.   I have clearer than ever before me my life's aim.

I have now a set of *resolutions* for the guidance of my life drawn up, which I read on my knees three times a day : and

I have also copied out from my Testament a number of promises and appropriate passages which I read over in my devotional exercises, always with increased satisfaction. O the word of God is precious; and the God of Grace is indeed kind ; but alas ! alas ! (I wonder He has *borne* with me so long) I am guilty, and careless, and trifling, and irresolute, and timid.

I have great reason to thank my gracious Father for His mercy towards me during the past week. On several occasions I have been wonderfully supported—especially in curtailing my hours of sleep—but *regularity* is still wanted here. Strength—real strength and nerve seem to be slowly finding their way into my being; but what a *load* there is of an opposite character ! Really, if I attempt a *good thing* in one way or another I am met by obstacles on every hand. Still, higher than my highest mountain of difficulty, stronger than my most inveterate foe, is HE who is with me —my sympathising friend and brother, Jesus the Son of God. And still, in the face of opposition and doubt and fear, *I will* hope for the best and go forward. I know His will with all my heart. I will endeavour to do it in all things ; and *leave the rest with Him.* I know He loves me very tenderly ; I have felt communion with Him inexpressibly sweet and precious ; and I am convinced He wishes me to pursue the course I am following. Do I wish more strength of mind— more dignified and exalted conceptions of Him and of His? Jesus wishes so intensely. Do I wish *power* and *faith* and *nerve* to fit for a great life? *Willingly* will Jesus bestow such upon the earnest suppliant. Do I want the influences of the Holy Spirit to be stronger within me and to enable me to realise my true position and rank as one of the Great Family? Jesus has promised the Holy Spirit for this purpose. O for the feelings which animate mine ELDER BROTHER ! I am so weak and forgetful. But I will be helped by my Jesus and my Father : yes, I am in safe hands : all will be well; eternity as well as time will testify to His unmixed *love* to me. O that I had His Spirit ! I ask strength for missionary work : to face *calmly* tempests ; shipwreck ; loneliness ; darkness ; temptation ; discouragements ; *heathenism* ; the death of an unknown obscure " servant of Jehovah-Jesus."

There is still a nervous agitation about my manner in society which nothing but a *nobler frame of mind* will cure. I am sometimes entirely above such things. I need food; I need light; new strength; or I will decline and *die*. Therefore I will give my beloved no rest till He doth arise and visit me with His richest blessing. This is a most critical period in my life. If Satan holds me, he has *the life of a man*. Since *Satan has lost* me he has lost the life of a man, for that life will be used against the power of darkness. He would still wound me, still detain me, by magnifying *lies* and presenting them to my mind; but Jesus helps me. I am faithless however.

I have resolved—determined—to live to Christ and to live like Christ. What a blessing and comfort to know, that, to do these two things, I may depend on His aid and encouragement. Why should I be afraid? Why cast down? If God be for me who can be against me? I have been wonderfully supported by God; and I feel encouraged to go on. Reverses have been occasioned by mine own weakness. The day of manhood is, I humbly earnestly trust, bursting upon me!

Saturday, 29th Dec.—Last week has been one of great conflict. O how sweet will Heaven be to me! And if I say this in my twenty-first year what reason may I have to say it when I'm twice as old! My mind having been dissipated by gaiety and social glee, Monday and Tuesday, I rose on Wednesday very weak both in body and mind, especially the latter; and yet I am not quite recovered. This of course is a lesson. If I ever get on in life it must be in comparative seclusion and in the atmosphere of prayer. It seemed awful to me on some occasions during the past week to have to live. O what would I not have given for a reprieve and a summons home! And I am sure this is far from my real wishes. I am desirous of a long life of hard work, of self-denial for Jesus.

God help me! I cried most vehemently with a heaving bosom in the following language: "O for truth! O for light!" over and over again. I saw my past life also, and wept over its deformity, regarding myself as the vilest of all His servants and unworthy of the name.

However great the difficulty, I find I must keep a stout heart to it, go much to the throne, and do my utmost in action: and the good Lord help me. I must conquer every evil habit: *that's settled*. Idleness, irresolution, carelessness, timidity, irregularity, all must be swept away. In the strength of the living God—the helper of the aspirant—I will set to work. NEVER DESPAIR.

Sunday, 30th Dec.—Preached again and with freedom from Luke xv. and 18. I observed tears. It is the salvation of the soul alone that I want.

Monday, 31st Dec.—Alone to-night on the cemetery-hill here, and by the foot of a fir tree, I poured out my soul to God. Reviewing the past year—its VICTORIES, its providential events, and its lessons. I was very much encouraged—never felt as I did then the power I really had. I saw obstacles give way, difficulties vanish, apparently the greatest and most insuperable ; seeming impossibilities surmounted, and the most unlikely things take place : and I knew that all this was *in answer to prayer*—taken, as it were, by violence. O there is something almost *awful* in the thought of having moved the Eternal Himself ! But yet it is so—in my case as plain and evident as a sunbeam. There is here a foundation for hope for the future as well as a ground for confidence that I am in the right, heaven-selected path of duty. There is here, above all, a powerful inducement to *importune God* for the blessings I need—to concentrate my energies, as it were, on a certain gift and to plead for it till Heaven is moved, and I am in receipt of it. If I prayed myself out of the *Courant* office, Elgin, at a season when everything seemed against me—to the astonishment, mistrust, and *alarm*, even of some who sympathised with me—may I not in the same way pray myself out of every bad habit of thought or action. If I prayed myself into a situation which I have reason to believe was my chief recommendation to the Directors of the L. M. S., and if I in that situation was enabled to live entirely *by faith*, not knowing whither I was going, may I not here in exactly such another situation, so pray and wrestle that, as I succeeded with the L. M. S. in the one instance, so in the other, I may pray myself into a situation where, with the blessing of God, I may be the means of special good to the Church and the world, and be the instrument in the Divine hand of doing a great work in His merciful scheme of reconciling the world to Himself. In my prayers on this solemn occasion (on the hill), I had only opportunity to state my case fervently and simply, *once*. I had not time to *plead* much when I was interrupted by the sound of approaching footsteps. I resumed prayer, however, in my study alone, and had much of the Divine presence.

I set out on the new year with the following special requests.

Kneeling down, I asked not only to receive a Christ-like spirit and manner ; resolute, immovable determination ; single-ness of heart and humility ; and courage in danger and diffi-culty ; but I asked also that I might be sent.

Saturday, Jan. 5th, 1856.—This week has been spent very much in prayer.

Delivered a speech at a tea-meeting lately, before my tutors. By the grace of God, I was enabled in some measure to dedicate that occasion not to the display of my powers, but to the delivering something which would be calculated to do good for eternity. I went there prayerfully, and I hope I did not speak for nought. I have been since told by a lay-preacher that he went home saying to his wife that Mr Mackenzie would be a man yet. In the strength of God alone, and for His glory alone, I WILL !

Saturday, 12th Jan.—Last few days have been seasons of wrestling. The kingdom must be taken by violence.

The impression is abroad here that I will not be long in Bedford. How it originated I know not. The Lord guide me and keep me here and elsewhere. I am in His hands. Without qualifying me, He will not send me. Let me look to Him with constancy of heart, and strive to cultivate all the graces necessary for the arduous life of a missionary.

An invisible God ! This doctrine has cheered me of late : I was struck by the words of Jesus on the Cross, " Father, &c." He addressed an invisible Being. He is present with me.

I preached from this subject with some freedom ex-temporarily.

I write on the 16th of February. My health has been very good indeed. I am about well. My spirit (my mind) has been more cheerful and *strengthened* than for years, per-haps than it ever was. My strength has come from God alone. Prayer has been my armoury. Before I can do greater things I must walk much nearer to God, close to Jesus, holding *communion* with Him, and keeping Him ever before me as an example.

Africa has engaged my thoughts recently.

I am still pleading for Faith, Light and Truth, Strength and Courage, even to fearlessness. A single humble Spirit (habitual). For what, indeed, will make me a Christlike man? My sole but sure confidence and ground of hope is *the love of Jesus, infinite, prompt, special.*

During the winter of 1855-56 the young Scotsman found his health growing gradually worse. Partly this may have been due to a change of habits and of climate, partly to the very long hours of work to which he gave himself while curtailing his sleep. But the most serious phase of his illness was due to the effort which he made to lessen the amount of his food. He resolved first to deny himself the mere pleasure of the table, and further to discipline himself to live on spare and simple diet in order that he might be ready for any emergency in his career as a missionary. And, as a guide, he wrote out a number of detailed rules for the regulation of his choice of dishes at table. The result, of course, was one which appears in the lives of so many who have made severe fasting a part of their spiritual life, that he was subject to great depression as well as thrilling elation of soul. Spiritual temptations fastened upon him also and gave him great distress, especially when they took the form of that haunting declaration that his life was doomed to be in vain, that he could never be of any service to the Kingdom of God. Indignantly do we find him remonstrating against the tyranny of this mere "idea," this "false idea." It was not until a visit to a London physician opened his eyes to his mistaken zeal, that health returned. So far had his experiment been carried that, though nearly of age, and not far from six feet in height, he weighed only eight stone. The climax and the deliverance are described in a summary of this severe experience which he wrote in London on May 18th, 1856. The following are extracts :—

3. *London, May* 18th, 1856. — He (Satan) has long studied by different methods, by calling up fears and

doubts and mistrust in my mind, with regard to my bodily health, which have *no foundation whatever.* In this proceeding he has had to shift his ground, but this he has done skilfully, and also too successfully. In answer to prayer I am now, blessed be God, in possession of *the truth* which sets the mind at rest: for I have eminent medical advice pronouncing me in good health, and *fit for any country.*

4. He calls up in my mind associations which have a tendency to shake my confidence in myself in whatever position I may be. He generally brings before me some scene in my past sinful life, and says, "These people know you not·; but you can't deny that you are the man."

5. Also in the matter of food my mind has been peculiarly exercised of late. The Lord has given me some strength, however, and some light, and I can now see mine adversary in the cunning of his wiles. So much was my mind taken up on this matter, that I could not raise my mind from it, and could only meditate on the different results of different kinds of food, and the effects of the food I myself had taken last. I was so particular, and thought so very much on this matter, that I almost counted the bites I took, ate every mouthful with a kind of terror lest I should not masticate it aright ; and to crown all, generally got into a confused flutter in settling whether I had eaten enough or not; Satan very often indeed persuading me I had, whereas everyone was at a loss to account for my conduct in not taking more food. I was reduced to a state of great weakness, both in body and mind, began to see I was wrong, lost confidence in some medicine I was taking, lost confidence in myself, and became thoroughly miserable, being at the time afflicted with a bowel complaint. I was all along enabled to study and to keep up with but six hours of sleep. From this position God in His mercy removed me by enabling me to come to London, where I have now been eleven days, and have recovered health and strength and confidence.

(I shall *note* this dispensation. I would fain write more upon it.)

6. I want very much love, true love to God. I come and pray earnestly to Him. But I wish to have the desire to be *with Him,* and the vision to *perceive* Him, and the spirit and heart to *address* Him, and really feel and recognise His presence, and not go to Him so much with the feeling of per-

forming a *duty*, or of escaping what is *evil*, as of enjoying the presence and partaking of the blessedness of the Almighty.

In July (1856) he journeyed to Morayshire by Glasgow, in fulfilment of a promise to spend most of his holiday with his mother. He found labouring in Speyside, a young student from the Congregational Theological Hall at Edinburgh of the name of John Douglas, afterwards the Rev. John Douglas of Glasgow, and for some time Secretary of the Congregational Union of Scotland. These two, with James Ross, spent much time together that August. They tramped over the district, visiting the people, preaching the Gospel. They made one long-remembered and oft-recalled trip to the top of Benrinnes, where they solemnly pledged themselves to the service of God. To Mackenzie this new friendship proved of immeasurable importance, for John Douglas invited him to pay a visit to his own home at Portobello. The visit was made in August of the following year, 1857, and in that home the prospective missionary found her who was to be the companion of his long labouring years in and for South Africa.

The session of 1856-57 was passed at Bedford with considerably more comfort in every way. The daily "jottings" indicate constantly that the prayer life was maintained in full vigour, but the descriptions of spiritual experiences are briefer and less quotable; references to the ground covered in study are more frequent, and show that hard and steady work was being done. Mackenzie opened his heart most fully at this time to his friend James Ross, with whom he felt complete spiritual sympathy. For example, speaking of his greatest mercy as being " the presence of the Lord Jesus Christ," he says :—

Jany. 7, 1857.—O let us live with Him—just in His sight —live in such a position as will admit of our speaking to Him. What a companion ! What conversation ! O one hour of this is worth far more than hours and days—spent as, alas! too many Christians spend them now-a-days.

I am persuaded we have not enough of devoted *personal* attachment to Him whom we call our Saviour. O let us be extreme on this point, let us *burn* with love, and *yearn intensely* to testify in actions the existence of this love.

In another letter (April 30th, 1857) he indulges in a characteristic speculation regarding that future life, to which he looked forward even as a young man, the hope of which influenced him very powerfully all his days. Evidently with him, as with all who have drunk the Spirit of the New Testament, that "other worldliness," when truly and purely cherished, produced profound and most admirable effects upon conduct and character in this world.

There are many thoughts which rush into my mind when I begin to write to you, Jamie. But I cannot write you a long letter—must not, indeed, say much more just now. Perhaps many thoughts which we would wish to communicate will never be communicated on earth; but if they are pure thoughts, truthful thoughts, then are they not imperishable? If our minds are to be expanded, our memories rendered unclouded to call up whatever of truth may have lodged in our minds, if these things happen to us in the higher and brighter world, perhaps what we know not now of one another's thoughts, we shall know hereafter. At any rate, it is sweet to think that even the *advanced* mode of communication by Post Office delivery will be effectually superseded in heaven. We shall be all *together* there ! No more to part ! To know God and to see the glories of His higher creation, the stupendous accomplishments of His Wisdom and Power and Benevolence. O my dear *fellowman*, this is our Eternity ! This is the "purchased possession" of the Friends of Jesus the Crucified ! Take courage, then ; for time is short and eternity follows. . . . We are loved by the Son of God. O look up, be noble, dignified, devoted, indefatigable : for *we* are *loved* by Him whom angels worship.

The holiday season of 1857 was also passed in Scotland. Part was spent in that momentous visit

to Portobello, where he met and became engaged to
Ellen Douglas, the fifth daughter and eighth child of
William Douglas; her mother's maiden name was
Anne Oliver Bruce. Not long after his return to
Bedford, Mackenzie was told that it was intended to
send him to South Central Africa along with a party
of five other missionaries who were appointed to be
pioneers and founders of new missions in the heart of
the dark continent, in a region which Livingstone's
first great journey across the continent had opened up,
as it seemed, to European influences. To the same
friend he announces the important event in the following way:—

It is now settled that J. S. Moffat and I form the mission
at Matabele—referred to in the last *Missionary Chronicle*.
There are other two going besides us, to a station farther
north; but arrangements as to site, etc., of missions cannot
be at present very definite. It is probable we shall sail in
February next. I hope to be in Scotland next month. I
daresay I shall see you by and by.

How different my life has been since I came to England,
from what it was when you and I used to take those long,
very long walks of an evening by the Lossie—discussing
earnestly, and cheering one another on. I suppose this
other thing is *life*, and that was its introduction or vestibule.
Are *you* the same Jamie of the olden time? I sometimes
almost doubt concerning my own identity, so great is the
change in my whole mental constitution. I'm afraid, if
there's a change in my spiritual state, it's not much for the
better, if any. God have mercy on me! And so I'm off to
Africa, and in a few years (God helping you) you will be the
Rev. James Ross, Congregational minister of ————, in
Scotland. Very well: we have only one life; His glory is
our highest object and end; in Scotland and in Africa let
us be the servants of Jehovah. Then, when we shall meet
before His throne, we shall be approved of Him.

Mackenzie had long desired to spend part of his
period of study in Edinburgh; but the attraction in
that direction was now intensified by the proximity
of that home at Portobello to the grey metropolis of

the north. He obtained the consent of the directors and went to Edinburgh in December. There he remained longer than had been expected, through difficulties met by the directors in making arrangements for the new missionary expedition. But he employed his time very fully in study. He made many friends, including several who proved most valuable and steady allies in years to come. Among these the chief one was undoubtedly the late Rev. Geo. D. Cullen, M.A., who was so long prominent among the Christian circles of Edinburgh.

At last it was definitely decided that the missionary party for South Africa should sail early in the month of June 1858. There remained nothing to do but be ordained and married, make the final preparations for the great undertaking, and then sail forth into the unknown future. The ordination took place on Monday, April 19th, in the Queen Street Hall, Edinburgh. Though a comparative stranger in the city, Mackenzie had made so many friends, and the enterprise in which he was about to embark had, partly through its association with the name of Dr. Livingstone, attracted so much public attention, that the hall was quite crowded on this occasion. On the platform, besides those who took part in the service, there were many well-known men, including " Rabbi " Duncan, of the New College, Edinburgh, and Rev. Drs. John Stoughton and Alexander Raleigh. Mackenzie believed that " it was the first occasion on which the three dissenting denominations had united in conducting such a service." The Rev. William Pulsford of Albany Street Congregational Church offered the first prayer, and the Rev. Geo. D. Cullen, M.A., " asked the questions." [1] An address on " Africa as a Field of

[1] The following were the questions which, according to Congregational custom, the young candidate for ordination answered in public :—
"(1) What leads you to conclude that you are a Christian ? (2) What induced you to devote yourself to the work of a missionary among the

Missions" was delivered by the Rev. Dr Harper of Leith, Professor in the United Presbyterian Divinity Hall, and the "charge" to the young minister was given by Rev. Dr Lindsay Alexander of Augustine Church, Edinburgh. The ordination prayer was offered by the Rev. William Swan, formerly missionary in Siberia ; an address on the claims of missions was delivered by the Rev. Dr Ewart, Free Church Missionary at Calcutta, in the absence of Principal Cunningham ; and a Free Church minister, Rev. Alex. Topp (formerly of Elgin), also took part in the service.

John Mackenzie and Ellen Douglas were married at Portobello on April 27th, 1858 ; a hurried trip was made to Morayshire, where the young bride was made known to her husband's relatives and his friends. The young couple reached London towards the end of May, and sailed on the s.s. *Athens* on June 5th from Southampton. The voyage was uneventful and, judged by modern speed, very slow, as they did not reach Table Bay till July 14th. During the voyage the four young missionaries, who were to be so closely associated in so great a work, had opportunity to know each other. Two of them were Welshmen, the Rev. Roger Price and the Rev. Thomas Morgan Thomas. One was from Yorkshire, the Rev. William Sykes. Mackenzie used the voyage for reading a variety of books, including Livingstone's "Travels" and for breaking ground in the Dutch grammar.

When the ship anchored in Table Bay it was immediately boarded by Robert Moffat and the Rev. William Thompson, the Society's agent at Cape Town, and the father of its present well-known Foreign Secretary, the Rev. Ralph Wardlaw Thompson. Dr Moffat gave the new missionaries a most affectionate greeting, and at once set to work with his untiring,

heathen ? (3) What are the Doctrines that you believe to be contained in the Scriptures ? (4) How do you propose to exercise your ministry among the heathen ? "

indomitable energy to prepare for the journey which lay before them all, as far as his own station of Kuruman.

Thus far we have found John Mackenzie to be a young man whose whole attention was concentrated on his own religious experience and on the effort to fit himself for the career of a missionary. While he tried to make his reading as wide as his opportunities would allow, his main intellectual life gathered about his religion and his chosen career. The answer which he gave at his ordination to the fourth question, indicates that he was by no means narrow in his views even at this time. By reading and conversation he must have already obtained that broad view of the missionary's career which he retained to the end.

" First of all," he said, " my proper work, the work of my life, is to preach the gospel of Jesus Christ in public and from family to family, instructing both young and old in the sacred Scriptures. I desire to do the work of an evangelist, and from this to turn aside neither to the right hand nor to the left. . . . In order to complete the work of elevating the people, he (the missionary) must teach them the arts of civilised life. If we exhort them to lay aside the sword for the ploughshare and the spear for the pruning-hook, we must be prepared to teach them to use the one with the same dexterity which they exhibited in wielding the other. If they are no longer to start upon the marauding expedition, if they are not to depend upon the precarious results of the chase, then we must teach them to till their own land, sow and reap their own crops, build their own houses, as well as tend their own flocks. Nor is the missionary to Africa content even when all this is accomplished. He longs to see the African united in friendly intercourse with the general brotherhood of the race. He desires to see the African ship, freighted with the products of African soil and the results of African industry, mingling in the great ocean with the ships of other lands and returning home richly laden with the varied treasures of commerce."

Notwithstanding this breadth of view as to the effects of the Gospel upon African communities, Mackenzie stands at twenty-three years of age on South African soil, the evangelist pure and simple, livingly aware only of one supreme duty and imperious call from the throne of God.

It is well to recall the fact that he had laid the deep foundations of a wider view of his mission in the close study of his own character. His evangelism was not of that purely emotional and superficial type which ignores the relation of divine grace to conduct and the organic structure of human life. He knew that the authority of Christ would mould his personal manhood into the likeness of Christ. His diary is full of this. It shows him quivering with painful sensitiveness to the disparities that show themselves to his own eye between himself and the great Model. He constantly recurs to certain sins and faults which were not harmonious with his relation to God in Christ. He speaks of his pride and love of praise, of his nervousness before others, his lack of nobility and dignity of manner. To him these were sins because they were unworthy of a Christian man. To him, as he said, " meekness was the first-born of nobility of soul " ; and nobility of soul, which he once called " a mild and dignified serenity," he conceived of as the natural and almost inevitable property of one who was united in the depths of his spirit to the Son of God. Those who knew him in later years will be amazed to learn that he who walked so humbly and unselfishly, ever battled with the devil of pride and vainglory ; or that he who was universally described as calm and self-controlled ever suffered from the sins of " blushing " with nervousness and of feeling confused when confronted by strangers.

There he stands at Cape Town, with his face to the far and gloomy north, nearly six feet in height, broad-shouldered but lithe and active, with his fair hair thrown back from a massive forehead, with a ruddy beard encircling his strong features, with those deep-set, light blue eyes, that could twinkle with amusement, or flash "sunbeams like swords" in a moment of moral indignation. Long afterwards an observant man who met him said, "I shook hands with him and he looked right through me!"

From those regions of drought and fever, of heathenism and strife, he often carried his memory back to a certain quiet nook in the Ladies' Walk, along the beloved banks of the Lossie at Elgin, where he knelt down one evening at the foot of a tree and uttered one strong and intense prayer, which he never forgot—"O Lord, send me to the darkest spot on earth." Neither had God forgotten it.

CHAPTER III

"WANDERJAHRE" (1858-1864)

WHEN our band of young missionaries landed in
South Africa they entered upon work which had
been already ennobled by their predecessors, during
almost sixty years of toil. The first of these, the
founder of the London Missionary Society's work
in South Africa, was J. T. Vanderkemp, a Hollander,
a learned linguist and man of science who, having
given his heart to the cause of foreign missions,
was sent to South Africa in 1799, at fifty years of
age. In 1815 there landed on those shores one
whose name was destined to be even more widely
known in connection with South Africa ; it was
Robert Moffat. In 1819 Dr Philip, one of the
greatest personalities associated with the history of
Cape Colony, appeared upon the scene. He gave
up brilliant prospects as a minister in the homeland,
to found mission work at Cape Town and to be
the general superintendent of the London Missionary
Society's operations throughout South Africa. He
was a man of indomitable courage, penetrating mind,
sympathetic heart, and clear conscience. He made
journeys in all directions throughout the colony, and
by the thoroughness with which he exposed the ill-
treatment of the native tribes by the white settlers,
he at once awoke the undying hatred of the latter
and set in motion many forces tending to improve
the condition of the former. To this day, it is hard
to obtain from South African historians anything
like a moderate and fair judgment of Dr Philip's

character and work.   He had been dead a few years
when our young missionaries arrived in Cape Colony.

But a new star was in the ascendant.   The name
of Dr Livingstone, already well known in South
Africa, had for several years gained fame in Europe
also.   He who had come out to be a medical missionary and had, as he thought, settled down for life
in Bechuanaland to spread the gospel amongst the
various branches of that race north of Kuruman,
was driven by strange events from his chosen fields
of labour.   The Boers of the Transvaal had, from
the time of the Sand River Convention in 1852,
considered Bechuanaland as finally handed over to
them by the British Government.   They knew what
missionaries had been doing for forty years in Cape
Colony ; how faithfully they had stood, in face of
every danger and opposition, for the rights of the
native peoples ; how remarkably their education of
the native peoples strengthened the latter and made
it impossible for the farmers to treat them as serfs.
These " immigrant farmers " of the Transvaal, therefore, very bitterly resented the energetic and successful way in which Moffat and Livingstone were
opening up Christian missions amongst the Bechuana
tribes, and they set themselves to destroy these
stations.   This was done deliberately and systematically.   Dr Moffat, in the end of 1852, describes
no less than four missionary stations which had
already been blotted out.   In each case the native
teachers were driven off, the people of the district
being plundered and slain.   Amongst these stations
was that of Kolobeng, where Dr Livingstone had
for some years been settled.   Dr Theal, the well-
known South African historian, amongst other attempts
to disparage the missionary point of view and redeem
from contempt the attitude of the Boers, has tried
to prove that the destruction of Livingstone's mission

was due to the inhabitants of Kolobeng and not to
the Boers. His bit of special pleading can convince
no one who knows the bare facts of the case. Amongst
these must be named this, that Dr Livingstone himself
shortly afterwards studied the evidence on the spot,
and described what had occurred in detail. To
imagine that the people amongst whom he had lived
on terms of intimacy and affection could unanimously
deceive him in such a matter is to make him out
to be one of the dullest of dull human beings. But
the fact is that visitors to the Marico district, in the
north-west corner of the Transvaal, from which these
plunderers went out, had for many years afterwards
abundant evidences given to them that the Boers
themselves were the depredators. Both the Rev.
J. S. Moffat and Mackenzie knew intimately the
leading Boers of that district; knew the men who
had led on that expedition to Kolobeng; knew the
houses to which Dr Livingstone's furniture had been
carried; and they knew, lastly, that the utmost the
Boers ever said for themselves was, *not* that the
natives had destroyed Livingstone's premises, but
that the rash deed had been done by the wilder
young men of the Boer commando without the approval
of their elders. It was left for ingenious historians
to suggest, without a particle of evidence, that the
Bakwena had attacked Livingstone's premises.

The effect of the pressure which the Boers exercised
upon the policy of the Bechuanaland missionaries
from the east, and the hindrances presented by the
vast Kalahari desert on the west, had been to direct
the eyes of the pioneers to the north and north-east.
The Bechuana mission gradually became a long series
of stations, extending from south to north many
hundreds of miles, from the Orange River up to the
Zambesi. The work of exploration which preceded
this extension of the mission was undertaken by

Livingstone. His discovery of a portion of the Zambesi in 1851 proved to him that the great water-way was being made a chief nourisher of the cruel slave trade. He therefore resolved to find some healthy spots in that region where missionaries could live, and from which would radiate the influences that ever prove fatal to slavery. In pursuance of this aim, Livingstone set out two years later, determined to find a shorter route to the coast, either east or west, than the long journey by ox-waggon from Cape Town. He reached the Makololo country once more, and found the chief Sebetuane as friendly as ever. These Makololo had been driven northward all the way from Basutoland by the terrific regiments of Moselekatse, the renegade Zulu warrior who founded the Matabele tribe. They had at last found a country where they were protected from the Matabele both by the river system and by a region infested with that tsetse fly, which is so fatal to cattle and horses. From Linyanti, the Makololo town, Livingstone went, attended by some Makololo servants, to St Paul de Loanda on the west coast, where he arrived on May 31st. From that place he returned to Linyanti in the faithful and self-sacrificing fulfilment of a promise to bring those servants back to their own town. Then he set out on his still more arduous and magnificent journey to Quilimane on the east coast, where he arrived on May 20th, 1856. Before he left Linyanti he got a promise from the chief that, when he returned to that region, the chief would lead his tribe out of their most un-healthy place of refuge to a higher country north of the Zambesi. Livingstone promised that missionaries would settle with them there ; and they, it was hoped would prove a shield to the Makololo, warding off any further attack from the Matabele. It was this agreement, made by Livingstone, which led the London Missionary Society to undertake the Makololo Mission.

In what we now call South Bechuanaland the work
of Christian missions had been already very fairly
established by such men as Robert Moffat, William
Ashton, Holloway Helmore, and others.   Through
their labours the entire Scriptures had been translated,
and evangelistic work had been carried on at various
centres. The school work, being the weakest spot in the
history of the Bechuanaland missions, had been begun ;
and in various towns native teachers laboured more or
less adequately to present the gospel to their fellow
countrymen.   One of the most interesting spots in
South Africa must always be the famous mission
station of Kuruman ; in 1858 it was from every point
of view one of the most important places outside the
Cape Colony.   The population was small, and its
chief by no means a man of power.   But the great
missionary, Robert Moffat, had settled there, having
obtained a most valuable grant of land from the chief,
on behalf of the Society.   The little valley, watered
from an abundant and perennial spring, he with much
toil and patience turned into one of the most fruitful
spots in South Africa.   Moffat's training as a Scottish
gardener stood him in good stead at Kuruman.
Traders in South Africa usually followed the " missionary road," and some store-keepers settled in time
at Kuruman.   Moffat's chief delight was in the work
of an itinerating evangelist. All other work he undertook as an inevitable but grievous diversion of his
energies from this. He therefore made almost ceaseless tours of all the native villages and towns within a
radius of twenty miles ; and when he formed the
church at Kuruman the converts of these outposts
became members of that church.   Thus was Kuruman
made, even for the native mind, a new kind of capital.
As the number of missionaries in Bechuanaland increased the importance of Kuruman increased.   For
there he lived to whom they all looked up as the

leader of their endeavours and the untitled chieftain of their circle. Kuruman, in fact, occupied in the minds of most people connected with the Bechuana mission, the position which the men of another Christian persuasion accord to the residence of a missionary-bishop.

The missionary party to which Mackenzie belonged received much help, in preparing at Cape Town for their long journey northwards, from Robert Moffat. They were all prepared like enthusiastic young men to array themselves under his inspiring leadership. Amidst their busy preparations they had time to study a little the conditions of life in that colonial capital whose inhabitants gave them a warm reception and watched their proceedings with intense interest. For it meant much to Cape Colony that it should be brought into living connection with the distant regions of the Zambesi. But the Christian people were prepared to welcome them for their work's sake, and gave them many a hearty God-speed. For this purpose a large meeting was held just before their departure, at which addresses were made by Cape Town citizens, and by several of the missionaries. This meeting has not yet been forgotten by those who took part in it, as letters received even since the death of Mackenzie prove. His own speech on that occasion made many friends for him, who never forgot his name and watched his career.

Mackenzie wrote a few letters from Cape Town to his home friends which, being the first despatched after his voyage, contain a few observations on the new world into which he had entered. He is much struck with the presence of the Oriental races and the celebrations of their own religious rites. He observes that nearly all the main branches of Protestant Christianity are represented in the religious life of the place. One letter describes a glorious day which some of them spent climbing Table Mountain. To

James Ross he sent the observation that American editions of standard British authors were being sold at Cape Town cheaper than in England (1858).

The missionaries were introduced to Sir George Grey, the Governor of Cape Colony, and were very kindly received by him. Grey was one of the few Cape Governors who have known how to deal fairly with the Cape Dutch and yet to retain their confidence and respect. He was at this very time about to set out on a journey to meet with some Transvaal Boers for the settlement of a dispute, and his mind was much occupied with rumours of the wide interpretation which these people had put upon that careless document, the Sand River Convention. They were already extending their aggressive policy northward and westward, and, as we shall see, even Kuruman was coming rapidly within the scope of their "practical politics." In view of all these facts it was a matter of some importance that the Governor publicly recognised the new missionary enterprise, and frankly expressed his good-will toward the representatives of the London Missionary Society.

Robert Moffat resolved to leave with his son and family before the rest of the missionary band, in order to prepare at Kuruman for their reception, and also to prevent the taking of too many oxen through the country at the same time. When the new men began their journey it was to meet with the severest forms of a South African traveller's loss and misery. The cattle which had been bought for them before their arrival turned out to be very poor ; and they perished in the terrible Karroo in large numbers. They were all, of course, struck with the monotony and slowness of the South African mode of travelling. "The fact is," wrote Mrs Mackenzie, "it is almost impossible to write while travelling, as we have to do in South Africa. There is an awful waste of time connected with it and we cannot help it ; we must get to our journey's end, and this is the only available mode of doing so. If poor South Africa is to be Christianised at an ox-waggon pace, what will become of the heathen children for many generations ? "

They reached Beaufort West on October 9th, and there were the guests of a Mr Frazer, minister of the Dutch Reformed Church, and his family. Mr Frazer had come from the north of Scotland, and was delighted to meet with one who had more or less acquaintance with a number of his old college friends and others. Mackenzie preached to the English-speaking people on the Sabbath and received an invitation to settle among them as their minister. The following brief extracts give an interesting glimpse of Mr Frazer's family, from which there sprung some well-known South Africans, including the wife of President Steyn of the Orange Free State :—

Although Mr Frazer has been in this Colony ever since he was a young man, he still retains his Highland accent. He has been married twice and has a family of ten, six sons and four daughters. His two eldest daughters are married, one in Cape Town, the other in Beaufort, to a very nice young Scotsman who has a general store. One son is studying for the ministry in Holland and another medicine in Aberdeen ; the others are quite young. Mrs Frazer is Dutch and speaks only that language, and you may imagine how awkward I often felt. She understands English quite well, for it is spoken regularly in the family, but then I could not always understand her Dutch. However, she is an excellent woman and was very kind to me, and there was generally some one of the children at hand to interpret. All the English-speaking people here speak Dutch, from the eldest to the youngest. It is amusing to hear the young children speak both languages. English parents, however, never allow their children to speak in Dutch at home. This I don't wonder at for it gives to their English a peculiar accent which indeed all the Africanders have to a large extent, and which I don't admire.

Who has adequately described life in an ox-waggon in South Africa ? There is a poetry as well as a misery about it to which no writer has yet done justice. Various missionaries and hunters have recorded their particular experiences, especially the hardships of special journeys. But it remains for some gifted pen, ere that peculiar mode of transport disappears, to picture its fascinations as well as its limitations, its freedom as well as its confinement, its constant human interest as well as its monotony. The following extract from a letter of Mackenzie's written in the first stage of this his first journey gives an all too rare glimpse of the actual life :—

MITCHELL PASS NEAR CERES,
September 1858.

Here we are, after a week's journeying by the ox-waggon, in a wild but beautiful part of Southern Africa. For the last few days we have been surrounded by mountains, some of the peaks of which are clad with snow, although lying under a sun which to us was actually broiling. Bain's Kloof and Pass, which we have just passed through, have many attractions to the lover of the grand and imposing in nature. Masses of rock have in many instances been blasted to a great depth, in order to form the road by which we travelled. I have never seen masses of rock so *ancient looking*, and yet they are chiefly sandstone.

We outspanned some days ago beside a brook, and really I thought more than once that Ellen and I were returning to the age of childhood. We went repeatedly together to wash our hands in the dancing stream, and as we sat there together after the genuine Arcadian fashion (do you know it ?), I felt sure that there were many people in this world of ours far less happy than this brother and sister of yours. We gathered wild flowers, too, day after day, and the top of my waggon looks rather gay I can assure you. We enjoy the company of our brethren and sisters very much. We form quite a village, and there is no loneliness where we chance to encamp. On Friday night we reached the highest part of Bain's Kloof, and outspanned where indeed the place seemed lonely. Baboons, too, came in numbers to gaze at the first of our party who reached the spot, but they soon retired, and their chatter was succeeded by the merry laugh of our men as they surrounded the fire and cooked our evening meal.   Ellen and I were detained a few days behind the rest in Cape Town, but came up to them after three days' travelling by ourselves.   They started on the Tuesday and we on the Saturday.   We met again on the following Wednesday.   Waggon-travelling has not had the slightest injurious effect on Ellen—indeed she enjoys it quite as much as any of the others.   We are all very busy while travelling.   There is always something to do.   Either we have to give the men their food, or sort something about the waggon, or get something cooked for ourselves.   We *have no time for writing letters*.   I am sorry for this, for almost every hour I see things which would be interesting if narrated. Ellen is also very sorry that she cannot write more to you and to all our dear relatives.   We both hope, however, that we shall be able by and by to write more to you all.   In the meantime don't let your pen rest, but send us many such letters as that which you sent from Portobello.

We are now inspanning, *i.e.*, inyoking our oxen.   We reach Ceres to-night, and this must be posted there in order to reach Cape Town in time for the September mail.

It is very hot, but we get some fine oranges at the farm-houses at the wayside, which are very pleasant and refreshing. Part of this letter was written under the shade of a bush, but my ink falling down the sloping bank, I changed my position and finished it in my waggon, which by the way we have named "Patience Lodge."

From Beaufort, Mackenzie sent a letter to the Directors of the London Missionary Society, from which the following extracts are made :—

LETJESBOSCH NEAR BEAUFORT WEST, S.A.,
October 9, 1858.

Mr Moffat, having interested himself in procuring waggons, oxen, etc., for the missionary party, left Cape Town on the 24th of August, accompanied by Mrs Moffat, Mr and Mrs John Moffat, Mrs Livingstone and sons, and Miss Jane Moffat, who is now returning from school in England.   On the 31st of August Mr Helmore, with the three young brethren, started ; but Mrs Mackenzie, having exerted herself too much in preparing for the journey, became quite unwell at this juncture, and, to the disappointment of both, the medical man would not allow us to leave with the others. On Saturday, the 4th of September, however, she had so far improved that he gave his consent to our starting, and we overtook Mr Helmore and party on the following Wednesday near Wellington. I am thankful to say that Mrs Mackenzie's health has continued good since commencing the journey, and I have no doubt but that with care and God's blessing it will continue so.

I shall not attempt in this letter to describe either the country through which we have passed, or the details connected with our waggon-travelling. On the latter subject, I shall only say that an ox-waggon is not particularly adapted for letter-writing, nor is it quite the place in which one who is fond of reading would choose to live. However, it is just the thing for travelling in this country, and this is our great object at present.

I am very sorry to say that the accounts which had reached England before our departure, concerning the high price and bad condition of oxen in this Colony were but too true. The oxen which were purchased for us at the Cape at a very high figure were, in general, miserable looking creatures, and as the event has proved, too weak for such a journey. We have not now half the number with which we started from Cape Town. One by one they have dropped down on the road, and in most cases we can do nothing with them in the way of doctoring them, for the disease generally is exhaustion. In the parched and barren Karroo great numbers have fallen, and all along the road there were evidences that travellers who had preceded us had been equally if not more unfortunate. In half-an-hour I have counted the skeletons of half-a-dozen oxen, as I sat on the front of my waggon, which vehicle, as you are aware, would not go over a great extent of ground in that space of time. At a place called Vlak Place, about eight days' journey from Beaufort, we held a consultation on the subject of our oxen, when it was found necessary to leave one-half of the waggons where they were, there being no oxen to pull them, while the other three should proceed to Beaufort and send back assistance. Mr Price, Mr Sykes, and I being worst off for oxen, it was thought fair that we should remain behind, while Mr Helmore's two waggons, with Mr Thomas's, should proceed. However, Mr and Mrs Helmore, thinking it unadvisable that Mrs Mackenzie should remain, recommended that I should leave my waggon in charge of my brethren, and offered us both a place in one of their waggons. Travelling thus we reached this place on Friday. I am now within a day or so of Beaufort. We have already purchased some oxen here, and hope that soon we shall be able to procure a sufficient number to send back for our brethren. They are pretty comfortably located beside a small river, and have a kind Boer in their vicinity, who will sell them sheep, etc., so with their own supplies there is not the slightest cause for anxiety.

The state of affairs between the Dutch Boers beyond the Colony and some of the native tribes is very unsatisfactory, and at times alarming. We have heard lately that the Kuruman is not considered safe, by some who reside there, but we fondly hope that such fears will turn out to be groundless. By and by we shall have full information on this important subject, which we cannot procure here in the desert.

At Victoria West the entire party were most generously received by a farmer in the neighbourhood. His brother had already given to Robert Moffat twenty-eight oxen to take him to Hope Town from Beaufort, of which only seventeen "were spared to return," as one correspondent quaintly expresses it. This farmer gave to Price and Mackenzie free pasturage for their oxen as long as they stayed there. Thus they received their first pleasant experiences of the far-famed South African hospitality. Mackenzie arrived at Kuruman on the first day of the year 1859. On March 1st he wrote a letter reporting the remainder of his journey, and surveying the whole of it.

KURUMAN, 1st *March* 1859.

My former letter from Cape Town conveyed the intelligence of the safe and speedy termination of the first stage in our long journey.

Had the second stage from Cape Town to Kuruman been equally prosperous with the first (we could not expect it to be so speedy), my present task had been both easy and pleasant. As the case stands, however, I feel it will be necessary to enter into the details, so far as they affect me, of a journey which has been disastrous and protracted, and therefore expensive and unpleasant.

I was detained a few days in Cape Town behind my brethren, on account of Mrs Mackenzie's health, which had been affected by her exertions in preparing for the journey. Starting on Saturday, the 4th September, we rejoined our friends on the 8th at a mountain pass called Bain's Kloof, a little beyond the town of Wellington.

I found that already some of the oxen had died from sheer exhaustion; in this pass more were added to this number; and when we came to the entrance of the Karroo, seven oxen were sold for £1 a head rather than bring them a little further, where we should only have got about half that sum for the hide.

In the Karroo our loss was fearful. At that season there was next to nothing for the poor animals to eat, and being in most wretched condition when they came into our possession, they daily fell down in the yoke unable to move another step. . . .

At Beaufort we disposed of nearly all the Cape Town oxen on very fair terms, and purchased others which were fresh and in good condition. In dividing these oxen amongst ourselves, we endeavoured to equalise the strength of the six spans.

It was thought advisable that Mr Sykes and I should travel together from Beaufort to Victoria, because at that time we both had white men as our drivers, who would not deign to sit at the same fire with their black brethren of the whip, but who being father and son, of course, agreed well enough at a fire by themselves.

Mr Price and I accepted a kind invitation tendered to the whole party by some friends in Victoria West, to rest and feed our cattle there before entering the dry and sterile district between Victoria and Hope Town. A large house was placed at our disposal rent free, and pasture granted for our oxen on the same easy terms. Our friends had only one request to make, to which we were happy to accede, viz.: that we should preach to them. We remained at this place, much to our own pleasure and the benefit of our oxen, rather more than a fortnight; and after all reached Hope Town three days after two of our brethren.

At Hope Town we found the Black or Orange River impassable at the ford eastward along the bank of the Orange River, until we reached the place where it is joined by the Vaal. There we crossed by means of a boat, emptying our waggons and taking them to pieces.

While at Hope Town, reports of a very warlike character reached us concerning the movements of the Transvaal Boers. It was believed by the agent of our Government at Hope Town, as well as by other gentlemen who had means of obtaining intelligence concerning the movements of the Boers, that Kuruman was about to be attacked. On reaching Griqua Town, Mr P. and I rode on to Kuruman to see for ourselves the real state of matters, and to get the advice of our brethren concerning the propriety of bringing forward our waggons. Being satisfied that there was no immediate danger, we returned for our waggons, which we brought to Kuruman on the first day of 1859.

As to the journey between Cape Town and Beaufort, it was managed entirely by Mr Helmore, who has no doubt advised you on the subject.

I attribute the success of the latter part of my journey to our having good oxen to begin with; to our *travelling rapidly* thro' the worst districts; to our travelling chiefly at night; and to our separating at Beaufort into parties of two waggons each.

As an incident of the journey, I may mention that while at Beaufort, I was invited to take charge of a church which the English-speaking population were desirous of having formed among them. A liberal salary was offered, guaranteed for five years, and other inducements held out. But my answer was ready, an answer which Mr Moffat had led them to expect when he passed through the place. In the full conviction that my work lay further north, I had pleasure in advising with them as to procuring another, and in commending them to the care and blessing of God.

The missionaries were soon engrossed in most earnest discussion of plans for the next stage of their journey. The plan as outlined was that Robert Moffat should accompany the missionaries to the Matabele tribe, these consisting of Messrs John S. Moffat, William Sykes, and Morgan Thomas. Along

with them would travel as far as possible those
who were appointed to the Makololo Mission.   The
man of experience amongst these was the late
Holloway Helmore, and with him were to go the
late Roger Price and John Mackenzie.   In the course
of their deliberations Mackenzie formulated a plan
which he submitted to the band, but which was
rejected by them chiefly through the urgent dissuasions
of Mr Helmore.   This he describes in a letter to the
Directors from which we have already quoted :—

(*1st March* 1859.)

As to the part of our journey still before us, we begin to
perceive, with all the force which nearness lends, the reality
of its difficulties.   Our minds were formerly occupied with
difficulties then present ; sufficient to those days were their
evils ; but now we are at liberty fully to contemplate what we
shall have to meet and contend with and through God's help
to overcome, between Kuruman and the north bank of the
Zambesi.

After giving my best consideration to our position, it is my
opinion that the Makololo brethren should, in the first place,
make a " bachelor expedition " to Linyanti, get the Makololo
to remove to some healthy locality on the north bank of the
Zambesi, build temporary huts for ourselves and our goods,
then retrace our steps to Kuruman for our wives and the
remaining part of our goods.   In the interim, if possible,
leave with the people a native teacher who, along with our
property left in their midst, would sufficiently attest that we
were not " gulling " them.

Of course, the greatest objection to this plan is that it
would take so much time in the accomplishment.   Now this
is an objection ; but it has to be balanced against others
connected with the bringing of females and children into that
country in the present uncertain state of matters.   From all
I can learn from those who have lived long in this country,
it is neither an easy nor a speedy matter to induce a native
tribe to shift its quarters, without force, even after they
have promised to do so.   Again, the position in which
the Makololo will be placed if they agree to our wishes will
be right in the teeth of their enemies the Matabele, a cir-

cumstance which, notwithstanding all the assurances which may be advanced to them, will not at all tend to hasten their removal. Further, the deadliness of the climate forms in itself a strong reason why the health of females, and especially of children, should not be hazarded until we have the sure prospect, with the blessing of God, of there establishing a mission.

The plans of the missionaries were much disturbed by the persistent rumours concerning the purpose and movements of the Transvaal Boers. M. W. Pretorius had but recently succeeded in reconciling warring factions and establishing the South African Republic, nearly six years after the Sand River Convention. In a recent message to his Raad he had given it as his decided opinion that the missionaries of the London Missionary Society had done and continued to do much harm amongst the natives ; and he asked his Raad to decide whether their continued labours and even their presence north of the Vaal River should be tolerated any longer. Pretorius acted on the theory that the Sand River Convention of 1852 had given over all the interior of South Africa to his people and government. The convenient phrase, " North of the Vaal River," was stretched by them very far westwards, and the spirit of the convention, as Dr Moffat in one of his letters pointed out, was interpreted by announcing to the chiefs in Bechuana-land that the Queen had handed them over to the Transvaal Government. Moffat received also a personal message from Pretorius, who was alarmed at the prospect of a large band of missionaries travelling through the interior to the Zambesi, in which he warned them not to begin their journey without express permission from himself. Rumours were sent flying across the country that the Boers intended to send an expedition westwards into South Bechuanaland, early in 1859. The prospect was so dark at one time that the Moffats sent a portion of their goods for safety to Hope Town, and Mackenzie deemed it imperative to take his wife into the Orange Free State.

Here it ought also to be recorded that Pretorius had formed the astute plan of settling German Missionaries in the interior to keep out and supplant the agents of the London Missionary Society. He succeeded in obtaining representatives of the famous Hermannsburg Mission, several of whom were already at work. If he had been successful in realising this plan he would have changed South African history profoundly. For German Missionaries, under the patronage of the Transvaal Government, would have made the interior of South Africa, Dutch or German permanently. Various events interfered with its success ; amongst these we must name as the most important a vigorous correspondence which was carried on with the officials of the German Society by the officials of the London Missionary Society, but most especially by Robert Moffat and John Mackenzie. These two sent repeated and powerful letters of expostulation and explanation. It is not too much to say that in this affair the missionaries took the first important steps towards opening South Central Africa to British supremacy ; which, as we shall see, they have done more than any other class of men to secure.

In view of the expected Boer raid, and his wife's health, Mackenzie went in May 1859 to Fauresmith. While there he heard, in June, that his brethren were preparing for an immediate start northward. He at once set out on horseback, accompanied by the Rev. W. B. Philip of Philippolis, and rode to Kuruman across the country which he was destined to traverse so often many years afterwards. He found that Mr Helmore's warm and impulsive nature had led him to declare that he would begin his journey at once, and must take his family with him. This vigorous action of course determined the movements of the rest,

Mackenzie excepted. For him it was arranged that he should return as soon as possible to Kuruman, remaining there in charge of the station, and follow with supplies in the next year.

At Fauresmith on July 16th there was born to Mackenzie his eldest child and son. He returned to Kuruman in August, and settled down to his work until the middle of the following year. The chief part of this consisted in the mastery of the Sechuana language, and in making various tours among heathen villages and towns, for preaching the gospel.

At length, on May 25th, 1860, Mackenzie set out on his momentous journey to the Zambesi. The experiences which he encountered have been fully described by him in "Ten Years North of the Orange River." In that volume he gives six chapters to narrate his own movements, his minute and accurate observations of native customs—especially among the Bushmen—the fate of the mission party which he was attempting to reach, and the extinction of the Makololo, the very people among whom they had hoped to establish a new mission. It is unnecessary to describe in any detail what he himself has recorded in these chapters.[1]

He tells us that he set out with four waggons, three horses, over seventy oxen and about a dozen men. Among his native servants, the most valuable was undoubtedly Mebalwe, the former servant of David Livingstone, who shared with him so bravely the dangers of the famous lion fight. It ought to be observed that, as the result of his method of organising the work of his servants, Mackenzie reports that his cattle did not stray once during all the months of their journeying. Mackenzie may be deemed especially fortunate in having crossed the desert regions, through which others passed

[1] "Ten Years North of the Orange River," chapters vii.-xii.

only at the cost of very great suffering and loss, without serious accident of any kind. This was due in very large measure to his own genius for organisation, to the prudence with which he foresaw and prepared for emergencies, and the personal influence which he exercised even over complete strangers from whom he sought accurate information.

As he passed through Bechuanaland, Mackenzie once more felt a deep surprise at seeing so many large native towns which were willing to receive a missionary, and to which none had been sent. The question arose more than once in his mind, whether it was wise to leave these regions with inadequate provision in order to reach those distant tribes to which he himself was going. At Liteyana he for the first time saw the well-known chief Sechele, whom Mackenzie describes as the "finest specimen of the Bechuanas"[1] whom he had yet seen; he was "tall and well made, with an open countenance, and unusually large eyes."

On July 20th he found himself in Shoshong, where he was destined to spend so many years of his prime; he found here a very large tribe gathered under a very able and quite unscrupulous chief named Sekhome. A German missionary had been at work there for a short time, by name Mr Schulenborg; he had been very successful, having formed a school and the beginnings of an organised church; among those whom he had baptised were the two sons of Sekhome, named Khame and Khamane. Here Mackenzie met Robert Moffat, on his way back from Matabeleland, who gave a very encouraging account of the reception given by Moselekatse to himself and the three young missionaries; this news made them both more eager to hear how it had fared with Helmore and Price on their more hazardous undertaking. In a few days Mackenzie started again, after making some careful plans

[1] "Ten Years North of the Orange River," p. 105.

for "the great thirst land" which they were about
to cross. We must content ourselves with inserting here a letter in which, on his return to Shoshong,
Mackenzie described to the Directors of the London
Missionary Society the dreary result of all the plans
and efforts to establish the Makololo Mission.

BAMANGWATO, *4th Dec.*, 1860.

Rev. Dr Tidman.

REV. AND DEAR SIR,—This note is written in a great
haste in order that it may be sent with some travellers who
leave this town to-day. I must, therefore, compress into a
few lines an account of my journey from the date of my
leaving this place in the end of July last.

Between Kanne and Nchokotsa there lies a most trying
country for travellers. The waters are far apart, and deep
sand intervenes. However, on Tuesday the 7th August we
reached Nchokotsa without knowing what thirst was, and
the oxen all right. From Nchokotsa we struck out towards
the north, spent Sabbath, 12th August, at Koobe, and on
the following Saturday reached Maila. After leaving
Nchokotsa we had employed guides, the "spoor" being
indistinct and often at night not traceable. When I asked
men to go forward from Maila to Kamakama, neither
Makalaka nor Bushmen would consent. I pleaded with
them, but they shook their heads, and pointing in the
direction of the places I had named, said, "There, there is
no water. Nothing but sun, nothing but sun. Your oxen
will be scattered and yourselves subjected to thirst in the
desert as were the Makoas of last year." This was the first
intimation I had received concerning the sufferings endured
by my brethren who had preceded me, which have not their
equal in the history of African missions, nor indeed in the
history of African travel, so far as I am acquainted with it.
Of course I could not think of returning, nor yet of lying
still, the rainy season being still distant. I resolved, therefore, to try to reach the Makololo country by some other
route. On questioning the Makalaka and the Bushmen, the
former offered to lead me into a road to the eastward formed
by hunters, by which I might reach the Makololo country.
This road leading to the S.-E. from Maila instead of to the
N. or N.-W., as I desired, my men and myself had consider-

able misgivings, but still, as the teacher Mebalwe remarked, one does not mind travelling by a roundabout road, provided it has water on it. I therefore engaged two Makalaka, and made ready to start. On Monday, before we were quite ready to leave Maila, Mokantsa, the son of Horoi, and a party of his Bushmen arrived "to greet us before our departure." A Bushman having the previous evening hinted that they knew a better road than that which I was about to take, I was very anxious that I should hear the merits of the two routes fairly stated, and therefore called all the Makalaka and Bushmen together, and, addressing myself to the two chiefs Mokantsa and Putse, offered them a reward if they would show me a nearer and better road than the one to the east. There followed a discussion among themselves, when Mokantsa offered to show me another lying a little to the west of that taken by my brethren. He counted on his fingers the number of valleys on the road containing water, and the number of wells having water sufficient for people but not for oxen, and mentioned last of all "the great river of the Makololo." We all thought we had now found the right road, and I thanked God, to whom I had repaired in this dilemma, for having thus assisted me. For some time after leaving Maila we kept the track of my brethren, but on the second day directed our course more to the west. The suspicion began to grow on me that the Bushmen were deceiving us, and this was confirmed when, after travelling three days, we found none of those waters to which they had promised to guide us. At last we reached a well, which we opened up after a whole day's work. On asking where the next valley was the Bushmen said, "the next water was the great river, and that it lay due west." This I was sure could not be the Mababe ; however, the question then was not how to reach the Makololo, but how to save the oxen by obtaining water for them. On Monday, 27th August, we reached a river which we found to be the Zouga, and not the Mababe. I beheld it with mingled feelings of thankfulness and disappointment, thankfulness that the oxen were saved, and disappointment that I was as far from the Makololo as when I was at Maila. However, I had now a river system before me, by the aid of which I hoped to reach the Makololo without risk to the oxen from thirst. The tsetse was my only obstacle, and I hoped to be able to secure guides who would be able to direct me how to avoid the districts infested by this destructive insect. I did not know then that a good Providence had brought me to the Zouga for special reasons. At Maila an old Bushman who had just arrived from Mababe was brought to me by the chief Putse to "tell me the news." The latter said, "Perhaps what he has to tell you is lies, perhaps it is truth. At anyrate I thought it my duty to bring him to you before you go forward to the country from which he has just come." The news was to the effect that Sekeletu had killed all the white people who had gone to them, and had taken their property. Of course, I laughed at the old man, being convinced Sekeletu was not the man to do such a thing. When we reached the Zouga, we met with a party of Lechulatebe's people going up the river in a boat. They told me the same tale—"all the white men were killed but one man and two children, who, they said, were now at Lechulatebe's." Knowing that the Batowana and the Makololo were enemies, I never heeded them. I viewed the story as one got up for the purpose of inducing me to turn aside to their master, instead of going to their enemy, Sekeletu. My men also were of the same opinion as myself, altho' we were all horrified to think that death should be so lightly spoken of by them and thus introduced without compunction into a story got up to serve their own ends. The four men left me for the lake, saying that they had never seen such a "hard-headed white man," assuring me at the same time that they would acquaint my friend of my arrival, and that they had no doubt I should soon receive a letter from him. I proceeded up the river, cherishing good hopes that I would soon reach the Makololo country. Although we heard the same dreadful story of the death of my friends at every village, neither I nor my men believed it. Their perseverance in the same story, after I had assured them I had got no ammunition for sale, we attributed to the strictness of their orders to allow no white man to pass to the Makololo. The history of Lechulatebe's dealings with Livingstone tended to confirm me in this view of the matter.

On Saturday, the 8th Sept., while we were moving along the river's bank, I beheld a party of men coming from the river and directing their course to the first waggon, which they stopped. On going forward and demanding their reason for stopping my waggon, the chief man answered that he came from the king and had brought boats to cross my goods over the river. I told him to be off about his business, that I did not intend to go to Lechulatebe's and therefore did not need his boats. " But I have brought the white man with me, your brother, the son of your own father." I answered, " Where is he then ? How can you tell lies so ? If you brought the white man to meet me, why do you come without him ? " " Because he is sick and tired and remained in the boat." I did not believe the fellow, and therefore answered, " I will go on just as I intended ; if you have got the white man, bring him to the place where we shall sleep, and where we shall rest to-morrow (Sunday) and then I shall believe you." The waggons accordingly went on. About sunset we drew near to the outspanning place. It was a beautiful, well-wooded spot, and the river gave a life and freshness to the prospect which those alone can appreciate who have toiled through the riverless, almost waterless, deserts of South Africa. I shall not attempt to describe my anxiety on nearing this place. Could it, after all, be true that my dear friends had thus been swept away ? I went on with the first waggon, engrossed in anxious thought, when the driver said to me, in a tone which made me start, " Ki ena " (" It is he "). I sprang from the waggon, and went forward to meet some one who, I could see thro' the trees, was a European. At length I saw it was my dear friend, Mr Price. " But can it be that all this which I hear is true ? " I hurriedly asked, almost before I had grasped his hand. Alas ! *I saw* what the answer would be before I heard it. " All is true." And then I had to break the news to Mrs Mackenzie that her beloved fellow-labourers, Mrs Helmore and Mrs Price, were no more. O, indeed, it was a trying hour ! Hopes which had cheered us during our long journey were now dashed to the ground, and high pictures which had often filled our minds with pleasure now gave place to one gloomy scene of desolation and of death. We sat down and wept for those who were not. Our men betokened their sympathy by their countenances, and the simple Makoba stood around witnessing the scene. Mr Price was very *unwell*; not at all the healthy person he used to be. His mind was also affected, for he would tell us the same thing twice in a very short time. He was holding Wednesdays as Sundays when we met him.

The following are the harrowing details of the mission at Linyante. Mr and Mrs Helmore and Mr and Mrs Price with their families arrived at Linyante on the 14th of February. On the 2nd of March, Malatsi, Mr Price's driver,

died; and on the 3rd the whole party were taken ill, with
the exception of Mr and Mrs Price and one servant. On
the 7th inst. Henry Helmore died, and on the 9th Mr Price's
infant daughter. Selina Helmore was next called away on
the 11th inst., and on the same day Tabe, the highly-
respected deacon from Likatlong, breathed his last. Next
day Mrs Helmore died. Before her death she said she
believed her work on earth was done, and that she had no
desire to live longer. On the Sabbath following their arrival
Mr Helmore preached to the people in the chief's court, and
went also for the same purpose on the Sunday following.
He was taken ill, however, while in the town, and returned
to the waggons, unable to conduct the afternoon service.
At the time Mrs Helmore died he was very ill, unable to
rise from his bed. Some time after this he got better, and
was able to go about a little, leaning on a staff. However,
a relapse took place, and on the 22nd of April he followed
his partner and two children. Another servant, an old man,
also died in March, when so many were swept away; the
exact date I am not able to give. Mr and Mrs Price were
also very ill in March, and also afterwards; but, as God
mercifully ordered it, the two were never very ill at the same
time. One or the other was thus able to minister to the
others, and they were the only persons able and willing to
do so. Mr Price was lying in a wet sheet, hardly able to
stand through exhaustion, when his infant breathed its last
in its mother's arms. In the language of a Mochuana who
has returned with Mr Price, they were all scattered about,
white people and black, those in their tents and these on the
ground outside, like logs of wood, unable to help themselves,
and indeed, many of them in a deep stupor from which it was
difficult to rouse them to consciousness. Mr and Mrs Price
had resolved to leave before Mr Helmore's death, but after
that event, feeling their increased responsibility, they were
still more anxious to return. They left Linyante on June
26th. The Makololo did not allow them to cross their river
until they had taken openly, or secretly stolen, almost every
thing in the waggons. Mr Helmore's new waggon Sekeletu
claimed as his, and all Mr Helmore's things; then Mr and
Mrs Price's things were taken, they with the utmost difficulty
obtaining clothing barely sufficient for the journey south.
After they had crossed the Mababe they began to breathe
freely again and to feel they were at last beyond the reach of

those who had so cruelly used them. On the 5th of July, however, Mrs Price died, after they had just begun to entertain hopes of regaining a more healthy country and more friendly people. Her body was laid in a grave in the wide African wilderness ; her soul, we humbly yet confidently hope, is in the Paradise of God.

I crossed the Zouga and went on with Mr Price in my waggon to Lechulatebe's at the Lake, leaving behind me the head waggon till our return. We met Lizzie and Willie Helmore at Lechulatebe's, it being impossible for Mr Price to take them with him in the boat. After preaching on Sunday, 22nd Sept., at Lechulatebe's, on returning to our waggons, I found my little boy ill with fever. Thro' God's blessing on the means used, the fever was checked. But we hastened our departure, after purchasing 9 oxen for Mr Price.

For a long time my child was ill, feverish symptoms constantly reappearing. One of the lads also took the fever after our return to the waggons which we left behind us, but he also recovered. These were the only cases of African fever I have witnessed. After prayerfully considering our position, we resolved to return with Mr Price and await fresh orders from the Directors, and accordingly began our trek down the river.

I must now conclude this hurried note. Mr Price would have written to you, but having the heavy task to perform of writing to his deceased wife's relatives as well as Mr Helmore's for the first time after these sad events, he has requested me to acquaint you with the circumstances of the Mission.

1. The chief men of the Makololo on several occasions stated their entire disinclination to remove to the north of the Zambesi. Sekeletu, Mameri, Motibi and others were unanimous in this. They said if they removed anywhere it would be to dispossess Lechulatebe of the Lake country.

2. The Mambari slave-dealers seem to have got a firm footing among them, and are received as friends, and feasting continues as long as they remain. The Mambari have evidently endeavoured to poison the Makololo mind against Livingstone, as they told our brethren they believed the Doctor was not now a Missionary but a ruler.

3. Mr Price and all the Bechuana servants believe that poison was administered to their party by the Makololo. This they ascertained from a man of influence who is always near the king.

4. Almost everything taken in by Mr Helmore and Mr Price has been stolen by the Makololo—waggon, guns, tents, boxes of clothing, etc. The last action performed by Mr Price's Makololo guides was to take him, on his way south, into a district full of tsetse, where his oxen were all bitten, and out of forty he has now only two! The guides ran away after they were fairly into the tsetse.

5. Much of the mischief done by stealing may be traced to the counsels of a servant of Tabe's named Mahoosi—a person whose very meat and drink seemed to be to create ill-feeling among the Makololo towards the Mission. He urged them to steal and even to kill every white person in the party.

6. The Makololo country can hardly be said to be accessible by the Kamakama road. It will always be a feat to reach it by that route. There is always plenty of water by way of the Lake, but the tsetse is on the road, and can only be avoided by the help of faithful guides belonging to the district. There is a road to the east of the Nchokotsa and Kamakama one, now used by hunters, which, I think, would turn out on the whole the best one.

7. Mr Price goes as far as the Cape with Mr Helmore's children, according to his promise before Mr Helmore's death. I returned with Mr Price feeling, that I would not be warranted to go on with waggon-loads of goods after what had happened. I have now laid the matter before you, and conclude with the question, "What am I to do?"

We are all pretty well in health. Mr Price and Mrs Mackenzie unite with me in Christian regards.

Before Mackenzie's letter reached England rumours of the terrible disaster which it described had already arrived; consternation spread far and wide in missionary circles, and a great deal of public criticism was now directed upon the entire plan and the mode of carrying it out. The original idea had been that the missionaries should arrive on the Zambesi at a time when Dr Livingstone expected to arrive there by way of the East Coast and the Zambesi River. It was to him that Sekeletu had given his promise to transfer the entire tribe to the higher and healthier districts on the north bank of the Zambesi River, if missionaries were brought to him.

When the missionaries reached him without Livingstone, and Livingstone owing to unexpected detentions did not arrive until after the rainy season, Sekeletu did not show himself as cordial as had been expected ; he was unwilling, naturally, to leave a position of great military advantage, although unhealthy, in order to settle in a place where he would be open to the attacks of his inveterate enemies, the Matabele. The inhospitable treatment which he gave to the missionaries stands out with unpleasant distinction in the history of the relations of missionaries to South African chiefs. Mackenzie has described [1] the destruction of the Makololo tribe which blotted this name from the map of Africa.

The Foreign Secretary of the London Missionary Society, Dr Arthur Tidman, wrote on April 5th, 1861, to Mackenzie as follows :—

LONDON, *April 5th,* 1861.

Under all circumstances, there is plainly no alternative but to relinquish the Makololo Mission for the present, and we consider you were fully justified in deciding to return to the South.

Until there has been an opportunity of conferring with the Directors on the whole case, I should scarcely feel prepared to indicate the course it may be incumbent upon you to pursue ; but it is more than probable that you and Mr Price will be recommended to direct your attention to the Matabele Mission. In the meantime you will be able, while at the Kuruman, to take counsel with Mr Moffat on the subject, and I hope by an early opportunity to convey to you more definite instructions.

On 23rd December, there was born at Shoshong, Mackenzie's second child, a son, whose arrival was hailed with great delight by the natives of the town. As this was the first white child born in that town, by general consent the Bamangwato gave him the name Mangwato, by which he was ever afterwards

[1] "Ten Years North of the Orange River," pp. 243-248.

known amongst the inhabitants of that country. It
may be added that the eldest child having been called
William, and usually Willie, his father and mother
were named after him, according to the Bechuanaland
custom. To this day Mackenzie and his wife are
known in Bechuanaland as Ra-Willie and Ma-Willie
respectively ; in the same manner Khame himself,
whose eldest child was called Bessie, is known amongst
his own people as Ra-Bessie.

After a brief stay at Shoshong, Mackenzie and
Price, who was very slowly recovering his health,
set out for the south. Both were much cheered by
the announcement that their friends in Cape Town
had set on foot a public subscription for the relief of
the surviving members of the Mission. This relief was
carried to them by Mr Moffat, who met them on their
way to Kuruman.

Mackenzie once more arrived at Kuruman, after one
of the most prolonged and trying experiences of waggon
life which have fallen to the lot of any but the pioneer
Dutchmen of South Africa.

KURUMAN, *Feb.* 29, 1861.

REV. DR TIDMAN,

Rev. and Dear Sir,—Again I address you from this
station. My journey into the interior is a thing of the past.
The waggons are unloaded, the men paid off, and we are
again enjoying the grateful shelter of a house. We have also
had the pleasure of again meeting those Christian friends
who, I at least thought, had been parted with for ever.

My last letter recorded the leading events connected with
my journey up to the date of our arrival at the Bamangwato.
I shall now resume that record. Our stay at the Bamangwato
extended over six weeks. On the 23rd December, Mrs
Mackenzie was safely delivered of a son in the home of
Mr Schulenborg. Altho' this residence had neither doors
nor windows, it had a good roof; and if it caused rather than
prevented a draught, it was delightfully cool, and was, besides, the hospitable home of kind Christian friends, whose
attentions we shall always gratefully remember. Our oxen

having in the meantime considerably improved in condition,
on the third week after the event just recorded, we pursued
our journey towards Kuruman, reached a place called Silinye
on the 19th, and on Monday, the 21st of January, we met
with Mr Moffat, who was on his way to look for us, and, if
necessary, assist us. Finding all whom he was seeking, he
turned his waggons towards home, and next day we went on
together.

In passing Sechele's town, that chief showed us great kindness, and agreed that his waggon, which I had formerly hired,
should go on to Kuruman, the only additional charge being
that I should repaint the waggon and make for it a new
sail, the material of which he gave me. I have pleasure in
mentioning anything like a disinterested action among a
people dreadfully selfish.

My mind naturally turns to the future. Altho' an invisible
shield seems to have been round both me and mine, and
altho' I make no claim to having endured anything very
severe, yet nine months loose, gipsy, waggon-life does not
leave one with much relish for that way of spending one's
time. I wait for that Hand to guide me to some sphere of
usefulness, as it has hitherto led me and sustained me. I
do not forget that I left my native land as a missionary to
Central South Africa. Altho' the Mission to the Mokololo
has proved so disastrous, there is a teeming population to
the eastward, in that district recently discovered by Dr
Livingstone, and you are aware what hopes the Doctor has
held forth to the Mission presided over by Archdeacon
Mackenzie. It seems to me that there is a greater prospect
of success in a Mission to some of these tribes approachable
from the sea-coast than there ever was in connection with the
Mission to the Makololo. Should the Directors resolve to
continue their efforts for the evangelisation of Central Africa,
I am quite willing to devote myself to the work. I think the
Mission to the north of the Zambesi has hardly received a
fair trial, there being high, all but insurmountable, obstacles
in connection with the Makololo. If the Directors resolve
to give it such a trial, and consider that I can be of service
to them in the attempt, they may depend upon me to the
utmost of my ability. It might take some time to establish such
a Mission on a permanent basis ; but if an agent or two were
directed to visit the country and to feel their way quietly, it is not
improbable that success might ultimately attend their efforts.

In the meantime I shall endeavour to do the work of a missionary among the Bechuanas while waiting for further instructions.—Yours sincerely, JOHN MACKENZIE.

Early in 1861 Mrs Mackenzie was attacked by a prolonged fever of a low and intermittent type. As a journey was itself on almost all occasions the best cure which Mackenzie could discover for this African fever, he resolved to go across to Fauresmith. While there he was once more confronted with the temptation to enter upon ministerial service in other directions. He received a very pressing call to the pastorate of the church at Hope Town. None of these proposals, although he frankly and earnestly considered them, presented any real attraction to him ; his eye was still on the interior of the continent, and his mind was set upon pioneer work. The Directors of the Society were themselves in great uncertainty, and found themselves unable for a considerable time to give him a definite appointment. During the remainder of 1861, he was at Kuruman, diligently engaged in educational and literary work ; he completed a school book on geography in the Sechuana language, and also wrote and printed a translation of Dr Newman Hall's famous booklet, "Come to Jesus." It was not until May 1861 that he received from the Directors a definite appointment to the station at Shoshong, and this was made under the impression, which turned out to be false, that the German missionary had left the place.

KURUMAN, 12 *May*, 1862.
REV. DR TIDMAN,
  Dear Brother,—I have to acknowledge receipt of yours of Feb. 5, recommending me to commence a Mission among the Bamangwato, in the event of Mr Price having gone to the Matabele.
  Since the receipt of your letter one thing is now settled in my mind, viz., that the Interior of Africa is to be the scene of my future labours. I am thankful after a season of perplexity to see my way thus far.

It will be necessary, however, to explain that this appointment has been given by the Directors while labouring under
a mistake.   I see by the March *Chronicle* that Mr Moffat
advises the step which you have taken, among other reasons,
because Mr Schulenborg was not returning to the Bamangwato.
Now the reports to which Mr Moffat refers turned out, as
most reports of the kind do in this country, to be without
foundation.   Mr Schulenborg *has not* rejoined his Society,
and *has* returned to the Bamangwato, with the intention of
living and labouring there.   Knowing the facts of the case
before the arrival of your letter, I was, of course, amused to
see that while you could not agree to my going to the East
Coast for fear of encroaching upon a district occupied by
English Episcopalians and Scotch Free Churchmen, it should
so happen that you were actually setting me down at the
same Bechuana Town with a Hanoverian Lutheran !   There
can only be one opinion as to the importance of the
Bamangwato District, both on account of its great population and its position.   Had it been unoccupied by other
missionaries as you were led to believe, there could not have
been a wiser appointment.

As matters stand I feel I cannot regard myself as missionary
to the Bamangwato, and I am sure the Directors, when they
know the facts of the case, would not wish me to do so.
Were the Bamangwato the last heathen town in Africa the
case would be different ; two or more Societies might en-
compass the last abode of heathenism in order to hasten the
progress of the Gospel : but the case, alas, is very different.
There are vast regions beyond the Bamangwato which are
the abodes of cruelty and degradation.   Into these countries
it was the object of the Society to introduce the Gospel, by
the formation of the Makololo Mission.   Adverse events,
linked together with singular fatality, baffled this endeavour.
But I am glad to find from the postscript of your last letter, that
the Directors still cherish the desire to introduce the Gospel
into these places, and thus to reward the evil received at the
hands of the inhabitants with the highest good.   It was and
is my opinion that efforts to this end could be best carried
on from the East Coast.   But such, I learn from your letter,
is not the opinion of the Directors.   I cheerfully acquiesce
in their decision.   Of course nothing must be done hastily,
nothing without due consideration.

Let me state to the Directors what I propose to myself to

accomplish in dependence on God's guidance and blessing.
Regarding my appointment to the Bamangwato as not likely
to be permanent, I look on some of the regions beyond as my
parish, accepting at the same time as my motto, "Festina lente."

I propose to go forward to the Bamangwato with the
intention of staying there for a time, and, should a favourable
opportunity occur, eventually to proceed farther. I hope and
believe this will meet with the views of the Directors. I
have written somewhat fully that they may perfectly understand my position. The first thing I hope to accomplish
and which will be of service to the Society at all events, is
this. With the assistance of Mr Herbst the missionary
artizan at Bamangwato, I intend to build a small but substantial house which, in the event of my departure for the
Interior, can be used as a store-room for the use of my
brethren as well as for my own. This plan was talked of
before we went into the Interior and the advantages of
having such a place are quite apparent.

When the traveller is going to the Lake, to the Victoria
Falls, or to Moselekatse's Country, he passes the Bamangwato.
Thus hunters and others could bring supplies so far, no
matter to what part of the Interior they were going; afterwards it would be easy for the brethren in the Interior to
send to the Bamangwato for such supplies.

While at the Bamangwato, I shall be able to command the
news of the Interior, so that I could not be in a better
position to perform the duties of a "scout." It will be my
endeavour as early as possible to open communications with
the Makololo and should I hear favourable reports I shall
pay them a visit. I would count it a great pleasure to tell
them that we owe them no grudge, but pity them and desire
their welfare. Should the door to the Makololo seem still
to be shut, and no inducement held out to increase the
number of the Matabele labourers, I might visit Lechulatebe
to see if there were no healthy site for a Mission in his
district, which would certainly be a splendid field for a
missionary. Lechulatebe expressed his willingness to receive
a missionary while I was there with Mr Price.

At the same time, I hope to do good among the
Bamangwato. The Directors will be glad to learn, that
judging from our past intercourse, there are grounds for
believing that Mr Schulenborg and myself are likely to get
on well together. I have no doubt as to our getting on as

friends, as neighbours, and as preachers of the Gospel; *as pastors* I am afraid we could not see eye to eye.

Such, my dear Brother, are the plans which occurred to my mind, and which I beg thus to communicate to the Directors. I ask their confidence and their prayers; let me work as it were in private; it may be the Lord will open up my way to the Makololo. At all events, wherever I am I shall endeavour to carry with me a savour of Jesus Christ.

Let me in conclusion state, for the information of the Directors, what has occupied my attention while in the Kuruman District and while awaiting their further orders. We returned from Philippolis and Fauresmith in August, after Mrs Mackenzie's recovery from fever. In October we visited the various sub-stations to the south-west of Kuruman situated among the Long Mountains (Langberg). In December I was at Hope Town, from which I addressed my last letter to you. In January I visited the Taungs District, partly in company with Mr Ross; and in February I visited Morokweng, a large town of Barolong, situated on the edge of the Kalahari Desert, and occasionally visited by Mr Fredoux of the Motito. During the interval between these journeys I taught a Geography Class and an English Class at Kuruman, taking also my turn in preaching. I drew up a First Book on Geography for the use of schools, and also set up the types of most of it. I also translated "Come to Jesus" into Sechuana, the MS. of which I have left with Mr Moffat, who has kindly agreed along with Mr Ashton to see it through the press.

When Mackenzie arrived at Shoshong in June, he found Mr Schulenborg still at work, and with no intention of leaving. Price, who had been refused entrance to Matabeleland, was also there trying to co-operate as well as possible, with his Lutheran brother. In these circumstances Mackenzie could not but regard his appointment at Shoshong as temporary and tentative, and his mind became employed upon fresh plans for reopening communications with the Makololo. But in the meantime, he entered as earnestly as possible into the missionary work of the place. He and his family lived in a

small two-roomed hut which had been built by
Mr Schulenborg at the very entrance of the kloof
or narrow gorge below which the town was built.
At the close of the year another letter arrived from
the Directors, showing that they were still uncertain
about Mackenzie's movements. They were carrying
on negotiations with the German sister Society,
which they hoped would secure to them the exclu-
sive right to work in Bechuanaland; hence, while
they did not disapprove of Mackenzie's attempts to
reach the Zambesi, they expressed their own desire
to establish other missions more broadly and thoroughly
in Bechuanaland, and their attention was especially
directed to the country of the Bamangwato. They
intended as soon as possible to send out more missionaries for this purpose. The following letter to his friend
James Ross states a number of these points clearly :—

BAMANGWATO, SOUTH AFRICA,
17th Dec. 1862.

MY DEAR JAMIE,—When you wrote to me last you
promised to send me another letter soon. I have waited
long, but the promised epistle comes not. It seems strange
not to know *your* address, not to know what you are doing,
except generally that you are preaching the Gospel somewhere in Scotland. However I have myself neglected many
promises as to corresponding, so that I am not in a position
to find fault.

I found out from an Elgin paper that you were in Inver-
ness. I thought you might stay there ; but I learn from John
Douglas that you are, or were lately, at Linlithgow. I am
glad you have some knocking about at the outset ; I should
think it will enable you to pursue a course of general study
with less effort than if you were fairly wedged into one pulpit,
and bound to preach service after service to a congregation
which you had "taken for better or for worse." It would be
a good thing if you could extend your rambles beyond Scotland. Live for a short time in England, and if possible, on
the continent. I'm not joking : take in stock, "everything
in the line," and your services are likely to have a freshness
and point which reading alone is not likely to give them.

You see I advise with the same liberty as when we went arm-in-arm along Lossie Bank.

As for myself, I am still "going to and fro" and (not walking) but tumbling "up and down" the southern part of this continent. Next time I write, however, will I hope, be from the north bank of the Zambesi. We leave this place in April next, and hope to cross the river, proceed to the site of our future station, which we must previously select, and erect some sort of house before next hot season comes on. We have *tsetse*, the Zambesi, and an unexplored country to the north, to pass through before we reach our destination; but I don't think we shall " stick." The physical difficulties, although not to be despised, are nothing to the moral obstacles which await us as missionaries to the Makololo. This tribe has obtained its position by a sort of Ishmaelite warfare: of late it has retreated to a natural stronghold formed by a river system on the one hand, by *tsetse* on the other. From this unhealthy den of Linyanti they have carried on their forays with impunity, have taken prisoners and sold them to the Mambari traders from the coast. Of course you know the sad history of the late attempts to open a mission among these marauders. In the interval Sekeletu and his people have been frequently visited by natives from the South; and I think by one English trader. From these parties they have learned enough to cause them to regret having taken the missionaries' property from them. As to the charge of poisoning those who died at Linyanti, they firmly deny it, and I give them credit for speaking the truth, for I never believed that my fellow-labourers were poisoned. When the hunters and traders went in this season, Mr Price and Mr Moffat and myself sent in a joint letter to Sekeletu, asking him if he would allow us to go direct to a place called Tabachow (or White Mountain) on the north of the Zambesi, and if he and his people would join us there. We have just received the answer, which is more favourable than we expected. He consents to everything, and urges us to hasten our coming. He is ill, and expects to be benefited by the white man's medicines. The people also are tired of the unhealthy place where they now are, and express their willingness to follow their chief and live with missionaries. It is said by all that the country to which we are going is not unhealthy, but of course this means, when compared with adjacent districts.

We go to try it, looking to God for His blessing and presence.
May we trust in Him with our whole heart, while we take
every precaution necessary in the circumstances. Pray for
us that the Gospel may have free course and be glorified in
Central Africa.

We have been staying here for some months, having our
eye on the North, and waiting the proper time to come round.
This is a large town, too large for one missionary. It is at
present supplied with a missionary who came to this country
in connection with Pastor Harms's Society. I had an appointment to this place, which of course became null through his
presence here.

I suppose you know that my third child was born on the
23rd September last. Since I began this letter, I had occasion to go for a short distance on horseback, so I took Willie
before me on the saddle. I sometimes ride with Johnnie also
behind me. Mrs Mackenzie is quite well, and sends her love
to you. Not knowing your address, I have sent this to John
Douglas. I thought there was no harm in doing this, especially
as I have not entered on any private topic. . . . My paper
fails me !

Affection and remembrances to the auld folks at Elgin, and
to our mutual friends in Edinburgh. Send me something
frequently ; an old newspaper will be new to me, and will only
cost you a penny, and the time spent in addressing it. *Write
at once.*—Ever yours affectionately, JOHN MACKENZIE.

The year 1862 proved another year of travel and
uncertainty to Mackenzie. On January 24th he wrote
a letter to Dr Tidman describing the negotiations
which were proceeding with regard to the occupancy
of Shoshong as a Mission Station by the Hermannsburg Society. Mr Schulenborg, their representative,
had gone on a journey to Natal, the South African
headquarters of that society, and Mackenzie was
occupying his little hut of two rooms in his absence.
And Mackenzie had written a long letter to Dr
Hardeland, the Superintendent of the Hermannsburg
Mission, explaining the policy of the London Missionary Society there, and urging that the German

Society should not send representatives to settle in the heart of a sphere already partly occupied by, and already fully mapped out for the agents of the London Missionary Society. In his letter to Dr Tidman Mackenzie added the following paragraph :—

I feel tempted to criticise the policy which overlooked as a site for a Mission Station such a central and in every way important place as the Bamangwato. What it is to-day it has been for more than twenty years. But there would seem to be some impediment in the way of the vigorous prosecution of Mission effort among the Bechuanas. Where are the two Missionaries who were to be sent out two years ago to reinforce the Southern District of Bechuanaland ? It would be useless to recapitulate the reasons for this re-inforcement which approved themselves to the minds of the Directors at the time. I may just mention, however, that a late personal inspection of the country indicated deepens my own impressions of the desirability of such re-inforcements, and further, that if the matter were left to the decision of your agents on the spot, there would be no voices raised against a more vigorous policy on the part of the Society.

In the month of March a dark cloud swept over Shoshong. The town was situated at the foot of a mountain kloof which had been selected as affording a military stronghold against the Matabele. Moselekatse, the fierce founder of that ruthless tribe, had often threatened to attack Sekhome, the chief of the Bamangwato, but hitherto his threats had been unfulfilled, and Sekhome's tribe had been growing stronger and stronger. At last the news reached Shoshong that their dreaded foe was moving for a determined attack upon them. This raid of the Matabele has been vividly described by Mackenzie.[1] That account amplifies a letter which he wrote at the close of the struggle to Dr Tidman, and which was printed in the *Chronicle* of the London Missionary Society at the time. The following is the main part of the letter giving the account of the raid itself :—

In more than one of my letters from this place, I have

[1] "Ten Years North," etc., chapter xiv.

been able to speak favourably of the prospects of the Makololo Mission. In fact, there was good reason to believe that before the end of 1863, your agents would be at work in a healthy locality on the north bank of the Zambesi, instructing the newly-removed Makololo. I am sorry to say that an event has taken place bearing most unfavourably on this project.

When the hunters and traders passed this place from Moselekatse's country in September and October last, it was rumoured that the Matabele meditated an attack on the Bamangwato. Altho' Sekhome had no reason for presuming on the friendship or consideration of the Ishmaelite Zulu chief, Moselekatse had so often pledged himself to Mr Moffat to give up his warlike policy that a certain impression was made even on the suspicious native mind.

It seemed to be the opinion of both Europeans and natives, that although the Matabele chief might continue to break his promise annually by sending his warriors to attack the Mashona and Makololo, who live on the north and north-west of his country, he would study to put the best face on such doings by keeping the peace with the tribes south of his territory.

On the 7th of March, however, Sekhome and his tribe received definite intelligence that a Matabele army was approaching, and that already several large cattle posts had fallen into the enemy's hands. Happening to pass thro' the *khotla* or court that morning on my way from school, I heard the first messenger, all breathless and excited, tell his tale, giving information concerning the Matabele. The war-cry at once resounded in the "kloof" where the Bamangwato live, and soon from all quarters men streamed into the khotla, some armed with guns and others with the assegai or spear, and ox-hide shield. The first thing to be done was to collect the cattle from the various posts, with the sheep and goats. Men having been despatched for this purpose, and sentinels placed at the various entrances to the Bamang-wato Mountains, Sekhome marched out of the town at the head of his men, and held what I suppose must be called a review; although it was certainly a different spectacle from what is indicated by that expression in civilised countries. There was no marching, no defiling, no sham fighting; but the chief squatted on the ground, dealt out ammunition, etc., to those who stood in need of it, inspected the faulty lock of one gun and the frail stock of another, all the while enquiring after the absent, conversing with those present

around him, and listening to the accounts of every newly-
arrived herdsman, who, leaving his charge in the hands of
the Matabele, had fled for his life. In passing my house,
after having this "review," Sekhome jocularly asked me if I
were going to help him against the Matabele? Replying in
the negative, I reminded him that I was a promulgator of
peace and goodwill amongst men; that I had no quarrel
with the Matabele; and that I was persuaded they also
would regard me as a neutral party. His reply was to the
effect that Matabele warriors did not make nice distinctions :
and that the colour of a man's skin was not easily discovered
in the darkness of night. He then informed me that they
expected to be attacked during the night or very early in
the morning. "In the olden time," added the chief,
"whilst our herdsmen were still informing us of the loss of
our cattle, the thieves themselves were wont to fall upon us
before we could make any preparation for self-defence; but
to-night they will find us ready; and should they enter the
town they will find it empty."

Sekhome having given orders that all the women and
children should take refuge in the mountains, and that all
property should be removed thither also, a strange and
melancholy spectacle presented itself to the eye; the several
narrow paths leading to the top of the steep and rugged
mountains were for some time densely crowded with women,
each one carrying a large bundle on her back, and the rest
struggling up the ascent before her. For some time the
women and old servants and old men followed each other as
closely as do people in Cheapside. That night Mrs
Mackenzie was the only female in the town of the Bamangwato ; and our children the only little ones who had not been
removed to the mountain fastnesses. People passed to and
fro, under arms the whole night ; every one was on the alert ;
and Mrs Mackenzie and myself slept as little as the Bamangwato. About ten o'clock the young chiefs paid us a visit
with several of those who attend church and school,
surrounded by whom I offered up prayer before our door,
in the bright moonlight. During the night we collected our
letters, accounts, portraits, etc., in a little box ; so as to be
easily removed. Although we could not sleep like our
children, we could commend them and ourselves to the
protection of God, our Heavenly Father, and enjoy the
repose of mind consequent on trust in the Almighty.

At length the morning dawned without any attack having taken place. The cattle, sheep and goats, from the outposts came pouring in, and were hastily driven up the mountains. The kloof for a time resounded with the lowing of cattle, the bleating of sheep and goats, and the shouts of their drivers.

In stating his plan of defence the Chief informed me that should the enemy make the attack from the plain, they were to be allowed to enter the town, and to set it on fire, if they chose ; that a number of cattle were to be kept in sight as a bait for the Matabele on the side of the mountain behind Mr Price's house, and right opposite my own ; and that the fight would therefore take place, as it were, on our premises. Sekhome said he was sure to beat them on this ground ; but if they approached from the plain he would not risk an engagement elsewhere. He added that he was sorry our houses were in the way, but he could not help it. In the event of the Matabele endeavouring to reach the town from the north which was nearest the scene of their depredations the Bamangwato were to meet them on a "haugh" in the heart of the mountains, and if beaten were to fall back on the vantage-ground before referred to.

After seriously considering our position in connection with this statement, and taking into account the merciless and bloody character of the Matabele, I came to the conclusion that it would be best for Mrs Mackenzie and the children to retire to the mountains, until the danger became less imminent. When I listened to one messenger after another narrating the cowardly, spiteful, and bloody deeds, enacted at the cattle posts my resolution was confirmed. While Mrs Mackenzie and the children were in the house I could not but feel uneasy as to the result of a midnight rush of such savages, everyone of whose spears had repeatedly drunk the blood of the aged and decrepit, the defenceless female and the tender infant.

Khame, the eldest son of Sekhome, kindly furnished me with a few men who carried up the hill the few articles which we had resolved to remove from the house. Accompanied by these people and by our servants, Mrs Mackenzie and the children took their departure. I followed with our cattle, and passed my little family squatted on the grass beneath a tree, their nearest neighbours on one side being the chief wife of Sekhome, and on the other Joseph and Koenraad de Buys, from the Transvaal Country. This was Friday morning ; it was Wednesday evening of the following week before Mrs Mackenzie left her " refuge " on the mountain top ; and the native women remained for two or three days longer.

It was not that life on the mountain was at all pleasant, for it was well known to be a haunt of wolves and tigers ; in fact, but a few days before, a sheep had been killed by a tiger in broad day light, not many hundred yards from where Mrs Mackenzie and the little ones slept in the open air.   But we heard nothing of such unwelcome visitors, and cannot but think that the overwhelming rush of people into their haunts must have driven both wolves and tigers to seek a lair else- where.   South Africa is a very thirsty land ; all its inhabitants are ever ready to welcome rain ; and many pretend to be able to conjure it from the reluctant clouds ; yet the showers which on more than one night aroused the sleepers on the top of the Bamangwato Hills were anything but welcome. The people disappeared in the crevices among the rocks : Mrs Mackenzie drew her little ones closer to her, and a karross, spread over their heads on the branches of the tree, formed a pretty good protection from the rain which was then falling in torrents.   It was my intention to remain in the house during the night, that, in case of an attack, I might be able to inform the Matabele invaders that the premises belonged to a missionary ; but such was Mrs Mackenzie's description of her first night on the mountains, alone with the little ones, that I considered it indispensable afterwards to form one of the party.   Our house was thus left without an occupant during the night : but a Makololo woman, whom I had saved from starvation a few months before, slept on the premises.   Being still weak and sadly afflicted with St Vitus's Dance, she preferred remaining among our pots to climbing the mountains, and we allowed her to do what she pleased. I have to record, to the credit of the Bamangwato, that although Mr Price's premises were entirely deserted, and my own every night left in charge of a single woman, no attempt at theft was made.   Of course so long as Mrs Mackenzie and the children remained on the mountain, my attention was divided between them and our premises.   The awkwardness of my position will be seen when I state that it would be much more easy to climb to the top of Arthur's Seat, Edinburgh, than it was to reach our encampment on the top of the Bamangwato Hills.   You will have a pretty good idea as to how I occupied myself between Friday and

Wednesday (and you will excuse the illustration), when I inform you that during the above period I wore down a pair of English made boots, and lamed myself into the bargain !

Fight between the Bamangwato and the Matabele

While we were scaling the mountain, the Bamangwato forces had assembled in the haugh referred to. It seems there was a good deal of talking ; and Sekhome (who besides being chief is also a " ngaka," or doctor or sorcerer) was earnestly engaged in reading his dice, and repeating his incantations, when he was interrupted by Khame, who very abruptly informed his father that he was taking up too much time with these things ; that as for himself (Khame) he wanted to fight and have done with it. The chief, who felt proud of his son, " pocketed " the insult which in his priestly character he had sustained, and immediately ordered out the two youngest " mepato " or regiments, viz., that of Khame and that of his brother Khamane. The people were so pleased with the conduct of the young chief, that several old men who of course did not belong to his regiment, tried to join it as it moved off, but were seen by Sekhome and ordered back.

The two chiefs next in rank to Sekhome also joined Khame's party, followed by a number of their men. The whole force under Khame did not exceed two hundred. Of these the majority had guns, and about eight were mounted on horseback. Before he rode off Khame was addressed by his father to the effect that he must not imagine he was going on an elephant hunt ; that he was marching against men, and not merely men, but Matabele.

It was late in the afternoon before they met the Matabele, who, contrary to their old custom, had been advancing slowly, apparently in no hurry to attack the town. They were marching in three companies, two of whom were together, and these the Bamangwato attacked. At first the " Machaga " made light of the guns, and imitated their report ; but they soon changed their tune. Moving in compact bodies, every ball told on some of them, so that when charged by those on horseback they gave way, some of them throwing down their arms and fleeing. These, however, were rallied by the others shouting to them that they were disobeying Moselekatse's orders, which forbade any of the warriors to run from the enemy. While the day was thus with the Bamangwato, the third company of Matabele, which had been following up a cattle track at some distance, hearing the report of firearms, hastened to the scene of action, and seeing how matters were going, crept along under the cover of the rank grass until they got close behind the Bamangwato. They advanced until they were discovered, when they sprang to their feet, and, raising their wild war-cry, rushed as one man on the forces of Khame. The retreating Matabele, finding that their comrades had come to their assistance, turned on their pursuers; so that now the Bamangwato found themselves surrounded by the enemy. Khame shouted to his men to stand; but his authority was soon at an end. Many of the Bamangwato had shown symptoms of fear from the beginning, and fought only after they saw that Khame and his young men were gaining the day. Now, when they beheld machaga on every side, the old fear of the Matabele seemed to return to them, and they fled in all directions, the horsemen doing their best to cover their retreat. The Matabele did not pursue them far; and the Bamangwato returned during the night, leaving about twenty dead on the field. The loss on the other side was much greater, according to reliable reports which have since been received from the Makalaka country; but of course we cannot ascertain the exact number. There were five of Moselekatse's sons in the fight, three of whom were killed and one supposed to be wounded. This information comes from Makalaka belonging to Sekhome, who at the time of the attack were on a visit to their friends living in a Makalaka town under Moselekatse, to which the machaga turned aside while they sent forward a messenger to the king to announce their return. As the men referred to were themselves Makalaka, they easily passed with the Matabele as natives of the town, and thus got to know the truth concerning the results of the engagement.

Out of many incidents which occurred in the fight, I shall narrate one or two. Pelutona, one of the chief men who went with Khame, being very fat and on foot, soon fell behind in the retreat, and would have been killed but for the gallant conduct of one of his men. This devoted heathen servant put himself between his master and his pursuers, saying to the former, "Take a good breathing now; they have to kill me first; and before they do so you will be well rested."

Instead of firing at once at the Matabele, this man kept them
at a distance by now and then presenting his gun at them,
until at length, thinking they were far enough from the main
body, their pursuers left them. I shall give another instance
of an entirely different description. In the course of the
retreat of the Bamangwato one of them found himself at
some distance from the others, and closely pursued by a
Letebele. His gun was loaded and cocked too, but he had
not courage enough to enable him to stand and fire ; so he
ran as fast as he could, carrying his gun on his shoulder.
To the surprise of both pursuer and pursued, bang went the
gun, its bearer still running at the top of his speed. Whether
the ball had passed somewhat near to the Letebele is not
known ; but at any rate, he at once gave up the pursuit,
evidently of opinion that he was altogether too dangerous a
fellow who could thus fire over his shoulder without slacken-
ing his pace ! Another man was brought to me some five
days after the battle with spear wounds on his arm and body.
He killed three men, but was surrounded while loading, his
gun taken from him, and he himself left for dead. Coming
to himself during the night, he crawled out of the way to a
place of safety ; but it took him five days to get home, as he
could not walk. He is now quite well.

The remainder of the letter described the futile
manner in which the Matabele regiments hung round
Shoshong for a few days. Mackenzie proposed to
visit their camp, but the Bamangwato leaders unanimously agreed that this would be a foolhardy adventure. As the invaders retreated, baffled for the first
time in their history by another native tribe, they
harried the country far and wide.

It was under these circumstances, when Mackenzie
had become known as Sekhome Missionary, and Sekhome's warriors had turned the Matabele from their
purpose, that the proposal was made to Mackenzie to
make another journey into Matabeleland. The proposal was made by Mr J. S. Moffat and his brother-
in-law Roger Price, who returned in the month of
June from the South. The Matabele Mission was
supposed to consist of three missionaries and their

families, who were all settled at Inyati. It seemed not impossible at this time that, through ill-health or other causes, two of these households, if not three, might be compelled to leave the country. This might have meant the total abandonment of the Mission, for Moselekatse, it was feared, would be unwilling to repeat favours which had been wrung from him only by the strong personal influence of Robert Moffat. Mr J. S. Moffat was especially urgent in pleading with Mackenzie to go in as a temporary reinforcement of the Mission. A second consideration was based upon Moselekatse's well-known attitude of suspicion towards missionaries, and his fear of their power in his land. It would help to familiarise him with their presence if Mackenzie appeared before him even for a while, and sought to gain from him some fresh favour for that work. In connection with this opportunity there was a vague idea in their minds that Moselekatse might be induced to give Mackenzie a new station in Matabeleland where, since the plans for the Makololo had failed, and Shoshong was at present pre-occupied by the Germans, Mackenzie might at least find it possible to settle down. He made it clear, in a letter written in the following year, that he had no personal desire to make the journey, and no real intention to settle in Matabeleland. He went, at some personal risk and much inconvenience, at the earnest and pro-longed solicitation of his brethren. This journey, however, was of great value to Mackenzie, as it gave him time in the months which he spent there to study very closely what nowadays would be called the sociology of a purely military tribe, and the per-sonality of its founder and chief. The result of this study is described at length in his book.[1] The follow-ing letter presents more briefly an account of this journey :—

[1] "Ten Years North," etc., chaps. xiv.-xviii.

INYATI, *Sept.* 1863.

Rev. Dr TIDMAN,

Dear Sir,—My last to you, written in July a few days after our departure from the Bamangwato, will have informed you of the reasons which influenced us to undertake a journey in the Matabele country. On reaching Mahuku's Town and receiving reliable intelligence of the welfare of our fellow-labourers amongst the Matabele, the first we had heard of them for nearly a year, I sent back a short note addressed to Mr Thompson of Cape Town, the contents of which have likely been forwarded to you.

It is the custom to announce to Moselekatse the arrival at his outposts of any strangers or travellers. Accordingly, on the Monday after our arrival, three Batalaouta were despatched by Shupeng, who is now the head-man at Mahuku's kraal, to inform Moselekatse of the return of Mr Moffat accompanied by another missionary, " who had come to see the King and his friends the missionaries at Inyati." We found that great stress was laid by the Batalaouta on the fact that I had been at Sekhome's during the late war, in fact that I was to be announced to the King as Sekhome's Missionary. While not caring to hide my connection with the Bamangwato I endeavoured to impress on their minds that I had only been one year at Sekhome's, that I had come from England at the same time as the Matabele missionaries, and that I was one with them in entire neutrality in all political matters. I learned afterwards, however, that my explanations were given in vain ; all that reached the ear of the chief was that " Yonie " (Mr Moffat) was coming, accompanied by Sekhome's Missionary.

Taking it for granted that Moselekatse would admit us, we did not wait at Mahuku's for an answer, as is sometimes done, but slowly followed in the rear of our messengers. After passing thro' in this way the beautiful " Makalaka country," as it is called, we entered the Matabele territory proper, now having an escort, or spy, a lichaga or warrior, whose town was on the road.

The messengers from Moselekatse met us one morning before we had inspanned near the Boherehere river. After saluting us, the principal man began to give us the " mouth of the King." First of all came a great number of questions concerning myself, summed up by, " The King wishes to know what is your business in his country ? " After having "catechised" for some time in this manner the messenger began, not without some confusion, to deliver the decision of his master. It was astounding, after having answered so many questions put by order of Moselekatse to be given to understand that the King had already made up his mind, and that I was commanded to return, that the King did not wish to see me. On inquiring into the use and wont of the thing, I found that it was quite customary to question people in this way, and yet, no matter what their answers might be, wind up the conversation summarily by announcing the previously formed decision of the chief. Further, my friends were of opinion that altho' my position was not altogether hopeless thro' this decision as to obtaining permission to enter the country, it was nevertheless nearly so, inasmuch as Moselekatse was very seldom known to change his mind. Altho' I might have returned at once, having ascertained that the friends at Inyati were all in good health, I confess I felt a strong disclination to do so. In the first place I did not relish the indignity involved in being sent about one's business in so summary a manner; but above all that I felt it would tend to enhance our character among the natives, who are all suspicious, were we able to pass over from one tribe to another in time of war. Altho' it may seem to those at a distance a small matter that we have succeeded in carrying our point, yet we on the spot see reasons to rejoice at it. Many of the heathen chiefs with their people are still wofully ignorant as to the true object of the missionary; we wish to teach them that in peace and in war we are the disinterested friends of all, having one simple object amongst them, to proclaim to them the gospel and to instruct them in its truth. I found on inquiry that one of the men was to return to the King with our explanation; so Mr Moffat and myself set ourselves to the task of unfolding to him our views and plans in so far as we deemed it necessary, reiterating the salient points so as to impress them on his mind. We found the messengers very respectful and well disposed; indeed we could understand that it was their wish that I should be admitted. Mr Moffat was struck with the improvement for the better which had taken place in his absence in the outward behaviour of the Matabele. In the course of conversation we learned some of the remarks which had fallen from the King when he heard that Sekhome's teacher was coming. Pointing to some cows in his cattle pen which had been stolen

from the Bamangwato, Moselekatse jocularly called to his
attendants to hasten and milk some of Sekhome's cows for
Sekhome's missionary, "for he must be hungry after so long
a journey." "Why, if I admit this man he will see everything in the country and return and inform Sekhome."
"Well, really," said a puzzled wife sitting near, "what crimes
do these white men commit, which cause them to flee from
their own country in this way?"

Being without water at the place where we received the
king's message, we suggested that we go *forward* and wait at
the first water for the king's final decision. To this the
Machaga agreed, altho' with reluctance, being evidently unwilling to allow me to advance without the king's consent.
On Friday afternoon the messenger returned from the king,
his feet and legs covered with dust, but with a smiling
countenance. Moselekatse's answer was that "I was to
come on; but where was my gift or present to him, and that
of Mr J. Moffat? He had not seen them." We reached
the camp of Moselekatse on Monday afternoon; but did not
see the chief till next morning. He was not living in a town;
but at the foot of a mountain near to a place called Sesentene.
His four waggons were drawn up near to each other; behind
these were the temporary huts of his harem and servants,
closed in by a hedge of thorn branches; and in front a large
pen for cattle and another for sheep and goats. Such were
the "quarters" in which we found the King of the Matabele;
and thus I am told he spends the greater portion of the year.
As in other things, his movements seem to be guided by
whims. After living for some time at a place suddenly the
order is issued to pack the waggons and yoke the oxen;
and before all of the attendants know whither they are going
the waggons are moving and the temporary huts left in a
blaze.

And now for my reception by Moselekatse. After passing
the little huts and the waggons we were shown into the sheep-
pen, at the door of which sat a number of Machaga. A fire
had been placed in the middle of the pen; near to this,
seated in an old-fashioned arm-chair, the gift of Mr Moffat,
sat Moselekatse. As we walked up and got each a warm
and very lengthy shake of the hand, the attendants kept
shouting "Great King," "Man-eater," etc. On taking our
places on the ground opposite the arm-chair we had a full
view of the object of this praise; and saw an old, frail man,

so frail that he is carried about in the chair by his wives, and whose only clothing then consisted of an English blanket brought loosely round his loins and a cadet cap on his head. An old great-coat, the original of which was to me matter of speculation, served as a footstool, and was removed with the chair, when the King desired to change his position. One could not help looking with peculiar feelings on the countenance of a man whose whole career has been so bloody, and so successful. We could imagine we saw evidence of that force of character, and cruel unscrupulousness, which have ever distinguished him. His features are still indicative of intelligence and force of character; while at the same time expressions occasionally flit across them which help us to realize that we are in presence of one who could listen to the voice of justice or mercy unmoved. No notice was taken of the two greatcoats which we had sent on the previous day; but immediate application was made for additional " help," as the expression here goes. However, our reception on the whole was gracious enough, as things go here. He recognised me as a missionary from Kuruman, or England, the differences or distances between these places not being very clearly understood by the Matabele. Not having an opportunity of speaking to the King in private, I did not introduce the subject of the war with Sekhome; for any public questioning of his policy is not at all calculated to produce beneficial results. Moselekatse has been noted for the hospitality of detaining visitors long after the time at which they desired to depart. But lung-sickness having considerably diminished the quantity of beef at his disposal, visitors are no longer guests fed at the King's expense; and in our own case, after a stay of two days, the chief's politely expressed reluctance at our departure was fully met by a promise of an early visit after we had seen our friends at Inyate. We hope then to have an opportunity of speaking to the chief on the subject of the war with Sekhome; but we cannot reasonably hope for much success, inasmuch as no one has ever succeeded hitherto in persuading Moselekatse to give up his warlike pursuits. It was at one time fondly imagined that such a result had been obtained, but a very short residence in the country convinced our brethren that this belief was altogether unfounded. Since your missionaries came into this country, only one year has passed unmarked by the departure of the Matabele forces against the native tribes to the east, north-east, and north ; and during that exceptional year, if the Matabele were not engaged in a foreign war, they were occupied with slaughtering one another. Interest was brought to bear with the King against Monyebe, the greatest friend of missionaries and most powerful man in the country after the King. He was accused of witchcraft, and put to death with all his house. Such being the past history of the Matabele, even after their connexion with missionaries, we cannot be very sanguine as to the result of our efforts to deter the King from prosecuting that war with the Bamangwato. However, we shall do our best.

We reached Inyate on Saturday, 29th of August, when we had the pleasure of meeting with our dear friends Mr Thomas and Mr and Mrs Sykes. This pleasure however had its sad alloy in the absence of Mrs Thomas. All we could see of her, except in the features of her two little boys, was her grave. However, she herself is with God, and doubtless feels no regret, either that she embarked in the mission work or that her remains are far removed from those of her kindred. I have the impression that Christian work among the Zulus in the neighbourhood of Natal, although extending over a lengthened period, has been sadly unproductive of results. My remark applies to the natives beyond British territory, who are under the despotic sway of their chiefs. If this impression is correct, there are others similarly situated to your agents in the Matabele country, preaching the word to a handful of people while the great mass of the people stand scornfully aloof. At the same time, the Matabele mission has been a trying one to your agents, and to all appearances their patience as well as that of your Directors will be tried for a long time to come before marked prosperity shall attend their efforts. I am glad to testify to the change that is taking place in the minds of the Matabele towards the missionaries. Received four years ago with the utmost suspicion, they are now trusted throughout the country, but especially in the neighbourhood of Inyate. The overbearing rudeness with which they were at first treated by all classes has now given place in most cases to respect. There are three out-stations in connection with Inyate, which the brethren visit weekly for the purpose of preaching the Gospel to the people. The whole population which thus comes under the influence of the missionaries is some 700 or 800, while of these about 150 constitute the

total number of hearers at the four stations, on any given
week.   Repeated attempts have been made in the way of
teaching the young, but hitherto without success.   Learning
seems to be regarded by the people with fear.   They are
not sure how Moselekatse would regard such a movement.
The work of your agents, therefore, has been to a great extent
of a preparatory nature.   They have had to eradicate many
weeds before they could sow the good seed of the Gospel.
However, the Word of God can be said now to be found in
the Matabele country ; it is preached regularly, and in the
language of the country.   And just as the life and conversation of the missionaries slowly disarmed the people of
suspicion and dislike, so the "little leaven" of heaven's
truth at present in course of being introduced into their
minds cannot possibly remain there long inert and unobserv-
able.   The soil however is emphatically a bad one.   The
training of the Matabele, their habits of plunder and bloodshed, and their social usages, all combine in their opposition
to the requirements of Christianity.   Your agents are labouring amongst a population the male portion of which has been
gathered from all tribes, knows little or nothing of home or
kindred, lives in barracks, robs and slaughters at least every
year, without reference to sex or age, and knows no law but
that of their King.   The females are also the children of all
the tribes and are as unpromising as the men, if not more
so, as subjects of the Gospel.   These things are mentioned
simply for the purpose of showing that the difficulties of this
field are of no ordinary description ; and considering the
amount of opposition and ill-feeling which has been overcome the directors and friends of the Society have good
reason to be thankful, although their agents here cannot
point to a single individual and say—"I have good hope of
this person," or "Here is our first convert."

When I left Bamangwato, I promised to Mr Price to
return in the course of the summer, provided that Mr and
Mrs Sykes were in such health as to enable them to carry on
the duties of this station in conjunction with Mr and Mrs
Moffat.   It was understood that only one inducement ought
to detain me in the country, the permission of Moselekatse
to occupy a new district as a field of missionary labour.
While my oxen are resting I shall endeavour to find out the
views of the head-men on this subject, and should I find
that they are decidedly opposed to the establishment of a

separate station I shall not make the request formally of the king. Should I meet with encouragement, however, and in the end obtain from the king a suitable place for a station, I think the Directors will agree with my brethren here and with myself that it would be of importance not to neglect such an opening. At the same time rather than attempt to *push* the matter, and rather than wait on, doing next to nothing, in the hope that a more favourable time may come, I conceive it will be my duty to return to the Bamangwato, which is at any rate a riper field than the Matabele country, and where I can resume direct and encouraging labours which were interrupted by the present journey.—I remain, ever yours truly, JOHN MACKENZIE.

Another letter which Mackenzie wrote after his return to Shoshong describes at greater length the negotiations which he carried on with Moselekatse, and the means which he employed for discovering the exact facts in Matabeleland from the missionary's point of view. He concentrated attention upon one object, to ascertain the amount of liberty granted by Moselekatse to missionaries on the one hand, and to his own people in relation to the missionaries on the other. He conversed especially with the head-men, through whom the chief carried out his will. In brief, Mackenzie found that, while the missionaries had nominally all liberty to teach and preach, *the people were warned that they must not learn.* Moselekatse knew full well that people who read the gospel could not remain true to his military system, and that men who learn to read could not be prevented from reading the gospel. When the chief, to the amazement of everyone, agreed to give Mackenzie a fountain for his new station, and empowered Mr J. S. Moffat to select one, Mackenzie used this as the opportunity for making one more urgent appeal to the chief to allow his people to become real learners. In this attempt he completely failed ; and, as it seemed to him per-fectly useless to open a new mission in a land practically closed to mission work, while in other directions many thousands of heathen people were hungering to be taught, he decided to return to Shoshong.

It was during this visit to the Matabele that the first bereavement fell upon Mackenzie's immediate family. In October his third child, born at Shoshong the previous year, died of croup at the age of fourteen months. Mackenzie's affectionate heart was deeply moved at the loss of little Annie. To the end of his days he referred to her with a loving and tender affection, and spoke of her always as still one of the family, and one of whose continued life in the unseen he was immovably convinced. He wrote at the time as follows :—

Now, don't grieve over us as if our affliction must have been so very much heightened by our being in a heathen land. We were among very kind friends ; and, above all, we buried our child with calm triumph, submitting to Death, and the Grave, and Corruption, in the light of the Gospel. "I am the Resurrection and the Life ; " "Suffer the little children to come unto Me." Altho' we say it with a sigh, still we are glad and happy that we have a child in Heaven, in that wondrous "House of the Lord." O for one glimpse of what she sees ! You know why we are here. We came as a "stop the gap" ; had we not come, and had our brethren here been in bad health, the Mission might have been dispersed for a time ; and it is not always easy to resume what has been given up in the country of the Matabele. It is not certain whether we remain here or not. Perhaps the likelihood is that we shall go out again. There is not freedom, and until there is, three missionaries are enough. The people here are the most degraded of all the tribes I have visited. The King has great power, in fact does what he pleases with his subjects, who fear him very much. This is the obstacle to the progress of the Gospel. Moselekatse has more at stake than many other chiefs in connection with the reception of the Gospel by his people. The whole social fabric of the Matabele must be completely changed, their whole policy, their whole course of life, when the

Gospel is generally received. The King is intelligent enough to see this; and it may be long before much is effected, for this very reason. Of course cases of individual conversion may take place, altho' they have not done so as yet. The Word and Spirit of God are omnipotent.

Shortly after Mackenzie's return to Shoshong, where Price had settled in diligent service, he received news that the German missionaries were to be withdrawn from all stations in Bechuanaland, and that Mr Schulenborg would not return to Shoshong. The way now was open to him to consider his appointment by the Directors to this station as final, and he forthwith set himself to the work which occupied him for more than ten years among the most powerful tribe in Bechuanaland, happy indeed to have done with the six homeless years of his wanderings up and down South Africa.

CHAPTER IV

THE FIRST PERIOD AT SHOSHONG (1864-1871)

MACKENZIE has given a very full account of the next period of his life.[1] We must be content with a more brief survey. He has described Shoshong in the following words : — "Shoshong, the town of the Bamangwato, contains a population of some 30,000. It is situated at the foot of a mountain range of primary rock stretching from east to west for more than a dozen miles. About three miles to the south of this range there is another basaltic mountain called Marutlwe, in the neighbourhood of which both sand-stone and limestone are to be found. The ground lying between the hills is occupied by the gardens of the Bamangwato. The main town spreads along the foot of the mountain, and some distance along the gorge in the mountain range, where the stream flows which supplies the town with water. There are also five divisions of the town in a beautifully sheltered position among the mountains. Again, there are small towns along the range to the west to the distance of some six miles, all being under one chief, whose decision is final." The comfort of life at Shoshong was much affected by the inadequacy of the water supply, for which the entire town depended upon a few springs in the bed of the river in the kloof. The river channel opposite the mission premises, and right through the town, was perfectly dry, except after sudden and abundant rains. Then the river came down in a flood, which however

[1] "Ten Years North of the Orange River," chapters xviii.-xxv.

speedily subsided ; after the rainy season was over no signs of it remained. Mackenzie would have liked for his own sake, as well as for the sake of the natives, to institute a small system of irrigation at Shoshong. Indeed, when he was home in 1870, he wrote to Dr Mullens, the Foreign Secretary of the Society, saying: " I wish some kind friend of the Mission would present me with a pump in order that through irrigation we might at least occasionally enjoy the luxury of a few vegetables at dinner." But he never had either the time or money to carry out so useful a project.

It was a picturesque sight, undoubtedly, which met the eye in the early morning, and especially at sunset, as the women of the town went up to the springs with large earthen pots on their heads to fetch the water supply for the following day. The interest of watch- ing this stream of human beings moving up and down the valley was for the missionary children only rivalled by watching the strange daily procession of baboons. These animals frequented the mountains overhanging the town, and possessed the singular habit of using the mountain on one side of the river for sleeping in, and the range on the other side for their daylight excur- sions in search of food. It was ever a matter of great interest to go up the kloof and watch these big human- like animals crossing the river to their sleeping apart- ments. That they had some measure and manner of family discipline was firmly believed by all who watched them, and who, almost every evening, heard the indig- nant speech of an adult baboon, the easily identified sounds of whacking, and the corresponding shrill replies of juvenile pain and resentment.

The town was also infested by wolves, or, more properly, hyenas of the usually cowardly and treacher- ous and filthy kind. They would creep after nightfall to the precincts of the town and steal whatsoever they could lay hold of, a goat or a child. Mackenzie tried to encourage the natives to reduce the numbers of these unwelcome scavengers. He several times set gun-traps, and once. he used meat poisoned with strychnine in order to get rid of some unusually daring depredator, and each time with success. His elder children still remember a weird hyena scene. One night, when several traders sat talking with Mackenzie in his parlour, his dogs started up suddenly with a unanimous howling and barking and a rush in one direction. This could only mean a hyena. Lanterns were procured, a gun was shouldered by Mackenzie, and they rushed out into the darkness. The sounds drew them to the rocks at the foot of the mountain immediately behind the house. There they found that the dogs, by harassing and worrying, had exhausted the energies of the hyena, and it lay panting on a flat rock almost in reach of safety. Mackenzie proposed to shoot it, when a little trader, whose diminutive size and bow legs created constant merriment among the natives, protested that the skin should not be spoilt, that he could cut its throat. Someone handed him a knife, which turned out to be too blunt. When his sawing at the throat with this unhappy instrument at last irritated the skin, the reviving energies of the hyena enabled it to snap at and hold the trader's toe within its jaws. The native crowd burst into an irresistible guffaw at the ludicrous scene. The imprisoned boot was quickly shaken free, and Mackenzie was allowed to shoot. A little boy is still remembered whose face bore the marks of another wolf's fangs upon it. He was out after dark, when one of these brutes caught him, and throwing him over its shoulder, made off for the mountains. The boy's right hand was, happily, hanging down and dragging on the ground, and it came upon a sharp stone. Immediately seizing this stone, this plucky little fellow so belaboured the wolf's face with the ragged edges that it was glad to drop its victim. One more wolf story Mackenzie used thoroughly to enjoy. It was of a trader who, on approaching Shoshong and finding the nights hot, protested against sleeping in his waggon. Having spread out a large kaross, or tanned skin, on the ground, he lay down to sleep, laughing in contempt at the idea that any animal could interfere with him. He awoke up suddenly to find himself still, indeed, on the kaross, but bumping along over the ground, hauled by an invisible agency of the darkness. His vigorous yells speedily aroused his companions, who were cruel enough to enjoy the event and to share their enjoyment with others. / 56117

The Bamangwato tribe, whose chief town was at Shoshong, had become powerful from about the year 1845 onwards. It owed much of its prosperity to a former chief, Khari by name, of whom Mackenzie says that, " brave in the field, wise in counsel, kind to his vassals, Khari was all that the Bechuanas desired their chief to be." His legal heir was Macheng, a son of his head wife ; but an elder son of a subordinate wife, Sekhome by name, usurped the throne, killed some of his rivals, and caused the flight of Macheng to Matabeleland. Under Sekhome, the tribe prospered until manhood was reached by his two sons, Khame and Khamane. These two had received Christian instruction from Mr Schulenborg, and had been baptised by him. Khame grew up to be a man of extraordinary dignity of character, his grasp of Christian morality being unusually strong and clear, and his loyalty to the Christian God profound and immovable. It was this noble-minded fidelity of Khame's heart, combined with an untiring charity, which led to some of the most dramatic situations known in the history of any native tribe. One can easily see that in the relations of Sekhome to Macheng, his brother, a more degraded heathen than himself, and to his Christian sons, all the elements were present of a long series of plots and counter-plots. Some of these we shall see unfolded in the following pages.

The gospel was first preached to the Bamangwato by David Livingstone, during his first journey north-ward to his discovery of Lake Ngami. The first regular teacher of the tribe was Sehunelwe a member of the Kuruman Church, who had been prepared for his work by Robert Moffat, and who was supported in it by a few friends in Glasgow. In 1858, Mr Schulenborg arrived, and worked faithfully for a short period ; his chief distinction, however, lies in the fact that he had baptised Khame and his brother. He formed a Christian church, but did so prematurely, in Mackenzie's estimation, and of such material that the foundations had to be relaid some years later.

Mackenzie set himself to the work of evangelising the Bamangwato people with all his heart and soul ; for a while he had as his colleague the late Roger Price, who in a short time, however, moved to Sechele's town, leaving Mackenzie with a task which he always felt to be far beyond the limits of one man's powers. In brief, his work consisted, first, in preaching, not only on Sunday but during the week in the king's court-yard and at various central portions of the widely-extended town ; second, in carrying on day-school teaching, for which he had no assistance ; and third, in putting up all the buildings necessary for a Mission Station. In 1866 he reported informally that he had 22 candidates for membership in the church which he hoped to establish ; he had about 60 *regular* hearers at his Sunday congregations ; he had one day-school whose attendance consisted of 30 adults and 8 children ; he had besides two district schools with similar attendance. It was impossible, of course, to carry on this educational work during the recurring wars which disturbed the people, and the building operations which necessarily absorbed his time and energy. The following extracts from letters give all too brief glimpses of this side of his work.

To Miss E. B. Douglas, Portobello.

SHOSHONG, 16th *March* 1865.

We are making a little progress here in our work. In the district schools which Mr Price and I started some time ago, we have had considerable encouragement. The young people are generally willing to learn to read; and the old people who are, alas! unwilling to do anything themselves, make a great virtue of giving their sons and nephews liberty to learn. The heathen rite of circumcision is now being celebrated here with great demonstrations. The old chief, by very unworthy arguments, has succeeded in inducing two of his younger sons who attended school, and one of whom was a very fair scholar, to cast in their lot with him and go to the ceremony, the celebration of which continues for some two months. We hope they will come back again after it is over. They are young and undecided, but with God's help, may eventually see their way to something better than the tomfooleries in which they are now engaged. The eldest son is really a nice lad, unassuming and manly; and the second is also a fair character, although excelled by his brother. There is a third son by the same wife, perhaps about 15, also a quiet, thoughtful lad.

It is difficult to say what were or are the religious practices of this people before their connection with white men. Of course, even the heathen are indirectly influenced by the opinions of the white people; and Morimo (God) gets credit for a great deal now that was formerly attributed to other agencies.

The Bechuana will appear surprised and sceptical when you preach to them the Resurrection from the Dead, and the Final Judgment; and yet they themselves are in the habit of resorting to the grave of an ancestor, and there offering up their prayers for the help of the departed one in any difficulty in which they may be placed at the time. This act is perhaps not frequently performed and I am not aware that it is practised except by the chief men. But Bechuana of all classes were in the habit in their journeys to select a very large tree in a forest, and there under its shadow offer up their prayers. To whom these prayers were made it is difficult to find out, but it was probably to their ancestors. Perhaps it is a faint shadow of that hoary and widely-spread ritual which in Britain is known as Druidism.

Witchcraft is to the Bechuana a terrible reality, although not to the same extent that it is amongst the Zulus. So uniformly have all white men ridiculed this article of faith, that it is universally admitted by them that we don't know how to bewitch. This is a fortunate thing; many an innocent Zulu is put to death through jealousy, etc., the pretext given by the king being that he is a "wizard."

Peculiar ideas are entertained out here about mad people. The word for mad is *tsenwa*, the passive of *tsena*, to enter, to go in. Our English expression "possessed" is pretty near to the Bechuana idea. Well when a person gets mad, he has got Morimo, and therefore some day he is Morimo. A poor woman lately became deranged, when hundreds of women flocked to see her with offerings of corn, etc. All the questions which gipsies and other adepts at palmistry at home are so ready to answer, were put to this demented creature, and answers of some kind obtained. As if they themselves were not satisfied with their conduct, these devotees in some cases explained that the woman was not God, but went to speak to Him on the mountain at night; and that He then instructed her what to say.

To the Rev. JOSEPH MULLENS, D.D.

SHOSHONG, 17*th June* 1867.

Like all Bechuana tribes, the Bamangwato have the name Morimo (God) in their language; but in their unenlightened state they had no knowledge of such being as the God of the Bible. According to them the dwelling of Morimo was not above but below on the earth. In this tribe a chief or a master is daily addressed as Morimo; and although all have now at least heard of the true God, even a missionary is still frequently shocked to hear himself addressed as Morimo, while some trifling favour is acknowledged or begged; such is the force of habit.

Life to these wretched heathen was, alas! and still is, full of imaginary dangers, crowded with things which are not "canny." Their own flocks and herds may be possessed with evil spirits bent on the master's destruction or that of his family. I have bought cattle which the natives would no longer keep. When the heathen goes to ' ₋nt he may meet with great misfortune by happening to gaze on a certain animal. Consequently, they have doctors who are said to be able to help them against these multiform evils, for a consideration. From these doctors they buy medicines and charms. They wear them on their heads, their necks, their wrists, their kaross, their ankles. Between the *ngaka* or doctor, who is also sometimes called *moloi* or wizard, and these numerous charms, there was little room left in the Bechuana mind for the position or action of Morimo. Indeed, if he had clearly defined attributes at all, they would seem to have been malicious ones ; Morimo was a mystery, or an object of dread, or both, to the poor benighted ones. It is worthy of notice also that in times of great distress the "last resource" was not to pray to Morimo ; but to repair to the grave of some powerful ancestor, and there lay their case in all its details before the departed and unheeding spirit.

In 1865 Mackenzie set himself to build a house. The following "statement of outlay" gives a very brief summary of the facts. How much personal toil was involved in this undertaking it would be hard to say, for Mackenzie had to discover a clay bed, make frames for his bricks, and then—the hardest task of all—had to train native workers to make bricks ; then he undertook the task of burning these, which involved not only the building of brick kilns, but the hauling of firewood in waggons for a long distance. His family can recall the intense anxiety with which he one day awaited the result of his first experiment. He set himself also to use lime, and, having discovered limestone, brought it in waggons to the Station, there burned it, and prepared it for making mortar. The astonishment of the natives at the action of the lime was amusing in a high degree. And, further, Mackenzie had to take his waggons out into the forest, cut down trees, persuade the natives to drag them into the waggons, bring them to the mission ground, and there saw them into boards. For the last purpose he dug a pit and taught two natives to use a pit-saw. The house which he built measured 38 ft. by 23 ft., and comprised five rooms, besides the kitchen and pantry.

STATEMENT OF OUTLAY IN BUILDING A DWELLING-HOUSE

I received valuable assistance from several Englishmen, who, with the exception of H——, who was hired by the month, would receive no wages. They of their own accord "gave me a hand" for weeks or months, as they had opportunity. They boarded at my table, of course, while at work. Having no garden here, and everything on my table except milk having to be paid for at high prices in the interior, I must in justice to myself make the charge of £3 per month for one man. The items are as follows :—

1865. W. H.—Wages, £14; board 3 months, £10 10s.	£24 10 0
W. F.—Board	12 10 0
F. C.— Do.	9 0 0
L. Do.	3 10 0
Paid native labourers in beads, etc. .	11 16 6
1867. M. for kitchen and pantry . . .	15 0 0
	£76 6 6

This outlay was met by myself at the time, and charged to the account of salary. I now beg to request that the above sum be refunded to me. I may mention that, after all, the chief part of the work was done by my own hands, the bricklaying and dressing the timber. I worked for months as hard as any labouring man. The brick-making was partially paid for by me to Sekhome, from whom I had four men hired for a heifer each.

SHOSHONG, 3rd July 1867.

In connection with the building of this house, a romantic incident took place which casts light at once upon the South Africa of those years, and upon human nature. There came to Shoshong one Tom Wood, an Englishman of the bluff and hearty type, who had been a carpenter and had made some money, and become a hunter. Between him and Mackenzie there sprang up a strong mutual confidence and regard. When they were discussing the best way of roofing the new house, Tom Wood urgently recommended the use of corrugated iron, which seemed an impossible, because expensive, plan to the missionary. The hunter, however, made a proposal, which won the day for his plan. He offered, if Mackenzie would lend him a waggon and some oxen which he needed for his own purposes, to make a journey through the Transvaal to Durban, do his own business there, buy the iron roofing, and bring it to Shoshong free of charge. This was agreed to, and Tom Wood set forth with the valuable small waggon and the loan of something less than a full span of oxen. It was intended that he should be back by September, when the rainy season might begin. September arrived and passed, but there was no sign of Tom Wood and no message from him. As days and weeks more went by the missionary had the sore experience of being told on all hands that he had been fooled, that he had no right to trust so much that was of value to a mere travelling adventurer. But Mackenzie felt certain that the soul of Tom Wood was true, and shaking his big head, said that his faith in him would yet be vindicated. That kind of certainty can only live on itself, and can give no reason but itself to others. In the meantime the wet season had to be met. It was known that the Boers sometimes use a certain soil called "braak grond," which contains salt, and from which, when rain falls, it runs off on the surface. Forth Mackenzie went into the forest and cut down hundreds of makuru trees. The central wood of this tree is so hard that ants do not eat it ; but its hardness made it difficult to work.   To saw this into planks was out of the question, so it was resolved simply to split up each tree with wedges, and then use the adze to smooth the inner surface of each half, and to remove the outer soft wood which the ants would enjoy.   As the wood is beautifully grained, these smoothed faces, when fitted close together, make a striking and ornamental ceiling.   Over them was placed a layer of clay, and over that the " braak grond " soil.   This answered fairly well.   Only a few showers came through into one room, over which the ants had worked through the clay at one or two points, and opened the way for the water.   Contentedly the family faced the rainy season in the new house, which seemed like a palace after the two-roomed hut.   The season of Christmas and New Year approached, and still no sign of Tom Wood ; and still Mackenzie shook his head emphatically, and believed in him.   Now, on last New Year's Day, the lost traveller had dined with the Mackenzies, and before he went off to Durban, he had said, " You'll see, Mrs Mackenzie, that I'll eat my next New Year's dinner with you."   Sadly they surmised that now that must be out of the question.   When New Year's Day came Tom Wood did come with it !

When he reached Durban, Tom Wood found that the firm with whom his money was deposited had failed and his money was all gone.   The brave fellow, because he was a true man and was trusted by another true man a thousand miles away, set to work at his own trade, and worked incessantly till he had made enough money to buy that roofing and his own hunting supplies.   After hard and silent toil he set forth to reach Shoshong in time to keep that appointment with Mrs Mackenzie for New Year's Day.

The following year, 1866, saw an almost complete

arrest of all ordinary missionary operations at Shoshong. The following letters give a sufficiently complete account of the remarkable events which occurred at that time :—

SHOSHONG, 19*th March* 1866.

THE REV. DR TIDMAN.

Rev. and Dear Sir,—Two years ago it was my duty to communicate the incidents connected with an attack on the Bamangwato by the Matabele. It is now my painful task to inform you that a division has just taken place among the Bamangwato themselves, which cannot but materially affect our work as missionaries in this part of the country. In order to a proper understanding of this quarrel it will be necessary to recall a few events connected with the past history of this tribe.

It will be remembered that Macheng, who was liberated by Mr Moffat from captivity among the Matabele, has a claim to the chieftainship of the Bamangwato prior to that of Sekhome. Macheng's mother was, it would seem, the chief wife of Khari, who was the father of both Macheng and Sekhome. Macheng, then, on his return from the Matabele was recognized as chief; but the tenure of his power was brief. Brought up among the soldiers of the Zulu despot, Macheng aimed at exercising a sway among his father's people equally despotic to that of Moselekatse. Sekhome fled for refuge to Sechele's with Khame and Khamane, his children. All property was declared to belong to Macheng, and nothing could be bought or sold except by his command or with his cognizance. By and by a petty chief was put to death by Macheng, upon which the head-men, who before this were tired of their new king, were now also in terror of him lest they should share the fate of him who had been summarily put to death. Secret meetings were held at which Chukuru took a leading part; and it was agreed to recall Sekhome. Overtures were accordingly made, and both Sekhome and Sechele were found to be agreeable, the one again to assume his position as chief, the other to aid with his men in the accomplishment of that end. Khosilintse was the head of the party of the Bakwena who reinstated Sekhome as chief of the Bamangwato; and he returned to Sechele's without the loss of a man, but driving a numerous herd of

Sekhome's cattle, which was the reward of his services. Macheng at first fled in the direction of Moselekatse, and begged help from his former master in the recovery of his lost chieftainship. Moselekatse refused his aid ; so Macheng fell back first on Selekas, to the east of Shoshong, and finally was received by Sechele, the very man who had driven him from his home.

Before his banishment, Sekhome had desired his eldest son to take to wife a daughter of Pelutona ; but Khame had conceived a dislike to this person and refused. On their return to the place, Sekhome recommended him to marry a daughter of Chukuru, to whom they owed gratitude for his efforts in recalling them from their banishment. Khame consented, and his wife has proved a helpmeet for her husband in his efforts to shake himself loose from heathenism, and not a hindrance, as is sometimes the case. Khamane the second son also married a daughter of Chukuru, with the approbation of Sekhome. This person never went through the rite initiating into heathen womanhood ; nor was she bought from her father according to the old custom. These things vexed Sekhome ; but Chukuru said, if the young people had believed the Word of God, he would never be a party to compelling them to go through the usual customs of their ancestors.

About fourteen months ago our prospects in this place were of the most cheering description. Besides the services in the church on the Sabbath, Mr Price and I conducted three schools in different parts of this large town, whose inhabitants we computed as being at least 30,000. We taught the two district schools three days in the week, and had an attendance of about 30 children and adults. We employed about 8 natives as assistants at these schools, amongst whom were six sons of Sekhome, three of whom were competent teachers of elementary classes, and very diligent in their work. The other two days we taught in the church, and here endeavoured to ground these assistants, their wives and others, in the elements of a good education. Some of them can read and write their own language well, understand a little of arithmetic, have a general idea of geography ; and, last and best of all, are comparatively familiar with the New Testament, especially the Gospels.

Yielding to the threats and entreaties of their father, two of Sekhome's sons deserted us about a year ago, and joined

Sekhome in the dances and other customs connected with the administration of the rite of circumcision. Sekhome was angry with the steadfastness of Khame and those who remained with us ; and by and by threats were heard that unless they also succumbed, their father would kill them. Inasmuch as Chukuru did not go the same length as Sekhome in his oppression, and doubtless instigated by jealousy against him who was now the father-in-law of his two eldest sons, Sekhome began to launch his curses and his threats against Chukuru also. It would be tedious to detail the course of this persecution and oppression on the part of Sekhome. Suffice it to say, that so far as Mr Price and I could see, the conduct of the young chiefs was all that we could desire. This was especially true in the case of Khame. His praises were in the mouth of the whole tribe for his skill as a hunter, his bravery as displayed in the affair with the Matabele, and his affability to all in the town. White men visiting the place were equally loud in their praises ; he never begged anything from them ; he never beat them down in their prices ; he was always polite and obliging. And these opinions were not insincere ; repeated and valuable presents testified to the sincerity of their respect and attachment to Khame.

Sekhome was jealous of Khame's popularity and formed the determination of bringing him entirely over to heathenism. Although the daughter of Pelutona had been given to another man and had borne to him two children, Sekhome swore that she must be his son's head-wife ; he must take her or die. Khame pleaded that he was a Christian, and farther, that he never liked this woman. Sekhome answered, " When I sought missionaries for you, I had no idea that their teaching would thwart me thus ; I thought you would just be taught to read and write, your habits remaining unchanged. But learn this : whether you like the woman or not, whether you are a Christian or not, I am your father, and am determined to exact obedience to my wishes. Either you or I must be master ; and who ever heard of a father governed by his own son ? What could I say to Khari and the rest of my ancestors if I succumbed to my own child ? " " Father, we obey you in all other matters ; we hunt the elephant and you get the tusks ; we kill the giraffe and the eland, and you get the meat and the hide : wherein do we defraud you of your right as our father ? Only in matters connected with the Word of

God we cannot obey you; we fear God, and would rather die."

Such is a specimen of repeated conversations between Sekhome and his sons. On the one side there was anger and vindictiveness; on the other firmness and gentleness.

About three months ago Sekhome thought to thicken his plot by bringing missionaries into it. I had five men from him hired for a year, the wages of each to be a heifer. When six months had transpired and my new dwelling-house was nearly finished, Sekhome made his appearance and demanded the heifers. "Their work was done, the house was finished." I reminded him of the engagement, the year was only half expired. He did not contradict me, but doggedly demanded the heifers. Of course I could only refuse, as it would have been a most pernicious precedent. The chief went away swearing by a whole list of his forefathers that he would take the heifers himself. He at once removed every girl or boy in the employment of Price or myself, and this threat with reference to the heifers was soon put into execution, the day selected being a Sunday. On leaving church that day, Khame was informed by his father that he had now paid himself by taking six of Mackenzie's cows. Khame and Khamane (who had charge of my cows) firmly remonstrated with Sekhome, and although he spoke defiantly at the first, he finished by saying he would return the cows to them, seeing he had taken them from their post without their knowledge. This affair has not yet been settled; I have offered a remuneration for the six months' service of the men, more than is usually given, but without result. The chief keeps this matter as a weapon against us. Some four or five weeks ago, Sekhome resolved to bring things to the issue of a fight. The two parties lay in arms the whole night. Sekhome repeatedly gave orders to fire, but no one was found who would obey. He himself loaded a double-barrelled rifle recently purchased, upon which Khame said to him: "You see I am unarmed. Fire if it is in your heart to do so; only I shall not fire at you but at your people." Seeing that general sympathy was with Khame, Sekhome ran and hid himself in his own back premises, shortly afterwards sending his mother to plead with Khame, assuring him that he should no longer desire to take Pelutona's daughter or to take a plurality of wives. What he could not give up was the death of Chukuru. Khame sent Mogomotsi, his uncle, to say to

Sekhome that they had no wish to kill their father and that
he might sleep in peace; only they could not consent to the
death of Chukuru, who was guilty of no crime. Although
this was a night of anxiety to us as missionaries and to the
Bamangwato, it passed over without any definite result.
Sekhome was not able to carry out his evil intentions; and
his sons were too forbearing to take any advantage of the
power they possessed.

Such was the position of affairs when our dear friends Mr
and Mrs Price started for a brief visit to Kuruman. I then
took occasion to write to Mr Moffat, that although the young
chiefs were at that time possessed of power, I had fears that
their father would yet out-manœuvre them. And this, I am
very sorry to say, is what has taken place.

Sekhome, seeing the popularity of his sons, had made
some secret overtures to his brother Macheng to return to
the Bamangwato, thinking that together their men would be
more than a match for their opponents. This step on the
part of Sekhome alienated the affections of many of his
most trusted men, for in the coming of Macheng they saw
a change of dynasty; they were assured that the chief's
cattle, of which many of them were herds, would be taken
from them by Macheng, and given to his own men, who
had been his companions in exile.

Sekhome was far from being sincere in his conciliatory
promises to his sons. He now put forth his best efforts,
not only as chief, but as sorcerer, to alienate the affections
of his people from his sons. To one he was generous
and kind, and profuse in his promises of future benefits:
to another stern and severe, mysteriously threatening awful
calamity to those who opposed his wishes; while to a
third he represented his sons as now bereft of all judgment and prudence as the result of his enchantments.
His sorceries and charms were in constant use. An ugly
bit of wood was always in the chief's hand, and supposed
to convey great blessings to him, and great disadvantages
to such of his adversaries as he might chance to meet or
address. A little of it was bit off every morning by
Sekhome, so that when he greeted his people their hearts
might be drawn out in love towards him. Then medicines were continually scattered in the young chiefs' dwellings and in the paths which they frequented. Sekhome
even went the length of asking two Englishmen who

arrived here a few weeks ago for some strychnine, or wolf-poison, as it is sometimes called in this country. It is certain he did not want this for the purpose he mentioned; and it is presumed that he had formed the diabolical purpose of poisoning his sons or their friends. But whatever were his wishes, they were never reduced to execution, for the Englishmen refused to give him the poison.

I had resumed the school for about a week, and was pleased with the new faces there in the alphabet class, as well as with the diligence of our old scholars, when on the evening of Thursday, 8th March, Khame came up to me hurriedly and said he had just learned that his father had made all his arrangements, and that he and his brothers were to be surrounded that night and to be put to death. It would seem that this bloody piece of work was given by Sekhome to the Matabele refugees who are in this town, and who number some 14 or 16. Khame met Lingake, their leader, after nightfall, and after some hesitation he admitted that such were the orders from Sekhome. The old chief had stolen a march on his sons. His men filled the crooked little paths at the back of Khame's houses; thus he could take up no position there, for it was in the hands of his enemies. He determined, however, to rescue his own rifle; and having done so, retired with his men to the neighbour-hood of the church built by the Germans here, but never finished; and which is now a ruin. Mɪ K———, an English-man, had a small shop close to this building, and here the young chiefs received their men and gave their orders during the whole night. The women and children were removed from the town during the night, Khame's friends climbing the eastern, his father's adherents the western side of the kloof. Mrs Mackenzie and the children retired to rest, and I believe slept soundly enough. Their slumbers were, however, rudely and suddenly disturbed by the report of firearms given in volleys. It was barely dawn of day, so we roused the children and put on their clothes, not know-ing what might happen. From all parts of the kloof were heard the sharp crack of the rifles, and deeper reports of guns of a wider bore. The natives never stint the powder; it is thrown from the horn into the hand by guess, and thence into the gun, so that the noise produced in this narrow kloof in the morning in question was really very great. The firing, we afterwards learned, was begun by

Pelutona's people, perhaps from a feeling that they ought to speak out first, seeing it was their daughter whom Khame refused. The young chiefs' ranks were so thin that they would have willingly postponed the fight. However, after having been fired at, they had no alternative. Khame himself fired the first shots on his side, which was the signal for those volleys which we have referred to. Our house is some little distance from the nearest huts, so that no firing took place in our immediate proximity. The small hill which is opposite our dwelling was occupied by some of Sekhome's men, who fired into the part of the mountain above Chukuru's town, which was occupied by Chukuru and his men. Then two men mounted the hill at the back of our house, and fired a few shots across the kloof. It was a singular spectacle as seen from the hill between Mr Price's house and my own. The old church was held during Friday by about 15 men belonging to Khame against 3 large parties of Sekhome's men. A constant fire was kept up by Khame and Khamane and part of their men, from the mountains opposite the khotla and Pelutona's Town. But altho' an immense quantity of powder and lead was disposed of, our first fears as to the number of casualties from such a galling fire were allayed, when we came to learn that on Khame's side not one was killed after that whole day's firing, and only four wounded on Sekhome's side. We have ourselves seen two dead bodies lying exposed, one of which was of a woman, shot while drawing water for the men who were fighting behind the cover of the huts. I learned that two or three of the Englishmen at present on the place had got involved in the fray, having shot for a time on Khame's side. Their shop was so near the church, that they and their property stood in danger from guns in the natives' hands, altho' they were aimed at the church. A ball passed through one of the waggons while young K—— was asleep in it; another passed C's head as he went behind the church for protection. Those, however, who had fired a few shots, as they say, in self-defence, made their way to my house, where they were in safety; only one of them stayed in charge of the goods, and I am happy to say no accident befell him.

The firing was continued on Saturday, altho' not with such vigour; and on Sunday it was all but silent. I had a sad prospect before me on that Sabbath morning, the town in possession of the enemy of the Gospel, its friends compelled to take refuge on the mountain top. However, my course was plain; I knew where I could obtain a willing and attentive audience, and resolved to climb the mountain to minister to those who, I felt assured, would welcome both my message and myself. The chief consented to my going, so I went up and held a short service with my friends who stood around, not, alas! with Testament and hymn-book in hand, but with gun and spear and shield. I learned that they regarded the affair as decided for the present, and against themselves. However they were not without hope. A dissension might arise in the camp of their enemies. Some of their people whose services they had not been able to secure in consequence of the shortness of the notice which they received, might join their ranks. At anyrate they would hold their own in the meantime, and leave the future with God. It had been reported with great glee, by Sekhome's party, that Mogomotsi was shot while climbing the hill. I was glad to see him at the service, and to learn from his own lips that he was not even wounded. Upon my coming down in the afternoon, Sekhome took occasion to refer to my refusing to give him the heifers, and said that I was quite on Khame's and Chukuru's side. I told him I was no party to their quarrels, it being my duty to remain unentangled with such affairs. At the same time I said I felt I could not but tell him that in my opinion Khame was innocent, entirely so. Whether it was genuine or affected, the chief answered with great emotion: "I am glad you spoke that word, Monare; Khame is my own son, my provider, during all these years; truly he is blameless. The blame is with Chukuru and Khamane."

I have twice visited Khame's camp since that first Sabbath morning. He looks weary, but far from despairing. He hopes to occupy the kloof yet, although it may be some time before he is able to do so. He thinks that even in his present position his followers will have freedom, and the force of his example in attending to the claims of the Gospel; and in this opinion I agree with him. At the same time Sekhome views my presence here with no favour, and he is jealous of my visits to the mountain. Even to-day, it seems, he told a trader that he was about to drive away all white men, missionaries and all; and that the Word of God was the cause of the present war. Of course that is a threat which he is not likely to try to carry out. While I write (midnight), my premises are surrounded by armed men who are on the look-out for messengers to us from the young chief's camp. However, we shall do our best not to offend Sekhome, and wait for the dawning of a better day. We shall be as assiduous as possible in our ministrations to Khame's party; and should the town be permanently separated, which is not likely, we hope to resume our labours among those who follow Sekhome.

In a review of this affair, it must be gratifying to you, as it is to us, to witness the forbearance with which Sekhome has been treated by his sons. In olden times the sons of both Zulu and Bechuana chiefs were not of this spirit, but were swift in revenge; and a troublesome father was not reckoned a very formidable adversary. Let us cherish the hope, and offer up the prayer that they whose cause is just, and who, in exercising great Christian forbearance, have been worsted by the heathen wiles of their father, may enjoy the presence of God's comforting spirit in their adversity; and that that adversity may speedily come to an end.—I remain, etc., JOHN MACKENZIE.

SHOSHONG, 3rd July 1866.
REV. DR TIDMAN.

Rev. and Dear Sir,—I have to acknowledge receipt of your favor of the 9th January.

My last to you, dated on the 19th March, contained an account of the rupture which had shortly before taken place in this town between Sekhome and his sons. I intend at present to continue the history of that disturbance, and to give you some idea of the present state of the town.

Khame occupied the stronghold on the mountain referred to in my last, from the 12th of March to the 17th of April. At first each party was content to hold its own, and no real engagement took place, but for the last eight days of that period Khame's position was besieged by his father, who also set numerous guards at all the waters in the vicinity, for the purpose of preventing Khame from procuring water either for himself or for his cattle. Twice did the forces of Sekhome try to take the mountain by storm, and were each time repulsed; but thirst eventually compelled Khame to submit to his father's terms, which were that he must return to the town with his people. It being known that Chukuru and some others had no prospect of mercy from Sekhome, a party was formed under Khamane of such as agreed to flee for refuge to Sechele. These having taken their departure in the darkness of night, Khame and his party descended from their fastness next morning and entered the town.

An event which seemed to irritate Sekhome and his party more than any other, took place about a fortnight after Khame left the town. Sekhome conceived that his unexpected victory over his sons had been brought about by means of his charms and his medicines; at any rate, he gave out that such was the case. Persevering in the use of so trusted an auxiliary, the chief prepared a large quantity of medicines, sufficient to fill a tsessebe skin, and despatched in the night four men with this wondrous burden, which they were instructed to throw into the water drunk by Khame and his people. Whether the contents of the bag were poisonous or merely charms, I am unable to say. I believe the men themselves were "charmed" before proceeding on this weird expedition, when it was said to them, "Go! It will be dark wherever you are, no one shall see you, nothing shall harm you." But, alas for witchcraft! the young chiefs' men in charge of the fountain that night heard the cautious footsteps of their midnight visitors, and reserving their fire till their enemies were close to them, the bearer of the medicine was killed on the spot. He was found next morning with the tsessebe skin above him. Nothing could exceed the vexation and rage which this event produced in the town.

And strange to say, instead of directing their wrath against their opponents, it seemed to find vent in bitter speeches against the white people on the place, and especially against myself. "What did the traders want with so much ammunition?" And they were sure they had helped Khame; and, as for me, they were sure I did not go up the mountain for any good on Sundays. If I preached from the Word of God merely, well, then the Word of God itself was bad, and was the cause of all the strife. So loud was the talk against me that an English gentleman thought it his duty to repair to my household one Sunday morning to warn me against the risk of going up the mountain again. A native woman also came to me in secret and told me that my death had been loudly demanded by Sekhome's mother and one or two head-men. Others proposed to whip me well, take my property from me, and send me away. This discussion was overheard by my informant's mother, who was in the employ of Khame's mother. Altho' hooted and called by very disreputable names, and altho' very sulkily received by Sekhome himself, I continued to get his reluctant consent to my going to preach to the poor people on the mountain, and did so to the last. My visits were always looked forward to by the little flock. As soon as I could see their features I could see a smile of welcome already there. I had a better congregation on these occasions than we have had on our usual worship since Sekhome began the present system of opposition. As time wore on this bitterness diminished, and I was able to go from one camp to the other with fewer insults, and at last had the happiness of doing something towards bringing about peace. Not being conscious of having wronged any one in the town, I felt pretty sure no one would harm me. One Sunday while I was taking leave of Khame on the brow of the hill, a man belonging to Sekhome's party got into position for taking a "dead aim" at some of us, laying his gun over an anthill and remaining in that position for a good while. At last he rose without firing and went away. I was told afterwards that as soon as I descended he came back to the same place, and *then did fire*. On another occasion Piet Jacobs, a Boer from the Transvaal, having business with Khame, got permission from Sekhome to pay the latter a visit. On reappearing at the brow of the hill he was fired at, as well as his two companions, and the firing was continued while they slowly led their horses down the steep path. They were unarmed, and certainly those who levelled their muskets at them were very bad shots, for they invariably missed them, altho' not further than 200 or 300 yds. It was Ralitlari who was guilty of this cowardly act, one of the sons of Sekhome who were persuaded by their father to give up attending both church and school.

I am sorry to say that Sechele has been so cruel and so false as, first, to write a very friendly letter to Khame and the head-men with him, promising them a refuge in case of emergency, and mentioning by name Chukuru, Khame's father-in-law; and then, as soon as Khamane and Chukuru made their appearance in the town, to put the latter to death under circumstances of great cruelty. Altho' Chukuru lived and died a heathen, he was much more friendly disposed towards the Gospel than Sekhome. He was also a man of ability, and in rank next to the chief. He was invariably kind to Mr Price and myself.

Altho' active warfare was brought to an end in the manner above described, Sekhome would not be satisfied, would not live in peace. Khame still went to church, still read the Bible, and until he gave up these he was not his son. Then in May a new element of discord appeared on the scene. When Sekhome believed that he would not be able to overcome Khame, he had sent in his desperation to his brother Macheng for assistance. Macheng naturally took some time to consider such an invitation, which, if sincere, was equal to an abdication of the chieftainship on the part of Sekhome, for Macheng is his superior according to the native way of counting rank. While Sekhome and his sons were at war, Macheng remained quiet at Sechele's, where he has been staying for some years; but as soon as the war was over, he announced his intention of yielding to Sekhome's request. I have no doubt that Sekhome was sorry that he had ever made such a request, but he could not recall it; so Macheng came. He was told in plain terms while at Sechele's, that he would be expected to put Khame and the rest of Sekhome's enemies to death. But instead of this, as soon as he entered the town he made Khame his friend; and now Sekhome is at his wits' end, for into the pit which he dug for his own son, it is not at all impossible that he may himself fall. Those who know both Macheng and Sekhome say that it will be impossible for them to agree together, but whether they will fight or quietly separate, the future must disclose. Macheng expresses himself at present as favourable to our work, but whether he would continue so had he full power as chief, is alas! a question.

We hope that those who continue true to Christ in this town, in this present distressing circumstances, will form a good nucleus for that church which we trust our Lord will yet graciously build amongst the Bamangwato.—I am, ever yours truly,   JOHN MACKENZIE.

One of the most thrilling events in this story of jealousy and intrigue, as well as of Christian forbearance and nobility of spirit, occurred as the result of Macheng's presence in the town. Sekhome's bitter

self-seeking could brook the domineering presence of
Macheng as little as the Christian disobedience of his
own sons. The result was that the crafty and cunning
chief began to plot against the man whom he had
invited to take his place among the Bamangwato.
When on a certain day he found his own friends so
reduced in numbers and so sunk in cowardice that
they would not smite his enemies, even after he had
given the signal in the public courtyard, nothing
remained for him but an ignominious flight. That
evening a sudden and strange excitement was observ-
able among the natives on the mission premises ; there
was a furtive pointing of the finger towards the
mountain, and a whispering in the ear, and a rushing
from one group to another ; men hardly dared to look
at a solitary figure climbing down the rocks behind
Mackenzie's house ; and yet all were fascinated, for
it was Sekhome ! He had often threatened to take
Mackenzie's life ; he had opposed with deep hatred
Mackenzie's Christian influence ; he had tried to cheat
him in the affairs of business ; he had been wont to
malign him amongst his head-men. But on this night,
when every man's hand was against him, and he
was a fugitive from his own people, a man doomed
to death, there seemed to him no safer spot in the
world or more attractive than Mackenzie's own house.
Once more he sat at the fireside of the faithful
missionary, who earnestly pled with him to trust in
the love and loyalty of his sons, and to cease from
listening to the evil counsel of bad men. Late in the
night he departed, was joined by a little group of
faithful followers, and fled for a distant town a
humiliated refugee.

In 1867 Mackenzie undertook the building of a
church. Hitherto his preaching had been conducted
in the open air, which was indeed in accordance with
the only possible native practice ; but he knew that

the best results could not be obtained until some one place was set apart as the spiritual home of the Christian people. He tried, of course, to èrect his church with the least possible expense, especially as he had not waited for the formal approval of his project by the Directors. He planned a building of 60 ft. by 24 ft., and it was one ambition of his heart that it should have lancet instead of square windows, the frames for which he made with his own hands. The following brief account of this work again fails to do justice to the extraordinary amount of personal labour and deep anxiety in which Mackenzie found himself involved before the building was completed.

SHOSHONG, *Dece·nber* 1867.

REV. J. MULLENS, D.D.

Dear Brother,—I beg to forward a statement of accounts connected with the new church here up to this date. The mason's charges were very moderate, carpenter work costs nothing; altho' no carpenter, I have managed the wood-work myself. The felling, sawing, and adzing of timber was done by natives of the place under my own superintendence. Some were hired for the articles mentioned in the account; others worked a stipulated time for repairs to the locks of their guns. I was glad to do anything so as to lessen expense. M., after living quietly and steadily in our household for about ten months, managed to procure some brandy from a trader, got very drunk, abused all and sundry, then got ashamed and asked his pay before finishing the plastering and flooring, and took his departure. I am at present busy finishing the plastering, and hope our church will be open for worship the first Sunday of 1868. You will notice with pleasure that Mr Stewart, a trader in ostrich feathers, etc., who was engaged to lay half of the bricks, returned one half of his pay, £15, as his subscription to the church. I ought to mention that besides this subscription I received from both natives and Europeans considerable assistance in the loan of waggons and oxen, etc.

I have already drawn on the Society £45 for church building; and £27, 12s. 2d. remain due. Our friends in Scotland will give a little for this object. Beyond this

I know no other quarter where help can be expected. It is true I have drawn the £45 without your sanction; but then I did not know of our Society's pecuniary difficulties when I began to build. We must have a church here; and the one now built is, I believe, suitable and substantial. I hope to hear from you on the subject, for it will be necessary to draw the £27 pounds soon.

With reference to our boys' subscriptions, Willie was the fortunate possessor of *one* ox from a cow which I gave him some time ago. We thought he ought to learn early to be unselfish and liberal, and laid the matter before him. It was not without an effort that he said he would give "Welshman" his much valued ox; but his mind once made up, he seemed happy in his deed. Then Johnnie burst into tears "because he had no ox like Willie." He had only a year-old calf, and it so went to my heart that I effected an "exchange" with Johnnie on the spot, giving him a young ox for his calf. It was thus that our boys were able to give £10 for the new church.

In attendance, the church is steadily improving, and a good many from the ranks of heathenism are learning to read.—I remain, ever yours sincerely, JOHN MACKENZIE.

On the completion of the church Mackenzie resolved to make the day of its opening and dedication one that should be remembered in Shoshong. This great feast day he has described in detail and with great sense of humour in his book.[1] Throughout these years of building operations Mackenzie was carrying on his missionary work as best he could. The wide range and variety of his relations to the people undoubtedly strengthened his grip upon the town, for they had come to know him not only as the teacher, but as the practical, strong-willed worker and master of men. His personality created an impression which is best illustrated by one significant fact. Europeans who resided in those regions knew that the natives had nicknames for them. These nicknames were often based upon some physical peculiarity, and

[1] "Ten Years North of the Orange River," pp. 461 ff.

were very seldom used in the presence of Europeans; and hence they were rarely discovered. Some of them were very apt and very amusing. Mackenzie never knew what his nickname was, until told, late in life, by one of his sons, who discovered it while moving one day among the workmen on a building at Shoshong. The boy suddenly heard the lazy fellows who had been loafing, calling each other to work. They pointed across the open to a solitary figure moving rapidly and powerfully toward them. He had broad shoulders, a tawny beard, strong, clear eyes, a deep voice that could shake a native defaulter to the heart. As they pointed they spoke of "him," pointed out how " he" walked, admiringly praised " his" strength. The secret was out. They were speaking in the tones and phrases used by natives of a lion. " Tau " (lion) was Mackenzie's nickname, and " Tau " was his reputation among them.

In the year 1867 South Africa and the world in general were startled by the announcement that a certain traveller, Captain Mauch, had found gold in the district of Tati, in the north-east part of the Bamangwato country. At once there began a movement of white people in that direction. The rumour spread that it was alluvial gold which was being found there, and that would have resulted, of course, in a great and sudden rush of gold-seekers ; but, as it ultimately turned out, gold in paying quantities could only be found in quartz. While this point was still under investigation the news that gold in any form had been found, led to the formation of prospecting parties and companies. Three separate claims to the sovereignty of the gold region were immediately set up by Macheng, Moselekatse, and the Transvaal Government respectively. The last named, in the year 1868, sent Commandant Jan Viljoen as a commissioner to Moselekatse, ostensibly to negotiate with

him for possession of the coveted district. While
Viljoen was engaged in this formal embassy the two
native chiefs were discussing their own claims. Moselekatse claimed that he had conquered all that territory even down to Shoshong. This preposterous
assumption was met by Macheng, chief of the Bamangwato, with the facts that his people had never been
conquered, and that, while a certain tribe whom the
Matabele had conquered *had* lived in that part of the
Tati district, the entire district had always been used
by Macheng's people, without dispute or disturbance,
as their hunting-ground and a valuable grazing country
for their cattle. Mackenzie thoroughly believed that
the weight of the argument was very clearly in favour
of Macheng. The prospect of an inrush of gold-seekers
roused him to explain to the chief all that such an
event must mean to his country. The matter was
gone over in one long conversation after another, until
Macheng clearly understood that if the gold-fields
proved rich there would grow up within his dominion
a large town of white men, most of them British
citizens, whom he would be utterly unable to rule,
and who, as things were, would be beyond the control
of any European government. He received from his
missionary the advice that he should immediately
communicate with the British Government, state the
facts from his point of view, and invite that Government to send a representative who should be a ruler
of the white people in the Bamangwato country. It
was of course reasonable that he should expect, as
the chief of the country, to have some share in whatever wealth the gold-fields were likely to yield.
Macheng very eagerly agreed to this policy, and on
March 29th, 1868, sent a letter to Sir P. E. Wodehouse, at that time Governor of the Colony of the
Cape of Good Hope. In this letter, after summarising
the facts that gold had been discovered, and that the

gold district was within his territory, he proceeded to
make his proposal in the following terms :—

Now I conceive it my duty, in circumstances of such
peculiar importance, to seek the counsel and aid of Her
Majesty's Government. The Transvaal Government, through
Commandant Jan Viljoen, desires me to hand over to the
Republic the district in question, and assures me, in return,
of the protection of the Republic should the gold-diggers
molest my people.   I shall decline to consider this or any
other overture, until I hear from your Excellency.

I. I beg, then, humbly to submit to your Excellency, as
Her Majesty's representative, that the gold-field or fields in
the Shashe district are situated in the country which belongs
to me, as chief of the Bamangwato. The boundary line
between my country and that of Moselekatse is at Makobe's
old town.

II. I would not willingly give up this territory without
compensation.

III. Having, however, no reason to believe that my claims
as owner of the district in question would be ignored by Her
Majesty's Government, I beg to state my willingness to leave
the amount of compensation, and the manner of its payment,
as questions for future settlement.

IV. Whilst I have hithero lived on terms of friendship
with English visitors, and with a few English residents, I feel
utterly unqualified to govern such a community as that of
gold-diggers is described to me to be. May it please your
Excellency, these gold-diggers are your people ; therefore I
invite you, and I beg you, to come and occupy the gold
country so far as it is at my disposal, and to govern the gold-
diggers, in the name of the Queen of England.

Meanwhile, and until I hear from your Excellency, it is
my intention to encourage such gold-diggers as make their
appearance, by granting them permits to dig, at a nominal
price, by enrolling the names of such permit-holders, and by
empowering one or more of their number to administer
justice in the gold-field. And these steps I shall take in
the earnest hope that speedily my weak efforts to sustain law
and order amongst British subjects may be superseded by
the advent of the power of England.

In an accompanying letter Mackenzie said that the

Europeans in that part of the country were, to a man very anxious that Macheng's proposals should be accepted and acted upon without delay. He pointed out that the country from the Orange River to Shoshong was occupied by tribes who were favourable to the English, and he believed that if the proposal were made to them by one in whom they had confidence, and if it were properly explained to them, even those tribes would unanimously vote for federation with the Colony. Thus early had this missionary, brooding on the problem of the influx and amalgamation of the races in South Africa, come to believe that the best thing for South Africa, the best thing for all the native tribes, would be that the British Government should gradually interpose a friendly and protective power between the native chiefs and the shock of European immigration. It is, in the light of subsequent events, a matter of interest to note, that at this time Mackenzie believed that the best plan would be to strive for this development of Bechuanaland through the Cape Colony, by means of some connection which he vaguely describes as " federation."

The excitement over the gold-fields involved Mackenzie in a great amount of anxious and sometimes exciting discussion and correspondence. He was used by the heads of distant prospecting companies as their best source of information. He did not shrink from doing all in his power to help those who were seeking most rapidly to occupy the new territory ; while he was, on the other hand, at the same time striving to secure for them the best possible form of government. He took great pains to secure specimens of the gold which was being found, and to forward these to the right persons, including Sir Philip Wodehouse. In the middle of that year, 1868, he made a journey to Potchefstroom in the Transvaal, for supplies. As this was the head-quarters of one of the most energetic companies that had been formed, he took with him specimen pieces of gold quartz. His arrival at Potchefstroom created an excitement which astonished him. A special edition of the Transvaal *Argus* was issued for the express purpose of giving the new facts which Mackenzie was able to convey to them.

TRANSVAAL, "ARGUS" OFFICE, 6*th July* 1868.

Potchefstroom was thrown into a state of considerable excitement last Thursday afternoon, the 2d inst., when it became known that the Rev. Mr Mackenzie, so anxiously expected here, had arrived. The excitement became intense when it was ascertained that the rev. gentleman had brought intelligence of a late date direct from the Victoria Goldfields, was a bearer of several letters from the diggers themselves, some of which we now publish, and moreover, had brought a sample of GOLD from the new diggings. Of course, we, too, went to see, having been attacked for the time being with all the symptoms of the gold fever. The sample was minutely inspected, and we now declare, on the sacred word of an editor, that the said sample requires but to be seen in order to dispel the strongest doubts of even the most sceptical. The "myth," as the gold discovery has been termed, has resolved itself into a stupendous fact. The samples produced by the Rev. Mr Mackenzie, which can now be seen at Mr Reid's, are two pieces of quartz, partly crystallised, very richly studded with gold, having solid pieces, some larger even than a pin's head, imbedded in the stone; and yet the richer pieces, parts of the same stone, had already been forwarded to His Excellency, Sir Philip Wodehouse, and also to Graham's Town. These pieces we have not seen, but the rev. gentleman assures us that they are richer far than those brought by him to Potchefstroom, and that all are parts of the same stone taken from the surface, picked up close to where the diggers are now at work—in fact, at the outspan place. These pieces of quartz fully prove the superior richness of these new and vast gold-fields, to which the name of "Victoria" has been given, in honour of Her Majesty the Queen of England.

One of the letters which he brought to the editor of the *Argus* from the captain of the prospecting party, announced that the gold-fields had been proclaimed British territory, and that the Union Jack already floated above the new district, which was called Victoria. So enthusiastic were the sentiments of the business people at Potchefstroom, and so grateful for the services rendered to them by Mackenzie, that they presented him with an address of welcome and of warm gratitude for what he had done on their behalf. In this gratitude they included his colleague, the Rev. Roger Price of Bechuanaland. The address was signed by sixty Europeans, including names which were unmistakably English, Scotch, Welsh, Irish, and Dutch respectively. On his way back to Shoshong Mackenzie was met by Sir Philip Wodehouse's reply to the appeal of Macheng. The Governor cordially recognised the great prudence of Macheng and promised to investigate the whole question, confessing that if the gold-fields came to be occupied by a considerable number of British subjects he would feel himself under necessity to provide for their good government. The matter was reported by him to the Cape Parliament, which voted £2000 towards the expenses of a Parliamentary Committee, which it was proposed to send north, and upon whose report an intelligent policy could be founded. At the same time, in a private letter, the Governor explained that he was laying the whole matter before the authorities in London. Alas! this was practically equivalent to an announcement that the matter was shelved.

In the meantime the Transvaal Government, without waiting for the report of its Commissioner, Commandant Viljoen, had actually issued a proclamation, claiming the entire territory as belonging to them. The proclamation, of course, did not do this directly by naming only and specifically the Tati district, but sought officially to define the extent of its dominions. These were said to extend as far north as Lake Ngami and right down the whole length of Bechuanaland, even to Kuruman. "This included," said Mackenzie to the Governor, "more than a dozen native chiefs, who have never owed any allegiance to the Boers." This astute but characteristic step was, owing to pressure from various quarters, never acted upon. But in the meantime Mr Viljoen strove his best to secure the gold country for his own people. Since he failed to obtain any recognition of Transvaal ownership either from Macheng or Moselekatse, he deliberately set himself to achieve his end by another method, which was also not unfamiliar to his countrymen. He wrote a letter to one Lee, a Boer, but a British subject, claiming him as his friend, and urging him as a man of influence in the Matabele country to try and stir up a war between the Matabele and the Bamangwato over the ownership of the gold-fields. He, in black and white, said that he specially desired to see the "vagabonds at Shoshong set on fire." Of course, if the Matabele had made such an attack upon the Bamangwato and secured the gold-fields, Commandant Viljoen and his compatriots would immediately have found it right, on humanitarian grounds, to attack their ancient enemies and possess themselves by righteous conquest of the Tati district. Into their hands in this way would also have fallen the territories of Mashonaland, where already it was known that gold abounded. The letter in which the Transvaal Commissioner made these proposals came into the hands of Macheng. Viljoen, on finding this out, immediately apologised to Macheng in the humblest terms, and offered, in reparation, to give him some cattle which, he said, he was about to get, or take, from another chief. Viljoen's letter Macheng did not answer.

As it turned out, the gold-fields at Tati were of such a nature as to require much heavy and expensive machinery. The companies which first attempted to work them were not very successful, their operations being of course greatly hindered by the enormous cost of transport. The result was that the expected "rush" did not take place, the Cape Parliament did not send its Commissioner, the British Government did not accept Macheng's proposals, and the whole subject for some years dropped out of practical politics. But it had considerably stirred up the minds of the native chiefs throughout Bechuanaland, and they henceforth thought of European ascendancy in South Africa with a new apprehension in their hearts. Moreover, the experience which he had received in these negotiations led Mackenzie to form still clearer and deeper views on the entire and vast subject of the relations of Great Britain to South Africa. Henceforth, it may be said that his mind worked upon the difficult problems which he saw looming on the horizon, with a definiteness and earnestness born of this brief practical experience.

In the end of 1868, Mackenzie set out on a southern journey with a double purpose. In the first place he must attend an important meeting of the Bechuana missionaries which was to be held at Kuruman in the following year, and thereafter he must go to Cape Town in order to send his two eldest children home to Scotland for their education. He had now a family of five children, consisting of three sons and two daughters. He was only a few days' journey from Shoshong when a letter from the Directors met him inviting him to go home on furlough. This unexpected invitation found him in many respects unprepared. He would have liked to see some adequate provision made for the work in Shoshong. Many things might have been said and done at that place to prepare the people, both black and white, for the management of various affairs in his absence. As soon as the news reached Shoshong messages were sent after him expressive of regret, and not only of regret but of apprehension, that while he was away troubles of various kinds were likely to arise in the town, which his presence had staved off.

At Kuruman a number of weeks were passed in pleasant intercourse with the brethren and in hard daily work on the Committee. The chief subject of discussion was the revision of the Sechuana Bible, with all the problems of translation and orthography which that involved. In the end of May Mackenzie arrived in London, and after a few days took his family down to his wife's home at Portobello, Edinburgh. This place became the headquarters of his family in the old country for a quarter of a century. His wife's mother and an unmarried sister, the late Miss E. B. Douglas, assumed the guardianship of his children, relieving him of untold anxiety. On the death of her mother, Miss Douglas continued this work of love and self-sacrifice. A lady of rare culture and deep piety she became to a very large circle one of those angel aunts to whom so many families have learnt to render a peculiar reverence and gratitude.

Mackenzie was of course speedily plunged into that strange form of recreation which the Christian world affords to its wearied missionaries and which is known as Deputation Work. He did not relish any more than others the constant journeyings and the endless series of meetings, at which the same story had to be told over and over again. His numerous letters to various members of his family, show that on this first campaign of platform oratory in England he was full of self-criticism and humility, almost of self-deprecation. And yet that he was successful in the work is proved by the importance of the appointments given him, as well as by the direct testimony of his hearers in different parts of the country. He related with immense relish the appeal which one good lady made to him while driving in her carriage from a large meeting where he had spoken. She told him that missionary supporters were looking out for a new hero—this one had died, and that one had retired—and that he seemed the one to take that place. For the sake of the cause they needed the popularity of a new man, and "Mr Mackenzie," she pleadingly added, "many of us think you are that man. But there is one thing you must do—you must talk more about yourself, you must tell us your own adventures instead of merely giving these addresses which we find very interesting, but in which you yourself have no place." Mackenzie fairly chuckled over the idea that he should stand up before an audience and talk about himself.

The list of deputation-engagements between March 8th and April 8th, 1870, shows that he had engagements at eighteen different places, at many of which he had to give two or even three addresses in one day. This is only a specimen taken at random from his records of the work, which he and other missionaries were and are expected to do month after month, during the larger part of their furlough.

In the spring of 1870, not without much hesitation and diffidence, after urgent arguments from many friends, Mackenzie gave himself to the task of writing his first book, which he sent out under the title "Ten Years North of the Orange River : a story of everyday life and work among the South African tribes from 1859 to 1869." It was published by Edmonston & Douglas of Edinburgh, in the spring of 1871, and has been for many years out of print. It was received with remarkable favour by reviewers of all types. In a style which had no pretensions, but which was characterised by clearness and force, he not only described his own experiences among the Bechuana and Matabele tribes, but also presented original and valuable studies of their political organisation, and their manners and customs. In an appendix of about fifty pages, he discussed the races of South Africa in a more scientific fashion, and also set forth the theory which he elaborated in after years concerning "the contact of Europeans with natives in South Africa." He believed himself to be the first writer who called attention to the fact which then was unknown and unsuspected, that South African races were not decreasing but very rapidly increasing under the British Government.

As soon as possible after the completion of this book the Mackenzies sailed again for South Africa in the month of March 1871, leaving three of their five children at Portobello. Before they left that place Mackenzie and his wife were invited by the members of several churches in the town to a social gathering in the Town Hall, at which some valuable gifts were made to them. These included a handsome gold hunting watch, which served Mackenzie with great accuracy to the end of his life.

CHAPTER V

JOHN MACKENZIE sailed the second time for South Africa on the s.s. *Sweden*, embarking at Dartmouth on March 10th, 1871. This vessel made what was at that date the fastest voyage on record, and reached Cape Town in twenty-seven days, thirteen hours. It is interesting to know that the very next vessel still further reduced the record by completing the voyage in twenty-four days, thirteen hours. Mackenzie sailed round to Port Elizabeth, and from there took ox-waggon through the Eastern Province. He made straight for Molepolole, which he was anxious to reach in time for the annual meeting of the Bechuana-land District Committee. When near Lovedale, in the Colony, he received from the Institution there the three young Bechuanas of whom he had had the care for some years, and who grew to manhood and womanhood in his service. Dr Stewart of Lovedale rendered an account for their board, lodging, and instruction since April 1869, in the following terms : " To charges, £0, 0s. 0d." The Committee meeting at Molepolole exerted an important influence upon the history of Mackenzie. Ten missionaries were present, and the Committee dealt with a large variety of subjects connected with the work of the mission. The most important of all was the establishment of a " Seminary for the education of young men as schoolmasters and native ministers." It is only necessary to say at this point that the Committee arranged for the immediate establishment of such an institution, and appointed Mackenzie to be its first Tutor. When he continued his journey to Shoshong, it was, therefore, not only with the happy anticipations of a return to his beloved people, but under deep concern over this new enterprise and his part in it.

During the months which had elapsed since they left England, the hearts of these parents had, of course, been much with the children whom they left behind in that distant Scottish home.   There began at that time, therefore, that long series of letters to his children into which Mackenzie poured all the tenderness and wisdom, and firmness and earnestness of his soul.   With children, as we shall see, he knew how to be playful as well as serious, and these letters written to his own children in their younger years reveal a true interest in the very matters which attracted their attention and affection year after year.   The following letter, written before reaching Shoshong to one of his sons, is thoroughly characteristic :—

MOLEPOLOLE, SECHELE'S TOWN.

MY DEAR WILLIE,—You will remember this place, I daresay.   We got here about ten days ago.   Our oxen were getting very tired; and I am very glad for their sakes that we are staying here for a little.   There are ten missionaries here at present, and we meet together as a District Committee, to consider all questions connected with our work here.

Bill and Plaything (two favourite goats) are with us.   We got them at Kuruman.   They are both quite tame, and allow me to scratch their heads.   They come running to you if you hold out your hand, hoping to get a piece of bread.   They eat porridge also.   Jamie is quite pleased with them, but he is a little afraid of them at present. Rosa (a dog) is here.   She is a great favourite with everybody, and is very beautiful.   Monk is now a large dog.   We left it, you remember, at Kuruman, a little puppy.   Garty (a much loved otter terrier) was at Kuruman, and came in with us, walking all the way.   He is getting old, and is a little deaf; but we shall take special care of it for your sake, for we remember it is Willie's dog.   I have also a fine large dog which I call Nero. Mr Good tells us there were lots of mice or rats in our house at Shoshong when he was in it; so we are taking in two cats from this place.

Ellen's cows are quite well. One is giving milk now; the other will calve in summer. I shall tell you about yours and Johnnie's when I see them at home.

Do you remember the Dam here? I have bathed in it three times. It was rather cold, it being still winter here. Little Rogie Price bathes with his father, and is quite brave in the water. By the by, I hope you are both very careful as to how far you go in the sea when bathing in summer.

At the time I am writing you are enjoying your vacation somewhere. We have been lately thinking and speaking much of you. When you get this letter the vacation will have again passed; and you will be at work with your lessons. Dear boys, continue to be diligent and persevering. Little by little—and whatever you do, do well.

I find that I am a little rusty in Sechuana. It will soon come back. At present the right word is not always at hand when I want it, so I have to express my meaning in another way. This happens once or twice in a sermon. I have very good news from Shoshong. The people are earnest about learning to read; and the church was nearly full when a native passed through, whom I saw yesterday. I am delighted with the idea of again preaching and teaching at Shoshong. Pray for us, my dear boys, that our work may receive the blessing of God. When you say "Thy kingdom come," think sometimes of the Bamangwato, and of your parents' work.

Be sure and continue in full love to one another. Don't keep secrets from one another. Don't quarrel. If you are angry with one another, make it up before you sleep. Stick to one another. And may your Father in Heaven Himself take care of you and bless you.—Ever your affectionate father, JOHN MACKENZIE.

When news reached Shoshong that Mackenzie and his young colleague the Rev. J. D. Hepburn were nearing the town, the young chief Khame and two brothers rode out twenty miles to meet them. They arrived on August 23rd.

Mackenzie received two letters of cordial welcome

after his long absence. The first was addressed to
him by Macheng, who was still chief of the Bamangwato, to assure him that he felt toward him as toward
an old friend and brother. These warm sentiments,
which at the time gave pleasure, alas! as we shall see,
did not continue. The other letter, so far as the
sincerity of the writers is concerned, was much more
valuable. It was signed by twelve European traders,
at that time residing at Shoshong ; as expressing
their spontaneous welcome to a missionary, whom they
as a class are usually supposed to dislike, this letter,
simple but earnest, gave Mackenzie much delight.

The missionaries were profoundly thankful to find
that both Khame and his brother Khamane had
remained faithful. They had personally maintained
public worship when no missionary was present, and
carried on the day school, with the result that the
congregation had increased. This remarkable fact
may be placed alongside the keen observation made
some years later by Mackenzie, that the native
Christians belonging to towns where no white missionary was settled, showed a higher average intelligence
in Christian affairs than those living under the
immediate tutelage of an ordained European. It
appears to be the case not only that the Church of
Christ has that sustaining spiritual force within it
which can maintain and multiply life even among the
rudest peoples, where the Word of God is openly read
and taught ; but that sometimes the continual presence
of an educated European retards the development
of intelligence among an ignorant and unlettered
people. The reason for the latter result probably is,
that he comes to be regarded too much as an oracle
whose every word is trusted, and whose assertion is
taken as authoritative. Naturally the word of a local
native teacher is more open to dispute, and is therefore
more disputed. The friendly discussions which his

teaching thus stimulates as well as guides, hasten the spiritual growth of the entire community. Of course, he himself has been taught by a missionary and he frequently makes a journey to the nearest Mission Station, where he discusses all those problems with the missionary, which his own parishioners have been hurling at his bewildered head.

Mackenzie found that the political atmosphere at Shoshong was peculiarly uncertain ; at times it threatened to break into a disastrous storm. Macheng who had begun, as may be remembered, by admiring and trusting the two brothers Khame and Khamane, and had striven to secure their co-operation and sympathy, gradually became jealous of them, as their own father had been. He was a self-indulgent and sensual man, and he grew in jealousy and greed. His greed led him to lay hold on as many " presents " from both white men and black as he could, while his jealousy led him to consult the young chiefs less and less. This attitude of mind was publicly revealed by various incidents, but by none more strikingly than that which occurred in connection with Kuruman, the claimant to the kingship of the Matabele tribe. Moselekatse, the famous Zulu warrior, chief of the Matabele, had recently died, and his head-men had made his son, Lobengula, chief in his stead. The latter immediately took steps to make his position secure, but was confronted by the fact that many of his people believed him to be a usurper. The true successor of Moselekatse was, they said, an older brother whom Moselekatse had sent away in his childhood southwards to be brought up where his life would be safe. Inquiries were made with the result that a young man named Kuruman, who had long lived with Mr Theophilus Shepstone of Natal, was announced as the eldest son of Moselekatse and the true heir to the chieftainship of the Matabele. Kuruman gave proofs which at once convinced large numbers, and he set out on the journey northwards to claim his kingdom. It may be a safe conjecture that Mr Rider Haggard, who was one of Shepstone's colleagues, founded one of the most interesting portions of his story, entitled "King Solomon's Mines," upon this very incident in South African history. Kuruman, however, lacked the wisdom and self-control of Mr Haggard's hero. When he reached Shoshong, and declared himself to Macheng, he asked for the loan of three regiments, announcing that he desired them not to fight against the Matabele but to act as an escort on his entrance into his own land. He appears to have taken for granted that Lobengula either would not fight against him, or if he did would be deserted by the entire tribe when they heard the simple announcement, made by chosen heralds, that Kuruman, their true king, was now in their midst. He went north in this foolhardy manner only to find that Lobengula had heard all about his movements, had paralysed those of the Matabele who were known to support his claim, and made arrangements to slay his heralds wherever they dared to lift their voices. This claimant to the throne was compelled to retire meekly to Shoshong, where he settled down for a time, and where his presence caused great disturbance of mind to his hosts. But his foolish movement made double mischief in Shoshong. For, in the first place, Macheng had placed those three regiments under an inferior officer, to the public humiliation of Khame, their real commander. And, in the next place, matters were complicated for Macheng himself, because some of Kuruman's servants had seized Matabele cattle and brought them to Shoshong. As long as Kuruman with his few soldiers and their plunder remained among the Bamangwato the latter felt themselves involved in what Europe would call "strained relations with a neighbouring government."

But to return to Macheng's domestic affairs, his relations with the young chiefs were brought to a head through the treachery of a half-brother of the latter named Ralitlari. This man was discovered in a deep plot to secure either that Macheng should attack Khame or that Khame should attack Macheng ; and he attempted to bring about an open warfare by acting as the friend of each, and assuring each that the other intended to murder him. When he was discovered, and he fled from the town with three of Khame's horses, the young chiefs made the strange resolve to invite their own father Sekhome back to the chieftain-ship. Sekhome, who had long been plotting for this very thing, in a most inexplicable way declined it, when the invitation was brought to him by Khamane. The young chiefs had a strong ally in Sechele, the well-known chief of the neighbouring tribe the Bakwena. Having promised to send them help he did so in a very effective way. His soldiers, with his own son Sebele at their head, arrived at Shoshong quite unexpectedly. The ensuing incidents may be given in Mackenzie's words as follows :—

Khamane arrived on Saturday, and the Bakwena were expected on the Monday night following. When Tuesday night came, and no Bakwena, Khame's anxiety was very great ; but in the middle of the night a scout arrived to announce that they were resting that night in the desert, some distance from the town, and that they would arrive next night. Strange to say, the secret did not leak out in the town. I never knew the Bamangwato keep a matter so close. Macheng was quite unsuspicious of imminent danger, although he knew that Khamane had been to see his father. He talked largely of the answer which he was to send back to Sechele ; and in the meantime ordered that a bag of sugar, the property of a trader, should be conveyed to his house, " as a present." In all such unworthy courses he was en-couraged by a few hair-brained youths who were his constant personal attendants.

On Wednesday the chief went unsuspectingly on his rounds

to visit the white men's shops, and to demand the customary basinful of brandy from each. But at gray dawn on Thursday morning Macheng's heavy slumbers were rudely disturbed by a discharge of musketry. He lay down, the sensual, stupid, but conceited chief of the Bamangwato; an hour after dawn he was an outcast, almost without a friend. As soon as he heard the discharge of fire-arms Macheng, partially dressed, hurried from his hut. He soon found himself in the hands of the Bakwena and Bamangwato, under Seretse, a brother of Khame. It was Sechele's desire that Macheng should be shot, but to this Khame refused to consent. "Kill his worthless and bloodthirsty attendants," said Khame, "but let Macheng himself go free." And so Macheng, when seized, was roughly told that he was indebted to Khame for his life, and was ordered to leave the town without delay. Six of his counsellors fell near to him. Several Matabele attendants of Macheng were also shot. Corpulent and indolent, Macheng cut a sorry figure on Thursday morning. Without shoes, without shirt, so overcome with fright and unwonted exertion that he was ready to fall down, he was driven from the town, forced to take refuge in the mountains at the foot of which it is built. Those of the Bamangwato who were taken by surprise, like their chief, hastened to that part of the town where Macheng took up his first position. Khame, however, afforded them an opportunity of retracing their steps and returning to the town. At the head of a party of horsemen he approached this harmless crowd, and shouted, "He who is for Khame, let him return to the town." The people came back almost to a man; and Macheng was left to scramble up the mountain as best he could. Twenty of Macheng's supporters fell in the engagement in the town, and two Bakwena. None of Khame's men were hurt, although they were always in the front. A native town is an awkward place for warfare; an enemy may be within some hut or behind some fence, and take dead aim at you before you are aware. So the Bakwena set fire to the town in order to dislodge its occupants. This is not at all the serious matter which the burning of European houses would be. The only grave part of it was the burning of the corn within the large clay vessels in which it is stored, and which are roofed over with grass, like a hut. The conflagration might have become a very serious one; but fortunately the wind soon fell, and Macheng's few followers were soon driven away; so the women were able to return and keep the fire from spreading.

In the afternoon some of Macheng's followers stationed themselves among the lofty crags overhanging the wells where the Bamangwato women draw water. This is not far from our houses, so we could witness the consternation among the water-drawers when the first bullet was fired amongst them. But Macheng's men did not confine their attention to the women in the river. Mr Hepburn was superintending some men who were sawing timber, when a bullet, evidently aimed at their party, passed close to Mr Hepburn's head and fell a little beyond the sawpit. Another struck the ground a few feet in front of Mr Hepburn's door. A third struck the ground close to where I stood. About this time a number of Bakwena had come to our premises to greet the two Bakwena students, and several Bamangwato men were also near our houses; perhaps this was the reason why Macheng's few followers directed their bullets as they did. Having annoyed us for about two hours, and effectually prevented our drawing of water during that time, they were driven from their stronghold by Khame and Khamane. After living for a few days in secluded retreats in the northern part of the range, Macheng turned toward the east, and while I write, is in the Machwapong hills on his way, it is understood, to Mankoroane's country. The unfortunate man has not a single friend among all the neighbouring chiefs. He quarrelled with everyone during the short period of his reign, and now he has to seek refuge in a country where he is unknown.

In the public gathering which took place after the fight was over, Sebele publicly informed the Bamangwato that Sechele had sent in his men not to assist Sekhome, but to assist Khame. Some of the Bamangwato head-men also declared in their speeches that "they saw Sekhome in Khame; they did not wish for another!" Khame himself spoke with great prudence: "I have not fought for the chieftainship; I have fought for my life. As to my father, I have asked Sekhome to come home, and sent Khamane for him; but he refused. I shall not ask him again. It is for you Bamangwato to send for him, and to bring him back again." He thus throws the weight of the responsibility upon the head-men. On the whole, I sincerely hope that neither Macheng nor Sekhome may ever be chief of this town.

One of the results of this revolution was that Kuruman had to leave Khame's country. Unfortunately the cattle which he had left at Shoshong were carried off by the Bakwena as their legitimate booty, a circumstance which afterwards involved some delicate negotiations with Lobengula.

It is surely a matter of intense interest that Mackenzie, at this crisis in the history of the tribe, retained the absolute trust of the leaders of all the parties who were warring against each other. At one and the same time he was keeping in safety some property for Sekhome, the exiled chief, and the originator of so much wickedness and mischief among the people; he was also made the depositary by Macheng of a considerable amount of money in English gold, and Macheng was Sekhome's rival and supplanter; he also acted as the trusted and most willing adviser of Khame, around whose personality the hatred of the two former for each other had been exasperated, and upon whom also it was concentrated. Yet none of these rivals for the chieftainship seems to have feared lest this missionary should use his power over their possessions, to the disadvantage of any of them.

Khame was now, to all appearances, formally established as the ruler of the Bamangwato tribe throughout its wide extent of territory, He entered upon his task not without anxiety, yet with a certain quietness and confidence characteristic of him. He was very speedily confronted with the two problems which, as far as his direct rulership was concerned, appear to have caused him the greatest perplexity. The first of these came from the fact that, as chief of the tribe, he was officially responsible for the performance of certain heathen rites and ceremonies. It was well known that, as a private man, he had even at great cost cut himself off from many of the traditional customs of his people; but it seemed to many that he would be compelled to give way to some extent when it came to the performance of those ceremonies which the entire people believed to be essential to their prosperity, and capable of due celebration only by the chief. The following account of the way in which Khame met this difficulty was given by Mackenzie.

Events soon transpired which showed Khame that his position would be one of great difficulty. On Saturday last he came to consult me concerning his first collision with heathenism; he informed me that some of the head-men, without meaning any offence to him, had suggested the performance of some heathen ceremonies in which the chief had to bear a part. The people, it seemed, were about to begin to dig their gardens. This was always done with ceremony and charm. The question then was, Were the people to be told simply to go and dig, without any ceremony, or could the seed-time be publicly inaugurated by a Christian chief in a Christian way? At harvest time there were also ceremonies. Now, the heathen ideas embodied in the ceremonies were good ones. In the spring-time by charm and spell and strict observance of use and wont, the heathen hoped to propitiate the Unseen and to get a good crop. When the chief began the harvesting, it was with feelings of gladness for the fruits which had come to maturity. Why should not a Christian Bechuana chief issue his "letsemma," inaugurate his seed-time, by public prayer to Almighty God the Maker of Heaven and Earth? And why not "loma" in the time of harvest, with thanksgiving and praise to Him Who crowneth the year with His goodness? Evidently such a public service would be a blessing to Khame himself, giving him an opportunity publicly to pledge himself as a chief to those customs which he had so faithfully followed in a less prominent position. From the standpoint of the old heathen people, such a service seemed also to be desirable. The town was not left utterly without a "custom"; there was something to which their ignorant minds might cling—something simple and better than the old charms. Then, as to the young men who are "adherents" but not Christians, such a service would be both a help and a pleasure to them, giving them an answer to those who would draw them back, and strengthening in their minds an idea of the suitability of Christianity to meet their requirements as a people. So I suggested to Khame that he should begin a new thing in the country, and issue his "letsemma" as a Christian chief in a Christian way. Inasmuch as every chief has the right to choose the nation from whom his son shall receive his doctors or priests, Sekhome had only exercised that right in choosing for his sons a missionary instead of priest. The teaching of the missionary was therefore entitled to at least as much public respect as that of any native doctor. By publicly acknowledging his firm adherence to Christianity at the outset of his career, I hoped also that Khame would escape molestation from the heathen party in the future.

So, on Sunday morning last, our church was empty. Khame assembled the Bamangwato in the public court-yard. The proceedings were commenced by the young chief in a short speech in which he emphatically announced his unwavering determination to adhere to Christianity. He did not prohibit heathen ceremonies, but they must not be performed in the khotla, and as chief he would contribute nothing towards them. The service in which the missionary was about to engage was his "letsemma"; after it they might dig where they pleased. Whoever wished his seed to be charmed or his garden to be charmed could do so, at his own expense; but he had no such custom. His speech, which was a very clear one, was well received: and I felt when he sat down that he was further from heathenism in his own estimation and in the minds of his people than before he made it. Then followed the religious service—similar to our ordinary morning service. We sang the Sechuana version of the 100th Psalm; I read the 33rd and 65th Psalms, and then engaged in prayer, which of course had reference to our special circumstances. Inasmuch as Khame had informed the people that I was not only to lead their prayers, but also to address them, I had an opportunity of making a short speech to the assembled Bamangwato. The points which I aimed at establishing were the suitability of Christianity as a "custom" or religion; that, therefore, under Khame's sway, they were not to anticipate calamity through having given up the public recognition of the old customs; it was a religion which had come to them from no mean nation, but one whose skill and prowess were patent to them ; it was not for one nation but for all ; and it had made their young chiefs truthful, kindhearted and brave— their praise was in every tribe. Let no one therefore hinder them or molest them in God's service in the future ; but rather let all learn to love and to trust the God of Khame and Khamane.

The speech was well received ; indeed audible applause was given to it. The service was concluded in the usual way, and thus ended Khame's public and solemn recognition of God and of Christianity among the Bamangwato people.

His other great difficulty Khame found among the white traders, who either had come to reside at Shoshong or passed through the town from time to time in large numbers. On the last day of December 1872, he went to Mackenzie to say that he wished to assemble all the white men in order to make known to them his laws with reference to strong drink. He had before explained his position to the traders as individuals, and a great improvement had resulted ; but fresh men brought the hated commodity in, and the traffic was therefore maintained, though in a mitigated form. He invited Mackenzie to be present at the meeting. The next morning early the chief again visited the missionary's house for further consultation, and they went down together to the khotla. All the white men, to the number of twenty-one, were brought together, several coming only after repeated summons had been sent to them. His speech, which was interpreted by Mackenzie, was a short one indeed, but very clear, direct, and authoritative. He simply and formally announced his law about " boyalwa " (strong drink). It was henceforth illegal to sell it in the town, or even to bring it into the country. After this warning, all brandy discovered in the town would be immediately destroyed, its owner would be fined, and expelled beyond the borders. Then Mackenzie made· a short statement, in which he explained that this movement had in no way been prompted by him, but was entirely the outcome of Khame's own thought. The traders, as a whole, appear to have approved of Khame's action. His right to make the law, and the fairness of the conditions under which he announced it, were universally acknowledged. Some of them rejoiced because their own servants would thus be delivered from temptation ; others, who were addicted to drink and had often disgraced themselves in the town, while they did not loudly acquiesce, were believed by those who knew them to be secretly glad that they themselves would be freed from temptation. The following sentences from Mackenzie's memorandum are of some interest, as illustrating at once the spirit of the traders and of the chief.

C—— said, "Well, now, there must be some loop-hole somewhere. We must not begin and smuggle, for if we do so, it will be worse for all parties than the thing is at present. We all like a little drink now and then, especially when we meet after a long separation ; we have been always accustomed to have a little drink. Does the chief mean to try and stop that ? "

I interpreted the question to Khame, who replied, " Ever since we saw the first white man we have been accustomed to see them pull out a bottle and giving one another something to drink. For a long time we thought it was medicine, and it did not concern us, for it was not given to black men. I do not want to interfere with your personal habits, so long as they do not become a nuisance in the town. But if, when you give one another drink, you turn round and give it to my people also, then I shall regard you as blame-worthy."

M—— said, "What the chief wants to put down is a canteen for black fellows, and I must say he is quite right."

I said I thought what he wanted to put down was a canteen for any fellows, white or black.

B—— made some reference to drink being allowed to pass. (He has some on his waggon.) C—— also wanted to know distinctly what was the law with reference to drink going through the country ?

Khame, in reply, said, "What other country do you want

to destroy with it? Why not let it alone? Why should it pass and destroy others? Are there not people like ourselves on in front?"

This did not, alas! end Khame's troubles in relation to this universally troublesome problem.

In the year 1873, Mackenzie found it necessary to make a journey into Matabeleland, in order to procure supplies of corn for the students of the Seminary who were now living at Shoshong. The journey was very rapidly made and the stay in Matabeleland was brief, but it enabled him to make a survey of affairs in that country alike from political, commercial and religious points of view. He recalled vividly the conditions which existed during his last visit in 1863 and made some interesting comparisons.

His purely private mission into that country was combined with an informal embassage on behalf of Khame. Since Khame's accession to the chieftainship of the Bamangwato several communications had passed between him and Lobengula, each chief being advised in the matter by the resident missionary. The result was that the negotiations even on delicate points had been carried on amicably. Khame disclaimed all desire to quarrel with his neighbour, and the latter wrote that his heart was "white" towards Khame, and that he desired to see his face. Notwithstanding these protestations of friendship, some of Lobengula's soldiers had attacked one of Khame's cattle posts, killing and stealing in the usual fashion. A letter on this subject was carried to Lobengula by Mackenzie. The Zulu chief made ample apologies for what he described as an "unauthorised movement" by his war party, for which he held them guilty. He repeated his invitation to Khame to pay him a personal visit, and he pledged himself for the future not to send a war party against Khame on any account, without first seeking an explanation of any difficulty that might arise between them. On the whole Lobengula behaved to Khame's missionary with great kindness and hospitality.

Mackenzie, in a letter to Dr Mullens (September 1st 1873), described his impressions of this part of South Africa, and made a most remarkable forecast regarding the fate of the Matabele tribe. He refers in strong terms to the beauty and richness of the southern part of Matabeleland, formerly known as the Makalaka country, where Buluwayo, the capital, was placed among the Matoppo hills. "From the neck or back-bone," he says, "near the Shashane river we obtained a view of the finest and most extensive landscape upon which I had gazed since I stood on the ridge of the Katberg and looked southward upon the beautiful scenery of the Kaffirland frontier of Cape Colony." On all sides he noted the evidences that this beautiful region had within a few years supported a large population. Alas! the terrible Matabele had swept them away, leaving only a "few scared Makalaka who came to our waggons to sell corn." Many of the Makalaka had taken refuge among the Bamangwato; the rest had been massacred, only the little children being spared to be brought up as Matabele warriors. He did not visit Mashonaland, that rich farming and gold-bearing country which lies far to the east and north-east of Buluwayo, but he heard much about it, and thought much concerning its relations to the future history of the country.

Mackenzie was confronted by the fact that the earnest and devoted labours of capable missionaries for fourteen years had not resulted in the baptism even of one convert to the Christian religion. Amongst these missionaries there was William Sykes, one of the bravest men who have touched South African history. It was he who on one occasion so incurred the anger of Moselekatse, the father of Lobengula, that everyone expected he would be put to death. The Matabele were amazed to find that he deliberately went on a personal visit to the enraged and savage monarch, and yet returned in safety. "I said to them," he reports, "as I had said to their chief on the occasion of his anger, that I never saw the man that I feared. I always did what was right to everyone and feared no one. I would do what was right to Moselekatse, but would not fear him." If this attitude of mind had gained the respect of the unscrupulous Zulus, it had at least failed to soften their hostility to the Gospel of Christ. In 1873 Mackenzie could find no increased interest in the message of the missionaries, although he met with a few who knew something about its contents. He attributes the toleration of the missionaries as teachers by the Matabele chief to the simple fact that none of his tribe had "as yet announced his serious intention of abiding by the law of Jesus Christ as his ruler for life. . . . So far as I could judge, it would at present be a critical business for either chief or head-man or common soldier to make such an announcement."

Concerning the future of the Matabele, Mackenzie made this most interesting prophecy. Just because the law of Christ would entirely overturn the whole structure of Matabele society there was no immediate hope of converting them ; and yet he adds, "As a tribe or collection of tribes they are probably doomed ; their sins as a tribe have been very great, and of late have been aggravated by the light which the Gospel casts on their cruelty and bloodthirstiness." "Is it not a most interesting problem," he proceeds. "What will the Almighty do with the Matabele ? For my own part, I look on with the profoundest interest to the solution of this question." He did not believe that the tribe could occupy for many years longer the position which it did. What would the end be ? It must be remembered that this letter was written in

1873, when only a few traders and missionaries had visited that region, and yet the following is the outline of coming events as they presented themselves to his eye. First, he knows that there is gold to be found in Matabeleland, even far to the north-east of Inyati. Further, he knows that there is a rich high-lying country to the east of Matabeleland, splendidly adapted for farming, which was formerly occupied by the Mashona, but was now unoccupied. Many Transvaalers to his knowledge had cast eager eyes upon this region, and an attempt had been made already to form a party of Boers who should " go there and occupy the country by force." From this quarter, from this deserted region, Mackenzie in that year conceived that the Matabele tribe would some day meet its fate. The white settlers in Mashonaland would begin to influence the tribal life of the Matabele. The question would then be, Can they " abide this shock and subside into a peaceable tribe," or will they " with blind fury rush against fate," in which case the tribe would be destroyed ? It is surely a remarkable fact that twenty years afterwards this fore-cast was fulfilled almost to the letter. It was the gold and farming regions of Mashonaland which first were occupied by the Europeans of the British South African Chartered Company. From their policy in this region Lobengula found his tribe involved in complications which led to war ; for they could not " abide the shock " of a European community on their borders ; they " rushed with blind fury against fate," and were destroyed. Let us hope that the other part of the prophecy is now being fulfilled—" In the de-struction of the tribe there will no doubt be found a remnant—humbled and ill at ease—to whom the gospel will speak with a power which it never before exercised."

From this interesting journey Mackenzie returned

to his work at Shoshong. Here he continued his teaching of the students day by day, and his close attention to the general work of the station. He was able to report in the letter from which we have just quoted that seven had recently been admitted to the communion of the church, and that one of these was a Makalaka, the "first of that people who has been baptised, so far as I know." He adds that there were others whose names were before the church, and whom they hoped before long to receive into its fellowship.

The atmosphere of politics at Shoshong continued to be very stormy. In the end of 1872 Khame and Khamane had for some inscrutable reason sent an invitation to their father Sekhome to return to Shoshong. Up to this time the two brothers had for the most part lived together in mutual affection and confidence, although their watchful shepherd-missionary saw some grounds for anxiety in their attitude towards one another. But as soon as Sekhome returned, his crafty and subtle mind proceeded to find a way of overthrowing his hated eldest son. His plan now was to sow the seeds and encourage the growth of jealousy in the heart of Khamane, the younger brother. Alas! he found in Khamane a disposition which he was able to adapt to this diabolical purpose. The two became very confidential, and carried out various little schemes which soon revealed to the whole people that they were allied in sentiment against Khame. Khame bore this new attack with his usual calmness and dignity. But at last, at the end of the year 1873, finding himself humiliated before the whole people by the attitude of his father and brother, he quietly left the town and went to a magnificent fountain called Serue, about 70 miles north-east of Shoshong, announcing that there he would receive any of his people who wished to follow him. To the consternation of the triumphant plotters, almost the entire

town moved out, and tramped to the camp of their
beloved chief. Khame got the best and the most of
his subjects around him, and was their actual chief,
without having to fight or even to denounce Sekhome
and Khamane. Finding that his position at Serue
laid him open to attack from other enemies, he resolved to make a still more daring venture, and carried
his tribe north with him as far as Lake Ngami, a
distance of more than 200 miles. His magnificent
generosity of spirit was shown even on this journey,
when, although a number of his cattle were carried
off by the emissaries of his father, he allowed a
waggon, with a most valuable load belonging to
Khamane, to pass through his ranks unmolested. In
a few months, however, he returned with a small force
to Shoshong in order to demand the property which
had been taken from him. When he saw how weak
was the influence of his rival relatives, and how deep
had been their duplicity and unscrupulous their
jealousy, he decided, during the brief negotiations of
this visit, to return as soon as he could with all his
people and take possession of the capital of his country
once more.

This purpose was carried out in the beginning of
the following year, when Khame brought the entire
portion of the tribe that had seceded with him back to
Shoshong. His movements were of course not
unknown to Sekhome. The latter had employed
the intervening months to good purpose in the way of
consolidating the people who remained under him, and
animating them with the desire to resist Khame's
return. He sent scouts in every direction to discover
the line of Khame's march, so that he himself might
choose his battle ground. Unfortunately for him none
of his scouts discovered the direction of Khame's
movements until the latter had reached Seshosho, the
main fountain from which the town derived its water

and from which it was named. When Khame sent a
challenge to his father and brother to come and fight
for the possession of this vital spot, they realised at
once that his strategy had given him the advantage.
The story of the fight which ensued has been very
vividly told in the volume of Mr Hepburn's letters,
entitled " Twenty Years in Khame's Country." The
following quotations from a letter by Mrs Mackenzie
to her daughter in Edinburgh will also help to put
the events more vividly before the reader.

We arrived home, after seeing dear Jamie (their third son)
off on his long journey, on Friday the 29th January. We
had hoped that during our absence Khame would have come
and had his fight over, but on nearing the town we were
surprised to see how quiet the outskirts of the town were—
no cattle, no goats or sheep or herds, or little children playing.
We at once suspected what was going on. Presently one
of the traders came out to meet us, and told us that Khame
and his army were close at hand, that the women were in the
mountain ; and we could see along the mountain sides groups
of armed men on the watch. This was not a pleasant
welcome, but it was what God had prepared for us.

Papa had a great deal of watching both by day and night ;
and all the while we were watching for the fight. On
Tuesday evening the war-cry resounded. Mr and Mrs
Hepburn and their two children came over for safety and
for company too. Their house is in a very exposed position.
Khamane's and Sekhome's wives also came for safety; they
occupied the dining-room. On Wednesday morning we
heard guns up the kloof, and before we knew what we were
about Khamane's men were flying "helter-skelter" down
the kloof, followed by Khame's men firing at them with
all their might. It was a dreadful hour, for we knew that
all these bullets were not being fired for nothing. In a
trice Khame's people were victorious and in possession of
the town. Sekhome and Khamane fled to the mountain
with a number of their people. At another part of the
mountain Khame, who had only some of the old men and
boys with him, fell into the hands of another part of
Sekhome's army and fared rather badly, and had to retreat ;
but of course the best of his people were here at the most

important part of the fight.   Khame came in the next
day, looking very thin and haggard.   He has had a great
deal of toil and anxiety, and longs for peace.   I hope it
is near at hand now.   Still the fighting is not over, and
a good many matters have yet to be settled.

But I must tell you of the danger into which dear Papa
was thrown.   That morning, when the alarm was raised,
our two herds fled.   Papa and some of the students took
the cattle up the kloof to give them water; before they
had done so they found themselves in the midst of the
firing.   Of course both parties knew them and would not
willingly have sent a bullet their way, but in a time of
excitement, and among so many "bad shots," we look
upon it as a great mercy that no harm came to them.
We shall not soon forget that day, nor the protection
afforded us all by our dear Heavenly Father.

The poor wounded fellows soon found their way to our
house, and Mr Hepburn and Papa have a busy time attending
to them.   There are nine now.   One died; poor fellow, he
was one of Khame's most faithful men.   One belongs to
Sekhome's party.   Papa, Mr Hepburn, and some of the
students went and buried some of the dead.

Among Khame's men we see some nice familiar faces
who used to be so earnest in learning to read and write.
Khame has brought a message from the chief of the Lake
Ngami people begging for a missionary to come and teach
them.   It is such an unhealthy place that it is not certain if
a European could live there for any length of time.

I am gradually getting stronger, but I cannot yet do as
much as I used to.   What with the children's illness, the
number of refugees in and around the house, the wounded
people and their attendants, the bolting of my cook, and
the excitement on the top of our arriving off a journey
and finding almost everything in confusion and dirty, the
last twelve days seem like a month, and many a time I have
not known where to put myself from sheer fatigue.   As you
may imagine, Papa has had his share of it all too.   He
and Mr Hepburn went up to see Sekhome and Khamane
in their place of refuge.   They were detained longer than
they expected, and had to come down the mountain in
the dark.   It was impossible to ride, the path being so
steep and rugged, so they had to walk and lead their
horses.   Papa fell, and hurt his back on a big stone.   He

did not feel that so very much; but on Sunday he went with one of the students to hold service at a village three or four miles off. The people were in their retreat on the mountain, and though they came half way to meet them, he had to climb a good way up the rough mountain, and that made his back a good deal worse.

Once more, then, Khame was seated in authority and power at Shoshong, and once more he behaved with extraordinary patience and generosity towards his father and brother. The extent and almost startling nature of this generosity can only appear when we realise, on the one hand, that no native chief scrupled to take the lives of all rivals, however close the relationship to himself, that it seemed to be a part of his function as a king to secure his kingship in this fashion; and, on the other hand, that Sekhome and Khamane had repeatedly broken the most solemn vows of loyalty, plotted in the most deliberate fashion for the taking of Khame's life, and, as we have seen, provoked civil war on more than one occasion, in order to secure their ends. Surely this South African native who, as a young man, broke with all the heathen customs of his life absolutely and finally, and who throughout his career refused to dip his hands in the blood of any relative to secure himself in the chieftainship, who yet when occasion arose manifested in the most trying circumstances true physical courage and noble moral heroism, must stand out as one of the most striking trophies ever won by the Christian religion upon the battle-ground with heathenism.

Throughout these years of storm and unrest in the political life of the Bamangwato, the two missionaries, John Mackenzie and J. D. Hepburn, carried on their work steadily and persistently. Mackenzie was now most absorbed in the work of teaching the students of the Moffat Institution, and for a considerable period had to spend time and strength in putting up houses for the students and a class-room. At the same time the work of preaching Sunday by Sunday in the church and in the king's khotla to the natives, as well as in the missionary's house to the white men, the visiting of surrounding villages for the same purpose, the incalculable miscellaneous work connected with interviews sought by white men and natives, alike on business affairs and on problems of spiritual experience, were continued without intermission. Mackenzie's work as tutor necessitated the spending of many hours in the study and in the class-room day by day ; and this sedentary life made it necessary for him, for the first time in many years, deliberately to seek active exercise in order to retain his health. As long as the climate spared several horses which he had brought from the south with him, horse-riding was his favourite recreation of an afternoon ; but the terrific scourge, known bluntly in South Africa as " horse-sickness," swept them away, even at last carrying off the hardiest and most beautiful horse he ever possessed.

The life of the Christian church prospered during these years at Shoshong.   Before his visit to England Mackenzie had found it necessary, as we have seen, to be very careful about the formal establishment of a church communion. But shortly after his return in '71, when the true Christian zeal and faith of so many had been proved, he saw no reason for deferring this act. It was with a peculiarly solemn joy that he therefore spread the table of the Lord, and for the first time welcomed to that feast of the soul a small group of the Bamangwato people. Amongst them, of course, were Khame and his brother Khamane. When the troubles came later which divided the two brothers from one another, Mackenzie repeatedly summoned them to his study, " questioned them, reasoned with them, prayed with them, and fondly hoped the

disagreement could blow over." We have already
seen that this fraternal rivalry and jealousy, which in
their years of adversity had been impossible, broke
out into great bitterness and open strife when the
years of prosperity had come. Then the missionaries
had the hard task of "disciplining" both Khame and
Khamane. In spite of this severe blow, the church
after a while rallied again ; more members were received, Khame himself returned into full fellowship ;
and gradually such momentum was gained that, in
later years, especially under Mr Hepburn's last period
of ardent service, the membership of the church
increased with great rapidity.

It would be foolish to hide and perhaps unwise to
omit the fact that missionaries in Bechuanaland were
sometimes in great anxiety regarding their own
domestic affairs. Their salary was never supposed
to be a salary, but was calculated on the basis of a
more or less definite experience as to the bare amount
necessary for buying food and clothing. Travelling
expenses incurred in the direct service of the society
were paid for as *extra*. But it must be remembered
that the price of food-stuffs and charges for trans-
portation, alike of food and all other goods, varied
much, and these variations caused oftentimes deep
care. At one time a missionary's small family, out
of their small salary, paid £15 a year for soap alone.
Corn had to be brought by the missionary a month's
journey, and was paid for at the rate of thirty shillings
or more for 180 lbs. When at last it arrived at the
mission station this corn had to be washed and
cleaned, ground and sifted—"if we can afford to sift
it," as one said—under the direction and constant
superintendence of the missionary and his wife. No
missionary in Bechuanaland had a private income, and
there were no perquisites. The only possible way of
easing what was sometimes acute distress was to be

found in the selling of a cow or a few trained oxen for a few pounds. This, however, was a plan which most missionaries adopted very reluctantly, for the Society had a strict law against trading, a law which had to be enforced on one occasion by the expulsion of a member of their staff. Nevertheless the most sensitive missionary saw clearly that, if he were reasonably careful of the cattle and sheep which he was compelled to own, he must have from time to time a few animals which he could dispose of. If he did not deliberately set himself to increase his possessions in live stock rapidly, for the express purpose of selling them and making money, so becoming a farmer in reality, any small transactions which came in his way were viewed as not only legitimate but necessary. In the case of most missionaries, and certainly of Mackenzie, this procedure was always so reluctantly employed as to do very little towards easing the burden of the household.

During these years it should also be added that Mackenzie had more than once to face the sorrow of parting from his children as he sent them home for their education.

In the year 1875 Mackenzie once more received a very earnest call to become the minister of a church in Cape Colony. This call came from Trinity Church, Grahamstown, and presented some very attractive features. In the first place Grahamstown is one of the pleasantest of South African centres, and has the great advantage of possessing schools of a high order, which would have exactly suited the parental hearts of the Mackenzies. Moreover, the salary which they offered amounted to about three times that which he was receiving as a missionary. None of *these* things moved him, and yet he took a fortnight to consider before he declined the offer. His hesitation was caused by the fact that for several years there had been disagreeable differences of opinion between the Bechuanaland missionaries and their Directors in London. These differences of opinion had very seriously interfered with the development of the work in several most important portions of the field. This is not the place to discuss the merits of the controversy which proceeded between London and Bechuanaland. Suffice it to say, that on both sides of the ocean it caused deep distress. Nothing could prove the pain of Mackenzie's mind more than the fact that, with all his passionate devotion to the missionary life, and his profound love for his own Society, he actually considered for a fortnight the possibility of accepting the pastorate over a European congregation. In writing on this matter (October 29, 1875), he said, "I have refused similar offers without one day's consideration. But I am free to admit to you in this quiet way, that the manner in which the affairs of this mission have been recently conducted has been a great grief to me. It is only deep love to the work itself—in spite of everything else—that has kept me where I am."

CHAPTER VI

' BY-PRODUCTS ' OF A MISSIONARY'S CAREER
(1871-1876)

THE number of traders and hunters who frequented
Shoshong increased year by year; indeed "Khame's
town" had come to be considered, in a small way, as
an emporium. Several roads from the south converged
upon it, and from that meeting - point the roads
diverged again northwards, making it a natural ren-
dezvous and a convenient base of supplies. Some
large wholesale stores were established here, and a
number of traders put up more or less permanent
houses and settled down for years. This entailed a
large amount of work upon the missionaries at that
station. For example, Mackenzie acted throughout
his residence at Shoshong as the postmaster. To him
the post-bag was always delivered, and through him
travellers in the north sent their letters southwards.
This work, while it entailed a considerable amount of
time and trouble, was very agreeable to him in that
it brought him into personal relations with almost
every one of the white men. Oftentimes traders fell
ill, either at Shoshong or in their journeyings, and a
number of these were nursed through their sickness
by both Mackenzie and his wife. Several men
were even taken into their house, and were brought
through dangerous crises only by the very closest
attention. Some of those who were thus helped back
to life showed their affection and gratitude afterwards
in most touching ways. It is an amusing fact that
some of the traders found it necessary even to transmit

money through the missionary. A trader, for instance who desired to send £20 to distant relatives had no means of doing so except by sending a draft for that amount to Mackenzie, and asking him to send another draft for that amount to the trader's friends. None of the inland business men's drafts were at that time negotiable at Cape Town, while those of the missionaries, because their Treasurer lived there, were always immediately honoured.

In addition to all this kind of work there must be named that which in some ways cost more than any other. A large proportion of the white men who went into the interior, especially those who tried to reach the Zambesi, died of fever. Some, of course, died from accident and other causes. When Mackenzie could discover the names and addresses of the relatives of any of these, he always immediately wrote to them announcing their sad bereavement. His letters were very considerate and very tender. As an illustration of the frequency of these events, the following extract may be given from a letter announcing the death of a young Scotchman in the year 1876.

Another young lad called C——, a young Englishman, died at the same time. Three died some time before ; and three gentlemen, who are now on this station on their way southwards, have made a narrow escape. One of the three is a trader ; he has not been successful, and declares he must return at once to try and pay his debts. If he does—contrary to all advice—he will certainly pay the penalty with his life.

It came to be almost an understood thing that where there was any property or money belonging to a traveller who died, Mackenzie should take charge of it and transmit it to his heirs. Where the deceased was a trader, whose affairs had been entangled with those of other men, this often entailed a large amount of intricate and puzzling work. He used, of course, the utmost care, as he more than once explained, to save expense and to send home as much as possible. In return for all this Mackenzie received letters full of the warmest gratitude for his labour of love, and in several cases this form of service brought him the rich reward of lifelong and most valuable friendships. The following letters reveal the manner and spirit in which he carried his sacred and delicate task. They refer to the death of Mr Frank Oates, who went to travel in Central South Africa as a naturalist. His travels and scientific observations were afterwards described in a memoir by his brother, Mr Charles G. Oates.

SHOSHONG, *1st March* 1875.

MRS OATES,
    Meanwoodside, Leeds.

      Madam,—It is not long since a letter from your son, Mr Frank Oates, passed through my hands, on its way to England. We expected soon to have the pleasure of again seeing him here, on his way out from the Victoria Falls. But his journey to the Zambesi had been delayed for one reason and another, until the unhealthy season of the year had arrived. Your son, however, reached the Falls in safety, and left the Zambesi in good health. But bad news concerning him has just reached us from the Zambesi road—news which I pray God to support you to hear. Mr Oates was seized with fever on his way out from the Zambesi, was ill twelve days, and then, near to the Makalaka Towns, and on the 5th of February, he succumbed to the fever and died. Dr Bradshaw, also travelling in the interior, happened to be in the neighbourhood at the time and attended your son, both as medical adviser and companion. It will be a great satisfaction to you to know that this gentleman was with your son to the last and that he afterwards superintended his interment.

    It is not, Madam, for a perfect stranger like myself to intermeddle with a grief so great and so sacred as yours. While leaving you and yours to drink the bitter cup thus suddenly presented to you, I would earnestly pray that in your darkness and sorrow, your mind may be visited by many cheering Christian thoughts—thoughts which, like balm, heal the wounded heart and stricken spirit.

Dr Bradshaw brought out Mr Oates's waggon to this place, and handed over to me his papers and personal effects. His agents in the interior have requested me to act as Trustee and Executor as regards the settlement of Mr Oates's affairs in this part of the country; and in the circumstances I have consented to do so. I may explain to you that there are only two classes of Europeans resident in Bechuanaland— traders and missionaries. It was thought that it would be most satisfactory to place your son's affairs in the hands of one not in any way connected with business.—I remain, Madam, ever yours sincerely,   JOHN MACKENZIE.

KURUMAN, *Nov.* 1, 1875.

CHARLES G. OATES, Esq.

My Dear Sir,—In my last letter to you (a letter on business, dated "Shoshong, 24th August 1875,") I expressed the hope that I should be soon able to report the final settlement of your late brother's affairs in the interior. "Soon" admits of degrees; and I am afraid that what we out here have come to regard as "soon" in the country of the ox-waggon, will be held to be slow enough in England. However, before leaving Shoshong in September, I was able to settle everthing connected with your late brother's accounts.

I am here attending the meetings of our District Committee of Missionaries, where we assemble to discuss matters connected with our work. A letter from your brother (Mr W. E. Oates, then in South Africa), was sent after me to this place. Your brother mentioned his intention of paying a visit to that spot which will be always so sacred in you estimation. Lonely the spot no doubt is in a certain sense; but in another, your brother's grave is surrounded by all the activities of the great Creator and Father of all. Flowers will bloom around it, though not planted by mortal hand; birds will sing over it and never weary in repeating the sweet notes which Nature has taught them. I have not been there myself, but I have no doubt the naturalist would not think your brother's grave a lonely spot, whilst to the Christian, such a spot is the quiet resting-place to which the body sank when the spirit was called away by God the Father.

I am writing to your brother to Natal; I shall be back at Shoshong before he will be there, and any assistance I can render him will be most cheerfully given.—I am, ever sincerely yours,   JOHN MACKENZIE.

Mackenzie's correspondence contains a large number of letters from the traders and travellers with whom he became intimate at Shoshong. He had the faculty of drawing men to himself; they would open their hearts to him, and receive from him the very word of warning and rebuke, of encouragement and consolation which they needed. Their letters make references to drink, to their success or failure in business, to the movements of other traders; or they inquire about letters, or ask help in a business transaction with the chief. They breathe unanimous affection and confidence towards that man whom God had set down at Shoshong.

This love of so many South African traders and travellers for a missionary found expression, not only in letters, but sometimes in beautiful deeds of considerate wisdom, and sometimes in ways that were at once pathetic and odd. It would be out of place, of course, to enter into particulars. But one case can, without any danger of harm, be briefly described.

Among the hunting traders who often visited Shoshong was an Irishman, known in South Africa under the assumed name of Fitzgerald. He was quite illiterate but very intelligent, tall, handsome, and powerful. He had formed drinking habits which he found it very hard to throw off. For a long time he made Shoshong his head-quarters and became most curiously and deeply attached to Mackenzie. The latter knew how to deal with such a man, to rebuke his weakness and rouse his manliness, give him condemnation and hope at the same time. Fitzgerald on one occasion quarrelled with a number of natives, who attacked him and nearly wrenched an arm off. This wounded arm he brought to the missionary to be doctored, and for a long while it needed close attention. Sometimes, when Mackenzie was absent, Mrs·Mackenzie would bring the rags and medicines and assist him in the dressing of the wound. "This," we are told, "went straight to Fitzgerald's heart, and in many ways and for years he showed that he had not forgotten it." The impulsive generosity of the man, and his determination to defend Mackenzie against danger is well illustrated by the following incident, which the latter relates.

On one occasion I let Mr C—— (another trader) have a little poison to kill rats in his waggon. The poison was used carelessly, and caused the death of a native's dog. Macheng came to C—— and demanded the medicine with which he had " bewitched," or killed, the dog, adding that only rascals had such things in their possession. " Why, I have none in my possession," said C——, not liking the chief's way of putting it ; "and the little I had I got from Mr ——" Mackenzie, he was going to say, but he was interrupted by Fitzgerald, who said, " From me, of course ; you know you got it from me "; adding, in English, " You dare to say you got it from Mr Mackenzie ! " And then again, to the chief, "I gave C—— a little poison, Chief ; it was only to kill rats." " You must pay a musket as a fine, Marikwe," was Macheng's answer. The fine was paid, and some time had passed before I heard anything of it.

Of course, there was no real need of concealing from Macheng the fact that the missionary kept a supply of poison on his premises ; that was already well known, as it had been used on more than one occasion for the purpose of destroying wild beasts. Fitzgerald made many thousands of pounds, but always squandered them, and he died at last, not only a poor man, but in debt. His end, like that of so many travellers who perished in South Central Africa, was tragic. He was far east, on the banks of the Limpopo, where he had been trading, when he was seized with a fatal sickness. There was no white man with him ; indeed, his last intercourse with a white man had ended in a quarrel at Shoshong, when he received a blow which, rumour said, hastened his death. As soon as he felt seriously ill, he lay down in his waggon and said to his servant, " Only take me, take me quickly, to Mackenzie." Alas, "poor Fitz's" strength was already well-nigh gone, and while the slow oxen dragged him, jolting on the rough waggon road, towards the one man whom he loved and trusted most, death came upon him.

One of the means by which Mackenzie at once served the white men and gained ascendancy over them was the Sunday afternoon meeting which he held in his own parlour. Even when there were only two or three traders in the town they were invited to the service. Here Mackenzie gave out psalms and hymns to be sung, read the scriptures, prayed, and gave a brief but very earnest and often solemn address. He knew the temptations, hardships, and disappointments which these men had to meet, and he spoke directly to their moral and spiritual needs. It was a bright spot in many a man's life, to which he looked forward and backward when away on his long monotonous waggon journey. Men still live who speak of it with emotion and gratitude. The following extract from Captain Parker Gilmore's "The Great Thirst Land," records, in a way peculiar to himself, the impressions which many others carried away from Mackenzie's Sunday afternoon services for the white people at Shoshong.

Mr Mackenzie is a tall, square-built man, about 5 ft. 11 in. in height, fair in complexion, genial in countenance, with great strength of character stamped on his brow, and an unmistakable Highlander, speaking the English language with wonderful purity and intonation. Mr Hepburn is taller but slighter, a Northumberland man, I should think, with great energy and resolution, and gifted with more than ordinary eloquence. The twain are a host in themselves ; and while our country is represented by men of their type it is bound to be honoured, in whatever part of the earth their labours are carried on. . . .

Sunday came round in course of time, and I could have known the day from all others, by the air of rest that lay over Shoshong. All was as peaceful as the village homes we

knew in our youth, on such occasions.   Missionary labour
may be slow in telling in South Africa, especially among the
tribes so far to the north, but when our religion is represented
by such painstaking, enduring men as Mr Hepburn and Mr
Mackenzie, it is bound to succeed in the end.

I shall never forget my Sunday afternoon at Shoshong.
Mr Mackenzie and Mr Hepburn had held service among the
natives in the morning, but intended having prayers and a
short discourse at three o'clock in their own house for those
Europeans who chose to come.   Not one of them did not
come ; and in the little parlour, where worship was held, the
presence of the Almighty might almost have been felt.   In
my early life I had regarded religion lightly, but when I
looked upon half-a-dozen stalwart men accustomed to everyday hardship and danger of life, our worthy pastor's children
and a few servants, giving their whole soul to what they were
engaged in, I more forcibly felt than ever I did before that
there was a great God above us—One who invited our
adoration and love.   The prayer was earnest, and such as
could have been desired, the address was strictly applicable
to the occasion.   There was no flowing language.   There
were no marvellous similes, it was exactly what was wanted,
and brought peace to the listener's heart.

That was the most solemn Sunday I ever passed.   No
cant or hypocrisy was here ; what I heard was an exhorta-
tion from an earnest, true, reflecting man, endeavouring to
make his fellow creatures feel the depth and height of
religion, and the consolation they could derive from it.

Another phase of Mackenzie's work among the
Europeans was described in a letter written in later
years to set forth his experience of the work of a
British Resident at the confluence of civilisation and
heathenism.

When I was residing there (at Shoshong), I used to
discharge many of the duties of such an officer.   Several
British subjects dying in the interior, their estates were
handed over to me, and their affairs settled in each case to
the satisfaction of relatives residing at a distance.   Sekhome,
Macheng, and Khame, in succession sanctioned the sitting of
a Court of Europeans to try cases which, to use their own
expression, would baffle the chief by himself.   For years I

acted as Chairman or President of that Court, assisted by Mr Hepburn, my fellow missionary. It was in reality a court of arbitration ; the first question put to the parties being, " Will you agree to the decision of this court, whatever it may be, and regard it as final ? " When they answered in the affirmative our course was clear—to go forward and do our best to give a just decision. The whole thing was in any instance explained to the chief, as far as he could understand it ; and where property had to be seized and caused to change hands, it was of course the chief's power which was called into requisition. Mr Hepburn and I declined to have anything to do with this court some time before I left Shoshong, because, in a case of insolvency, the traders in Shoshong resolved to seize what they could lay their hands on of the insolvent's goods, pay themselves so much in the pound, and then leave creditors at a distance out in the cold. Goods unpaid for, fresh from the sea-coast, were then unloaded from the waggons at Shoshong, and sold by public auction ; and the firm which had supplied these goods on credit got only what was over, after men on the spot had received payment in full of all their debts. This transaction was not sanctioned by the chief ; it was an arrangement among the traders themselves. Shoshong was a capital place for creditors to stand at and waylay their debtors as they came out from the interior, from trading or hunting trips. If the man tried to slip past, the creditor was sure to hear of it, and fleet horses soon enabled him to overtake the ox-waggon. The style was then for the creditor, mounted and rifle in hand, to go forward and stop the front oxen pulling the waggon and literally compel a settlement of accounts.

There were certain matters which a missionary had to pass by, which a British Resident could have treated in a very different manner. At that time British subjects beyond the border of the Colony were completely at the mercy of the Boers and the natives, and it was well known that no redress would be obtained from the English Government. It was my sad lot more than once to know that parties of slaves passed through Shoshong on their way to the Transvaal, having been bought in the interior, chiefly on the Lake River, by Boer inhabitants of the Transvaal. I took what steps I deemed suitable at the time to put a stop to this ; but my circumstances precluded my doing what a British

Resident could have done; for the Government at the time was flooded with information on this subject, and yet did nothing; whereas to write in the papers would have been to consign myself to the fate of two early missionaries, who were driven from the country by the Boers for exposing their evil ways in the newspapers.

In closing this chapter of Mackenzie's life, we must give two illustrations of the fact that already he had studied the political problems of South Africa very deeply, and held in his mind that ideal of the relations of Great Britain to her great· dependency, which in after years completely absorbed his energies. The first is an extract from the address which he delivered in 1875 as Chairman of the Bechuanaland District Committee. After a historical survey of the relations of the Imperial Government to South Africa, Mackenzie proceeded as follows :—

Is it too much to expect that England should take a comprehensive view of what is going on in South Africa? Taking up the question as the undoubted friend of the weak and the helpless, there is an immediate and pressing work for her to do. The experience of the past may prevent the recurrence of needless bloodshed and of cruel outrage. Viewing this movement in the interests of her own children, England has a great and incumbent duty to perform. It is within her power to cause that the European population of South Africa shall be as loyal and attached as in Australia or Canada. On the other hand, it is quite possible for her to see growing up beside her Cape Colony, states whose bitter dislike to her Government shall equal, if not exceed, any such feeling entertained now or at bygone times, by the people of the United States. England is at this hour the paramount power in South Africa. To know the English language is held to be a necessary qualification by inhabitants of Continental countries who come out either as missionaries or as men of business. England is colonising Southern Africa. Why should history have to recount that she did it unwillingly, unwittingly, and in a left-handed manner? It is not in accordance with her high name and character that she should retreat from an obligation. Let

England then come forward and avowedly take charge of
and direct the northward progress of Europeans in South
Africa. She has been hitherto very unwilling to do this.
The sum of £2000 was recently voted by the Cape Parliament for the exploration of an auriferous country of great
extent in the interior. The expedition was never sent. "If
I went up to your part of the world," said the Governor of the
Cape of that day, addressing the missionary of the District,
"I feel sure I should never come back." His term of office
had well nigh expired; he did not wish to answer in Downing
Street for the sin of adding to English territory; he was unwilling to explore, for explorers might be successful; then he
would have no end of trouble; and, as he said, he might not
be able to retreat from the country.

The missionary is usually in advance of everyone else in
South Africa. He is soon followed, and is occasionally passed
by the trader. In future the responsible agent of the British
Government ought not to be long behind. At present, without doubt, there ought to be a British Resident in Matabeleland on the East, and Damaraland on the West. With the
increase of the English population the native chiefs find
themselves unable to cope with their responsibilities. Fully
qualified to decide on all matters occurring in a native town,
they are unable to understand or to decide upon civil cases
which occur among the European inhabitants of their country.
One chief requests the white men on his place to form themselves into a court of arbitration, with the missionary as chairman; and (engages?) that the decisions of such a court shall
have his sanction. Another chief who had attempted to
understand and to adjudicate in such matters himself,
disgusted and thoroughly alarmed at the changed and constantly changing aspect of affairs in his town, assembled his
European traders, and to their astonishment informed them
it was henceforth unlawful for them to build, or to
occupy, houses or shops in his country. Why should they
wish such large and substantial houses? They were to
go back to their waggons, and trade from them, as they
did in the olden time. Of course this was not carried out,
but it exhibits in a striking light the helplessness of the chiefs
to cope with the events which are gathering around them. As
a result of a wisely-pursued policy on the part of special
Commissioners or British Residents, the chieftainship of such
towns would in the course of time, and without a drop of

bloodshed, pass into the hands of the English magistrate, in whose presence the common people would have pleasure from the first, and to whom the chiefs themselves would in the end become accustomed. The British Residents ought to be supported by the Government which sent them. The magistrates would be supported, as in Basutoland, by local taxation. They ought to be very carefully selected; and, while men of the world, ought to be Christian gentlemen.

Our Society has rules which rather tend to discourage her agents from taking an active part in political affairs. No doubt the rules are the expression of wide experience in the various countries where the missionaries labour. Still we do not hesitate to say that the highest type of missionary in Bechuanaland must assist the chief with whom he resides, in political matters   He finds himself the confidential adviser and probably the secretary of the chief in the most natural way, and before he thinks anything about the rules which he may be breaking. I do not think our Society's rules are really aimed against such political connexion. If they are, we submit with all respect that it is a mistake. Who may be said to have been the makers of the Basuto tribe? Undoubtedly, our brethren the French missionaries. By their teaching of Christianity alone? Nay, also and as a powerful auxiliary to their teaching, by their active assistance to Moshesh as his advisers and his secretaries. Those who care to go into such matters, know from Blue Books which have been published, that the letters of the French missionaries commanded the respect of those with whom they corresponded; and thus, by their instrumentality, the correspondence was raised to a higher platform, and was conducted between equals. British Basutoland is no doubt destined to flourish under the mild and equal sway of Britain. But the Basutos themselves have grown from an insignificant tribe to their present proportions, under the moral protection and fostering care of the French Protestant Church.

I am sorry that matters have not taken place so happily in our own district in this connexion. Had the Griquas and the Batlaping been content to have had missionaries as their advisers and secretaries, and had the missionaries seen it to be their duty thus to act, the present wretched disputes about land boundaries had never taken place.

I would here direct your attention to one aspect of this aggression of the Europeans, which can only excite sorrow

and disappointment. We have said that no power would
seem to be able to arrest the white men in their northward
progress ; no power could prop up or keep together the
declining heathen communities. It does not follow, however, as part of a Divine plan, that wherever you find a
Dutch pioneer there should be a waggon-load of Cape smoke.
The English trader and hunter is not bound to descend to
be a canteen-keeper either for natives or for his fellow-
traders. No doubt, if it would only pay as well, we should
find opium as well as brandy-waggons plying an equally
nefarious traffic. And no doubt some would choose to eat
the opium or drink the laudanum while others might prefer
the alcohol. Is this hideous excrescence on English society
to follow unquestioned and unchecked into every new country
in which they spread ? Some native chiefs have the good
sense and foresight to forbid the sale or consumption of
strong drink within their country. Should their territory
at some future period be handed over to the English, would
it not be fair that such a law should be respected and
enforced under the new regime ?

And how far, some one will ask, would you have the
English to go in this work ? I answer, why should a nation
be afraid of genuine healthy growth ? With due subdivision
for the purposes of local government, I profess to be quite
unable to say how far such growth might or might not
extend. English society is at present so constructed as to
facilitate the work of making money, and the pleasure of
spending it in luxurious living. It is not so constructed as
to encourage large classes of her population to remain at
home. England is at present heedless of their leaving her
shores in thousands ; but it would be unnatural and suicidal
policy for her to give no thought to her children in the
distant lands of their adoption. We are not at present
speaking of money, nations do not always or often fight
for money, but of sentiment and feeling ; and we assert,
without fear of contradiction, that it is worth England's while
to retain her children's loyalty, no matter how distant may
be their present home. Indeed, there is little doubt that
England will or will not be prominent among the nations
of the future, according to the relationship in which she
stands to her numerous colonies and dependencies.

In directing your attention to this subject, you will quite
mistake my meaning if you imagine that I wish to divert

your attention in the slightest from our own great and transcendently important work as missionaries. But I feel that we can do our own work all the better if we reflect that along with its heavenly sanctions, which alone moved us to engage in it, it is also part of a great movement which is going on in the country, going on as we believe under the guidance of a merciful Providence. It is ours to evangelize, to teach, to educate. Our work remains the same whoever become masters in the country. We are not in any sense responsible for the advance of the white men behind us. But we find ourselves present where the meeting of the races is taking place, and it is in our power to assist the weak, to guide the ignorant, to rouse the slumbering and slothful on the one hand, and on the other, and as far as we can, to restrain from evil and from wrong the enterprising and sometimes reckless European. It were pleasant to find a native chief so far advanced in intelligence as to desire to join and form part of this great South African Commonwealth; this pleasure would be greatly increased were the chief or his brother, or some member of his tribe, qualified to act as magistrate, so as to give satisfaction to all classes who might come before him. The higher education which as a Society we hope to introduce may do something in this direction.

The following letter speaks for itself—

SHOSHONG, 2d *May* 1876.

SIR HENRY BARKLY, K.C.B.,
High Commissioner in Southern Africa.

May it please your Excellency,—I beg to draw your attention to the condition of certain parts of the Interior, from my own point of view as a Christian missionary and as a loyal subject of Her Majesty, Queen Victoria.

The aggressive movements of certain inhabitants of the Transvaal Republic are assuming an importance which, I think, demands your special attention. While I write there are over 40 ox-waggons lying on the Limpopo River—about two days from this place—the owners of which were until recently burghers of the Transvaal and inhabitants chiefly of the district of Magaliesberg. They are of the religious persuasion known in S. Africa as Doppers. They are "trekking," and most,

if not all of them, have sold their farms in the Transvaal.
They are under the leadership of one who signs himself
" Veldt Cornet."   They are waiting for their friends to
come forward, to the number, it is said, of some 800, from
other parts of the Republic and from the Free State and
some say even from the Cape Colony—when they intend to
move forward.   It was first given out by them that they
were bound for Damaraland.   They told Khame, the chief
here, that they had heard of a land in that direction which
was without inhabitants, and they said they were on their
way thither.   Recently, however, I hear they declare that
they are going to march on Mashonaland, lying to the east
of Matabeleland.   Of course there is no unoccupied country
in Damaraland, so far as I can learn : and although a large
tract of country has been devastated by the Matabele in
their wars with the Mashona, the country itself is claimed by
its conquerors, who will no doubt fight with the Dutch for
its possession.

Here then we have a party of armed men publicly avow-
ing that they are about to enter some part of the interior as
an army ; and that they will seize upon and if possible
occupy one or other of the countries already named.

The Chief Khame has given permission to these men to
pass through his country to Damaraland.   A few waggons
went on last year ; but I believe they have not gone much
beyond Lake Ngami.   Khame does not refuse the road ; but
of course he will dispute any aggressive act on his country
itself.

The second matter to which I would beg to direct your
attention is the condition and habits of the Matabele tribe.
I am sure the outrages perpetuated continually, and as a
matter of course by that people, are not known either in
England or in the Colony.   In a little work published some
five years ago and called, " Ten Years North of the Orange
River," I endeavoured to direct attention to the subject.
The Matabele may be truly described as a horde of bloodthirsty savages who every year make wars upon the Mashona
and other weaker neighbours, murdering all who fall into their
hands, except young boys and girls.   Old people and those
in their prime along with children too young to walk to the
Matabeleland, all are put to death.   While they are powerful
enough to carry on such heathen warfare with their neighbours, the Matabele have deteriorated in prowess since they

occupied their present country. An army of 800 Dutchmen would no doubt overcome them. The tribe is also weakened by the existence of a rival to the present chief, in the person of a man who calls himself Kuruman, and who is now living in the Transvaal Republic. It is supposed that should any respectable force accompany Kuruman to the Matabele country a large party of Matabele would at once desert Lobengula and join Kuruman. Missionaries of the London Society have been labouring among the Matabele since 1859; but, alas! without having had as yet the pleasure of baptizing a single convert.

When gold was discovered at Tati some years ago, the chief of this place at that time addressed your predecessor, Sir Philip Wodehouse, offering to the British Government the possession of the auriferous district on terms which might afterwards be agreed on. I believe £2000 were at that time voted by the Cape Parliament for the purpose of sending a special commission to thoroughly explore the country producing gold—both in the Tati and Mashona districts. Sir Philip, however, never availed himself of this grant. His reason, as given to me privately in Cape Town, was that "if he once went into those regions, he would never come back" —that is, if a Commission went north, it would only be the beginning of the occupancy of the country by the English.

In connexion with the events which were transpiring at that time, your predecessor was kind enough to say that he would be glad of all information which I could communicate, along with such explanations and statements of opinion as I might be able to send. As your anxiety to do your duty as Her Majesty's Representative in this country is well known, having been tested for years, I make bold to express my opinion upon the crisis which at present obtains in the interior; and perhaps I ought to premise that I have had considerable opportunities of making myself acquainted with the peoples concerning whom I am speaking.

1. I have no hesitation in saying that the Matabele tribe is not worth preserving in independence. The country which they now occupy, which they of course took by force, has been theirs for about 30 years. They form a dead wall to the progress of the missionary as well as the trader and hunter. In short in their corporate capacity, they are a nuisance in the country. It would not therefore be a good action *merely to hinder the Dutchman* from taking Mashonaland,

and perhaps dispersing the Matabele. On the lowest ground the Dutchman would be infinitely better than the Matabele, better both for the Matabele people themselves, and for their neighbours.

2. But I do not write to suggest an inactive policy. From my point of view this is an important crisis and one which will have the most extensive issues. If the Dutch settle in Mashonaland as an independent people, there will never be one united South African Government. On the other hand, there will speedily grow up a large community or communities, richer and more powerful than the countries under the English Crown, agreeing in one thing if not on others— in dislike of their English neighbours. Allow me to say that it is now in your Excellency's power to checkmate all this. At the same time, in performing your duty as the friend of the oppressed and of the slave, I cannot help thinking that you are bound to interfere on the part of England to put down the outrages perpetrated from year to year by the Matabele. And surely your duty to England and to the various English colonies in South Africa calls upon you to prevent if possible the addition to its territory by the Transvaal, of a country fairer and even more fruitful than the South African Republic itself.

The Dutch can be checkmated and the outrages of the Matabele gradually put down, by the prompt appearance, in the interior, of a British Commissioner or Resident, especially appointed and sent by you, as representing Her Majesty's Imperial Government in this country. Should the Dutch know that there is a special British Commission in Matabeleland they will never go there. If the English power once got fairly to the north of the Dutch they would be forced to settle down and till the soil, yielding themselves to the influences of the European civilization from which, in point of fact, they are now fleeing. Exercising a protectorate over the Matabele, and eventually occupying and possessing the country, your Excellency would find that the whole question of English supremacy had been settled finally; and the Dutch would probably become in South Africa what they are in the United States.

Should the appearance of an English Commissioner lead to the preservation of Matabeleland from the Dutch, it would only be reasonable that the Mashona Gold-fields, at present a territory entirely uninhabited, should be handed over by

Lobengula to his preservers.   This would lead to the settlement of farmers in the very beautiful and rich country of
Mashonaland, a great part of which is also at present uninhabited, having been denuded of its population by the
ceaseless wars of the Matabele.

I may mention that Major Stabb, of the 32nd Light
Infantry, last year visited Matabeleland and the Victoria
Falls, and will be able to give information as to the social
condition of the Matabele.

Perhaps some of the sentences in this communication may
appear to be too strongly expressed.   My apology must be
my sense of the magnitude and imminence of the question,
which alone could have induced me to write at all.—I
remain, with every expression of respect, your Excellency's
humble servant,   JOHN MACKENZIE.

P.S.—For obvious reasons connected with my residence
in this country as a missionary, I beg that this letter be
regarded as a private communication.

At last the time came to which Mackenzie had
looked forward with so much dread, when he must
leave Shoshong and his much-loved mission station
there.   The progress of the Institution buildings at
Kuruman had reached such a stage as to demand his
presence at that place.   He would for himself have
much preferred to remain at Shoshong, and to carry
on there the work of the Institution as it was shaping
itself under his hands, and the work of the mission
station in which he was so largely assisted now by
Mr Hepburn.   There had been staying with him for
some time the well-known Austrian traveller and man
of science, Dr Emil Holub, whose medical skill was
freely given to those in need, during his visits to
Shoshong.   He threw himself with great energy into
the work of packing up all the belongings of the
Mackenzie family and loading the waggons with them.
On June 13th, 1876, the dreary feeling of the
travellers was expressed by Mrs Mackenzie to one
of their sons in this way :—

This is post-day, and we are in the midst of packing. You would be sorry if you saw the dear old house all but empty, and an enormous buck-waggon filled with boxes at the door, and another waiting to be filled, and our own waggon waiting to be filled and furnished for their journey. We do not like this moving any more than you do. To us Kuruman seems a desert waste as compared with this, that to others seems so dreary and inhospitable; but we are going where duty calls us, so we try to go through it contentedly and cheerfully.

The sorrow among the Bamangwato was deep and extensive. Not only the Christians felt themselves bereft of their pastor and friend, but the very heathen knew that they were losing from the town one whom their chief loved and whom all trusted. They expressed their grief in native fashion, numbers of them turning out to watch the waggons as they moved down through the kloof and the town out upon the flat. Many of them, including Khame himself, rode out for ten miles or more with the waggons, as an evidence of their affection and their regret. As they stood watching John Mackenzie go past, and saw their chief's sorrow expressed in word and look, they would utter their soft and beautiful Sechuana farewells, "Tsamaea señtlè, Ra"—"Go nicely, Father"; or "Tsamaea ka pula, Ra"—"Go with rain, Father."

CHAPTER VII

THE MOFFAT INSTITUTION (1871-1882)

WHERESOEVER Protestant missions have been established they have found it necessary to begin the task of education ; and wheresoever they have been carefully conducted, education of a thorough kind has been made a prominent feature of their work. All the more strange is it to find that in Bechuanaland this part of missionary enterprise was for a long number of years peculiarly neglected. This is not the place to attempt to fix the responsibility for this disastrous lack. Probably no one man or set of men is responsible. Throughout the letters of missionaries to the Directors and of Directors to the missionaries we find frequent references to the matter of education and the necessity for its development. And yet years passed into decades, and the decades multiplied without any one efficient school being established throughout the whole of Bechuanaland. In each mission station there was, of course, some school work done ; there were always some natives who were learning to read, and a few learned to read well. The chief Sechele, for example, was wise enough to send his son Sebele to Kuruman, where he received a good grounding from Dr Moffat and his family, and he has been always recognised as one of the best-educated Bechuanas. But in no station or village was school work carried on by men set apart for that work who were capable of doing it thoroughly. One can only try to imagine how great a difference it would have made to the entire history of those tribes if, during all the years

179

which passed before the general influx of Europeans
took place, the natives had been widely and thoroughly
aroused to the desire for education.   If those native
chiefs, and at a later date numerous native farmers
who owned valuable lands, had been able to read and
write well and had mastered the elements of arithmetic,
they would have been saved from many a cheat, and
would have retained for their own legitimate use
extensive and richly productive estates, which, through
their ignorance, they have lost.

As we have said, every missionary tried to do something in the way of education ; but in South Africa,
where so much time was lost in the making of long
journeys and in the putting up of houses and churches,
it was by no means easy to concentrate upon this
work, and still less easy to carry it far, single-handed
and burdened as the labourers were.   The Directors
of the Society in London appear to have realised very
inadequately how much was needed to perform this
work, and how far behind Bechuanaland remained.
For even in the year 1875 their brilliant and powerful
foreign secretary, Dr Joseph Mullens, wrote to
Mackenzie, " It was for those rudimentals that we
want you to have a schoolmaster (not Mr X., but
a *good native*).   We value our English missionaries,
and want to see them occupied in the *highest duties
available* to them."   One hardly knows whether to be
amazed most at the notion that an English missionary
would not be doing the highest duty available if he
were engaged in Christian education, or at the
expectation that a native could be found to do the
work at that time in Bechuanaland.   Concerning this
very sentence Mackenzie writes to his friend, the Rev.
James Ross, " There is not a single native taught by
the London Missionary Society in South Africa who is
at all qualified to do anything of the kind."

At last however, practical steps were taken at the

meeting of the Bechuanaland District Committee held at Kuruman in January 1869. The Committee had before them a letter from Dr Mullens, written in August 1868, in which a number of questions were submitted for the consideration of the South African missionaries. These questions included a request for proposals of any new methods which might be employed to "call out the zeal and consecration of individuals" in the churches. To this the missionaries replied that effort should be made to direct the minds of promising young men "to the work of Christ," to "forward the education of such as become interested in the matter, with the view of their becoming schoolmasters and native teachers." This general recommendation led on to the specific and important demand for "the speedy formation of an institution for the training of native agents." The Committee further requested the Directors to sanction the establishment of such an institution, and to release "one of the missionaries now in the country from his present duties," and to appoint him as Tutor. It was recognised that the Directors would have to provide an additional sum of money annually for the expenses of this new work, and they were reminded that the Rev. Robert Moffat had "for some time past paid the Society the sum of £40 per annum towards the support of such an institution." The Directors responded favourably to these proposals of their Bechuanaland agents, and urged them to take the necessary steps for the establishment of the Seminary which they had proposed.

It was not, however, until the meeting of the Missionary Committee at Molepolole, in July 1871, that this was found possible. But there, after another very full discussion, it was resolved that at once "an institution for training evangelists and native ministers" should be established. The report which they made

to the Directors goes on to say, " Having submitted
the selection of a Tutor to the ballot, it was almost
unanimously decided to recommend the Rev. John
Mackenzie to the Directors for that office." . . . " As
a temporary measure it was decided that the institution should be commenced on a small scale at
Shoshong, inasmuch as it is Mr Mackenzie's present
residence." Regulations were further drawn up with
regard to the admission of students and the course of
study through which they should be carried. Only
those were to be admitted who could read and write
Sechuana, and who had a fair knowledge of the Scriptures. They must be suitably married, and bring their
wives and children with them for their period of study.
The course was at first only intended to last two years,
but it was found necessary to lengthen this to three.
In general the subjects taught were to include arithmetic, geography, and history, Scripture exegesis, and
theology, as well as instruction and practice in the
making of addresses.

As soon, therefore, as Mackenzie reached Shoshong,
he began to arrange for the erection of buildings which
would be needed while the institution remained at
Shoshong. He and his brethren felt considerable difficulty about his accepting the appointment, acting
upon it, and spending money upon the buildings,
before they received news of the approval of the
Directors in London. Already some signs of vacillation in that quarter had caused them a little
hesitation. Nevertheless they had behind them the
explicit instructions of the Directors, and it seemed to
them only wise to begin the work at the earliest possible moment. Seven cottages were erected for the
students as well as a class-room ; and five students
were enrolled, these being selected with very great care.

Much to the relief of the Tutor and his brother
missionaries, the reply of the Directors to their pro-

posals was a very cordial approval of all that they had undertaken. The Directors suggested " that there should be attached to " the institution " the honoured name of the Rev. Robert Moffat." This suggestion was well received, of course, by the missionaries, and their approval was, if possible, made still more warm by the news which arrived later that a proposal to establish such an institution as a memorial of Dr Moffat had awakened great interest throughout England and Scotland. Churches and individuals began freely to subscribe the necessary funds, and these increased rapidly until, where the missionaries had hoped for hundreds, they now heard that the institution was supported by thousands of pounds.

Mackenzie found his first class of students to be on the whole intelligent and earnest men ; and he reported that they were very anxious to get on. The fifth among them was Khamane, the second son of Sekhome, who did not intend to become an evangelist ; his career as a student was cut short by his subsequent political ambitions and disloyal intrigues against his brother Khame. Throughout the remaining four years of his residence at Shoshong, Mackenzie was daily engrossed in this work, and deeply anxious to fit his men in every way for the position which they were afterwards to occupy. He trained them in the work of building houses instead of huts, and other practical affairs. He talked much with them concerning the political excitements and changes in the Bamangwato tribe, and strove, by direct precept as well as example, to show them how they must avoid in their future careers the danger of becoming partisans, and yet how they must not shrink from declaring themselves the friends of righteousness on every occasion.

In a letter written to the Secretary of the Society he says :—

You will be glad to hear that I feel encouraged with reference to the work of the Institution. The six men now at Shoshong work conscientiously, and are very anxious to learn. I hope that moderate expectations with reference to their future usefulness will not be disappointed. There is a general feeling of curiosity in the country with reference to them. What have they been learning? Why was not one, or at most two years, a long enough period to teach them in? The constant political changes among the Bamangwato have supplied an occasion for the students to endeavour to exercise that neutrality which is required of the messenger of the Cross who is the friend of all parties.

When in 1876 the first four students passed the final examinations of the Committee, and were appointed to various important fields, it was felt that a good beginning had been made with good and intelligent men. Throughout their subsequent years they most fully justified that hope.

The Bechuanaland Committee of Missionaries at the first left the question of a permanent site for the institution open, although the Directors in London had from the beginning suggested that Kuruman should be selected. In May 1873, the missionaries decided that this was the wise course to pursue, and sent a recommendation to London to that effect. To their surprise they received a letter from London asking them to reconsider this decision. They carried further their investigation into various possible sites, and reconsidered the matter at Kuruman in May 1874. Once more they decided that Kuruman was the only site that was available and, on the whole, convenient. They proposed that buildings on a moderate scale should at once be put up so as to be ready for occupation in October 1875. They also decided that if the institution was to be made a permanent and an ever-growing success, a thoroughly good Youths' School should also be established at Kuruman.

On this whole matter of the site for the institution Mackenzie, while he supported the almost unanimous decisions of his brethren and defended them, never formed any very strong conviction of his own. He was not at all enthusiastic about Kuruman, as it seemed to him too far south, and yet he was unable for various reasons to fix his mind upon any other more suitable place.

So sure were the missionaries that the London Directors would approve their action, that they appointed a sub-committee to superintend the work of building. Mackenzie and Mr Ashton proceeded to arrange for the gathering of material and the engagement of workmen. The former went to Klerksdorp, where builders were engaged. To the consternation of all, a letter was received from the Directors which forbade their proceeding farther with the work. The letter was so emphatic that there seemed nothing to do but to countermand all orders and break all contracts. As one of the leading business men at Klerksdorp remarked, when he acted as intermediary in the cancelling of engagements, " This affair in the eyes of an outsider looks bad, and will more or less damage Mr Mackenzie in the eyes of the workmen. . . . It places Mr Mackenzie in a very awkward position ; he will no doubt be grieved, and may be a little angry, for being treated in this manner." The reason for this unexpected action seems to have been that at this time the Directors began to receive so large a sum of money for the Moffat Institution that they saw their way to do something grander than the humble missionaries on the field had intended. But it was very perplexing and drew from Mackenzie a letter to Dr Mullens which contained the following passages :—

I regret much, as Tutor of the Institution, that the erection of the permanent buildings has been so long delayed. Indeed, I believe at the time I write, absolutely nothing is being done in the matter. At their meeting in April last the Committee contemplated rearing the Tutor's house and the cottages for married students, so that we could begin work at Kuruman in October of the present year. The main building and schoolmaster's house were to follow, after the fullest consultation with the Directors. The Committee's plan admitted of being carried out piecemeal, and they availed themselves of this. It was thought the approval of the Directors would be to hand before an actual commencement would take place; and it was thought that there could be little difference of opinion about the Tutor's house and the cottages, while we knew, that as to the place itself, there was no other site available. The movement had long been delayed; it was to be delayed no longer. Every member of the Committee was interested in the work; and everyone undertook some work in connection with it. But (speaking for myself) I was much pained to find that all this hearty work was crushed by the Directors—I cannot think but *ill-advisedly*.

By this time business had been done, engagements made, all which had now to be receded from, as far as possible. This was unpleasant and humiliating work for grown-up men to set about. But it was got through—with scant grace. And the members of the Committee now naturally turned their eyes to London. . . .

The Directors have announced their approval of Kuruman as a site. A beautiful plan, based on that of the Committee, has been sent out for the Committee's guidance! This is good news. At length the Directors and their Committee see eye to eye. I pray earnestly that this may continue. May nothing—may no one—come between the Directors and their agents in the field! May there be mutual helpfulness and mutual confidence!

While the missionaries were discussing their modest plans, the Directors had engaged Mr E. H. Robbins, a London architect, to draw up plans for the Moffat Institution. He carefully studied the topography of Kuruman with Dr Moffat, making pencil sketches in his presence, and then drew up plans for an institution such as the Directors and Dr Moffat had described to him. These drawings he took to Dr Moffat for his approval, and reported that " with a few slight alterations the plan met his view exactly." As soon as possible these plans were sent out to Bechuanaland, and the missionaries were instructed to erect buildings as therein described. As a matter of fact the designs were extravagant, and the careful Bechuanaland District Committee reduced some of their most expensive features, thereby saving hundreds, if not several thousands, of pounds.

The work was begun under the superintendence of the Rev. William Ashton in the year 1875. In the following year Mackenzie decided that as the buildings which he and his family would occupy must be near completion, he ought, after attending the Committee meeting at Molepolole, to go on to Kuruman and begin the new session where henceforth his work was to be carried on. When all had been arranged, and while he was engaged in the work of packing, another letter arrived which amazed him exceedingly. This letter suggested that he should remain at Shoshong for two or three years longer, " during these building operations at Kuruman." If that had been the only reason or argument given it might not have caused much surprise, but the Secretary of the Society added a sentence or two of which it was very hard to understand the real significance. " We all identify you with Shoshong, with the Bamangwato, with Macheng and Sekhome, with Khame and Khamane, and with the great social advance of the tribe. I can't bring myself to fancy you at Kuruman, even in the important position assigned you there. However, we shall see what two or three years bring forth. And besides, you are a man of so much weight and spirit that you would find far too little to do in training two or three novices ; you must of necessity spend a large portion of time on rudimentals." These sentences certainly seemed to contain the suggestion that the Directors did not expect the institution to grow to much, and that they did not desire very warmly that Mr Mackenzie should leave his mission work at Shoshong to be the Tutor at Kuruman. Much perplexed and disturbed, Mackenzie nevertheless resolved to abide by the decision of his brethren. They agreed that he should, upon the explicit appointments and approvals already given them by the Directors, proceed to Kuruman. Here, then, he settled as Tutor of the Moffat Institution in September 1876.

From this time until the end of 1878, John Mackenzie found himself once more involved in the irksome task of building. The extensive and expensive plans which had been sent out by the Directors from London would have required the entire time of a fully qualified and salaried manager. To save this expense the burden was laid upon the Tutor of the Institution, who therefore endeavoured to carry on his task of daily teaching and of superintending the large works which were proceeding. He had associated with him as consultants, the Rev. John Brown and the Rev. A. J. Wookey ; but next to himself, the man upon whom the heaviest burden fell, was the Rev. William Ashton, who was now stationed at Barkly. The letters which passed between Barkly and Kuruman are innumerable, and deal with every detail in the purchase and transport of material, the engagement of workmen, the payment of wages, etc. The work was carried on by these missionaries with the greatest energy and unfailing patience, although Mackenzie did confess to one of his sons that he found it very hard to teach and to build at the same time. It is a curious fact that for so long a period the supreme work of teaching was allowed by the Directors to be interfered with by the work of building, when the latter could have been carried out by specialists. In a letter of that year (1878) he gives a glimpse of his perplexities, inasmuch as he is compelled to keep ox-waggons on the road between Kuruman and Kimberley and Barkly carrying necessary materials.   At one time six waggon-loads have accumulated at Barkly, and yet nearer at hand he says, " It is all I can do to keep the masons and plasterers supplied with straw, bricks, clay, etc." In still another letter to his friend the Rev. G. D. Cullen of Edinburgh, he says, " I have under my oversight nine masons and plasterers, three carpenters, one squad of brick-makers, two squads of reed cutters (reeds for thatching), besides two classes of young men who have just been examined by my brother missionaries." His difficulties were not all merely mechanical, nor were his worst troubles with the native workmen. During the period of building, two of his contractors died, another decamped.   " Drunkenness," he says, " among the European workmen has been one of the difficulties with which I have had to contend ; and I am sorry to say that natives are always found who are willing to bring the brandy for these men, although they have to go seventy miles for it."

At last, however, the work drew to a conclusion, and in the month of January 1879, the tutor and builder of the Moffat Institution was able to send in a report to the Directors, which described the structures as practically completed.   It occurred to him that it would be only fair to the subscribers in Great Britain and to the Directors that they should receive an independent and authoritative report of these buildings.   Through the kind assistance of Major (afterwards Sir) Owen Lanyon, Administrator of Griqualand West, he was fortunate in securing the services of Sergeant-Major Ellison, who was at that time in public service at Kimberley, and who was highly qualified as builder and surveyor for this work.   He went to Kuruman, and very carefully investigated the entire series of buildings. In his report, after describing each building in detail, he adds :—

I have gone through the accounts and examined the invoices and bills for material and labour, also the agreements for small contracts with the several men, and I consider there is very great credit due to Mr Mackenzie, who has the management of the whole works, for the zeal and ability with which the several works have been carried out. He has spared neither time nor trouble to get everything done at the most reasonable cost. I have been for the last two years in charge of the public works in Kimberley, and for fourteen years superintending large works and buildings under Government, at home, in the colonies ; and from my experience I have no hesitation in stating that the works at Kuruman have, with a few slight exceptions, been carried out in the most efficient manner, reflecting very great credit to those concerned.

In his own final report, Mackenzie said, " Brethren, I cannot say that the work which you devolved upon me has been easy or pleasant ; I hope, however, that it is work which will remain, and that a good educational work will be carried on within these buildings long after we are forgotten."

The desire and great aim of the Bechuanaland missionaries from the first had been for inexpensive buildings and a sufficient staff, and this was very specially emphasised on several occasions by Mackenzie. As it was, they got expensive buildings and an insufficient staff. They had, however, been compelled by the will of the Directors to enter upon the extensive building enterprise which absorbed so much energy during these valuable years. But they were encouraged, even when they saw the cost of the buildings to be approaching £10,000, by receiving a letter from the Directors, in which they invited the missionaries to consider and report on an enlarged scheme of educational development. With great joy they undertook this grateful task at the Bechuanaland

District Committee meeting of February 1879. They outlined a scheme for overtaking the work which the institution, as now reared at Kuruman, seemed to make both necessary and possible. In connection with their suggestions, and in view of the beginnings of retrenchment which the Directors began to propose very soon after that proposal of enlargement, Mackenzie wrote as follows :—

KURUMAN, *2nd April* 1879.

MY DEAR DR MULLENS,—Your communication of Feb. 6 arrived at Barkly while I was in that neighbourhood, travelling for the benefit of my wife's health.

We were five weeks away from Kuruman, and I am happy to say that Mrs Mackenzie has derived considerable benefit from those great doctors, fresh air and change of scene.

The instructions of the Directors with reference to the expenditure on the building of the Moffat Institution shall be attended to. The carpenter and painter has not finished his work. When he does so there will be a balance to pay to him. Then one waggon-house has still to be roofed, and the second waggon-house and mealie store has not yet made much progress. But it is to be of sun-dried brick, with thorn-wood roof, and will not, therefore, cost much. It is of importance not only as a waggon-house and store-room, but one end of it is to be appropriated to the boys of the boarding school as a dormitory, as it is not advisable that they should sleep in their class-room, if that could be avoided.

I wait with anxiety your report concerning irrigation and the raised furrow. (For which a skilled agriculturist had been asked by the Committee.) I have the utmost sympathy with the position of the officers and Directors of the Society at this time of distress. Still I beg to remind the large-minded and far-seeing friends of Christian work that our beloved Society is on the threshold of a great work in South Africa in connection with this Institution, a work often attempted, but not hitherto attained to in this country, but which the Society is carrying on with much advantage to the natives in the South Seas, in Madagascar, and in India. It is gratifying to read of instances of individual liberality in stimulating to evangelistic effort, and the breaking up of new ground. Would to God some generous man would thus interest himself in your educational work here, and enable you fairly to launch it, by sending out the labourers still necessary to make up the Institution, and necessary to carry on its operations successfully. If it should come to be a question between sending out the necessary staff of workers and sanctioning the outlay in raising the dam, etc., by all means let us have the staff of workers, and let us hope on for better times as to the raised furrow; that is if one or the other must be given up. On no account give up the work in its broadness and importance. It was delayed at least *one generation* too long in Bechuanaland; in the name of our blessed Lord and Master let it be delayed no longer.

I thank you for your kind expressions concerning the services which, along with my brethren, I have been able to render to the Society in the matter of its property at Kuruman and elsewhere. I regret that we have not been able to obtain a settlement as to the Eye of the Fountain property. It may be of importance to remind you that when Col. Warren spoke favourably of your claim to "the Eye," it was with a distinct understanding that we should carry on here a really good and serviceable educational and industrial establishment for the benefit of the natives.

．　　　．　　　．　　　．　　　．　　　．　　　．

If you give the Institution the staff of men asked by the Committee it would be possible—I had almost said easy—for them so to arrange as that visits to the out-stations should be paid by them after some kind of plan, and *as a break to them in their work of teaching*—say once every three or every four months. Thus it is not necessary to have a European Missionary at Kuruman, who shall be only pastor. *Every European connected with the Society at Kuruman ought to have a place and a work on your Institution Staff*, and that Staff with the students will attend to the pastoral and itinerating work of the district. I am willing to take the responsibility of this as Tutor and Pastor of the Kuruman Church; and I do this trusting to the co-operation of my European co-workers here.

In the meantime, I have to report that there are now scarcely any of the usual Langberg out-stations to visit, owing to the "unsettled state of the country" to which you refer in your concluding resolutions as an element which might cause your arrangements to be open to revision. For instance, many of the people of the Langberg are now living at Batlaros; and the village of Hamohara, where a student from the Institution had resided some three years, is now removed to a spot within six miles of Kuruman, and is regularly supplied by the students who have, in all, four preaching stations which they regularly visit on Sunday.

.   .   .   .

The surprise and dismay of those upon the spot may be imagined when, under a sudden change of atmosphere in London, letters arrived from the Directors which dwelt upon the expense of the buildings, and criticised the smallness of the educational work. One of the periodical depressions had come, affecting the income of the Society from the churches, and the Directors did not feel themselves in a position to pay for the staff of so lordly an institution as they had erected at Kuruman. It seemed to be held by some that an advanced theological college could be in a trice established in a land where elementary education had not been seriously tackled, and yet it was even hinted that the teaching of English in the boys' school was a work of supererogation. It was in answer to such a letter that Mackenzie addressed the following words of remonstrance :—

In making the remarks which follow, I am not to be supposed to have little or no sympathy with the Directors of the Society in their pecuniary difficulties. I am greatly distressed on account of those difficulties, and especially that they should occur at such a crisis as the present in the history of this mission. As I understand the subject, the Directors resolved to accomplish three objects in building the Moffat Institution here. It may not be out of place to consider how far these have been secured, or are in the way of being secured, and good for all practical purposes.

I. Memorial to Dr Moffat.
    1. Bricks, as proposed by local committee, were exchanged for stone which was undoubtedly more suitable for a memorial.

2. While the general idea of the Committee's plan was adhered to, Mr Robbins, in consultation with Dr Moffat, changed, improved, and beautified it very much. This also added to its suitability as a memorial. But here also comes in the second object of the Directors as announced in the Foreign Secretary's letters at the time the plan was sent out, viz.—

II. That the building itself should be an educator in the country on account of the style of its architecture.

III. The third object, and the original one, upon which the two former were engrafted by the Directors, was to supply suitable premises for conducting a Theological Seminary and a boarding school for boys.

Now, brethren, the two first of these objects, which have entirely originated with you in England, have been secured to a great extent, as you can see from Mr Ellison's plan: although *two wings* remain to be built before your plan would be a complete thing. But, in the meantime, here the Memorial stands in good masonry and durable material, as a thoroughly qualified inspector has certified to you; here it stands to perform its second or silent educational work. It has already been instanced publicly in Kimberley by Sir Bartle Frere, in laying the foundation stone of the Presbyterian Church there, as a stimulus to well directed Christian liberality. The first remark of skilled men such as Col. Warren of the Royal Engineers, on first seeing the Institution, has been one of unfeigned pleasure and surprise. They had heard they were beautiful buildings; they had expected something far short of what they saw. Such sums as £20,000 and £25,000 have been hazarded as "what it must have cost:" and that, too, by practical men. As to the first two objects therefore, the Directors have perfectly succeeded in doing what they resolved to do.

As to the third object in view—the schools, cottages for ten married students, and the two teachers' dwelling houses, are very suitable. As summer residences they are perfect. In the bitterly cold winter weather the height of the walls (fourteen feet under beam), renders the schoolroom almost unbearable to the natives: in the plan the height is fifteen feet: the one foot of masonry taken off all round represents a considerable saving in money. But every foot taken off detracts from the gracefulness of the building as a Memorial, rendering it of a more homely character ; and it must always be remembered that we were forbidden in the letter accompanying the plan to make important alterations in the plan without the express sanction of the Directors. As the buildings made progress, and now more than two years ago, a number of queries were sent out by the Directors accompanied by an encouraging letter. We were asked to sketch out the work which as a local committee we thought might be advantageously carried on here ; and to give to the Directors an idea of the cost. Most unfortunately our local committee postponed its sitting for more than a year ; and when at length it meets and sends home a sketch of the work which might advantageously be carried on at Kuruman, I can only say that it is not received in the spirit which was uppermost in the Directors' minds when the sketch was asked for. This leads me to wish that our committee meeting had been held sooner, in the sunnier days when the questions concerning our work here were put to us. The opposing ideas may be put thus : " Having built such an expensive Institution we shall spend no more money there whatever : we feel inclined to think the money has been wasted." The reply to which is : " Not a penny has been wasted, so far as reliable evidence goes ; only our wishes as Directors have been carefully and skilfully carried out. *Having built such an expensive Institution,* let us not suddenly stop short there ; especially when a little further consideration and outlay would complete a worthy scheme." The first mission-house is empty : were a lady teacher at Kuruman now, she might commence her work among the girls at once. Were a printer sent out—a good man all round—*it would be like pumping life-blood into shrunken veins.* Acres on acres of arable land are lying waste before our eyes ; it is usually the first thing a traveller says, Why don't you reclaim that morass ? The agriculturist would soon more than pay for himself ; and would place the property of the Society here in such a position as that the special work carried on here would be little or no expense to the general fund. Therefore, dear brethren—

1. Send us a lady teacher *in redemption of your own proposal*—I believe in 1873—when Miss Waterston offered her services, and the Committee declined the offer, hoping to get the services of (another lady).

2. Send us a printer—because your mission at its present state cannot make progress without one.

3. Send us an agriculturist—*to save money.*

It was Mackenzie's profound conviction that the greatest work could be done now for Bechuanaland, so far as the Missionary Society was concerned, by appointing a competent and adequate staff of teachers and workers, who should co-operate at Kuruman in laying the foundations for an educational system over the whole country. With a thorough woman teacher over a girls' boarding school, and with a good boys' boarding school, efficient superintendence of the printing office and development of the farming lands which already belonged to the Society, as well as with his own continuous labour among the students in the Seminary, it was his conviction that a great enthusiasm for education would be awakened throughout Bechuanaland. Moreover, this craving could gradually be satisfied in every town and village, as the Moffat Institution year by year sent out intelligent and devoted native teachers to spread the work abroad. This staff of men and women would have had in Kuruman and the surrounding villages a splendid field upon which to employ their evangelistic energies with greater concentration and continuity than had been possible before. Even as it was, the Moffat Institution sent out men upon whom Mackenzie had directed his whole energy for three years each, and this continued until he left the place in 1882. Most of these men are labouring to-day all over Bechuanaland, from the Orange River to the Zambesi. What might have happened if the Directors had responded, or had been able to respond, to the demands of the Bechuanaland missionaries, if they had set themselves with great energy to the development of this educational work, it is hard to say. Possibly this might have made all the difference in Mackenzie's own plans and the important decisions which were so soon forced upon him. The subsequent history of education at Kuruman and in Bechuanaland would seem to indicate that a great, a very great, opportunity was lost at this time.

With the year 1879, when the buildings of the institution were almost completed, Mackenzie assumed the full charge of the Kuruman Mission Station. This involved, of course, regular preaching, much organising and constant pastoral work. As we shall see later, disturbances among the natives lasted for the next three years, and resulted in war against British forces ; the whole country of South Bechuanaland was for long kept in a miserable turmoil and unrest. This brought upon the pastor of the Kuruman station an enormous amount of spiritual as well as political labour. It is with the former that we are at present concerned. More than two hundred pages of large size note-paper remain, which are, for the most part, covered with notes on individual cases, to prove the minuteness, the care and the tenderness with which Mackenzie laboured amongst the natives through those years. These pages contain the names of candidates for baptism inquirers and applicants for church membership, as well as particulars of various kinds of discipline. The student of religion and of society is, in the reading of such notes, brought in a most vivid way to realise the immense power which the Christian Church exerts in a heathen land. The jottings show that on almost the whole range of what we call the moral life, the Church was the only institution in the Kuruman district which could teach the principles of right living and use forces that would help to secure it. The pastor studies each case, notes down the salient points of each personal history ; then he reports these to the native deacons and discusses everything with them ; then he presents them to the Church as a whole, and guides the Church to a right decision on Christian grounds in relation to each man and woman whose name is presented. These jottings comprise particulars regarding the station in life, the education or no-education, and the Christian experience, as well as the moral standing of these Bechuana people. They show that the tumult of the war had led many astray into cattle-stealing and depredations of other kinds; even some church officers had for a time lost their balance. These records prove again that one of the greatest tasks of the Church in such a land is to strengthen the marriage bond. Constantly cases of desertion by husband or wife are recorded, and these are dealt with by the Church.

It is when one reads the life-story of these missionaries in heathen and primitive lands that one realises the breadth and the strength of grasp which the Christian religion lays upon human society. The missionary presents in his personality and in his actual work that synthesis which some economic students of our day discuss so much, and about which a few of them have so many dreams. Here is a man who at once is a builder of houses, showing people a new ideal of permanence and beauty in the structures which he rears; he is at the same time the agriculturist, giving them new ideas and desires in the development of lands which have been for ages treated as waste lands; he is the teacher, labouring to awaken the intellect of picked men and lead them at least into the vestibule of the intellectual life; he is also at the same time, as we shall see, the ruler, who, for a long time, actually represents the British Government among them, and to whom natives of all classes come from many towns in all directions for help, and to whom Government officials look for information and for advice; he is also the preacher, proclaiming the Gospel of the Grace of God in Christ Jesus, believing in his heart of hearts that that is the root and crown of all human experience, and that all his other work receives its true interpretation in the light of this fundamental relationship ; and we see finally that he is the spiritual shepherd of a very large flock, striving to know each sheep by name and disposition, giving every week many hours of his congested days to that which he believes to be his supreme task, viz., dealing with the characters of men and women in the light of the Law of God and the Cross of Christ.

The following letter to the Directors was written when the first and most acute stage of the disturbances had passed away, and will, in Mackenzie's own words, illustrate what has been said :—

KURUMAN, 1st *August* 1879.

Rev. J. O. WHITEHOUSE, Acting Foreign Sec'y, L.M.S.

MY DEAR MR WHITEHOUSE,—The Directors will have understood that this station and neighbourhood has been a rallying point and place of refuge for the natives during the late disturbances. During the past year there has been probably a larger population on the Kuruman river-course than has been seen there since the time when the Batlaping were united and living there. It is a matter of thankfulness to us that we were enabled to hold on here during the time of the disturbances : for the large congregation of people to which I have referred has assembled on account of the proximity of this station, and the confidence which the people of all classes have in those residing here.

Inasmuch as the people would soon separate and return to their former places of abode, I judged it to be of great importance to enter into all questions affecting their Christian character and standing in the Church while the events were fresh in people's minds, and before they broke up.

I therefore announced from the pulpit that I would devote a certain portion of one day in the week to meet with any refugee Church members who might wish to speak to me. Up to the present time I have seen and examined over 160 connected with outside churches. Of these I have received back into the Church 117 people, several of whom have already removed to Griqualand and elsewhere with their

certificate of membership in their possession. Of the
remaining number there are those who have been engaged
in aggressive warfare : and among them I am sorry to say
there are four deacons or teachers whose conduct has been
highly unsatisfactory. Two have been engaged in open
warfare of an aggressive nature, one having been persuaded
to join an attack on Campbell, the other to join a similar
attack on Griquatown. The latter had all but succeeded in
re-entering the Church through deception—he having striven
to keep it secret that he had been one of this party. Whilst
keeping back such men—over whom the old cattle-lifting
spirit has got the mastery—I have endeavoured to do so in
such a way as not to lead them to be unduly discouraged.
And I am happy to say that all who have called on me, and
who are still under discipline for the part they have taken in
the breach of at least the sixth and eighth Commandments,
show some symptoms of shame, and some of them, I trust,
of repentance for what they have done.

Several admirable cases of steadfastness came to my
knowledge during their examination, in which Christian
men had had the courage to oppose the war-party. Others
had been simply bewildered : others saw what was coming,
but were weak and half-hearted : others again actually used
their influence in the wrong direction. It is pleasant to
think of the village of Hamohara, with its teacher from this
Institution—in a small scale like Kuruman itself—as a place
of refuge for Europeans as well as for well-disposed natives.
When teacher and people actually left Hamohara, it was for
fear of the war-party among their own people, and they came
as a body and settled down in our neighbourhood here.

I shall give a single instance of the state of things which
obtained in this country last year. The village of Tlose,
25 miles east, presided over by old Molete its chief and
Holele his eldest son, was for a considerable time untainted
by the war spirit. Great kindness was shown to forlorn
Europeans who had escaped from the murderers at Daniel's
Kuil. Waggons were sent for survivors, and for their
property. Clothing and food were given to the destitute
Europeans by Holele, who did his best for them. But
some of the murderers themselves approached the town :
Griquas fleeing from the European forces also crept in.
There was no lack of beef at the encampments of these
strangers. They rode beautiful horses ; and it was here

understood that horses and cattle were the property of the
white people.   Holele protested; old Molete spoke sharply;
and soon these people would have had to seek other quarters.
But fresh arrivals took place—among them one of our native
teachers, an old man, along with another of Molete's friends.
Holele now found himself alone in his town : his father and
his own brothers went over to the war-party, and soon the
attack on Campbell was organised, and those engaged in
it departed from Tlose in spite of Holele's efforts to the
contrary.   This change in the disposition of his father
Holele attributed to the evil counsels of a man called
Likatshane and our native teacher Jonathan, all of the
young men of whose family joined the attack on Campbell.
On his first arrival here Holele gave me an account of his
difficulties, and how he had left his own kith and kin and
had proceeded to Hamohara rather than be mixed up
with the cattle-lifting, etc.   He also expressed his great
disappointment at the kind of influence which Jonathan
and the other men had had on his father.   Time passed
on ; the cattle-lifters fell in the several engagements, or
gave themselves up, were fined or imprisoned, or otherwise
punished: and intimation was given that the refugee Christians
who wished to be recognised as Church members must call
on the missionary and explain to him their history during
the past few months.   Among the rest came Jonathan, who
was confronted with the facts which I had learned, but without
mentioning the source of my information.   At first he
demurred to the truth of the report which I had heard ; but
afterwards admitted his great shortcomings as a Christian
teacher at such a juncture.   He said he saw now that he
might have done better.   I was amused and gratified also,
to see the well-disposed Holele make his appearance one
day desiring a private interview, which I granted at once.
" About Jonathan, Sir ; I have come to say that I hope you
won't think too hardly of old Jonathan.   My father and
brothers were greatly to blame ; I don't know what possessed
everybody at that time ; but I hope, Sir, you won't think too
hardly of old Jonathan."   I went over the *events* which had
transpired, and asked if these things had taken place ?   " Yes ;
they were all true."   " Then," I said, " kindness to Jonathan
must teach him what harm he has done before we receive
him again among our number."   I might give you many an
interesting story, as unfolded to me at these interviews ; but

the above must suffice to describe the kind of thing with which we have had to do.

I have just returned from paying a visit to Griquatown, which I undertook with a view to complete the work of re-organization, and also to inquire on the spot into certain charges brought by some of the Church members against our teacher there, Jan Sepego. I found that the charges had not been proved, although the conduct of Sepego had not been altogether satisfactory. I was nearly a week in Griquatown ; some four days at Daniel's Kuil, where we have now a considerable number of Church members, being one Sunday at each of these places. As I did most of the travelling on horseback, my waggon following me, I was only a fortnight away from home. Having heard all that they had to say against one another at Griquatown, and seeing that there was more ill-feeling than wrong-doing, I reached down the large Dutch Bible from the pulpit and read to them the text, "And forgive us our debts," etc. This had the desired impression : the idea was startling that if they were living unforgivingly they were not forgiven of God. At length all had spoken in a friendly way except Sepego and the woman who was his chief accuser——his chief helper as she called herself. I read the verse again. The woman said she would go home and think of it. Jan was silent. Their hearts were sore——having spoken much against one another. I asked how they proposed to live any length of time not forgiving one another. Both rose as of one accord, a good expression came into their faces, and they shook hands over the past. I told them there, assembled as a Church, that I had found things in such a state that I did not feel it to be my duty to administer to them the ordinance of the Lord's Supper on the occasion of that visit ; but that I would endeavour to return in say three months, and that then, if I found they were all living in love and good works I should have pleasure in calling them together to com-memorate their Saviour's death.

Wishing you much pleasure and satisfaction in your work as Secretary during Dr Mullens' absence.——I remain, my dear Mr Whitehouse, ever yours sincerely,

JOHN MACKENZIE.

When in 1882 Mackenzie left Kuruman for his second visit to the homeland he little thought that he

was starting on a furlough which would separate him
entirely and finally from his beloved work at Kuruman. He had already proved, as we shall describe
later, when temptation to forsake the Society and the
Institution came before him, how profound was his love
for that work. He especially valued the task assigned
to him to instruct and mould the men who were to
become the native ministers and teachers of their own
land. These men were selected from a large number
of applicants with very great care by the Seminary
Committee. They were picked men upon whom
great confidence could be placed, who had shown
themselves both intelligent and earnest in their
Christian faith. The care with which they were
selected and the determination not to run up expenses
had kept the numbers down, so that up to the year
1875 only six regular students had been admitted.
In 1875 and 1876 owing to the removal to Kuruman,
and the task of putting up the new cottages, no
students were admitted. But from that date the
numbers increased, so that in 1882, when he left his
work, Mackenzie had two classes which comprised in
all eight students. There was at that time every
prospect that the number would increase, for the
recent disturbances and the advent of large numbers
of white men had quickened the desire for learning,
and had made large numbers of Christians more
zealous than before. The future of the Institution
was bright indeed. But during the years 1879-1881
he was drawn into another kind of work, which was
forced upon him by the political and social history of
South Bechuanaland. And that work, now appearing to him as inevitable (but inevitable for the next
ten years), became the supreme and absorbing burden
of his heart.

CHAPTER VIII

KURUMAN — AN UNPAID ADMINISTRATOR
(1877-1879)

GREAT BRITAIN for more than twenty years faithfully observed her compact with the Transvaal Government that she would not make treaties with any native tribes north of the Vaal River. But two events occurred which brought her, even against her will, into relations with these tribes. In the first place, the famous Keate Award, which was the result of a dispute between the Transvaal and certain chiefs, fixed or seemed to fix, a definite south-western boundary for the South African Republic ; and, in the second place, the annexation of Griqualand West, the territory which included the Diamond Fields, extended British territory north of the Orange River into Bechuanaland itself. In addition, we must reckon the rapid accumulation of European inhabitants in the Diamond Fields district, with the increased stimulus which they gave to farming operations as well as general commerce. More Europeans than ever spread themselves over the country, and the work of sweeping the natives out of the ownership of their lands proceeded apace. Many were the stories of downright robbery which were told from village to village, and which awoke burning indignation in the hearts of native chiefs, who saw their own prerogatives invaded as well as their people wickedly impoverished. To make these experiences somewhat vivid it may be well to cite two instances, besides that which Mackenzie relates in " Austral-Africa." [1] The first of these was minutely

[1] P. 117.

investigated by Mackenzie at Kuruman in 1878. A native, named Sebelego, owned a farm called Skuy Fontein and held a title to it dated 1866, which in the year 1877 he handed over to Mr Roper, the British Civil Commissioner at Griquatown. Now, in the year 1867 one Solomon Kok had coveted this land and tried to establish a title by the well-known land-grabber's method; he simply proceeded to plough part of it. This claim was disallowed by the Griqua chief of that date. But as soon as the English Government arrived the same man claimed this farm under another name. The rival claims were of course investigated by the British magistrate. To the consternation of the poor native, in 1877, and after he had given up his title, Solomon Kok brought him before the magistrate's court at Griquatown on the charge of burning his, Solomon's, hut and kraals, and filling up certain wells. The only evidence produced in support of the former charge was rendered by immediate relatives of Solomon's, while Sebelego pleaded not guilty. As to the second charge, he confessed that he had filled up the wells, but explained that they were on his own land, and had been originally opened by himself! For this he was fined the large sum of £64; part of this he had to borrow; and, as usual, when he came to pay what he had borrowed he found that a further charge was made against him for expenses. The poor frightened man was driven from pillar to post by schemes like this and actually made a fugitive from his own property, contrary to the law and against his will!

Another example must be given as Mackenzie described it to Col. Lanyon :—

Jantye (a native chief) has a ground for complaint which he never fails to mention when I see him. The friendliness of " Government " is very good, he admits ; but there is a Mordecai sitting in the King's gate whose presence extracts all the pleasure and satisfaction which the kindness of your Government would otherwise convey. Mordecai is Mr G—— (a Dutchman), who, as you are aware, lost his case as a claimant for Likatlong (Jantye's town) in the Land Court; and again in the Court of Appeal. But all this Jantye says is in the "Kantoor," or Court-house; outside the Court-house and at Likatlong itself G—— still possesses Likatlong, and says he means to stick to it.

It is almost beyond my powers of belief; but it seems when Luka, Jantye's son, came from the Interior he found this G—— occupying his (Luka's) house, and told him to leave it, as he had now returned and wanted his house. On G——, or his servant, refusing, Luka proceeded to put the things outside and to take possession of his house, when he was informed that the police were coming to apprehend him for breaking the peace and assaulting a white man! Luka fled, and, I understand, has scarcely been over the line since.

G—— has been repeatedly ordered or requested by Jantye to leave; but that person seems to have great confidence in his power of staring Jantye out of countenance, and declines to go. Impudence and brow-beating of this kind ought to get their appropriate reward; and I am surprised that this fellow is still allowed to remain at Likatlong against the wishes of Jantye, to the embittering of native feeling against the Government, and to the discredit of the English administration. The man has lost his case in an English court after a fair trial. What would he have more?

These incidents, when taken as examples of a procedure which was only too common, and which almost invariably ended in the defeat of the native even when he was a man of importance and education, will account for the feelings of unusual distrust and unrest which began in 1877 to make themselves felt throughout South Bechuanaland.

Griqualand West, including Kimberley, was under the administration of Colonel (afterwards Sir) Owen Lanyon, who made it his aim to meet these growing evils as fairly and firmly as possible. He was in constant correspondence with the High Commissioner, Sir

Bartle Frere, who also entered into the entire problem of British relations towards border tribes with characteristic insight and enthusiasm. He had reports made to him from various directions in South Africa upon this subject, and made up his mind on the main issues involved with great clearness and assurance. His convictions led to action which involved him in the Zulu war and in other proceedings which awoke criticism at home. Sir Bartle Frere was one of those unfortunate Governors of South Africa who saw so deep into British responsibility, and so far ahead into coming history, that they outlined a policy at once bold and intelligent. Because it was bold it began with trouble ; because it was intelligent it would have ended in peace, permanent and widespread. He it was who in 1878 began to report to the home Government on the condition of affairs in Bechuanaland. In one passage he evidently agrees with those who held " that it will be found necessary, sooner or later, to extend the British dominions or protectorate, in some form or other, over all the tribes between the Orange River and Lake Ngami, and between the sea and the present Transvaal frontier, and the longer it is deferred the more troublesome will the operation become." He adds the following vigorous and most true observations : " By refusing to accept the position of a protecting power, habitually acting as arbiter in tribal disputes, we escape nothing save the name and responsibility. Its reality is already incurred, and when at length we unwillingly undertake the burden of dominions, we shall find it greatly aggravated by delay and neglect." [1]

In another despatch he shows his grasp of the facts by pointing out that the establishment of two British officers, say in Kuruman and Shoshong, " would enormously strengthen the Transvaal and Griqualand West

[1] C. 2220, p. 35.

Governments." This was after the annexation of the Transvaal.

Mackenzie became deeply interested in all these occurrences, and was drawn into an ever-enlarging correspondence with the British authorities upon the subject. He, with the other missionaries, had long given close attention to the question of land-owner-ship among natives, and had induced many natives to become farmers in a real sense of the term ; they encouraged them to use the plough and to transport their crops and drive their cattle to suitable markets. Some natives succeeded in this, and their success was very likely to spread and to create a community of Bechuana stock-raisers and grain-producers, both pros-perous and law-abiding. It was such men whom the missionaries saw, to their chagrin and bitter disap-pointment, ousted from their possessions and driven into poverty and degradation. As a matter of fact, these natives were sometimes so enterprising that their influence was beginning to be felt upon the Kimberley markets ; undoubtedly their very pros-perity awoke the special resentment of their heredi-tary foes, the Boers.

Colonel Lanyon had already begun to experience serious trouble. Some of the Griquas, as well as the Kaffirs who lived within his province, still resented the displacement of the Griqua Government by the British ; and their resentment was fanned by such instances of wrong-doing as we have related, as well as by the insolence of English officials and even of policemen, who despised and humiliated them at every turn. The bitter feeling became so widespread and so strong that at last it broke out in open rebellion. For the double purpose of helping to quell the re-bellion, and to deal with the whole subject of land claims, Colonel (afterwards Sir) Charles Warren, R.E., was brought to Griqualand West.

Meantime disaffection was rapidly becoming warfare beyond the British border in Bechuanaland itself. Here matters were complicated by the fact that a certain chief named Mankoroane had for some years been officially recognised as " paramount chief," by which Bechuanas understand one thing, while the Boer and British Governments at that time understood quite another.   Among Bechuana tribes, what we call paramountcy simply means the dignity of the chief whose standing by birth is the highest and whose tribe is the strongest.   If several tribes unite against a common enemy he will be recognised as leader of them all ; if a number of chiefs and head-men meet in council he will naturally be their president.   But this paramountcy does not interfere with the complete independence of the separate tribes, nor with the authority of their chiefs within their own territories. Paramountcy was vaguely supposed by Boers and British at one time to imply much more than this, so that treaties or agreements or purchases of land arranged with the paramount chief were assumed— absurdly, from the native point of view—to bind the action of the separate tribes, or affect their ownership of the soil.   Now this Mankoroane, who really belonged to a younger branch of the royal family of the Batlaping tribes, was not at all loath to act in line with the assumptions of these foreigners, since they conferred on him much dignity, and seemed to multiply his power.   As soon as the Transvaal was annexed by Great Britain in the spring of 1877, Mankoroane, advised evidently by certain Europeans who hoped to make much out of their intrigue with him, issued a bombastic pro- clamation.   In this he calls himself " paramount chief of the Batlaping nation and all other tribes and peoples living within the limit of my country as defined," etc.   He proceeds to declare that the time had now come for laying aside the passive attitude which he had maintained, "owing to my august ally Queen Victoria's Government's advice!" The whole tone of the proclamation indicates the determination in his mind to assert what he calls his "rightful authority," even in places which, according to native law, were beyond his jurisdiction. Several of the native tribes of course defied him. When therefore Colonel Lanyon asked Mankoroane for permission to enter his territory at the head of an armed force, in order to punish a certain chief (Botlasitse) who had defied British authority within British territory, and who at the same time resented the so-styled paramount chief's assumption of authority over him, Mankoroane gladly consented. This gave him one more proof that his authority and power were recognised. Colonel Lanyon undoubtedly had a right to make this expedition, since Botlasitse had carried off cattle from within British territory, and in such a manner as, from the native point of view, to make his act a declaration of war.

Into these local disturbances there was introduced a very serious complication from the far east. The apparent success of Sekukuni against the Boers had become exaggerated as accounts of it spread across the country. Agitators of a reckless kind did not shrink from going about assuring the natives in the Cape Colony, in Griqualand West, and in Bechuanaland that it would not be impossible to drive the white men out of their land, and that if they would only rise at once, and all together, the great deliverance could be accomplished. From village to village these suggestions were whispered, and the air became thick with schemings and threatenings and personal ambitions. The chiefs of the various Bechuana tribes of course differed in character amongst themselves. Some, like Jantje of the

Kuruman district, had long lived in more or less close association with missionaries and other white men, and were not easily deceived ; but others like Luka, Jantje's own son, were of a wilder and more adventurous spirit ; and yet others, like Morwe, were wavering time-servers, ready to side with the victor. A few successful cattle raids inflamed the greed, and the success of one or two early skirmishes with white men inflamed the pride of the disaffected chiefs.

Early in the year 1878, roused by the very evident signs of a restless spirit and dark purposes among the natives, Mackenzie wrote to Colonel Lanyon suggesting that he should secure the appointment of a Commissioner or Commissioners to reside with the native chiefs who were near the border of Lanyon's province.

At the present juncture it is of great importance that you should have such an agent. Perhaps Taungs would be the best place for him to reside at, but he ought occasionally to visit the various chiefs on the line, and be able to keep you informed of the state of things ; and if he were the right stamp of man he would no doubt succeed in keeping the chiefs out of scrapes. I am afraid that some officials have expected raw natives at once to act like Englishmen ; and if they don't, punish them for it. This is a snobbish way of acting, and is not in accordance with the true English mode of treating natives. The one policy reminds one of the rude blow of a big, flat-headed hammer ; the other is the quiet action of the thick, wedge-end of a crow-bar. The one shatters everything to pieces ; the other moves and changes without destroying.

Unfortunately, no such Commissioners were appointed, although one white man, Mr Samuel Edwards, of distinguished South African experience, was employed to gather information by Colonel Lanyon.

While he was in Kimberley early in 1878, Mackenzie saw a troop of volunteer soldiers leave to serve

under Colonel Lanyon against certain marauders—
Kaal Kaffirs and Griquas—in the Province of Griqualand West.   This troop was surprised by the enemy
and defeated with considerable loss.   That was enough
to set the veldt on fire.   Rumours of what was in the
native mind had of course reached the ears of various
missionaries ; but none of them believed that after all
these years of peaceful life and careful instruction the
natives of South Bechuanaland would attempt to meet
the might of the Briton.   They even discounted the
effect of that little victory of the Griquas.   Mackenzie's
confidence was shaken when one or two leading men
came to him at Kuruman, and in a confidential, dark-
faced whisper, said, " Monare, we do not want you to
be afraid.   No harm will come to you or to your family."
This assurance of his own safety seemed to convince
him that the danger was greater than he had suspected.
Then, like a thunder-clap, fell the news upon Kuruman
that about sixty miles south-west, at a place called
Daniel's Kuil, a well-known and highly respected man
named Burness and his family had been murdered and
his farm looted.   A white woman, whose husband was
away from home on a journey, had fled with her six
little children into the bush, and nothing was known
of their fate.   The marauders were, of course, said to
be an army, and this murder was described as the signal
of a general war.   Kuruman was to be the first point
of attack, and all the white men there and everywhere
else in South Bechuanaland were to be destroyed.   The
neighbouring mission station at Motito had to be
abandoned by the resident missionary, Rev. A. J.
Wookey, who left with his family for Kuruman.   When
on May 29th, 1878, they reached the latter place,
they found the European population in a state of great
alarm.   The deserted mission station at Motito was
destroyed, and Kuruman was cut off from communication with the outer world.

The European traders were naturally much perturbed, for it seemed as if they would soon be overwhelmed and destroyed. They urged Mackenzie to send a formal request to the British Government for help, but this he declined to do. He held the doctrine that the missionary who goes into a heathen land goes at the risk of his life, and has no right to call upon the home government for help when his life seems in danger. And this is surely the doctrine most generally held by British missionaries and statesmen. Whatever other governments may have done, it has not been the practice of the British Government to treat the murder of missionaries by heathen peoples as calling for the interference of the sovereign ; and yet, wherever it is possible, that Government would of course be glad to deliver any of its subjects from such a danger as that which threatened the white people of Kuruman. Although Mackenzie declined to send the petition for help, he did not prevent others from acting on their own convictions in the matter ; and such a request was sent, although without his knowledge.

In the meantime it was decided that all the Europeans should take refuge within the institution buildings. It is a strange fact that when the natives several years before saw these, as it appeared to them, large and strong buildings being put up, they asked one another what they could mean ; and the answer seemed obvious, that these were not houses but strongholds, and that the white people were now taking possession of their land for ever. This idea had, of course, been carefully destroyed by the explanations which Mackenzie gave to them concerning the real purpose of the buildings, and their minds had become accustomed to his explanation ; but many of them, especially the dark-minded and heathen amongst them, recurred to their former belief when they saw that as soon as the buildings approached completion they became useful for the very purpose which they had at first ascribed to them. There were no fewer than twenty-six European men now living in the institution buildings, besides women and children ; every room in the Mackenzies' house was occupied.

When Morwe, the local chief, arrived with a band of soldiers and pitched his camp within sight of the institution, upon the old mission station of the Moffats, it looked as if there was no escape from an actual battle. Mackenzie, nevertheless, did not fear an attack at any time. The buildings were too solid and strong to be carried by storm by any number of natives so long as they did not possess big guns. And moreover he felt certain from his intimate knowledge of these people, that while they might have perpetrated a surprise massacre, the publicity which their plottings had attained was itself a most powerful deterrent. The real feeling of the best of their own people was against their plot, and against the infliction of any injury upon the missionaries. The chief danger was that some desperadoes might set fire to the thatched roofs in the dark of night. To prevent this all the men, including the native students, who all remained thoroughly loyal, were divided into groups and watched throughout the entire night at every point of danger.

An act of courage was performed by Mackenzie which astonished the natives. When one night some horsemen arrived from Kimberley, he saw at once that Morwe, whose scouts no doubt knew their number and the hour of their arrival, would conclude that reinforcements had been sent for ; Mackenzie resolved to walk over to Morwe's camp and state the facts. The traders and others were much alarmed and tried to dissuade him. But he went right into the enemy's camp, and announced that these men had come to see them and make sure of their safety. He long afterwards remembered vividly that on this adventure he saw what he had recognised on one or two occasions at Shoshong, the passionate lust for blood looking at him greedily from the eyes of native men.

In the end of June, Mackenzie wrote a letter to his sister-in-law, Miss Douglas, rapidly reviewing the situation in which he and his family found themselves :—

We are in a very critical state here.   I don't mean as to ourselves—although there are those who think that too.   But the people have gone absolutely mad on the subject of war and of cattle-lifting.   They are getting payment in kind.   A large English force is in Griqualand, and has completely scattered the rebels there : and we hear that 200 men (Volunteers) are on their way from the Fields to this place.   Their object is to secure the murderers of the Burnesses, and to get back cattle stolen, or an equivalent for them.   We are afraid they may come to blows.   The natives blustered greatly—while the English were far away.   But they are now changing their tone, and no doubt by and by will be very humble. I have done my very best for old Jantye the chief, or one of the chiefs of the district.   But it has been of no use, except that the old man has turned round upon me, and denied having written a certain letter to the English Government, in which he promised to do his best to recover stolen property, and to secure the perpetrators of the dreadful murder at Daniel's Kuil, some fifty miles from here.   They are all here in his country, and no one lays hold of them.

You know, dear Bessie, I would be the last to spread anything like an alarming report; but there is no doubt that there was a general movement in the native mind in Griqualand West and in the surrounding districts to rise upon the white men and to massacre them.   You need have no fear ; the thing has come to light.   But the traders are especially uneasy about it : and there are some twenty-six Europeans (men) now in the Institution : many of them having wives and children also.

I hope Col. Lanyon will turn up while the Volunteers are here, so that some permanent settlement may be come to. I could not have supposed that the Bechuanas could have been such fools as they have proved themselves in this matter. It is also particularly distressing to hear that more than

one of the murderers of the Burnesses is a baptised person
and member of this Kuruman church.   May good government be established in our midst and that speedily !

The students turn out very well in this trying time.   The
two eldest, who belong to this district, have particularly
exerted themselves to assist Jantye to do what is right.   But
the old man has bad sons ; so he promised to do the right
thing, but alas ! has not performed it.

We still mount guard every night ; the students have one
of the stations to guard.   We are afraid of fire, as the
Institution has a thatched roof—that is, every part except
the student's cottages, which are roofed with corrugated iron.

Had we been alone here, we should have gone on in our
usual way, but as there were a good many other missionaries
and others who considered themselves in danger (and perhaps
rightly), we could do nothing else than receive them here.
Ours is a place of refuge.   We are non-combatants, of course.
But we have quietly made every preparation against attack,
but do not expect any will be made.

In another letter written a little later to his friend,
the Rev. James Ross, he again comments upon the
situation in the following manner :—

I have been waiting with much anxiety just now to know
what settlement Sir Bartle Frere and the English Government
will make in Bechuanaland after the fighting is over.

Here, as in other parts of the world, a few restless spirits in
" high life " can throw a whole country into war and confusion.
The body of the Bechuana people did not, and do not, want
to fight with the English.   But others did ; and by and by
the foolish hope was more and more begotten generally in
the peoples' minds, that the English were being conquered
in some places, and could be conquered everywhere.   They
would not listen to me here.   Old Jantye did, but his son
Luka, the real ruler, laughed at my advice.   Our country is
now in the hands of the English.   We have an English
garrison here.   The reign of feudalism is over.   The question
is—What position are the body of the people, small farmers,
stock-grazers, etc., to occupy ?   I have written a memorandum
propounding a bold and new plan (in this country) viz., to
give the farming population back their farms as tenants
under the Queen.   This is in preference to the " location "

plan which keeps the natives together in a pseudo-feudal manner, professedly under the Queen, but really, as the last war has shown, under their own chiefs.

I always was somewhat sanguine. It would be a great pleasure to me, as I have no doubt it would be to you as an onlooker, to have something to do with the great work of showing practically *how* the coalition between the two races of Europeans and Africans can take place, with profit to both sides, and with the minimum of friction and heart-burning.

To treat an African other than as a nigger, destined to be shot down by the white man, is odious to some. A wounded commandant lying in my study, as a hospital, is of this opinion. "Make a boundary line, and drive them over it, and keep them over it, and don't care or heed what they do over that line, and among one another!" That is the old Colonial policy, which caused, with other factors, some half-a-dozen Kaffir wars. A step higher and better is the location one, the present policy of the Cape, but one concerning which there is considerable uneasiness and distrust among those who administer the Government. To conquer a country in Europe does not mean to drive out the body of the people out of the land; would not mean even to degrade the farmer class, to make practically serfs of them. But this is what it would mean here, if they don't change their policy.

Mind, I hope they will. We could not have a better man than Sir Bartle Frere, and Col. Lanyon is also a fair-minded man. We shall see.

There is still fighting to be done. And there will come what I consider the real tug of war, to devise a wise policy, get the right men to carry it out, and get the people to trust that you are sincere in what you are doing. Post time.—Our love to you all,   JOHN MACKENZIE.

Write soon. Don't be beat by a missionary.

When the Europeans at Kuruman took refuge in the institution-buildings in their alarm, they hardly realised the extent to which other people far from them became alarmed on their behalf. At Kimberley the excitement grew intense as rumours came flying across the country announcing that the missionary

and traders' families at Kuruman were cut off; and
later, that they had been attacked; and later still,
that they were all murdered "except Mackenzie, and
Mackenzie had fled." The coolest and wisest men
of course distrusted these rumours, but the situation
was serious enough to call, as it seemed, for energetic
action. Mr Ford was accepted by Col. Lanyon as
the organiser and leader of a band of volunteers, who
rode quickly across the country to Kuruman. They
had a sharp battle with the natives at Ko, before they
reached their destination, in which some of the white
men were killed, and Commandant Ford and his son,
along with others, were severely wounded. The
wounded men were taken to the institution-buildings
at Kuruman, and henceforth for months the home of
the Mackenzies and other rooms of the institution
were occupied by wounded soldiers, who were brought
thither from one fight after another. Poor Ford and
his son lay together in Mackenzie's study, and there
the young man died. At a later date, one of the
wounded bore the well-known name of Arnold, being
a grandson of Dr Arnold of Rugby, and brother of
Mrs Humphry Ward. He died of his wound, and
was laid to rest in the little mission cemetery.

The victory at Ko still further roused the hopes of
the wilder natives, and great confusion resulted. Many
of the rebels in Griqualand West, consisting of Kaal
Kaffirs and Griquas, had already fled northwards and
westwards through the Kuruman district, driving large
numbers of cattle which they had stolen from British
subjects; among their number were the murderers of
the Burnesses. They found a ready ally in Luka, the
bad son of Jantye, and he with them brought pressure
to bear upon many of the peace-loving Bechuanas,
forcing them into outward alliance with themselves.
Luka was very indignant when Mackenzie sent messengers from Kuruman amongst his followers, with

the broad and open announcement that they were
all blundering, and that it was his wish that all who
had no personal desire to fight should at once forsake
Luka and return to their homes. The result of this
message was a large decrease in the followers of Luka.
But the victory at Ko had produced another and
opposite effect, for it brought Colonel Lanyon and
Colonel Warren immediately upon the field. Without hesitation they now passed across the border
into South Bechuanaland with a sufficient force to
carry all before them. They came avowedly upon
a punitive expedition, and one which, according to
native law and custom, they had every right in the
circumstances to make. Their immediate purpose
of course was to deal with the Griqualand rebels and
the murderers of the Burnesses ; but as we shall see,
when they found themselves actually in Bechuanaland,
the extent of their operations spread from town to town
as the Griquas fled before them ; and their own task
was changed insensibly, and even beyond their purpose, from that of a punitive expedition, to that of
a peace-making and re-organising administration. As
Colonel Warren in the ensuing months pursued the
Griquas and other rebels from place to place, he
found that the spirit of war had laid hold of considerable numbers of the Bechuana people. Several
sharp engagements took place. It was the object
of Colonel Warren to be at once severe and kindly ;
severe towards the real objects of his pursuit, and
kindly towards all who submitted and brought their
pleas before him. It is safe to say that few soldiers
have ever succeeded so well as he did in carrying out
this double policy. Mackenzie appreciated his work
in the very warmest manner, and he was able to
point to it ever after as having produced upon the
native mind a profound sense of the fairness of the
Queen's representatives, who desired only to punish

wrong-doing, and not to rob anyone of life or property. The work of Colonel Warren went far to
confirm Mackenzie's faith in the effect of a direct
Imperial control of native territories. It was found
necessary to leave small bodies of border police at
various points, while the chief force was placed at
Batlaros, about ten miles from Kuruman, under
Major Stanley Lowe. This officer remained in the
country for about three years, and he too gained the
warm approval and goodwill of all who watched his
methods of dealing, alike with the natives on one
hand, and with the invading European farm-seekers
on the other.

From the first entrance of the British officers and
their men into Bechuanaland, the labours of Mackenzie
were enormously increased. He carried on, with very
little interruption, after November 1878, his full work
as tutor of the institution and pastor of the Kuruman
church and district. But in addition he was now forced
to undertake work of a political nature. It was inevitable. To him the white men and the natives alike
looked for information and advice. He received, sometimes daily, letters from Major Lowe and Colonel
Warren, advising him of their movements, informing
him concerning the natives with whom they dealt,
asking him to take various steps which seemed necessary in order to pacify hostile leaders, and to win
over wavering chiefs, and to investigate the evidence
for complaints which were brought before them for
adjustment. To him also the native chiefs came, or
sent messengers, stating their troubles, defending themselves from crimes of which they were accused, or
seeking some way of repentance.

This work received official recognition in the following manner. On August 1st, 1878, he addressed a letter
to Colonel Lanyon, as Administrator of the Province
of Griqualand West, and the invader of Bechuanaland,

frankly placing the circumstances of the country before him. It seemed to him that since the power of the chiefs was broken, and British officers were now, even against their wills, *de facto* rulers of the country, it was their duty to plan for the future. How were the natives to be treated under these altered circumstances? The two plans previously employed by Europeans in South Africa were described as follows :—The first says, " Having conquered the natives, deprive them of their country, and let them go elsewhere, or hire themselves out as labourers. This is the old plan, and it always led to war." The second plan, which had been adopted in recent years by the English Government, consists in assigning to every native tribe its own location, where, under the general protection of the English, they live practically very much as they did before. This plan, so largely employed in Natal and in some parts of the Transvaal, has its own peculiar and real dangers ; for, in the first place, it perpetuates the tribal or clannish manner of life, and, inasmuch as the population increases more rapidly under this system, and no effort is made to advance them in education and civilisation, a dark and dangerous heathenism is perpetuated in the very midst of a European country.

Mackenzie urged that a new plan was evidently necessary ; one which, on the one hand, would avoid permanent continuance of the tribe, and bring the people directly under British control, and, on the other hand, would not degrade a people who already were mounting visibly and steadily towards civilisation. He could point to the fact that already among the Bechuanas there were to be found a large number of men who constituted a farming class. These men led out water from their fountains, and annually raised a little wheat as well as Kaffir corn and " mealies." This work of irrigation meant, in some cases, much hard work. " Surely," he urged, " these men have a right to go on as farmers. Why should they be degraded as a class? They hold their fountains under some kind of tenure from their chiefs; let them continue to farm under such tenure as might be arranged." His proposal was, that to all natives who could show that they had actually tilled the soil, leases should be granted for a period of say ten years, during which they would pay rental, and at the end of which their standing could be carefully revised. An essential feature of the scheme was that not more than say six or eight huts should be built on one farm. This would effectually prevent an ambitious chief from attempting to collect a large number of poorer or weaker people around him as his vassals or slaves. It would thus break down the tribal system, without injustice or hardship. There was another essential feature of the scheme, that the leases should be unsaleable, which would protect the tenant-farmer class of natives from being imposed upon and robbed by clever and unscrupulous land-jobbers and land-agents. Practically Mackenzie said, Treat these people as children who need paternal care; watch over them until they are further educated and able, in ten or twenty years, to manage their own affairs without the immediate tutelage of a white officer. At the same time he made it clear, now and later, with great frequency and carefulness, that he was no indiscriminate lover of the blacks, that he did not seek to pet them or treat them with undue consideration, as he was afterwards so often accused of doing. He insisted, on the contrary, that every native who proved himself unworthy of his lease should be ejected. "Let him sink to his own level among the inferior labouring class." What this missionary stood for and demanded was simply justice, bare justice to a class whom he and many others had laboured for many years to uplift, and who were being visibly and confessedly raised to a higher rank in life.   As he pointed out in a later communication, the reports upon the state of Bechuanaland, made by unbiassed and careful English officers, showed that many of the natives were now living, " practically much after the mode of the Dutch Boers."   There can be no doubt that many of these natives were beginning to read and to write, to plough the land, and to prepare their cattle for the market, which means that they were as civilised as many of those ignorant Boers and other Europeans who rushed in upon their lands and drove them from possession of their farms.   And they were very often better men. The only conceivable reason that could be given in justification of this process of civilising South Africa by robbing the natives of their farms, was that the one set of men were white and the others black. Mackenzie claimed that this reason ought henceforth to be condemned by the British Government, and its operation made impossible by a new departure in policy.   And yet he only claimed justice, bare justice, for men who occupied or owned farm lands, diligently tilling the soil and disposing of the produce in a civilised manner.

Colonel Lanyon, while he was in Kuruman, held many long and earnest conversations with Mackenzie about these matters.   He, of course, urged against the assumption of the government of South Bechuanaland, that the British people disliked any more annexation, and that many of them were sensitive about interfering with the inherited rights of the native chiefs and tribes. To this the convincing answer was given in a twofold manner.   Bechuanaland was not and never would be fully occupied by the natives themselves ; there was abundant room for both Europeans and natives ; but, on the other hand, " the word annexation is misleading. The real movement is that which is happening before our eyes, in the country, in the spread of the whites.

That *is* the annexation!" What therefore he con-
tended for was simply the formal and authoritative
regulation of an annexation which neither native
chiefs nor European governments could put a stop
to, which was "happening before our eyes." No way
could be found which would more certainly dispossess
the natives of their land than for England to refuse to
occupy the country. No way could be found more
certainly to conserve the rights of the natives and to
uplift them than by sending British officers and magistrates to see that bare justice was done between the
white man and black.

The result of these communications and conversations was that in September 1878, Colonel Lanyon
asked Mackenzie to aid the Government by acting as
its agent in Bechuanaland. The following was his
reply :—

With reference to your proposal or inquiry as to my
assisting the Government in the settlement of the country,
I have given the matter my best consideration ; and the
following are some of my thoughts on the subject.

If there is one name more hateful than another to a native
of this part of the country, it is that of agent, "ah-gent" as
they call it. For a missionary to leave his work and become
an "agent," would be to descend to another level in native
eyes ; he might be better or worse than other agents, he
would not be regarded by them any longer as their fast and
trusted friend.

But, if I understand you aright, you do not propose that I
should appear to the people in any other capacity than their
missionary and trusted adviser. If this is so, I am willing to
place whatever influence, etc., I may have, at the service of
the Government. Indeed the work which you sketch — of
carrying through a plan by which the Bechuanas can become
accustomed to British rule and, at the same time, go on
making progress in agriculture, etc.—is, perhaps, at present,
the most urgent undertaking connected with the welfare of
the natives. Once done well in one district, this work could
be copied elsewhere with local modifications. Tribes in the
interior would scrutinize it, and I hope, see its advantages.

Now, speaking frankly, I should be glad and thankful to be connected with such a work ; and feel that thus I should be doing a permanent service to both Europeans and Bechuanas. You see that I have full confidence in the sincerity and the good intentions of the Government, that it is their wish that the Bechuanas should take root in the country and occupy it.

Were it possible that this could be changed and that retrogressive measures should be adopted, with the view of driving the natives out of the country, the Government could, of course, expect no assistance from me in carrying out such a policy.

If then Sir Bartle Frere as representing the Imperial Government, joins in your view that while discharging my work as Tutor in the Moffat Institution, etc., I could be of use to the Government in the present peculiar state of affairs in Bechuanaland, I am willing to meet these views and do my best in the service of the Government. The fact that the best and most influential young men among the Bechuanas are under my care as Tutor and that native ministers who have been in the Institution, are anxious to keep up intercourse with their old teacher, are all means which might be used for the good of the people.

(You will remember that Matsau, our minister at Mankoroane's, of his own accord rode through on horseback, to be with us in our difficulties when shut up here,—as soon as he arrived, quietly taking his turn as sentry, etc., as if he were still a student.)

Stipulating that I must not be called an " agent " (ah-gent) —that the duties expected of me will be such as could be performed along with those I am now discharging, and that the work to be done will be such as is sketched in your letter ; generally to induce the Bechuanas to settle in Bechuanaland, under the Queen, in some such way as in the scheme I had the honour to forward to your Excellency some time ago—I am willing to accede to your proposal, if it is deemed advisable, and to give the Imperial Government my hearty and earnest service.

I thank you for the compliment involved in the proposal ; and pray that if the work is given me to do you may have no cause to regret that you made it.

From this time forward, for about eighteen months semi-officially, and down to April 1882, actually,

Mackenzie carried on the work thus undertaken at the instance of the Administrator of Griqualand West. As he afterwards explained to the Directors of the Society, he never allowed this to interfere with his distinctively spiritual and educational responsibilities ; although he felt in his heart of hearts that it was work which some one must undertake, if the conditions were to be preserved under which the mission work in Bechuanaland could be most successfully carried on. Moreover, he found that far from interfering with his influence as a missionary, the kind of work which he did enormously increased it ; for the natives now saw in him a man, who not only preached the Gospel and not only advised faith in the English Government, but who himself acted effectively and authoritatively as their friend. Wherever he saw wrong-doing, in white or black, he rebuked it ; wherever a black man robbed a white farmer, or a white land-grabber coerced a black farmer, he stood unflinchingly for justice and righteousness. Such work could only raise the esteem of the natives for the missionaries and for the religion which they professed. It also carried Mackenzie's name over the Transvaal, where the true significance of his policy was well understood, far better indeed than at Government House, Cape Town, or in London ; and where the ultimate issues of that policy were alike foreseen and feared. Only let Mackenzie do what he was now doing for another ten years, and Bechuana farmers in South Bechuanaland would be as firmly established in their ownership, and as prosperous, as most Boer farmers were then in the Transvaal.

It should be added that for all the work which he thus performed Mackenzie never asked, and was never offered, any compensation by the Government which he served.

CHAPTER IX

THE hard work of 1878 extended into 1879. In this year the number of students was considerably increased, and at the same time the political work was multiplied. Mackenzie's devotion to missionary labours was not curtailed by the continual consultations which went on between him and native chiefs and farmers on the one hand, and British officers on the other. He continued to discuss, of course, the political problems of the situation both in letters and in conversation with Colonel Lanyon and Colonel Warren. He also forwarded to Sir Bartle Frere a memorandum containing a certain plan for the government of Bechuanaland, which he had been gradually working out in his own mind, and which the experience of these months, as well as his complete knowledge of native laws and the native mind, proved to be thoroughly practical. This scheme was described by him in many various forms at various times; but nowhere with more clearness than in a letter which he drafted for the Bechuanaland District Committee of missionaries, which they adopted and sent to Sir Bartle Frere. They did this in answer to a request from His Excellency for suggestions regarding measures which they thought calculated to promote the advancement of the races amongst which they laboured. Before giving this document, it may be well to emphasise the point that the main source of trouble among South African races had ever been the question of land tenure. From the days when the first Dutchmen began to graze their herds and dig their gardens on the lands around Cape Town, which Hottentots had previously used as their own, down to the days when Boer commandoes picked quarrels with native chiefs, then fought them and seized their fountains, dispossessing them of their lands, and making it illegal henceforth that one of their colour should own land in his own country ; or when English land-jobbers made natives drunk and got them to sign away their property under the influence of liquor, or drew up deeds of sale in English, which they professed to translate into Sechuana, and persuaded the native to sign, under the impression that they were deeds of another kind—these poor, ignorant, and yet often intelligent, sometimes hardworking and trustworthy, men, had been steadily deprived of all rights, and had been made practically serfs under the white man's rule. Their original land system was a simple form of feudalism. The land belonged to the people, the chief assigned to each his fountain and his garden ; but land, according to native law, was inalienable, and all deeds of sale to white men were therefore in fact illegal, and all to whom land was assigned must render military service to their chief. But this system was now broken down, for the chiefs had lost their power, and the strongest took what he desired, and there was no law.

The method which Mackenzie proposed was intended to make the transition, from the broken-down feudalism to the European method of private ownership in land, entirely safe for those native peoples. But let this be described in the language adopted by the missionaries of Bechuanaland, and communicated by them to Sir Bartle Frere. The following is part of their document :—

I. Our first suggestion has reference to the land. We submit that both Griquas and Bechuanas stand on an entirely different platform as to civilisation from that occupied by Kaal Kaffirs or by Zulus. It is no exaggeration to say, and your officers who have made acquaintance with the country, will bear us out in the assertion, that the population affected by the war in and around Griqualand West, have attained a respectable position as to civilization.

II. In their dwellings, in their gardens and corn-fields, in their possessions, in their clothing and personal habits, you have infallible evidence that the people have long left the ranks of heathen. Let the spoils of Langberg, Gamoperi, Takong, etc., testify whether or not the English were fighting with people who had a right to be called civilized.

III. Many of the fountains of South Bechuanaland have already been opened up and led out by the people.   Indeed, Bechuana society had reached an interesting crisis before the war. The people, who were devoting more and more of their time to farming, were constantly harassed by their chiefs, who wished them to live together in the town in the old style. Missionaries advised the chiefs to yield to the inevitable and sanction this farming, or scattered life, among their people, with the understanding that they all came in from their farms once or twice in a year.

IV. Having then to deal with people in this condition, we respectfully submit that they ought to meet with treatment corresponding to their degree of advancement, and not having reference to their colour.

V. Those who have made themselves acquainted with the conditions of these people, prior to the advent of missionaries among them, and contrast that with their position in 1878, will be encouraged with reference to their capability of improvement.   Indeed, such a glance at the past of the people would encourage a just mind to hold out to them inducements to follow the same peaceful and industrious manner of life which has been characteristic of many of the people.

VI. Proceeding upon the supposition that the country comes under the English Government, we would respectfully suggest—

    1. That, except in special cases, such as chiefs or other men who have made themselves obnoxious, natives who have been in occupation of an irrigable garden or small farm, be placed in similar circumstances under the English Government.

    2. We do not recommend that saleable title-deeds to farms be given to Bechuanas. The land has

hitherto belonged to the tribe as such, and has
been unsaleable. We would propose that a similar
law should still obtain ; that is, that natives who
have irrigable gardens or small farms should
obtain a lease of them under the English
Government for a certain number of years, say
ten ; and that under this lease they pay an
annual rental to Government as landlord.
That it be understood that there shall be no
eviction at the end of the lease, if the tenant
has conducted himself well, and has cultivated
his ground in an industrious manner ; but that if
the opposite has been the case, if the farm has been
neglected, or criminal charges have been preferred
against the occupant, that the officer of Government appointed to such questions have the
power to refuse a renewal of the lease, should
he on the whole decide to do so.

VII. The Committee anticipate that a plan of this
description would effectually obviate the numerous and
serious difficulties which immediately arise, when speculators
in land are allowed free course to act upon native landowners. In the latter case the native is induced to sell his
farm—sometimes by presenting a long bill and threatening
imprisonment ; often while under the influence of strong
drink, and unaware what he is about.

VIII. Some of the Bechuanas with whom members of the
Committee are acquainted have expended considerable
labour in leading out water furrows. In one case which
occurred a short time before the outbreak, the native farmer
received labourers from all quarters to work at his furrow.
He was able to get them and to keep them, during the time
when the Moffat Institution buildings were in progress. He
paid with money and with stock. Such men would be seen
to get on well under the English Government. Others of
equal enterprise, but of less means, would no doubt avail
themselves of government loans for such work, as soon as
they understood thoroughly what that meant.

IX. It is of great consequence that some such policy as
that here indicated should be carried out in South Bechuanaland, for other reasons than those connected with its own
inhabitants. The tribes in the interior are watching with
the closest interest the steps which Government will take

with reference to land. . . . If the tribes in the south are allowed to remain in virtual possession of their land under the British Government, complications will be less likely in the interior. The people will know that private property will be respected; as for the waning of the power of their chiefs, they will get accustomed to that also, provided a good position is secured to them as respectable subjects of the Queen.

X. The Committee would strongly recommend to Your Excellency that the canteens be closed, which have been open for trade among the natives of Griqualand West. The most respectable Griquas petitioned Your Excellency to this effect some time ago. No ruler would willingly allow to be opened a canteen among such a people as the Griquas and Bechuanas—provided that his object was the highest good of the people themselves. Canteens are unmitigated curses to all connected with them, and in reality frustrate the highest work of a good government. The Committee would anticipate the best results from shutting up "Canteens" throughout the country, and trust it may speedily take place.

XI. Into the detail of the scheme for the government of these people we do not enter. It is evident that the success of this or any other scheme would greatly depend on the character of those to whom working out will be entrusted.

It is one thing to get men accustomed to treat all natives as "niggers" or "black fellows," with indiscriminate contempt and carelessness. It is quite another thing to get a magistrate who would be filled with the idea that as a servant of the Queen he would be bound to treat all her subjects with justice, and to show courtesy to all.

Sir Bartle Frere, who had already been in communication with Mackenzie, was profoundly impressed with the wisdom of the plan now submitted to him. On his return from the Transvaal, *viâ* Kimberley, he invited his missionary-correspondent to meet him at the latter place, where he expected also to confer with Colonel Warren. There, then, Mackenzie, for the first time, met face to face one whom he had long admired and with whom he formed, from that date, a warm friendship. Sir Bartle Frere decided that the scheme

submitted to him ought to be at once adopted and
put into operation ; but he saw that it would require
to be begun by one who understood the entire situation, and in whom the natives would have deep
confidence.   He accordingly proposed that Mackenzie
himself should accept the position of Commissioner
for South Bechuanaland, at a salary of £1000 per
annum, that he should have under him a number of
magistrates, and be supported by a body of mounted
police, probably to number about 200.   If Mackenzie
agreed to undertake this work, a proclamation was at
once to be drawn up, and, with the consent of Her
Majesty, was to be issued, announcing that the region
concerned would henceforth be treated as a " Territory "
under the British crown.   To the proposals thus made
to him the man who twenty years before had been
ordained to the life of a missionary had only one
answer to give, and it was given firmly and decisively.
He could not give up his life-work, even to undertake
a position of such importance as this.

So anxious was the High Commissioner to secure
the services of Mackenzie, that another plan was proposed which seemed to the latter both feasible and
consonant with his life-purpose.   According to this
plan, Mackenzie was to be appointed as native commissioner, with the same salary as before, and with a
group of magistrates under him, it being understood
that he was to continue as missionary and Tutor at
Kuruman, giving only part of his time to the service
of the Government.   It was further understood that
his civil appointment would only continue for two or
three years, until the whole of the region affected had
been brought under the new system of law, and British
officers had become accustomed to its working and
had gained the confidence of native chiefs and their
peoples.   Mackenzie agreed to this proposal, with the
understanding that it must be submitted for ratifica-

tion to the Directors of his Society in London, so far as his part was concerned, as well as to the Colonial Office, so far as the Imperial aspect was concerned. So anxious was Sir Bartle Frere to see this plan adopted that he wrote a letter to the Directors, earnestly requesting them to allow their missionary to do this special work for the sake of the country in which their missions were placed. Mackenzie, on June 3rd, 1879, wrote to the Directors, describing the whole situation and the proposal which Sir Bartle Frere had made :—

As a loyal agent of the L. M. S. I do not wish to embark in anything, even for the direct benefit and elevation of the people, without laying the matter before the Directors. What I do, brethren, for the pacification and settlement of the natives in the country, I would do in the same spirit in which I would doctor their bodies, or perform for them any of those numerous kindnesses which it is in the power of a missionary to do. It is my opinion that, *as a missionary,* I could do the work from a vantage-ground—a work which is evidently for the general benefit. It will probably be accomplished in, say, two years, when it is to be hoped there will be a population here thankful, not only for the spiritual instruction they have received from the L. M. S., but also for the scheme of settlement devised and executed for their benefit by one of your agents. I am aware that by acting as I propose to do I am stretching the letter of some of our rules ; but I think the position in which I am placed is quite an exception, and I trust the broad-minded Board of Directors of the London Missionary Society will sanction the present endeavour to elevate and establish a people who have already received from them so many blessings. Of course, I am aware that in undertaking these duties I entail upon myself a great amount of hard work ; and it is possible that health, or ability, or something, may give way. In the meantime I am not at all afraid ; but hope that at this crisis in the people's history, with God's good hand upon me, I may be able, along with my usual duties, to accomplish this special and incidental work. In concluding this necessarily egotistical letter I beg the Directors to understand, that my promise to the High Commissioner is to give three or four hours per day to the settlement and government of the country. It is not intended that I shall have judicial functions; there are four English magistrates to be appointed for this work. The administrative work which I am asked to do will be of great consequence at the commencement of English rule over Bechuanaland; but when the vessel has passed the first sandbanks, the special pilot will, I hope, be no longer needed.

The reply to this letter, from the Directors, consisted of further inquiries in a series of questions which called forth from Mackenzie, on September 25, 1879, a very full set of corresponding explanations. The most important of these are as follows:—

KURUMAN *via* KIMBERLEY,
25th Sept. 1879.

I. How has the land been acquired by the Government?

The country has been partly conquered and partly ceded to the English Government by its chiefs. It is the intention, I believe, to proclaim South Bechuanaland as under British "protection"; so that as a "territory" the unbending and letter formality of English law might not at once be brought to bear upon the natives.

II. Opinion and feeling of natives on annexation.

The more intelligent part of the people of Kuruman were long ago in favour of being under such an equal law as they understood that of the English to be. . . . In my opinion, the common people and the vassals are rejoiced at the advent of the English rule.

I am in correspondence with chiefs of the surrounding tribes. They are undoubtedly uneasy; the best people are anxious to have a settlement; the bad people endeavouring to spread evil reports. *There is one cause of uneasiness*—what is to be done with the land? So far as the governing of the country is concerned, the chiefs and the people have advisedly given themselves up to the English Government, but they are anxious as to the fountains; the present delay and apparent hesitation detract so far from the English character and position.

III. Are the natives hostile or suspicious towards the missionaries?

So far as I am concerned I never regarded the natives as hostile to missionaries. It is a fact that in their late conceited

uprising the word was given by the natives on the Orange
River that not even missionaries were to be spared; but that
order was given with the idea of making "siccar" or thorough,
rather than on account of anything charged against the
missionaries. . . .

Under this query I may mention that, when I came here
in 1876, the *work* which I had to do in building the Institution
was very unpopular. . . . There is now the best feeling towards
us in the Bechuana mind. I have received spontaneous
messages from chiefs and head-men living at a distance, in
which they warmly thanked me for what I was doing in the
country for peace, and for the establishment of the people.

IV. Is it understood that you will be a Government official
with a salary? What will be your probable work? How far
have you been doing this work up to the present time?

I should be a Government official, and have a salary.
From its point of view, the Government desires more than
an outside helper—one on whom they can rely. Should
the sanction of the Home Government be obtained, it was
intended to proclaim the ceded and conquered territory as
far as the Molopo river. This country was to be divided
into four magistracies: one at Taungs; another at Sehube
(East Molopo); a third at Morokweng (West Molopo district), and the fourth, who should also be a local judge, and
review cases of appeal, was to be stationed at Kuruman, or
rather Batlaros. In the meantime, these magistrates were to
be captains of police composed of Europeans and trustworthy
natives. All this was to be under a "Commissioner" (or
whatever he might be called), who in turn would be under
the Administrator of Griqualand West and the High Commissioner at the Cape. This office of Commissioner is the
one offered to me; and the one I have accepted in the
manner and to the extent related to you in my former letter
on the subject. The territory from the Molopo to Griqualand West, and from the Hart river to the Kalahari, would
be under my care. The office would be purely administrative; the judicial functions would be performed by the
magistrates and judge, assisted in the first instance, and no
doubt for years, by the various native chiefs; and, if my
policy were carried out, I should consent to be held in
the usual sense responsible for the peace, government and
progress of the territory. For about a year this work has
been virtually in my hands, having been placed there by the

Administrator and the Acting Administrator of Griqualand West.

Some important movements and many little matters, which taken together make a policy, have been directed by me, and have been carried out by the officers and men of the Border Police on the one hand, and by native chiefs, trustworthy native messengers, etc., on the other. But I think it right to inform you that, although such has been my position up to the time I write this letter, I have never received a penny of Government money. On the contrary, although I have had severe losses in cattle and sheep while the disturbances were going on, and captured cattle are constantly passing the station, I positively declined repeated invitations to put in my claim for compensation. So that I am not beholden to the Government in the way of personal obligation; the services which I have been able to render have been, from the Government point of view, worth a good deal. I may mention also that I had made the promise I gave at Kimberley before the question of salary came up. The salary offered to me as Commissioner is £1000 per annum.

VII. How will taking this work affect your missionary position and influence, and that of other missionaries?

The circumstances of the Batlaping as to the land question are such that my own position and influence as a missionary, and indirectly that of my brethren, would be strengthened and increased were I able to carry through the policy as to land, which I have already explained to the Directors. It would be regarded, and justly, as a case of the missionary coming to the assistance of the native and getting for him his rights.

VIII. If released from missionary connection and work for say two years could you at the end of that time resume our work?

So far as my judgment goes, my work as Commissioner would be far from lowering me in the natives' eyes; what would tend to lower me would be the statement which *the enemies of that work* would delight to spread " He is no longer a missionary now, he is just like the other Government servants now." If that could be said with absolute truth it would tell against me so far—in cases in which no explanation would be given as to *why* I had left the Society; and the people who are unfavourable to the natives and unfavourable to their rising in society would no doubt keep back all

explanation which would be to my honour. It is my idea
that I could best do the work as a missionary.

IX. How am I to do it—how can I give three or four
hours daily to this work without sacrificing the interests of
the Society, in the duties laid upon me by the Directors?

By downright hard work. This is the only explanation I
can give. I may however add that having, as Tutor, to do
with students who have no literature to which they can refer
after leaving the Seminary, I made it a point at Shoshong to
write out my lessons to them in every department, which
they copied for after reference. Although one sees reason
to add to or improve such lessons, they are now extant, and
do not need to be re-written. I *could not* have done the
work which I accomplished during the first years of my
teaching at Shoshong, with the political work which I have
done for the people here. The thing would have been
simply impossible. But as at Shoshong I was the tutor and
the missionary during the day, easy of access to everybody
and anybody, while at night I was the student and lecture-
writer; so here by day work and night work I manage to
pull along.

There are some duties here which have devolved on me
from the force of circumstances, and not by any appointment of the Directors—for instance the superintendence of the
agricultural work connected with the Institution gardens
which are 13 in number. I believe that I have shown that
I am willing to do *anything* for the Society; and in acting
as builder of the Institution I was doing work as much outside pure missionary work as is the agricultural department
still in my hands, or that of Political Commissioner which I
am also transacting.

I take it for granted that those who freely mingle in
politics at home—having before them their great and worthy
aims—must have sympathy with the missionary who is not
afraid to go, as it were, bodily into the conflict of frontier
society, addressed now by the European, now by the
native; now by the chiefs and head-men, then by th
Colonial Government; who strives to have a kindly and
straightforward and helpful word for men all round.

Some English dealers will cheat and take advantage of
legal forms unknown to the native; almost all the natives
are ignorant and therefore suspicious, and liable to go off at
a tangent under a misapprehension. In some cases the

missionary sees all this take place, deploring that it is not
his work to interfere, contenting himself in a paragraph in
his next communication to the Directors, in which he describes his own trials and the peoples' sufferings from
the abandoned white men or from the misgovernment
and misconduct of European officials.   In other cases the
missionary is a man, at whatever station placed, to whom
men of all opinions and colours go for his advice and
assistance when they need it; thus called upon he is not
afraid to go into their grievances and difficulties, exposing
now the white and then the black man; for it is *not* the case
that the fault is always on one side.   In this case the missionary becomes a power in the country.   Europeans seek
his advice and assistance, chiefs and people with a real
grievance know where they have a friend.

Perhaps it will simplify matters, if I now formally request
the Directors to be allowed to accept of this Commissionership while retaining the position which I at present hold as
an agent of the L.M.S.   *During the past year I have done
the work of this office :* no one has hinted to me that I have
neglected any of my duties as Tutor, etc.   As practical men,
therefore, the Directors will, I hope, hold this to be a con-
clusive answer to *theoretical* objections or *surmises* of evil.
The whole case is on the face of it exceptional ; and will no
doubt be thus judged by the Directors.

The Commissionership means the social establishment of
the people in civilized life ; the Tutorship means their moral
and spiritual development and elevation.   Solemnly, I do
not know which is the greater work.   I aspire to the honour
of doing both ; and say to the Directors, let it be tried ; if I
fail either as Commissioner or as Tutor it will soon be
apparent.   Pray that in this and all our affairs the will of
the Lord may be done by you and by me.

During the ensuing months, while the Directors in
London were considering this proposal and its effect
upon the future of their missions in South Africa,
Mackenzie continued his work as the adviser of the
representatives of the Queen in Bechuanaland, and
was indeed practically carrying on the work, as he
had been doing for more than a year, to which it was
proposed now formally to appoint him.   He wrote

various important letters and memoranda to the High
Commissioner, to Colonel Lanyon and Colonel Warren,
and also to the Colonial Secretary in London, discussing the various aspects of the Bechuanaland
problem as they presented themselves month after
month. Towards the end of the year 1879, he was
alarmed to find that the authorities had begun to
discuss the withdrawal of the police from Bechuanaland,
and that their number was being then actually reduced.
It has been urged that the British could do nothing
else than withdraw at this time, because they had gone
into Bechuanaland on a punitive expedition against
robbers and murderers. They had, indeed, in order to
accomplish this, been forced into relations of various
kinds with the native chiefs at whose towns the
fugitives took refuge, and, in order to allay the excitement which had broken out, they incidentally
found it necessary to settle some quarrels over
rights of property. But the whole matter, it is said,
must be viewed as a military operation which gave
the Bechuanas no right to expect that the British
would remain, nor gave the latter the right to remain
without a formal proclamation from the Queen.
Whether or not this be the strict letter of the law,
the substantial facts seemed to Mackenzie, and must
seem probably to all fair-minded people, to put
another interpretation upon the responsibility of
Great Britain at that time and in that region. The
effect of the military expedition had been to shatter
finally all semblance of native rule. There was not
to be found in South Bechuanaland a single native
chief who now had as much authority over his own
people as before the advent of Colonel Lanyon and
his volunteers. The successful military operations of
Colonel Warren, and above all his patient and humane
and kindly and wise dealings with the natives in
settlement of their difficulties and in prevention of

various attempts of white men to rob them of their lands, had made him and his officers practically rulers of the land as representatives of the Queen, and had won the hearts of the people. Already, in 1878, Mackenzie had written urgently to Colonel Lanyon to say, "I repeat it, we are entirely without government, and no temporary chastisement will meet our case." Colonel Lanyon afterwards found this to be the case, for he himself wrote to Sir Bartle Frere,[1] saying :—

My own opinion is that Mankoroane is powerless here for good or evil, and is, like all other Batlaping chiefs, a mere puppet in the hands of the mischievous natives of his tribe. In either case, however, it would seem desirable that some steps should be taken for placing those territories hitherto under his charge under some more powerful government, which would naturally be that of Her Majesty.

And Colonel Warren also discovered gradually how complete the disintegration of native government had become. The following extracts will illustrate his impressions :—

Makolokue states that he has been unable to control his people ; that some of them went down to fight at Campbell in June. . . . I am endeavouring to make such arrangements as will allow all the people who are quiet to go on with their plowing at once, so as to prevent a famine in the land.[2]

And again,

Kuruman : I have issued a notice that while there is military occupation in those parts, and pending the just and lawful settlement of the land claims, no sales of land or houses are to take place without the sanction of the officer commanding the field force. This is to prevent land-jobbers coming up here to buy up all the land at low prices, and to ruin the natives, as they have been ruined in Griqualand West.[3]

Mackenzie gives an interesting illustration of the

---

[1] C. 2454, p. 27.   [2] C. 2222, pp. 111-113.   [3] C. 2252, p. 3.

extent to which this disorganisation had struck the natives themselves :—

One of my messengers, an important member of Sechele's tribe (in North Bechuanaland), where the chief is a chief, was very much struck with the absence of all government or supremacy of anyone at Morokweng. The discussion in the khotla, or court yard, was not decorous or respectable, according to this native messenger's idea. Everyone spoke at the same time, people turned their backs on their chief, shouted and talked while their superiors were trying to make themselves heard.

The chiefs not only knew that they had lost control of their people, but knew also that the best blessing which could come to them would be annexation to the Queen's dominions. Of eight important chiefs with whom Colonel Warren came into personal communication, and most of whom he personally visited, no less than six sent in petitions praying to be taken under the government of Queen Victoria! Obviously Great Britain was now in possession and in actual control of South Bechuanaland, and both whites and blacks took it for granted that no retreat was possible. To all alike it appeared clear that the British Government had come under moral obligations to carry on what she had begun, and that now to withdraw would be practically a criminal course. Colonel Lanyon put the matter in a nutshell when he expressed his opinion to Colonel Warren :—"One thing is, I think, quite certain, that it will never be left again to the state of anarchy which prevailed there before." While then Bechuanaland had been occupied for military purposes, it was evident that the occupation had resulted in a displacement of the pre-existing native administration and the substitution, for the time being, of British authority in the country. The dismay of all concerned was very great, therefore, when it began to be whispered that the British police were being withdrawn before any arrangement was made for the government of the land.   Mackenzie, in December 1879, addressed a strong protest to the High Commissioner as well as to the Administrator of Griqualand West.   In this protest he described the anarchy of the country so far as the chiefs were concerned, and their dependence upon the presence of Major Stanley Lowe and his body of police.   He urged that a withdrawal without explanation would make matters worse than they were before, especially since the Imperial Government had not yet decided what to do with the territory.   When this decision was reached, and if it led to the abandonment of the country, the fact ought to be publicly announced and explained to the native chiefs and peoples.   At present the native chiefs were at a loss to account for all this delay in the settlement of their country.   Nevertheless, had it not been for the encroachments above referred to, both chiefs and people were willing to believe that all would come right, especially in connection with the "provisional" acceptance of the surrender of their lands by Colonel Warren.   To them the word "provisional" had no meaning when they saw power actually lost by them and actually exercised by others.   Their chieftains' authority was lost, not "provisionally" but absolutely and for ever, their farms were being grabbed, not "provisionally," but finally and unconditionally.

In his letter to Sir Bartle Frere, Mackenzie gives fresh instances of the cruelty and the absolutely unprincipled methods which Europeans, most of whom were Dutchmen, employed, in order to obtain possession of the most desirable farm lands in the country.

Later in the same month (December 1879), Mackenzie addressed an important letter both to Sir Bartle Frere and Sir Garnet Wolseley, who were both High Commissioners in South Africa at

the same time, according to that curious arrangement which paralysed the former, and made the
subsequent war of the Boer revolutionaries in the
Transvaal shorter and easier.   In this letter he discusses the entire subject of the relations of Great
Britain to South Africa, and especially to its native
territories.   At this point only the following extracts can be given, but they will suffice to show
how practically he was studying the problem, not
only as it affected Bechuanaland, but all other parts
of the country as well.   For years Mackenzie had
been brooding, dreaming, praying, working over
"South Africa" or "Austral Africa," from Cape
Town to the Zambesi, and from ocean to ocean.
The letter discusses some matters which have now
passed beyond discussion, but the following sections
refer to problems which are still very much alive,
and for that reason are selected here :—

In arranging for that "fresh departure," which ought to be
the sequel of recent complications, disturbances, and wars,
in various parts of Southern Africa, it is of the utmost importance not only to know the widely different character and
wants of the races with whom the English Government has
to deal, but to profit by the experience of the past, and to
have a carefully considered scheme for the future, eschewing
all haphazard or improvised policy.

Responsibility is thrust upon the English Government in
Southern Africa.   It is impossible to avoid it, except by
abandoning the country altogether.   The northward progress of Europeans in South Africa has been steady and
rapid in the past.   It takes place with the consent, and at
the request, of the native chiefs and people, who welcome
missionaries, travellers, and traders.   They have a keen
sense of the benefits flowing to themselves from this contact.   But the government of the country by the chiefs
becomes more and more difficult after the advent of the
Europeans in numbers.   The new wine of European
energy, persistence, and sometimes recklessness, cannot be
contained in the old skin bottles of tribal laws and
customs.   In several instances the chiefs have recognised

this fact, and have asked for the help of the English Government. Such a reasonable request has usually been refused. The Government could not consent to "Annexation," or "increase of responsibility." The new wine and the old bottles are therefore let alone by the Government. Thieving, murder, war, inevitably follow; thousands, it may be millions, of pounds are now spent; precious lives are lost; recriminations take place as to who was to blame, as between political parties both in England and the Cape Colony, and occasionally as between the Home Government and their officers in South Africa.

Now the blame lies with the English Government, to the extent that England has no South African policy worthy of the name; and in so far as it has one, viz., to let things alone as they are, and to shrink from responsibility. It is worse than no policy, for it is practically impossible, while it so far hampers the Government in South Africa as to cause them to do things in a shuffling and uncertain manner.

Will Your Excellency allow me to explain that, coming to this country as a missionary in 1858, my great desire, apart from the spiritual aspect of my work, was to help to elevate some tribe of Africans, so that they could endure the shock of meeting the wave of European cultivation, etc., etc., and not be driven away by it? Close and careful study of the subject led me in the course of time to see ,that politically it would be impossible for my wish to be fulfilled; the constituent elements of the tribes would remain, but the tribal laws and policy were destined to pass away. I noticed that events were taking place rapidly in South Africa a hundred-fold more rapidly than similar events had moved forward in the history of Europe; events over which no government had control, but which occurred with such rapidity and force, that they may be regarded as "a law," or as the "will of God." And in this light I have come to regard the mingling of the races in Southern Africa. I believe that it is the will of God that it should take place. No one can prevent it. The question therefore comes to be, How is it to be regulated, and by whom?

Having made the subject a special study for many years, I beg to offer a few remarks upon it at the present crisis. Sincerely wishing well to all classes and colours in this country, I desire that English rule should be gradually, and with due caution, extended over the native tribes; and that it

should be done in such a manner that England should regard
her work in this land with pleasure and with pride, instead of
impatient bewilderment, as at present.

BECHUANALAND

The Bechuanas are like the Basutos, but divided into
small tribes, and inhabiting a less generous country than
Basutoland.   They have made considerable progress in Christianity and civilization, and the wealthy men are living after
the fashion of farmers or Boers—having opened up fountains
and led out the water for the irrigation of their lands.   The
poorer men are good servants.   There are no labourers or
herds so much thought of in the Colonies as the Maccatees
or Mantatees, as the Colonists call Bechuanas.

The chiefs are favourably impressed towards the English
Government in the southern districts.   Those who were disaffected have been subdued, and their country is still
occupied.   Almost all the Bechuana chiefs have been in
correspondence with the English Government, and have expressed at some time the desire to be under English
protection.

Their ignorance of the English language and of our
English laws and modes of procedure render it undesirable
that they should at once be brought entirely under their
unbending, and often to a native, incomprehensible routine.
To step at once from native to English law, as was recently
done in Griqualand West, would be unfair to the Bechuanas
and would have the effect of placing them at the mercy of
designing men.

PROPOSED TERRITORY SYSTEM

It is well known that in the political economy of the
United States, a "Territory" is a state in embryo.   I propose that in accomplishing a nobler and more Christian
work in Southern Africa than Europeans have placed before
themselves in America, England should institute a provisional government over tribes or districts conquered or
ceded, by means of which justice could be administered
and peace preserved, while at the same time the people
would be trained to understand and to appreciate our
English law and procedure.   This is what I have called the
"Territory" system.   The same standard would be before

the Administrator of a Territory as before the Governor of a Colony; the same code of laws would be the guide of the Territory Judge or Magistrate as of his Colonial brother; but in the former case the mode of procedure would be simpler, and more adapted to a people emerging from an uncultivated state.

I take the liberty to propose that Bechuanaland should be proclaimed to be under the British Government as a "Territory," and not as completely under our laws. Further, I would suggest that magistrates should be appointed at suitable places, and that taxes should be levied. The land should not be saleable in said Territory; but occupants of fountains should receive a lease for say ten years — to be renewed on approval of an imperial officer, after personal inspection; but if said officer on visiting the farm found that improvement had not been made as to house‑building, enclosing, irrigating, etc., or that that occupant had become by habit and repute a cattle-lifter, and his farm a den of thieves, the lease should not be renewed to this tenant, but should be given instead to one of a list of applicants for farms kept by the Government.

By this system you would also secure a contented labouring population; for while some members of such a native farmer's family would stay on the farm and work it, others would go out and work for wages.

In the course of time, when the English language was known by the people, when they had become instructed as to our laws and modes of procedure, the "territory" system might cease; and union take place with some neighbouring colony or province.

By this scheme, to which any Bechuana chief would give his ready consent, you would allow the natives who are industrious, energetic, and intelligent to rise in society; and thus, instead of being the bitterest and most dangerous class among the natives, as they have been in some parts of South Africa, you would make them the warm friends of the Government under which they had risen. At the same time you would, by the prosperity of these successful men, stop the mouths of the ill-disposed natives who would wish their fellow-countrymen to believe that it was hopeless to look for prosperity under the white man's rule.

A copy of this memorandum, which dealt also with

Zululand and other parts of South Africa, was forwarded to the Colonial Secretary in London, Sir Michael Hicks Beach.

In the beginning of 1880 Mackenzie received the announcement from London that the Directors of the Missionary Society did not agree to his accepting the position and doing the work offered to him by Sir Bartle Frere. The Directors appear to have been under a misapprehension of almost all the main points which Mackenzie had tried to make so clear. His reply to their refusal is given here, not to prove that they were in the wrong, but because Mackenzie speaks his soul out in these paragraphs with the warmth of an earnest and unselfish heart. The fact is that the Directors made the mistake of arguing their case. If they had simply said, " We will never under any circumstances allow one of our agents to do Government work, however deeply it concerns the welfare of the natives and of the mission, because we must at all hazards avoid creating a precedent," there would have been nothing to say. But they went into the merits of *this* case, and an answer was possible.

KURUMAN, 10th Feb. 1880.

MY DEAR MR WHITEHOUSE,—I have received yours of Nov. 27, conveying to me the decision of the Directors on the question of my performing certain political functions while doing my work as a missionary, tutor, etc., at Kuruman.

I acquiesce in that decision in accordance with my statement to that effect to Sir Bartle Frere, and to the Directors themselves in my letter to them on the subject. Their decision was to settle the question ; and it has accordingly settled it.

What I had feared however has happened. I did what I could to show that the case was an exceptional one, and that, in ordinary circumstances, I should have no desire to do Government work. The answer of the Directors, however, as I read it, is not to an exceptional case at all, but to the general question of the union of such offices.

You appear to have misunderstood my full and unreserved statement concerning written lessons or lectures. I explained that it was by hard work and self-denial that I could do this Government work—more especially by night work. My illustration was that at Shoshong I was in class and at the disposal of the people during the whole day, and that my lectures were chiefly written at night. *Not having still to write these lectures* I felt that so much time could be given to other work. In no part of my letter did I suggest or imply that I would make my written lectures alone or chiefly do duty for the work of a tutor. I thought that I had made it plain that my intention was to teach as I had done, but, not having now to arrange and "get up" the lectures, the time I had devoted to that could be given to something else. I have always been fully convinced of the absolute necessity of oral instruction in the case of the young men in the Institution, with written lectures to be copied by them to secure exactness, and for after reference at their stations by those who have no literature. I must confess to a feeling of surprise that you should have felt called upon to make such remarks to me on this subject as occur in your letter. Upon reflection I think you will agree with me that if I had thought lightly of my work here, I would have given it up; and that, refusing to give it up, it is at least not likely that I should perform its duties in a slovenly or perfunctory manner, as hinted by you.

Another remark I would refer to. You are sorry that I have been doing this Government work, and believe that my doing so has meant much loss to the Mission. Nothing could show me more plainly than this statement that you are *labouring under a complete misapprehension* as to the nature of the work which I have been doing. If you knew the details it would be *impossible* for you to make that remark. It is far from the truth. In effect I have been fighting for the natives. You say in effect that I am to let this alone; and you expect, among other things, that the natives will think more highly of me and my brethren in consequence! Were the policy carried out one opposed to the interests of the natives, and I gave it my support, then your remark would have had foundation. As it is, those who dislike my influence and work are the land-jobbers and white claimants for farms. It is distressing to them that I should be trusted, both by the natives and the Government. When you say theoretically, " So much work done in the settlement of the people, so much loss to the mission," you never made a more inapplicable remark.

I feel however that only personal intercourse could place the Directors and myself in full sympathy on this subject. Correspondence would seem to have failed. Expressions of thankfulness and confidence come to me from chiefs and people on account of what I have been doing. This is fact, and it is quite in the teeth of your theories as to the result of such work. When missionaries let alone things and they went deplorably wrong, they were suspected and blamed by the ignorant people for having helped to bring about the evil, because what had happened was to the benefit of Europeans. On the other hand when a missionary comes to the front and speaks and acts in behalf of the people, and endeavours to secure for them a good position under English Government, he, of course, secures the confidence both of heathen and Christians. Mark my words : if things go wrong in Bechuanaland, the missionaries will be blamed by the natives, no matter how innocent they might be. Things are not likely to go right without such active assistance as I have been able to give. There are few who are both able and willing to carry through such a policy.

Before I leave this subject I wish formally to say to the Directors : In refusing your consent to my formally assisting in the political settlement of the affairs of this territory, *on certain principles favourable to the natives which were explained to you*, I think you have made a grave mistake, in the interests of the natives and in the interests of the mission, which are one and the same.

Throughout the year 1880 the affairs of Bechuana-land remained, as he said to Mr John Noble of Cape Town, " in awkward suspense." A provisional acceptance of the surrender of their territories by the various chiefs had been granted by Colonel Warren in 1879, but these documents of surrender having been forwarded to head-quarters, *were never heard of again.* Even the courteous refusal of the wonderful gift of a kingdom was withheld ! The chiefs waited on with deepening chagrin. They communicated with Mackenzie, who strove as best he could to encourage them, even when his judgment was perplexed and his heart sore with protracted disappointment. The Home Government did not know its own mind. The Zulu war, owing to mismanagement, had brought discredit alike upon Sir Bartle Frere, who was not responsible for the mismanagement, and on the Home Government. A general election was imminent which, it was felt, would probably result in the return of Mr Gladstone to power. He and others of his party had so spoken on South African affairs as to make confusion in that part of the world worse confounded. No one could possibly foretell what policy would be adopted in any part of South Africa. What would be done with Zululand, or with the Transvaal, or with Bechuanaland, or with Griqualand? These regions were all in need simply of firmness and justice and wisdom; their names were made the occasion of party strife. And this resulted in the worst blunders of misgovernment. The police force in Bechuanaland was gradually reduced, until at last, in April 1881, they were finally and completely withdrawn. On this Mackenzie has said [1] :—

The reader can imagine the weariness of these years of uncertainty. The question was ever, "Has not the mouth of the Government come yet?" "No, we hear nothing," would be inevitably the reply. And to our shame as an Imperial Power, be it said, when the last policeman left Bechuanaland, he did so obeying a mere local police order. No warning from the High Commissioner was given to the chiefs; no reply to their offer of obedience and submission; no advice as to the future; the policemen just left—the military occupation of three years ended; and Bechuanaland became what every confidential adviser and commissioner of Her Majesty had said it would become—the abode of anarchy, filibustering, and outrage.

In this year (1881) the retrocession of the Transvaal took place, and the Pretoria Convention was drawn up

[1] Austral-Africa, vol. i., p. 118.

and signed.   In the course of negotiations which led
to this Convention the western boundary of the
Transvaal was carefully discussed and its course was
defined anew.   The reader will remember that one
of the main features of this Convention, which gave
back self-government to the Transvaal, was the provision that a British Resident should live at Pretoria to
control the relations of the Boer Government to the
native races, alike within and outside the Transvaal.
Mr Gladstone made, with reference to this arrangement,
the extraordinary prophecy that it would enable Great
Britain to exercise a more direct and actual control
over the treatment of the natives by the Boers than
she could exercise even in her own colonies !   Sir
Evelyn Wood, one of the Commissioners at Pretoria,
who showed more insight and more independence of
judgment throughout the proceedings than any other
representative of Great Britain, foresaw that this
was an impossible arrangement.   He urged, for
example, that provision must be made for the
appointment at once of British Residents among the
tribes both on the western and south-western borders
of the Transvaal.   These Residents would report on
native affairs to the Resident at Pretoria.   Such a plan
would have so far agreed with the general policy
which Mackenzie had for years been advocating, and
perhaps would have helped to fulfil Mr Gladstone's
prophecy in a small measure.   But it was overruled,
and the result was that these native tribes were left at
the mercy of the Boers.

Not long after the last British policeman had left
Bechuanaland, that pitiable country began to suffer
painfully from the change.   A large number of Boers
from within the Transvaal began immediately to deal
with the Bechuanas in the old and familiar ways ; and
the Resident at Pretoria, in spite of Mr Gladstone's
prophecy, was absolutely powerless.   These Boers did

not act, of course, officially; but their names were well known, and some of them were men of influence in the Transvaal. All representations made at the seat of Government were turned aside with clever excuses, put off with vague promises, or simply dropped with silent contempt. The invasion of Bechuanaland took place at two main points, and it was carried out in an exceedingly cunning and effective way. In the southern part where Mankoroane held sway, an ancient quarrel between him and Massow, a chief who lived nearer the Transvaal, was revived and aggravated. The Boers, under G. J. Van Niekerk, at this point offered themselves as volunteers to Massow, who accepted their service for the purpose of crushing his rival. But as soon as these volunteers found themselves in Bechuanaland with the natives at their mercy, and the British Government was now 6000 miles away, they proceeded to settle down and form themselves into a Boer republic which they called Stellaland, the capital town of which was named Vryburg. Further north, in the country of the Barolong, there lived an ancient foe of the Boers, by name Montsioa, who had as his rival on the Transvaal side of the border a young upstart called Moshette. Moshette was of course made the object of the warm regard of the Boers, and was assisted by a number of volunteers. The country of Montsioa was invaded under the redoubtable Gey Van Pittius. Near Mafeking, which was Montsioa's capital, another republic was going to be established under the Biblical name "Goshen." Now Montsioa, like Mankoroane, had for many years cherished the deepest faith in the British Government, and had over and over again petitioned to have himself, his people, and their country taken under British protection and control. He had more than once fought against the Boers, had showed himself a

clever diplomat, and through many years of pressure and persecution had succeeded in maintaining
his freedom.   In the war of the Boers against
Great Britain (1881) he, as also Mankoroane, had
steadily refused to aid the former, even when much
threatened and hard pressed.   When people speak
of those who fight for their country and their
independence, pitying a race that has its land
snatched from their grasp, and piously invoking
Heaven's curse upon those who rob them of Heaven's
best blessings, surely they must shed many tears for
heroes like these !   These men too, although black,
loved their land, ruled their people with fair success,
tilled their soil, herded their cattle ; not without honour
to themselves they were increasingly prosperous, eager
for education ; and withal they had for long been most
loyal to the distant " White Queen " whose ways with
them disappointed them so much.   These men were
heroes, if any have lived in South Africa. Can any one
blame those Europeans who, as they watched the fate
of such chiefs and their people, felt themselves roused
to a white heat of indignation?   They knew that the
advent of Boer republics meant the advent of the
Grondwet of the Transvaal Republic, with its law
that no native could have equal rights in church or
state with the white man, meant that Montsioa and
Mankoroane would either be cooped up in narrow
and famished locations, or would be reduced to the
position of a degraded serving class without the
right to own land in their own land!   The question
which was uppermost in the hearts of men like
Mackenzie and Sir Bartle Frere at this period of
South African history, was simply this : Does Great
Britain realise that by refusing to accept the free
gift of South Bechuanaland from its own people,
she is allowing that vast and rich region to be
annexed by lawless hosts of Europeans, and the

real owners of that country to be robbed of their ancient possessions and trampled under the feet of such men as Van Niekerk and Van Pittius?

Throughout 1881 Mackenzie maintained the battle for his people by means of letters and communications sent alike to the new High Commissioner, Sir Hercules Robinson, at Cape Town, and the new authorities at the Colonial Office in London. Early in 1882 he received permission from the Directors to return home for his second furlough. To this he refers in two letters to Mr Charles G. Oates.

KURUMAN, *Jan.* 18*th*, 1882.

MY DEAR SIR,—I have much pleasure in acknowledging receipt of your letter, informing me that you had sent to my address a copy of your book describing your brother's travels in this country. I thank you much for remembering me in this way. Without reference to its own merits I shall treasure the volume as a memento of him whose steps in South Africa it traced. The volume itself has not come to hand, but my experience is that, while such things often move very slowly in this country, not many are lost. . . .

You kindly inquire about our residence here and our surroundings. In the language of the advertisements, this is quite a "desirable residence," especially if compared with our house at Shoshong. Besides the pastoral care of a wide district dotted with village churches (I mean small Christian communities and not ecclesiastical structures, for the last have not got beyond the wattle-and-daub era), I have the oversight as Tutor of an Institution recently established for training native ministers and evangelists. The missionaries select men of experience, who have been tried, and who are trusted. They come with their families and live in cottages which have been put up for their reception. During their stay the wives get some instruction also, as well as the children, who are old enough to go to school. We carry on things in a quiet, unpretending way, and trust that the presence of these men in the villages throughout the country will have a very beneficial effect. Christianity has been long enough an exotic; our effort is to make it indigenous.

I thank you for your invitation to Meanwoodside; at

present it may be looked at by me as one of the pleasant
possibilities of my sojourn in England.   Our Society pre-
scribes to its missionaries a visit home every ten years; and
it is in connection with that rule that our visit takes place.
At the same time it is of great importance to us as a family
to be able to go home at this time.   The children left in
Scotland eleven years ago are grown up now, and about to
leave the University to enter life on their own account.   We
wish to be together as one family, if it please God, even for a
little while.—With kindest regards, I am ever sincerely yours,

JOHN MACKENZIE.

KURUMAN, 22d *April* 1882.

MY DEAR MR OATES,—Since I wrote to you I have
received "Matabeleland and the Victoria Falls," and I
have perused it with great interest.   You have succeeded
in producing a beautiful book. . . . I rose from its perusal
with deep regret that the traveller himself was not spared to
tell his own story.   You have done your best; and you will
allow me to say that your success is gratifying, and to me,
knowing the circumstances under which you worked, even
wonderful.   But no one knows what hidden ideas were indicated by the dry notes which came before you for your
guidance.   How suggestive they would have been to him
who penned them !

Let me again thank you for the handsome volume, which I
shall always prize.   And allow me to express my gratification
at the kindly manner in which my name has been mentioned
by you. . . . We have begun packing up, and hope to leave
this place in a month or so.   I am afraid the Transvaal will
again force itself into notice.   Their borders are already disturbed.   *The truth* as to recent border affairs does not seem
to be known at home.   One set of statements is welcomed by
Her Majesty's Government, and distrusted by the Opposition.
An opposite story is published in Opposition papers, and is
stigmatised as "Jingo lies."   This does not seem to me very
admirable as a method of government.   I should think
thousands of Englishmen, when they think of the matter
at all, feel inclined· to ask, "Politics aside, and political
struggles aside, what are the facts with reference to the
Transvaal and the natives ? "

The Transvaal *Government* is not at war—the Republic is
at peace ; but a few days ago a party of armed Boers stole

cattle and shot some dozen herds within fifty miles of this place. At their "laager" there are said to be some 200 or 300 armed and mounted Boers; their leaders men of influence and position in the Transvaal.—With kindest regards, I am ever yours sincerely, JOHN MACKENZIE.

With a heavy and sad heart Mackenzie left Bechuanaland, dark days lowering before it. He was well received at Cape Town by Sir Hercules Robinson, who paid close attention to his evidence, his proposals, and his arguments. But his mind, as he sailed from Cape Town, was fixed on London, and the determination was already forming in his heart that he would, if God gave him strength, so place the entire facts before the Government and the people of Great Britain as to bring about a reversal of the disastrous policy which had been adopted in South Africa.

CHAPTER X

THE MISSIONARY AS POLITICAL EDUCATOR
(1882, 1883)

WHEN John Mackenzie landed in England, in July 1882, he entered on a new career. All that he had done hitherto in the way of political work had been incidental, and had been ever kept subordinate to the various responsibilities of his position as Tutor of the Moffat Institution and Pastor of the Kuruman Church. But he was now to enter on a course of work which gradually reversed the relations of these two supreme interests of his public life. He has described, in " Austral Africa," the atmosphere of England, on the question of South Africa, when he began to breathe it in that summer of '82. It was enough to stifle hope. The Liberal Government was then in power, under Mr Gladstone's leadership, and Lord Kimberley was at the head of the Colonial Office. The public mind had been dazed and the public heart disgusted by the events of the preceding four or five years in South Africa. The only people who knew that they had an opinion, even when they had no real facts on which to base it, were those who openly triumphed over the retrocession of the Transvaal, and who preached the doctrine that Great Britain ought to leave South Africa to the Dutch. This section of the Liberal party were definite and vociferous, whensoever any aspect of South African policy was raised ; to be at once definite and vociferous is always very impressive.

For the rest, Mackenzie found them all in deep
ignorance of the facts ; all vaguely felt that " some
one had blundered," that the true solution of the
problem had not yet been proposed, but did not know
where to turn for light or for a leader.   The general
trend of feeling among the Conservatives was that of
people who having blundered are struck dumb, or
who prove ineffective as critics of those who commit
fresh blunders by way of correcting theirs.   Mr
Gladstone had tried to atone for a badly managed
annexation in 1877, by a worse managed retrocession in 1881; and Lord Kimberley was now trying
by mildness and generosity to win the trust and
elicit the faithfulness of the Boers, whom Lord
Carnarvon was supposed to have driven into fear
and suspicion.

Mackenzie was therefore confronted with a perplexing situation as he stepped into the political life of
London.   We have seen abundant proof of the deep
love which he cherished for his family, of the yearning
with which he looked forward to that reunion with
those whom he had left as children and would now
greet as men and women, learning to call them his
children still.   It is characteristic of his unselfish
spirit, that sending his wife and family down to
Scotland, missing the first flush of that joy, he
remained in London.   His " King's business," the
salvation of Bechuanaland by the British Government
from an impending destruction, required haste.   Within
a fortnight he organised and held his first meeting,
and made his first public speech.   The meeting was
called by the Directors of the London Missionary
Society, and was held in the Westminster Palace
Hotel on July 25th.   Mackenzie's speech was a clear
recital of the cruel facts of the case in Bechuanaland.
He proved to his audience that the Bechuana people
were not savages.

Not long ago a certain town in Bechuanaland was looted.
The spoils of that town were put up to auction. They were
much the same as the spoils of a colonial village : you could
not, through many of the articles, have discovered any black-
ness about their owners. There were the ploughs and
agricultural implements of farmers, presses, Staffordshire ware,
and such things as belonged to small farmers : and I was
told that some Europeans purchased the new and made-up
clothing, and wore it.

He recounted the relations of Great Britain to that
country, from 1878 to 1881, and the innumerable
proofs which those tribes had given, through their
chiefs, of their intense desire to be protected by the
government of the Queen. He then described the
manner in which Boers from the Transvaal had been
invading and swallowing up the lands, and seizing the
individual farms of these defenceless people. Much
stress was laid upon the impotence of the British
Resident at Pretoria, that official through whom Mr
Gladstone had prophesied that the natives would
receive, so completely, the watchful oversight and
strong help of Great Britain.

I feel there is nothing that I, as an individual, would not
do to give these people the right to the fountains which they
are using and the land which they hold. I do not wish
them treated in any special way, but only in the light of
English Christianity and justice. Many things I might
have said or written at an earlier date in the history of
these disturbances, but I judged it best to be silent.
Under the present circumstances, however, silence on my
part would be a crime.

The speech was printed and widely circulated as a
pamphlet.

From that meeting Mackenzie hurried down to
Scotland, got off the train when it stopped at Portobello for " taking the tickets," and there met his two
sons, one of them taller by several inches than himself,

bearded fellows now, whom he had not seen since
1871. Only those who have gone through it can
tell what those trying first hours in a reunited family
must be. However frank and sincere and full the
correspondence has been, there is something of a
bitter experiment involved in that meeting. " Are
they our children still? " the parents ask each other
when the day of severest strain has ended. And the
hearts of loyal sons and daughters have been wondering
too in their silent depths, and have been asking and
answering questions of the keenest kind all that day
long, such as it would be disloyal for others to face
who had never passed through that long separation
to this supreme day of trial and, please God, of
unspeakable joy. To John Mackenzie it was unspeakable joy.

For six short weeks he had all his children, who
numbered nine (three sons and six daughters) under
his roof, four of these weeks being spent in the village
of Urquhart, near his own beloved Elgin. One day he
walked with one or two of his boys into Elgin. When
they had passed the " Institution," where he had
his schooling, and were in the narrow part of High
Street, before it widens around the Parish Church, he
suddenly stopped, struck the pavement with his stick,
and exclaimed, " I smell Elgin! " His laughing boys
looked round and accounted for his discovery of Elgin
by several shops—odoriferous—which had clustered
opposite that spot in his boyhood, and by which he
must often have been arrested as he passed five and
thirty years before.

On the 4th of September he took part in the
ordination of his eldest son as minister of the
Congregational Church at Montrose. He offered
the " ordination prayer," and himself led in the
" laying-on of the hands of the presbytery." It
was a great satisfaction to him that in this ordain-

ing act the ministers of five or six different sections of the Evangelical Church took part ; as also that Dr Lindsay Alexander of Edinburgh, who had " delivered the charge " at his own ordination in 1858, did the same for his son in 1882.

In September, Mackenzie resumed his work of informing the British public about Bechuanaland. The journeys which he had to make as a representative of the London Missionary Society enabled him to address a large portion of the most influential Nonconformists in the country.   And for several months thereafter Mr Gladstone's Government was made the somewhat unwilling and astonished recipient of strong resolutions from all parts of England, in favour of firm action in Bechuanaland and of Imperial protection of the native races.   In Birmingham Town Hall a large meeting showed a very real and earnest interest in the matter.   From Leeds, Bradford, Bristol, Ashton-under-Lyne, in the months of September and October, and from other places such as Bolton and Farnworth, in February, this demand was made.   At these meetings the resolutions were discussed at length by well-known men.   And at most of them Mackenzie was himself present to give full information both in public and in private.   He of course organised the movement at each of these places.   Between September 10th and October 24th, he visited twenty-nine places, frequently giving two, and even three speeches or sermons in one day.

At this time, acting on the advice of many friends, he wrote a letter to Mr Gladstone on the state of affairs in Bechuanaland, forwarding his pamphlet, and earnestly asking the Prime Minister's personal interest in the question.   " In spite of all that has transpired," he urged, " it is my deliberate opinion that it would be easy for England to govern South Africa if a certain course were followed." Mr Gladstone's reply seemed to indicate a personal indifference on the subject, and merely referred his correspondent to the Colonial Secretary.

One of the most valuable allies whom Mackenzie found in the provinces was the late Dr R. W. Dale of Birmingham. With his usual force and clearness of judgment, Dale studied the case, and frankly gave his aid to his missionary-brother. Some of Mackenzie's best letters were addressed to him, and they were well repaid by various timely and well-placed services which Dale rendered to his cause.

3 BUCKINGHAM VILLAS, CLIFTON,
BRISTOL, 18*th Sept.* 1882.

MY DEAR MR DALE,—Thanks for your letter, which I got last night, after coming home from the day's work.

I went this morning to "take up the spoor," or track of the discussion, and see where the *Pall Mall Gazette* was on this question. I have read the *Times*, the two notes in the *Gazette*, and your letter in the latter.

Your position is quite impregnable behind a signed Convention. That of the *Gazette* quite disgraceful; and such writing has been the fruitful *cause* of deeds of wrong in South Africa, inasmuch as lawless men see how the land lies; and that they will be left to do what they like.

"Do you mean War?" This is supposed to be a poser to a Christian minister. What did the Royal Commission, the Liberal Government, mean when, leaving the subject of the natives *within* the borders of the Transvaal, they proceeded to treat of the natives *outside* that country? In case outrage or wrong should be committed by Transvaal people the settlement should be in the hands of the English Resident and the English High Commisioner, and *their decision should be final?*

Taking the sneering remarks of the *Pall Mall* as one's guide, the opinion is forced on us that an immorality was perpetrated by the English Commissioner and English Government when they signed the Convention. They professed to do one thing; and posed before the religious public of England and of Europe as the benevolent doers of it. "As heretofore, England would reserve for herself the protection of native races," etc., etc. Now, it seems this was all bosh and only meant to deceive, and carry forward for the time the religious public of England.

It seems to me impossible to harmonize your position and that of the *Pall Mall*. The one is the open truth; the other is the sinister and sneaking inuendo-making expediency of a hand-to-mouth policy.

There is a practicalness about the step which was taken in Birmingham which will commend itself elsewhere, I have no doubt. The work of the religious public of England in an African district is in imminent peril through the marauding inroads of Boers, in the teeth of a Convention signed by them and by our own Government. What sort of people are the religious people of this country, if they would quietly and meekly submit to that without giving any sign?

And what sort of Government have we got if they will righteously and piously make due and formal provisions for doing a thing which they have long prided themselves on doing—inwardly resolving, all the while, that what they openly promise they will secretly deny?

What was conceded to the Transvaal was *self-government*. What was advisedly and formally kept from them was management of native affairs, either within or beyond the Transvaal. If the English Government were to say openly and earnestly: We will support the Convention, the marauders must leave Bechuanaland, there would be no "war." It is the sneers of the *Pall Mall Gazette* people which make wars.

By the way, what has become of the Anti-Annexation Society in the Bechuana matter? Why don't they give the Bechuanas their "moral support?" I asked this of someone in London, and his reply was that the Bechuanas were better without it.

My wife told you about the powder. That, of course, is not the main question. The main question is the open breach of Convention by both Transvaal and English Governments in the present state of things in Bechuanaland.

As a matter of fact and law, all powder sales in South Africa are transacted after getting permits from government officials. These permits are *refused* to black men, and to traders living among them. These permits are *granted* to Boers, and to traders living among them. This is not referred to in the Pretoria Convention. Without breach of it powder might be freely sold.

It was specifically referred to in the Sand River Convention —no powder was to be sold to blacks, and *no treaty was to be made with them by England.* By the way, have you ever seen that delightful document? It would raise your opinion of your native land to peruse it. Its provisions as to powder were relaxed by Colonial and Transvaal Governments, that is to say, practically. Natal has always professed to be strict as to the sale of guns, etc.

In Bechuanaland, so strictly is powder law now observed, that the wild beasts are fast gaining ground upon the people; they had come back quite near to Kuruman before I left.

I have seen Mr Arnold Thomas and talked over the matter. Don't know yet what they will do. But I feel sure in my own mind that good will come out of the agitation. Mr Thomas said something as to the advisability of having the matter before the Congregational Union, at its meeting here. I mention this as being his thought, that you may consider it.

Trusting that the blessing of those who are ready to perish may find you out and be yours,—I am, ever yours sincerely,

JOHN MACKENZIE.

But it was in London of course that this battle must be lost or won. There were three directions in which he looked for help—the press, the philanthropic societies, and such members of Parliament as he could at once reach and influence. He early found a most intelligent and hard-working friend in the late Mr F. W. Chesson, who was at that time Secretary of the Aborigines Protection Society With his help a "South African Committee" was formed which included some very strong men, and that committee proved to be a powerful instrument both for educating the public mind and moving the will of the Government. The Lord Mayor, Sir R. N. Fowler, M.P., was on the committee, and speedily called a public meeting at the Mansion House to consider the affairs of South Africa.

In his attempts to use the press, Mackenzie employed two methods. One was to convince, by means of personal interviews, the editors of several of the most influential journals; the second was to contribute articles of his own to the columns of certain others. His first article was accepted by the *Scotsman* on October 10, 1882. Thereafter he wrote very frequently for that paper as well as for the *Leeds Mercury*. Mr Talbot Baines of the *Mercury* became one of his staunchest and most encouraging friends. Among the London papers his attention was early directed to the *Pall Mall Gazette*, which at that time was edited by Mr John Morley. We have seen in his letter to Dr Dale how deeply he resented the tone in which that paper discussed South African affairs. It frankly, almost cynically, advocated the "letting go" policy. In this case, the only plan seemed to be to convert the editor, and this could only be done by means of a personal acquaintance. Mr Morley won Mackenzie's heart with his kindness, his perfect sincerity, his willingness to listen to the other side, his judicial fairness. For a time it looked as if Mr Morley might be gained; but to the defender of Britain's South African Empire there came the great disappointment of seeing Mr Morley at a later date stand up in the House unconverted, and hostile still to the new policy which was then beginning to win the attention of the Government.

The following letter to his eldest son gives an account of his effort to convince Mr Courtney, one

of the most determined advocates then and since of
the policy of abandoning South Africa.

11 Queen's Square,
Bloomsbury, 26th Nov. 1882.

Dear Willie,—I have just come back from Mr John
Morley's house, where I spent the night. . . . I went between
3 and 4 p.m. It was a visit of great pleasure to me. All
the people were nice; but the Morleys are all very nice. I
hope I shall like Courtney on ahead. I can't say I do so
just now; but he is a very fine fellow, says Mr Morley, and
I believe it is so.

Had a long talk with Morley before dinner. I think
he is more interested in "my view," or "scheme," as he
called it. He said some warm things in its praise when
summarizing on more than one occasion. I judged of his
feelings and position very much by the intense interest he
showed in Courtney's face as I was talking to him after the
ladies left the room. I could see, or fancied so, that Morley
wished me to get on well with Courtney, and watched the
effect of every "point" I made.

Dear Willie, Courtney made "no bones" about admitting
right off, that those who think with him want to "clear out"
from South Africa entirely, and openly said he believed the
natives would "go as the Choctaws had done," after the
English Government had left Africa. This is exactly what
Lord Kimberley said on my second interview with him. He
(Courtney) expressed an opinion that this entirely "letting
alone" would soon be announced publicly. His position
argumentatively is this: We never could govern South Africa
in the past. We had as fine men trying as any we are likely
to have now or in the future. The lowering of the suffrage
in this country has rendered all government more difficult
—especially of such outlying governments—the pressure of
work being so great. "We can't do it—it's impossible, and
by and by the suffrage will be still more widened." I joined
issue as to the African fact that fair effort had been given to
the work there. The enquiry was a historical one, and was
ascertainable with niceness. Gladstone, I said, was on my
side here, and publicly admitted they had had no South
African policy—only "staving off the evil day." "I daresay,
like one of his speeches." "And then, sir," I said, "your

opinion supposes that we cannot go beyond those who preceded us in attainment; and that we cannot learn from history and from their mistakes." At Morley's suggestion I then briefly sketched my plan. "Couldn't possibly do it with our changed constitution or mode of—I forget exact expression—doing public business. You see, a few years ago we had the aristocratic class doing that work, according to their light, and finding it to be, as they thought, their vocation. All that is now changed—our democracy is an entirely different thing."

Well! there were several answers that suggested themselves here. The one I gave, I think, was that to press that argument was to show that unless it cleared its way and got more time to do its real work the English Government would be effete altogether, even for insular work; that my scheme of sending a Department of Downing Street, as it were, to South Africa, was in the nature of improving that mode of procedure. I afterwards spoke very seriously to Morley about this view as a complete giving up of the cohering English Empire, and the abnegating, as I thought in an unworthy way, of duties and responsibilities which Providence had imposed on England : and that the character of our people must suffer, if they came under the active power of such motives; they would shrink into something very little indeed. " I grant yours is far the nobler position and begets more worthy and chivalrous feelings," was his reply.

But that about the Choctaws, and the way it was put, went to my heart like a knell. At Morley's instigation I told how the Bechuanas had improved—irrigation, ploughing, etc. " Quite surprising in such a short time ; I am much interested," said Morley. But Courtney was silent. Evidently, here, Morley was helping me in a kind way. Mr Morley is not satisfied that my scheme has been fairly understood by Mr Courtney. Suggested that I should have another interview with him—he would arrange it. I said I thought there was little hope, he had made up his mind. I then reminded him of my social disqualifications—nobody, etc., yet a missionary. He insisted on it, however ; only perhaps Mr Courtney himself will be of my opinion, and not wish any more of it—though, even if that were the case, I should think he would find it hard to deny his friend.

We breakfasted early this morning—sitting down at table at a quarter to 8 o'clock.   Mr Morley's work demanded this. Therefore he goes early to bed.   Spoke about meeting again —arranged about my writing a magazine article—and so parted.   With love.   J. M.

In a few days the matter was up in the House of Commons and Mr Evelyn Ashley, who was then Under Secretary for the Colonies, asserted that the Government could and would do nothing.   Next day he was visited at the Colonial Office by the terribly earnest missionary, who had begun to haunt that home of Imperial officers with an untiring persistence.   The following letter to his second son describes that visit and reveals something of his method and the secret of his success :—

London Missionary Society,
Blomfield Street, London Wall, E.C.,
1<i>st Dec.</i> 1882.

Dear Johnnie,—I got your nice letter.   I want to jot down the events of last night and to-day.

Mr Ashley gave a flat denial to the suggestion that more should be done by the Government than had been done.   "They were not to do more."   Well, I have seen Mr Ashley and I wish to jot down about it while it is fresh.

He was very dry indeed when I went in.   Did not say, sit down.   "Well, Sir, anything fresh—more than we know?" "No, nothing fresh, except that I saw from your answer last night you were not aware that those fellows were now acting for themselves, without any chiefs intervening."   "We have not heard that.   But sit down—let us talk about it.   What I do say heartily and earnestly is, Mr Mackenzie, that I wish all your meetings and resolutions, etc., would go further, and tell us what are we to do.   I would forbid the right of criticism, for my part, except when accompanied by practical suggestion."   "Well, Sir, the meetings which I attended always gave practical suggestions.   In the first place, it was suggested that the Convention should be more stringently applied, since it became known that a number of these men

were in Bechuanaland ; the Directors suggest that Her
Majesty's Government and the Cape Colony should combine
to establish order there. These are practical suggestions."
" But do you mean that we should march an army thro'
the Transvaal for the purpose ? " " No—nothing so extreme ;
something much more practical. The Cape Colony naturally
dislikes taking the lead. That is the position of *this* Government. But if Her Majesty's Government would take the
lead in co-operation with the Cape Colony, they might enlist
men at the Fields, or find the Border Police already on the
Border enough for their purpose." He was silent—apparently interested. " I don't underrate the difficulties of the
Government. I wish, as far as local knowledge goes, to
assist as far as I can. In this country I have never ' pitched
into ' the Transvaal at any public meeting, but have always
taken the utmost care as to what I said. But when I am put
up before a public meeting and asked to tell the people
about Bechuanaland, I must say something. In a small
way, you can see that I have my difficulty too." " Oh, yes,
I can see that. Well, I should like you to read the Blue-
book which will be out to-morrow. Come again and have
a talk after you have done so. Tell me then what you think
we ought to do there."

Excuse haste in ending. Ladies' meeting on.

J. M.

A letter to his wife, dated December 5th, gives still
another further glimpse into the alertness with which
he seized every opportunity and used every instrument that seemed available.

12 QUEEN SQUARE,
5th Dec. 1882.

DEAREST,—I got your welcome letter this morning enclosing William Walker's. . . .

I can't get at my article. I have written two for *Christian
World* and *Independent*, which they may or may not accept
of. There is given in the Blue-book a very striking article
from the Cape *Volksblad* strongly upbraiding the Transvaal
Boers with their criminality and foolishness in reference to
the Western Border. " Don't you see that you are alienat-
ing from yourselves the respect of the very people in England

who may be said to have given to you your self-government ?
They insisted upon your getting your rights.   Depend on it,
they will insist with equal force on the natives getting theirs."
It is a great gratification to me to see this leader.   It establishes my position with Lord Kimberley as to the two classes
of Boers.   There has been *much done since we reached Cape
Town.*   The Blue-book shows that.   Sir Hercules Robinson's despatches are very strong.   It was he who sent
home the leader from Cape paper for Lord Kimberley's
information.   The Transvaal *stands discredited* in this latest
Blue-book.

But I don't want the Boers interfered with in the Transvaal.   Let them govern themselves, if only we could get
some kind of hopeful government for Bechuanaland.

Mr Morley yesterday enclosed a letter from Mr Froude
stating his opinions, and saying that, such being his
opinions, I may not think it worth while to call, but if
I do call, he assures me it will give him much pleasure
to go over the matter with me.   I shall call to-morrow.
In the meantime, for the fun of the thing, as Mr Morley
asked me to return F.'s letter, I have done so with the
"other side" as to every statement which he makes, in short
compass.

All the resolutions from Birmingham, Bristol, etc., are
given in this Blue-book.   There is no shutting our eye to
the fact that *much* has been done.   I sometimes think a
more rabid and unscrupulous man might have lashed
up public opinion sooner—telling all the atrocities, etc. ;
but such spasms do little good ; at any rate, I could not
do it.   People ought to be convinced, so as that they
can continue to uphold their views to-morrow and the day
after.

I sent a copy of pamphlet to Sir Bartle Frere.   Letter from
Miss Frere in a day or two to say that her father would be
very glad to see me at lunch some Saturday, and would
Saturday next suit ?   So I have written to say I shall be
most happy, etc.   Lord Carnarvon writes from some Castle
in Wales to say he has perused with much interest, etc.
An acknowledgment also from Lord Shaftesbury—Ashley's
father—and he says he will give it his "early attention."
However, I must go at this article now.   And I am going
down to the Mission-House to-day to stir them up about the
circulation of the pamphlet.

When am I coming home? Don't know. Can't say. Wish I were there. Feel strongly inclined to put in a sort of "To be continued"; but have not got to that stage yet.

Very much love to you and to all.   J. M.

The Christmas of 1882 Mackenzie spent with his family at Portobello, and worked from there for the first few weeks of the New Year. He maintained his battle with unrelaxing courage. Not without some sickness of heart indeed; for he could not learn to look with inward indifference upon the policy of those who were most actively opposed to him. "However," he says in one letter to his wife, "I am tried somewhat to-day, and the selfish worldliness of the other side—the 'For Ourselves' style of the thing — is saddening." It always seemed to him that the policy of withdrawal from South Africa was dictated, partly by a certain pessimism regarding the continued power of Great Britain to carry its enormous load of Imperial responsibility, and partly by a certain 'doctrinaire' attitude of mind which applied the abstract theory of national freedom to the Dutch in South Africa without a careful scrutiny of the facts concerning the rights of other races, black and white, in the states, colonies, and dependencies of that region. Africa had cost a great deal and paid back little; therefore let Africa go—that cry he met. The Dutch wanted to be free, therefore give them their freedom, more of it, if they want more—that cry also he heard. Great Britain had enough to do elsewhere, and ought in any case to confine her attention to her own home interests, which must be neglected by the bestowal of so much time upon the rest of the world—even that cry also met him. And Mackenzie, who had spent twenty years of brooding in South Africa upon the might of the British Empire, the high integrity of her officers, the brilliant genius

for administration displayed by them in India and
elsewhere, who had worked out a broad plan by
which South Africa might without war and with a
minimum of Imperial expenditure be built up into a
great Commonwealth or Dominion, faced these cries
with that mingled courage and grief which comes, not
from shallow optimism, but from a hard-won faith, to
the defence of a great cause.

About the end of January he received a letter from
Mankoroane, the chief at Taungs, in which the latter
stated the grievous condition into which he and his
tribe were being brought by the inroads of the Boers,
and pleading with Mackenzie most piteously for his
intercession.

> Speak for me to the English people and to the Govern-
> ment of the Queen. So far as I know I am suffering all this
> because I said, "I belong to the Queen." It is well known
> that, during the war between the English and the Boers, I
> received and protected the Queen's people who had fled
> from the Transvaal. My Teacher, all my confidence is
> still in the Queen's Government. Plead for me! Help
> me! If the Government does not help me, I am de-
> stroyed. . . . If they delay to think of me I shall have
> passed away.

Mackenzie at once communicated the contents of
this letter to the Earl of Derby who had just succeeded Lord Kimberley as Secretary of State for the
Colonies. He also proceeded to write a pamphlet,
entitled " Bechuanaland, The Transvaal, and England,"
to which he appended the letter from Mankoroane.
In this pamphlet he described the situation from the
point of view of Bechuanaland. He first sketched
what England had done for the natives religiously and
educationally, and stated some of the results in their
improved social position ; then he described the active
relations in which England stood to Bechuanaland

from 1878 to 1881. When England deserted them the chiefs were left powerless, their tribes disorganised and left to the tender mercies of land-agents and secretaries, and Boer "freebooters." Lastly, an account was given very frankly and yet not passionately, and without invective, of the part which the Transvaal was then playing in Bechuanaland. Their conduct was contrasted with that of the Cape Colony and the Orange Free State.

It is now for the English public and for English legislators to compare their former ideas of the Boers, as men who were nobly longing for freedom, with the careful terms of the Pretoria Convention as to the protection of the natives, with the advice and warning of the Royal Commissioner at Pretoria, 1881, given through its President, and with the disgraceful wars and raids in Bechuanaland which have prevailed for more than a year.

In the month of February Mackenzie began to draw encouragement from the attitude of Lord Derby. He writes on February 23rd to his eldest son :—

Did you notice Derby's speech? Hopeful between the lines. Protection is not scouted, as Kimberley scouted it.

He also felt himself surer now in expounding and defending his own policy. The natural hesitancy and even diffidence which he felt when he first began this work were giving way under the experience of his success in persuading others to a reasonable confidence in his ideas. In the same letter he says,

I am certain of my ground now, I mean the policy I propose. I have fought it out with some tough customers here ; and last Saturday night witnessed my first conversion, quite a startling one too.

On April 27th, 1883, Mackenzie celebrated his silver wedding by attending that of his eldest son

in Upperby Parish Church, near Carlisle. In a
letter written next day to his new daughter, with a
playfulness and a depth of feeling which he knew so
well how to mingle, he pretended that she had neither
seen nor appreciated the various wedding scenes, and
proceeded to describe them to her. He recounted a
few characteristic words which he had uttered at the
breakfast, which, as being autobiographical, have a
place here.

Do you know what I said when thanking them for drinking
my health ? It was this : That my son and daughter-in-law
would work out their own day's work as everyone should,
according to their own ability ; but that, as far as happiness
was concerned, I could not wish for them greater or truer
than by praying that their conjugal life might be as
happy as my own had been for twenty-five years. This
means that you may *do* more, fill higher places, and so
on, but that I cannot conceive of your being more to one
another

In May 1883 Mackenzie had the satisfaction of
addressing the British public through the pages of
the *Nineteenth Century*. His article was entitled
"England and South Africa," and it extended to
thirty-one pages. It was divided into five sections,
in which a rapid and concise account was given of
the leading historical facts and the main political
features of South African history since the purchase
of Cape Colony from Holland in the beginning of
the last century.

Section I. discussed "England and the Cape Colony ;
Europeans." The social and educational progress of the
colonists was described, and it was shown that : "Found in
degrading bondage to a commercial company, from whose
authority part of the population were in actual rebellion, the
European inhabitants of the Cape Colony have enjoyed a
period of increasing prosperity under the government of
England." Section II. was on "England and the Cape

Colony; Natives." It sought to bring out "the two-fold aspect of the question, the effect of our policy on the natives themselves, and the reflex result on the European colonists." The facts connected with serfdom, slavery, and emancipation, were recounted. Nowhere have more beneficial results followed to both masters and slaves from emancipation than in South Africa. Even from the point of view of deliverance from the practice of slavery with the wrongs and wars it would engender, the blessings conferred on the European population in South Africa by their connection with England have fully equalled those conferred by that power on the native African races. Section III. passed to "Our Border Policy in South Africa." The principal lesson of this section was that there had been no border policy. Uncertainty and vacillation, rather than a mastery of the subject, characterized the attitude and action of Britain throughout the century. With great force this conclusion was driven home by instance after instance, ending with the ever shameful treatment of the Bechuanaland chiefs and their tribes. "Thus a people begs for our help in the establishment of good government; they agree to submit to us, and to pay the necessary taxes. We turn a deaf ear to them, and see them shot down by irresponsible filibusters, whose base of operation is a country of which we have the sovereignty!" In Section IV., "Northward," the irresistible movement of Europeans was set forth. "There are reasons for it deeper than political ones; it is a movement which can be counted on and legislated for, but not arrested. In America those who move westward never think of severing their connection with the East; and if they did think of it, the United States Government would insist that there should be no such separation. England unfortunately has never recognized this northern movement as a fact in South African history." This movement is then sketched to show on the one hand how steady it has been, and how our zigzag ways of dealing with South African affairs led to the dangers, disasters, irritations and disgraces, of that which should have been controlled by the Central Power from first to last.

Thus the writer was brought to his last Section V. "The Lessons of the Past; Our Future South African Policy." The policy is based on the assumption that " England will not retire from South Africa, but will retain her position as the Central or Supreme Power having, as hitherto, the native policy in her own hands." (1) The first step would be the selection of one head . . . we may call him Governor-General. The Governor of the Cape Colony would exercise that office and nothing more, and so in the case of Natal. (2) The Cape Colony would be relieved of its burdensome task in managing such outlying territories as Basutoland, Transkei, Griqualand East, etc. The Colony would contribute its quota towards defraying the expense of upholding the peace of its borders. It would have enough to do with a large native population within its borders. Responsible government would then have a fair trial at the Cape, which it has not had hitherto. The native territories would be placed under administrators, each in direct correspondence with the Governor-General and magistrates, assisted in certain cases by native chiefs as assessors. Under this provisional or territorial government, taxes would be raised to defray local expenditures, and territorial law would be administered. Each territory would be expected to pay its own way and to contribute towards the central government. . . . The native territories would pass through this stage to the higher grade of Colonial Government, which would be reached when Education had made some progress and the people had become familiar with civilized procedure as to deeds, titles, etc. Under territorial law, for their protection, natives would not be allowed to sell land ; which would inflict no wrong, inasmuch as that is their tribal law already.

Of course this plan meant annexation. Any satisfactory solution of South African difficulties must take into account the northward movement of Europeans. This movement is itself the annexing or aggressive force ; our scheme seeks to control it ; and its tendency would, on the whole, be to curb rather than to stimulate forward tendencies. The present proposal introduces no change in our relations to any colony or state in South Africa. They would deal with a Governor-General of South Africa instead of with a High Commissioner, who was also a local governor. In such a scheme as that now sketched, there would be the true nucleus of a United South Africa. Gradually there would grow a general council or parliament representing all colonies and states, and assisting the Governor-General in the management of the general affairs of the country. At present we have mere *disjecta membra* in the South African body politic, the head being one of the disjoined parts. He concluded with the confident belief that when England establishes some such government as that which we have here imperfectly sketched, she will at length have solved the problem of governing Europeans and Africans in mutual helpfulness.

Before the appearance of this article, and in reference to it, Mackenzie wrote a letter to Dr Dale from which the following extracts may be made.

12 QUEEN SQUARE, BLOOMSBURY,
LONDON, 28*th March* 1883.

MY DEAR DR DALE,—My article suggests the doing with the right hand what England *has done* left-handedly and with much irritation in the past.

I believe you have the choice of adopting some such general line of South African policy! or leave the country (practically) and see one race-war after another till the blacks are—in the language of one of your leading men of to-day— "where the Choctaw Indians are."

.   .   .   .

I have met with great personal kindness from Mr John Morley, to whom indeed I owe the introduction to Mr Knowles of the *Nineteenth Century*. But his late speech and his recent articles are to me very sad. They mean the total relinquishment of duties and responsibilities in South Africa. They mean nothing else. If we were deciding whether or not we should go there, they would be in place. I consider there is a deadly shrinking from fact and duty and obligation, which, as a factor in politics, does not augur well for the prosperity of the country in which such views come to the front. "For ourselves" would seem to be the motto of this kind of writing and speaking. But who are "ourselves"?

"I know we signed something but we never meant to keep to it, and we won't either," said a gentleman to me, when speaking of the Pretoria Convention. "Then," I said, "you will forgive me for saying it; but you are a bad lot."

Only one man of all I have met with has spoken out such unmitigated falseness as that. It is however, at the bottom of the whole attitude of the government at present. I am no partizan.

.   .   .   .

CHAPTER XI

ENGLAND—THE TRANSVAAL DELEGATES AND THE LONDON CONVENTION (1883, 1884)

MUCH of the summer of 1883 was spent by Mackenzie in Scotland. In the earlier months he was engaged in " deputation work " on behalf of the London Missionary Society, which took him through part of Aberdeenshire. He was also busy with the production of his little book entitled " Day-Dawn in Dark Places " which the Directors of the Society had asked him to prepare for them. It was to be used as their annual gift-book to Sunday School children for the year 1884. The book was an account of his missionary life and work in South Africa, and hence in part consisted in an adaptation of his earlier volume " Ten Years North of the Orange River." It dealt also with those later experiences in Shoshong and Kuruman which as yet lay buried in the archives of the London Missionary Society. The little book was published by Cassell and Co., and had a large circulation, which that enterprising firm extended to America. For the holiday month of August 1883, Mackenzie took a cottage at Hillside, near Montrose, where once more he was able to see all his children gathered together at one time.

But in September Mackenzie was in London again, preparing for the fiercest of the fight. Ominous signs of a hard struggle were in the air. It had become known in June that the Transvaal Government wished to send a deputation to England to deal at close quarters with Her Majesty's Government. Lord Derby very readily consented to receive them, but warned them that the Conference could not take place before the end of October. In the month of September, therefore, Mackenzie found himself in at once a more strenuous contest and a better position to carry it on. The visit of the deputation was about to hasten the decision of the British Government and to make it take a final step—into Bechuanaland to remain there, or out of it for ever! But just because the whole matter was about to be decided the voice of the best-informed man in London, perhaps anywhere, on this specific subject acquired a public authority.

The delegates were sent by the Transvaal Government to Europe, in the first place, to raise a loan. The fact is that the wheels of State were beginning to grind heavily, and the drivers saw themselves sinking into that condition of bankruptcy which had helped to make annexation in 1877 seem inevitable, and which would have made history, sooner or later, repeat itself, had not the discovery of the Witwaters Rand goldfields transformed the economic situation. In relation to Great Britain the delegates had another plan. They determined to urge that the Pretoria Convention had failed, and that a return must be made to the Sand River Convention of 1852! In particular, they were prepared to make four demands upon Great Britain. First, that the name "South African Republic" should be recognised; second, that part of the debt to Great Britain, over £250,000, should be cancelled; third, that the system of British control of the treatment of natives within and without the Transvaal, of which Mr Gladstone had prophesied so triumphantly, should be abolished; and fourth, that the Western boundary of the Republic should be carried so far west as to include all Bechuanaland within its limits.

Mackenzie was alarmed by these proposals. With his intimate knowledge of Boer feelings and ambitions, with his estimate of the recently formed Afrikander Bond and its future influence on South African history, with his convictions about the character of the leaders of the Transvaal, he saw that the real substantial question now actually raised was that of the paramount power in South Africa. He stood almost alone in this belief at first. And to the end he failed fully to convince Lord Derby, or even Sir Hercules Robinson, who was happily in London to take part in the conference. But the subsequent history of Transvaal ambitions has proved that he was right. His estimate of the situation is most vigorously expressed in a letter to Dr Dale.

PORTOBELLO, 22 *Sept.* 1883.

DEAR DR DALE,—I hope you have been able to follow recent South African events, especially those connected with the Cape Colony. The extreme anti-English party in the Cape Parliament has been shown to be a small one. There was danger at one time that their hands would have been strengthened by the extreme Hammer and Tongs English party at the Cape ; but this did not happen. The Scanlen Government is not a strong one ; but on the Basutoland question it actually secured votes from those adverse to its general policy.

There would have been universal approval of the Basutoland policy of Mr Scanlen's Government, if anything like confidence had been felt as to the intentions of the English Government. Could her promise be trusted to ? How much must be discounted from what she promised ; or did she promise anything ? The result of the Basutoland arrangement is beginning to be felt in that country, and good will appear as confidence is restored to men's minds by the action of England.

Now the Transvaal envoys are on their way to this country. What is the question which they come to decide ? Whether the Transvaal is or is not to be left without restraint, and if thus left, to become the paramount South African State. It is not a question of " freedom," as that word is usually understood ; much less is it a question of self-government. It is a question of paramountcy. Is it to be retained by England, with and for the Cape Colony and the more civilized South African communities, or is it to be handed to the Transvaal ? The Cape Colony appears to have awoke to the imminence of the peril in which she stands of being shut out from the trade of the interior, and shut out from the great possibilities connected with having a voice in the settlement of the immense unoccupied and beautiful countries to the north. But the attitude of England is surely too coldly supine. The men who would be glad to see England out of South Africa altogether are having it all their own way. At least it would seem so. An intelligent German, well acquainted with South Africa, recently said to a friend of mine, " It is deplorable how England fritters away her influence for good in South Africa."

At such a juncture as this the hands of the government ought to be strengthened in connection with the Pretoria Convention. What has failed ? Where is the mistake ? Where is the Transvaal wronged ? South African affairs need a head ; and that head is the English Government in the meantime—along with and, perhaps, to be succeeded by, the government of the Cape. Modify the Convention if you like by removing internal interference in Transvaal (I say this reluctlantly, but to gain a point)—if you are to modify, do it there ; but as to setting the Transvaal free and irresponsible, and undefined as to its borders, it would be a moral wrong for England to do it. And history would point to the action as an illustration of cold-blooded and short-sighted selfishness.

Now I want to ask your advice as to what ought to be done in this most important matter? The Cape Colony has given up Basutoland—how can it take over Bechuanaland ? It could only do so with the understanding that England assisted the colony with Bechuanaland as with Basutoland.

The Missionary Society lately addressed a letter to Lord Derby on this aspect of the question. His reply was, that Her Majesty's Government were waiting in this matter the action of the Cape Government.

My position is that with a Viceroy (as the *Spectator* called the official whom it also recommends for South Africa) and a central government, South Africa need never cost England anything in money or men—except some of her best sons as administrators and civil servants.

Now, before I have done, just consider the issues that are at stake just now. Who is to be supreme in South Africa? What sort of views as to native races are to have power in the future? With reference to the London Missionary Society, is it to expect better treatment at the hands of the Transvaal authorities than the French missionaries met with from President Burgers, when they were detained as prisoners and then sent back to Basutoland, on the occasion of their *desiring to pass through the Transvaal* to reach the tribes beyond? What are we to make of our useful Bechuana Mission and native ministers and the possibilities of our northward work, if law and justice retreat from the country, and might is left to assert itself as right? And but for the attention which Bechuanaland has received in England— feeble and uncertain as that has been—where would our Mission have been? Ask the ruins at Kolobeng, at Matebe, and at Moilwe's—the stations destroyed by the Boers, shortly after the signing of the Sand River Convention. England is surely interested in the right of way to the interior of South Africa, so that peaceful men, whether missionaries or traders, or scientific explorers, should have a free right of way, as they have had from the native chiefs.

Now, if you have followed me thus far, I think you will agree that there is a case for the attention of those who are better known than I am. Please to think over the matter, and suggest something practical and something worthy of the greatness of the question.

I remember in May last you seemed to have mastered this question. I hope it has not been buried under later and more absorbing questions. But if it has been covered, it is still there in your mind. I look to you for help to do good in a far-reaching way, and in a work which I think will abide. I shall be glad to hear from you.—Believe me to be, ever yours sincerely,

JOHN MACKENZIE.

Mackenzie had now found several most valuable allies in the London press. The editorship of the *Pall Mall Gazette* had passed from the hands of Mr Morley to those of Mr W. T. Stead, who proved himself at that time a most vigorous and useful propagator of true Imperialism in South Africa. One of the papers which from the first showed a profound grasp of South African affairs, and which has maintained its first clear insight through all the tumult and confusion of intervening years, was the *Spectator*. Mackenzie had no direct relations with the *Spectator* beyond having met Mr R. H. Hutton and Mr Townsend, but was ever deeply grateful for its sympathy and its constancy. Both of these papers used their full power to prevent the political blunder, the moral disgrace, which the Government seemed not unwilling to perpetrate in South Africa. The columns of the *Pall Mall* were used by Mackenzie frequently, and a number of trenchant editorials appeared there from the pen of Mr Stead, with the result that people were thoroughly aroused to see that an important event in Great Britain's Imperial relations was about to occur.

The delegates, soon after their arrival, committed the error of publishing boldly a statement of their claims, and supporting it with what professed to be a history of their relations to Bechuanaland. They found, to their astonishment, that opposition to their plans had been already unwittingly prepared by Mackenzie's long campaign since July 1882. They also found their curious "history" and their political claims confronted by the same man, with an accurate and moderate and unanswerable statement of the real history of Bechuanaland, and with a sound estimate of their real ambitions. They had friends, of course, such as Dr G. B. Clark and others, who had so long, so curiously, acted as champions of the Transvaal; and these tried to create a public movement favouring Mr Kruger and his companions. They failed however. Even the Lord Mayor of London, Sir R. N. Fowler, M.P., who was a member of the South African

Committee, and a student at first hand of South African affairs, declined to invite them to a Mansion House banquet, when it was proposed to him to do so. Shortly after their arrival Mackenzie wrote a letter to Mr Stead, from which the following may be taken :—

It is commonly supposed it is "freedom" which the dear Dutchmen want. I'll tell you what it is.

It is not self-government; that they have had, and have. There has been no real interference by England with their internal affairs since the Convention.

It is not independence (like the Free State). But, in order to meet them, this *might be given them*, and Mr Hudson removed from the Transvaal, and Bechuanaland administered by Cape Colony and England.

But what they want is the supreme political position in South Africa, to be the empire State among its states, the highway into the interior, to have native policy of the Future, etc., etc., all in their hands.

Now if England is out of the country, do let Cape Colony come to the front, and be in the front. Let civilization and intelligence get ahead (as to influence) of dull ignorance, prejudice and bounce.

Why does not Dr Clark work for the independence of Cape Colony? That the frontier men of South Africa should be independent of the rest of the Europeans out there is what every true friend of South Africa would protest against. It is impertinent as to the Cape Colony and Natal that Englishmen in London should work for the Independence of the frontier men of our European population in South Africa.

.   .   .   .

At the same time they would have been none the worse of the Mayor's wine.

We need not here recount the story of that long Conference between Lord Derby, assisted by Sir Hercules Robinson, the High Commissioner for South African Affairs on the one hand, and these delegates of the Transvaal, President Kruger, the Rev. S. J. du Toit, and General N. J. Smith, on the other hand. The conference was carried on almost exclusively in writing. The first pretension of the delegates that they were about to make a treaty with Great Britain was abruptly turned down by Derby, who defined the difference between a treaty and a convention. The convention was an agreement under which Her Majesty conferred upon certain people who had been formerly her subjects the power of self-government, on certain conditions. With great ease the delegates found themselves receiving—handed over to them with the proverbial hauteur and uncalculating, and therefore ignorant, self-complacency attributed to the typical Englishman—three of their four great boons. A large part of their debt was remitted; the British control over the Transvaal's treatment of its native population—Mr Gladstone's prophetic dream notwithstanding—was withdrawn; the Transvaal was formally recognised as " The South African Republic." There can be no doubt *now* that Lord Derby went too far, that in making the last two concessions he put actual and immeasurable power into the hands of what was, at heart, a hostile power, and that he gave the Transvaal an international standing. This international standing was of course further confirmed and dignified, when to these he added yet another boon, that of making treaties, with only the right of veto reserved to the Queen. Mackenzie saw with deep sadness the gradual investment of the " Frontier Boers" with such power and prestige; he saw the day of the Boer's hope dawning. For, as his letters have shown, he already knew that the deep design of Mr Kruger was to make the South African Republic the paramount power in South Africa. Very few were the men whom he could convince of this as a living policy, and a living danger; and, alas! none of these was in the Colonial Office.

There remained the one greatest desire of the Transvaal heart, namely, the extension of their western border over Bechuanaland.   What they said alike before, at, and after the London Conference shows how far they saw into the future.   They knew that this alone would settle the question of paramountcy in South Africa.   The other concessions would help them wonderfully towards the fulfilment of their racial dream ; but without this, those others might prove futile ; with this, they would certainly make the Transvaal supreme.   It was the discussion of this matter, the fate of Bechuanaland, and in that the fate of the British Empire in South Africa, which prolonged the Conference from the beginning of November 1883 to the middle of February 1884.

A few men in Cape Colony and England had already begun to appreciate the far-reaching importance of this Boer movement westwards, such as Mr Cecil Rhodes and Sir Thomas Scanlen at the Cape, Mr W. E. Forster, Sir T. F. Burton, Earl Grey, Sir Bartle Frere and others at home.   Mr Rhodes, indeed, proposed a motion in the Cape Parliament requesting the British Government " in the interests of the Colony to appoint a Resident with the Chief Mankoroane."   This was mild enough surely ; but it was lost.   The Africander Bond, whose rallying cry was " Africa for the Africanders," and whose membership included the leading Dutchmen in the Transvaal, Orange Free State, and Cape Colony, was now organised and its momentous history had begun.   As an immediate result, the racial elements in the Cape Parliament were being rapidly changed, and Mr Hofmeyr had opened his career as the Bond leader without whom no Cape politician might hope to gain or to hold for long the office of Prime Minister.   So strong had the current already set in against British " inter-

ference," that a certain well-known member of the
Cape Parliament—an Englishman—refused to present
a petition which proposed to keep the trade route into
the interior open, because the petition affirmed that
England ought to be the paramount power north of
Griqualand West!

It seemed at one time as if Mackenzie might have
a direct and official position in the Conference. For
Mankoroane, the chief whose territories lay nearest
to Cape Colony, who had been very true to Great
Britain and had suffered for his loyalty, and whose
land was now being seized by inhabitants of the
Transvaal, claimed the right to be present at the
Conference. He began his journey and reached Cape
Town, when he was informed that he should go no
further. He then asked that Mackenzie be allowed
to act as his official representative. This also Lord
Derby refused, but he wrote to Mackenzie to say that
all information which the latter might have regarding
Mankoroane and his rights would be received and
carefully considered in the course of the Conference.
In this way Mackenzie was put in a position of actual,
though unofficial, power. As the Conference was
carried on almost entirely by the exchange of documents and letters, and by private and personal interviews, Mackenzie, to whom those avenues were thus
fully opened, had a very real place in the Conference.
His conversations with Sir Hercules Robinson, Sir
Robert Herbert and others at the Colonial Office
were very frequent. Every new proposal by the
delegates, every argument which they made, every
historical assertion which they risked, was submitted
to Mackenzie for his criticism. He used his oppo-
tunity, not merely to deal with the claims of the
Transvaal, but, as these were successfully rebutted,
with the new position in which the rebuttal of those
claims put Great Britain. That Government, it was

plain, must do much more than waive aside the proposals of the Transvaal; it must say what was to be
done with, and what was to become of, the native
tribes whose territory was now being "eaten up" by
the Boers.   You do not dam back a flowing tide by
drawing an imaginary line and forbidding its advances,
nor would you stop the unrighteous and murderous
annexation of Bechuanaland by Boers from the Transvaal, by drawing a line on maps in London and
having it "ratified" at Pretoria.   The only possible
plan was British action instead of Transvaal action.
The trade route could only be kept open through the
actual occupation of the country by those for whom
it was to be open.

In the beginning of December Mackenzie sent in to
Lord Derby a memorandum describing the kind of
government which Great Britain could, and ought to,
adopt in Bechuanaland.   It was his old well-pondered
system of territorial government, which had capti-
vated Sir Bartle Frere, and convinced other wide-
viewed men.   To his great joy, Lord Derby confessed
himself impressed by it.   " A policy, such as you have
indicated, would doubtless, if firmly and judiciously
carried out, avert many difficulties and dangers."
That marked a great advance upon the attitude which
Lord Derby had himself taken less than a year before,
when the same principles were submitted by Mackenzie
for his consideration.   Lord Derby made British
action depend upon the action of the colonies and
states of South Africa.   It was his view that such a
scheme could only be carried out by them.   This
visionary notion was characteristic of the British
statesman's knowledge, and his theorising about
South Africa.   No one who knew South Africa could
possibly consider it as possible that the colonies and
states would combine, in those days, to carry out so
broad a policy of native territorial government.   For

one thing, it would mean the complete transformation of the Boer spirit, and for another it would mean that rival states and colonies should at once unite on purely humanitarian grounds, upon a work which is the most difficult in South Africa. Mackenzie was much cheered by Derby's letter, notwithstanding this restriction. To his eldest son he writes of it as follows :—

11 QUEEN SQUARE
(Undated.)

DEAR WILLIE,—I got the enclosed last night before going to bed. It was good news. I caught myself singing when dressing this morning, which I have not felt inclined to do for some time.

When you remember that I ask no new responsibility, and when you consider the attitude of the Cape Colony asking for what Lord Derby says he is inclined to grant if colonies and states agree to ask it, the thing is most gratifying. God grant that nothing go wrong—no ill-wind blow on this decidedly practical and masterful attitude of Lord Derby. It is personally very pleasing to me to get his commendation so far to my scheme.

The *Contemporary* is to try and get some big people to endorse my view in the *Review*, perhaps Sir H. Barkly and Sir B. Frere.

Do pray earnestly that this tendency in the right direction may be strengthened till it become a policy. I have seen Mr Scanlen, and showed him the letter. He was pleased. It was new life to him. I told him he must look up my communication and see if he approved of it, in which case a great point would be gained. He is likely to do so. Sir H. Robinson does so. I read it to him in MS.

Must stop to catch post. Love to all in Portobello and in Montrose.—Your affectionate father.

J. M.

Mackenzie did not confine his agitation during the Conference to the Colonial Office and communications to the newspapers. Knowing the value of public meetings and the effect upon a Government of resolutions from important and representative gatherings all over the country, he continued this kind of work. The most important of all the gatherings was that held at the Mansion House, London, on Tuesday, November 27th, 1883. The Egyptian Hall was full to overflowing, and the " platform " was most distinguished as well as numerous. It was held under the auspices of the South African Committee, whose secretary, Mr F. W. Chesson, put his whole heart and his great organising powers into the effort.[1] The Lord Mayor (Sir R. N. Fowler) occupied the chair. The principal speeches were delivered by the Earl of Shaftesbury, Mr W. E. Forster, Rev. John Mackenzie, Sir Henry Barkly and Sir Thomas F. Buxton. Mr Forster's speech was long, but full of fire, and produced a very great effect. The speakers all dealt mainly with the following points : the commercial value of the Bechuanaland trade-route into the interior, which the Hon. R. Southey, former Lieutenant-Governor of Griqualand West, estimated at one million pounds sterling per annum ; the rights of the Bechuanaland tribes and the obligations of Great Britain towards them ; the policy of the Transvaal towards natives and the *virtual* slavery so long practised in the Transvaal. Mackenzie's own speech was very well received. It produced such an effect on one great man that he (Lord Shaftesbury), in shaking hands with Mackenzie at the close of the meeting, said emphatically, " You have a great career before you ; I'm sure you have a great career before you." On the night of that meeting Mackenzie sat down and wrote the following letter to his eldest son, which throws much light upon his work at this time :—

[1] An important pamphlet was published by the Aborigines Protection Society (1884), entitled "The Bechuanas, the Cape Colony, and the Transvaal," which contained a good report of the speeches at the meeting, besides other documents of importance to the discussion.

11 QUEEN SQUARE,
27th Nov. 1883.

MY DEAR WILLIE,—I am addressing you to-night, as I feel it is indeed a long time since we interchanged thoughts. I have just come home from handing in MS. of my speech to the *Times*. Their reporter came up and asked if I would like to supply it, and saying how much space they could afford. I have sent much more than he said in the hope that, having it there cut and dried, he will let it go in and save himself trouble.

Well, the meeting has been a marvellous success, to use the kind of expression which you hear on such subjects. I came far short of my own idea as to what a speech ought to be. Lord Shaftesbury was in his usual vein, and was, of course, very well received. Next came Mr Forster. You will read his speech. He gave it them hot on all sides. You can have no idea of the enthusiastic reception which he met with. I think this question has done good work for Mr Forster, as certainly he has done good work for it. You know what I mean. He has shown those points as a politician which English people dearly love—fearless rectitude and strong denunciation of mere shiftiness. The people were very kind and appreciative all through. I was quite astonished at the heartiness of the meeting. I was very careful in what I said. I did not have time, however, half to go over the ground which I had chalked out, as others had to come after me, and Forster took a frightfully long time. However, I said some of the things I wanted to say, but omitted how many! I am assured the meeting was an unusually enthusiastic one—this from Londoners!

Sir Henry Barkly is a good speaker. It was opportune also that Hon. R. Southey, the first Lieutenant-Governor of Griqualand West, should have been there to say a few words.

The *Aberdeen Free Press* is evidently in communication with Dr Clark, the Boer advocate—if, indeed, he is not writing for it. I was very glad and thankful for that leader in the *Scotsman*. I sent it to the Colonial Office.

I had the impression that I had described my visit to Lord Derby; but as your mother asks me about it in her last, I must have done it in my dreams only.

I found Lord Derby and Sir Evelyn Ashley, with Sir

Robert Herbert, the Permanent Secretary, in the large room
—I suppose, Lord Derby's. They had just been glancing
over my statement in behalf of Mankoroane. Lord Derby
came forward and very courteously met me, etc.—But surely
I must have written all this to some one.

We were close upon an hour together. What did
Mankoroane want? The establishment of order and
government in his country by England or failing that,
by the Cape Colony.

The map was referred to; places, etc., pointed out.

ASHLEY. But Mankoroane has not lost any of his good
land, only his outlying hunting veldt. At least, I said so
in the House of Commons, and no one contradicted me.

I. I'm afraid your inference is not warranted. I'm afraid
you could say a good many things about Bechuanaland and
not be contradicted in the House of Commons.

DERBY (laughing). Very true. No doubt of that.

I then explained what he had lost, and how the people
had begun to live at their farms before this trouble, so that it
was really their homes which had been broken up.

ASHLEY. Why don't all these people unite—they are so
numerous—they could soon settle the matter themselves?

I. Well I should be glad of a settlement, but, to say truth,
I should not be glad to see people ranging themselves in an
hostile attitude in South Africa—blacks, because they were
blacks; and whites, as whites.

DERBY. Very true. I agree with you—it would be a bad
thing. How would you do this?

I then sketched how I thought the thing might be done.
Increase (with the active sanction and consent of the Cape
Colony) the Cape Border Police, and make that your *force*
for all practical purposes in Bechuanaland. You must
recognize that this is an old affair, and has been let alone.
Claims to land held by white men might turn out to your
Commissioner to be valid. In my opinion the Commissioner
would not dirty his hands, or compromise himself by dealing
with these men. All that has been done already by the
Government. The highest morality compels me to say they
ought all to be cleared out. But the past action of the
Government compels me to make the above suggestion as
the only one feasible.

I should have European magistrates, under a Commissioner
—but territorial as distinguished from colonial law, etc. I

did not go far into this.   But I think I shall request a short
talk on this very point about *land*; it is so important, and my
arrangement is so unlike everybody else's, or rather, nobody
has anything to propose that is new.

I took occasion to mention the fallacy of some of what I
knew to be the Boer position—*e.g.*, that if they got more
ground they would be more peaceful, etc.

You would see that by Sir Bartle Frere, in the *Pall Mall*.
I asked Chesson about him and the meeting.   " If you like
to spoil it let him come," was the answer, " the Conservatives
would cheer him, and the others hiss him."   " If any hissed,
and I had the slightest chance I should certainly stick up
for him."   " Yes, and spoil the meeting."   When I found
that no tickets had been sent to him, or his family, and all
so deeply interested in the question, I sent some down to
them, and Lady Frere was kind enough to send up an
express, with a note of thanks.   Sir Bartle was away in
Nottinghamshire, and wrote a note to me which I got in the
morning.   Of course he did not know about the tickets, as
he was away from home.   Do you know, although I don't
agree with what the Conservatives and he were doing, I do
admire the man, and feel intensely sorry for the calamity
which has come upon him after a life-time of devoted service
to his country.   It is his indomitable pluck which captivates
me, and his really noble bearing in his present trying
position.   However, I did not mean to go into this.   But
Sir H. Barkly was there and spoke well; Sir H. Robinson
was quoted by Forster; but poor Sir Bartle was nowhere.
Mind you it is a warning—but not to governors only, I
should think, but to those who send them; for I think
he was a good and loyal servant of the Conservative
Government.

Sir Fowell Buxton was very kind, enquiring where I was,
etc.   And what do you think ?   The Lord Mayor has asked
me to dine with him to-morrow week, to meet Mr Scanlen of
the Cape Colony.   Perhaps it will be all over before that
time.

We shall see ; but I should not be surprised if the meeting to-night does help the cause of eventual peace and good
government in South Africa.   I am sending this, *via*
Portobello.

Another important meeting was held in Edinburgh
on January 31st, 1884. Mackenzie was the leading
speaker and he was followed by the late Professor
Henry Calderwood of Edinburgh University, the late
Bishop Cotterill, Professor W. G. Blaikie, the biographer of Livingstone, Mr John Gifford, the Rev.
G. D. Cullen and others. Dr Calderwood described
Mackenzie's speech as a " very clear, very calm, and
very important statement."

Mackenzie secured a place for his second *Review*
article in the *Contemporary* of January 1884. It
was entitled " England and South Africa," and extended to twenty-six pages. It was divided into four
sections, in the course of which the author tried to
put into the hands of any intelligent Englishman
all the material which he would need for making up his mind as to the claims made by the
Transvaal and the responsibilities of Great Britain
in Bechuanaland.

Section I. introduced the discussion by asking why the
Pretoria Convention had not succeeded. " The delegates
have declared, since they came to England, that they are
willing to observe towards the native tribes all that human
or divine law would dictate. Under what category are we
to reckon the Pretoria Convention, which the Transvaal has
so flagrantly broken, and now wishes to rescind?" Section
II. "The Transvaal and Bechuanaland," traced the history
of the relations between the Transvaal Boers and the tribes
whose territories they now wished to obtain. The legal
status of the blacks in the Transvaal is once more referred
to, and the following telling comparison is made. "The
Transvaal is a would-be Republic; so are the United States
of America. But the one may be justly said to be in some
respects the opposite of the other. The inequality of men
which the Transvaal people left the Cape Colony to secure—
which they have written in their constitution in the Transvaal—is the very doctrine which has been removed from the
laws of the American Republic, after sacrifices such as the
world never heard of before. Americans have freed their

own Republican doctrines and carried them out. The Transvaal may come to do so, but in the meantime it has no right to be classed with governments which are its antithesis in doctrine and practice." A little later Mackenzie says, " I am exceedingly sorry that duty compels me to affirm and to show that the historical researches published under the name of President Kruger are entirely unreliable." This he proceeds to do at some length, tracing the history of Bechuanaland from 1812 to 1883. Section III. dealt with the " Political Condition of South Africa." Natal, the Free State, and the Cape Colony were briefly described, and then nearly five pages were given to one of those full and, it may be presumed accurate expositions of the relations, characteristics, and political problems of the native tribes of South Africa, which make Mackenzie's books and articles of first-rate importance to future students of that subject. Section IV. once more outlined his ever-developing plan for " The Government of South African Native Territories." After describing once more the need for a High Commissioner released from the trammels of a local Governorship, he set forth successively his definition of a " Territory," the system of territorial law, the knotty problem of land tenure in a " Territory," the certainty that a territorial government could be paid by local taxes and upheld with a simple system of police. Finally, he dealt with the possibility of war in the carrying out of his scheme. His main points were that in a country like South Africa occasional disturbances may be looked for, but that a strong government would always prevent them from growing into "wars"; that Great Britain cannot "run away from difficulties . . . from the shadows of her own mistakes in South Africa," but that she need never have on her hands in South Africa a disturbance which could not be quelled by means of South African Police. " If you have several native territories under your Government, you will always be able to find fighting men ready to your hand," when any tribe becomes rebellious. The article concluded with the following sentence : " There is annexation which is mere theft ; that we abhor. But in the successful government of South Africa there would be wise provision made for a process which in our scheme would be like growth, and not like theft. The land would not be stolen, and yet expansion would gradually take place. Black men would come southward,

white men would go northward—under control and peacefully.   There is a responsibility in accepting such a scheme ;
but there is a responsibility in rejecting it ; and there is the
gravest responsibility in letting things alone.   The present
condition of South Africa is a disgrace to the character and
the known administrative ability of England.   And yet with
intelligent treatment, South Africa, as it has been the most
difficult, and is to-day the most unique, may also become the
most interesting of English dependencies, and the crowning
effort of her successful administration."

The editor of the *Contemporary Review* secured
letters from Sir H. Barkly and Sir Bartle Frere, to
whom this article was submitted in proof, and their
comments were printed in the same number of that
Review. It had been announced in December that
Lord Derby had expressed his substantial agreement with Mackenzie's policy, and that fact no doubt
added to the interest with which his article was
received.   In a private letter Sir Bartle Frere made
some useful suggestions as to the dissemination of
the *Review,* and added, " It is far the best paper
on South African affairs I have seen for a long
time, and ought to be read and carefully studied
by everyone who is going to speak, write, or vote
on the subject."

From November 1st, 1883, when the Conference
began, more than three months elapsed before an
agreement was reached on the first article of the
new Convention, the article which determined the
boundaries of the Transvaal.   Lord Derby aimed
at and secured a compromise.   He agreed to the
annexation of a rich and extensive portion, about
2600 square miles, of South Bechuanaland to the
Transvaal.   Mackenzie of course opposed this, not,
as he says in an unprinted manuscript on the Conference, " not in an inimical spirit to the Transvaal,
but rather in its highest interest."   He held that
for so scattered a population as the Transvaal, and

for a Government so inefficient in departmental work, the addition of territory was no boon, but a burden. At the same time, he pressed the argument that the two native chiefs, Moshette and Massouw, although they had been induced to employ Boer volunteers, did not desire annexation to the Transvaal. Nevertheless, Lord Derby having remitted a quarter of a million pounds sterling, having recognised the significant title, " The South African Republic," having agreed to surrender the British right to control the Boers' treatment of natives, having granted the right to make treaties with foreign powers, subject only to the Queen's veto, went further still in this broad and unparalleled policy of " generosity " to the Transvaal, and " gave " that Government the right to govern the territory of those two native tribes. All through the discussions Mackenzie feared to assume too hostile an attitude, lest he should seem to be a mere partisan ; but with his clear conviction regarding the ultimate purpose of Mr Kruger's policy, he regretted deeply that the power to realise that purpose was thus put into those hands with a smile of security and of Imperial self-confidence.

When the Conference at last resulted in the " Convention," that document embraced no less than twenty articles, drawn up in English and Dutch. Several of these have acquired strange significance from subsequent events. For example, the fourth article forbids the South African Republic to conclude any " treaty or engagement with any State or nation *other than the Orange Free State* . . . until the same has been approved by Her Majesty the Queen." That singular exception, which was allowed with contempt, has produced sinister results. Article IX. provides for the continuance of complete religious freedom for all denominations, " provided the same be not inconsistent with morality and good order." Article XIV.

is the famous one which became the basis of dispute between the Transvaal Government and the Uitlanders in after years. It provides for the freedom and equality as to property and commercial rights before the law of "all persons, other than natives, conforming themselves to the laws of the South African Republic." Natives are dealt with in other articles (VIII. and XIX.), where slavery is forbidden, "or apprenticeship partaking of slavery," and the South African Republic "engages faithfully to fulfil the assurance" given to the Transvaal natives by the Royal Commission at the great Pretoria Pitso, or assembly of native chiefs and headmen, in 1881.

The second Article was the one which, along with the first, "saved the face" of the British Government, and South Africa from becoming a Dutch Republic. The first half of it was as follows :—"The Government of the South African Republic will strictly adhere to the boundaries defined in the first Article of the Convention, and will do its utmost to prevent any of its inhabitants from making any encroachments upon lands beyond the said boundaries. The Government of the South African Republic will appoint Commissioners upon the eastern and western borders whose duty it will be strictly to guard against irregularities, and all trespassing over the boundaries. Her Majesty's Government will, if necessary, appoint Commissioners in the native territories outside the eastern and western borders of the South African Republic to maintain order and prevent encroachments."

Lord Derby decided that, in view of the whole circumstances in Bechuanaland, the provisions of that Article must be acted upon at once. Order must be restored in that land, a debt of honour must be paid to Montsioa and Mankoroane, the two loyal chiefs, and the trade route must be occupied in order to be kept open. To this decision Derby was led, not merely by a consideration of the rights of the case, but by the argument that the Cape Colony was profoundly interested in the matter, was prepared to share the expense of occupying the country, and might ultimately consent to its annexation. The Premier of the Colony had been in England during part of the negotiations, and virtually pledged himself and his colleagues to see that the Colonial Government bore its part of the cost. Lord Derby, while convinced of the wisdom of Mackenzie's scheme, was never thoroughly convinced that the British people would sanction the expenditure of Imperial funds to secure Bechuanaland or maintain British supremacy in South Africa. His timidity on the point was no doubt increased by the urgency with which that little group of Liberals still pressed what Mackenzie called the "clear-out policy."

When Lord Derby and Sir Hercules Robinson were deciding what to do with Bechuanaland, the latter recommended that Mackenzie should be sent out as Deputy Commissioner. At first Derby hesitated. He clearly foresaw the kind of criticism which would be made upon the appointment of a missionary to so important a task, and he invited Robinson to name some one else. But Sir Hercules had made up his mind, for the time at any rate. He had been very closely associated with Mackenzie for some months now, and was evidently under the influence of his strong personality and his intellectual grasp of the situation. A few months later, when other strong personalities were busy around him and bearing down upon his too pliant will, he gave the following as the reasons for his nomination of John Mackenzie : " Mr Mackenzie was selected for the post because it was assumed that, having regard to his well-known influence with the natives, as well as to his successful advocacy of Colonial interests, his appointment would have commanded the confidence of the colonists as well as of the natives over whom it was proposed to establish a Protectorate." The following is the letter to Sir Hercules Robinson, in which Mackenzie indicated his willingness to accept the appointment if offered to him by the Government :—

11 QUEEN SQUARE,
BLOOMSBURY, *8th Feb.* 1884.

DEAR SIR HERCULES,—With reference to your kind offer to recommend me to Her Majesty's Government for the Commissionership in Bechuanaland, I beg to express my thanks and my willingness to do my best in that capacity, should your recommendation receive the sanction of the Government.

I am, however, more interested in the initiation of a Native Policy in South Africa by the English Government which would pacify the country, lead to union, and establish our own rule there, than I am with reference to any other question, even my own personal affairs.

The government is getting the credit with the public of facing this subject somewhat on the lines of the article in the *Contemporary*. I meet with indications of this on all hands, and I feel sure they themselves will feel bound to look at it in this light.

I shall be content with the smallest honest and avowed beginning of this policy ; and will cheerfully, and under a full sense of duty, take any share in working it out, for which they and you may think I am qualified.

Trusting I rightly interpret the attitude of Her Majesty's Government towards this most important and hitherto most perplexing and vexatious question, I place myself at their disposal in connexion with it.—I am, dear Sir Hercules, ever yours sincerely,

JOHN MACKENZIE.

P.S.—If Her Majesty's Government will only give this a fair chance, and gradually, cautiously, and intelligently develop the policy I refer to, I hope to live to see a practically united South Africa, and England relieved of the present irritating responsibilities in that part of the world.

On February 21st Mackenzie received Lord Derby's formal offer of the post, and he at once replied in the following letter, which summarises the main conditions of the appointment. The salary named to him was £1200 per annum, and necessary travelling expenses.

LONDON, 21st *February* 1884.

THE RIGHT HONOURABLE THE EARL OF DERBY,
    Secretary of State for the Colonies.

MY LORD,—I have received your Lordship's letter of this date, stating your own views and those of Sir Hercules Robinson as to my fitness for the proposed office of Resident Commissioner in Bechuanaland, and desiring to know if I can undertake that work " under those conditions which the circumstances of the case render necessary."

Your Lordship's description of those circumstances is, that the intervention of Her Majesty's Government in Bechuanaland is of a tentative and experimental character ; that therefore, present arrangements cannot possibly be of a permanent nature ; consequently, that your Lordship cannot guarantee the permanence of the employment which you now offer me ; but that either party may retire from the arrangement should he see fit to do so.

After giving the question the most serious consideration, I have come to the conclusion to accept of the offer with which your Lordship has honoured me. As I do so, the importance and the difficulty of the work are vividly before me. I face it with diffidence, but with a clear feeling that I am in the path of duty in the course which I now take.

Your Lordship seems to be of the opinion that I could do the work required of me, while still connected with the Missionary Society. This was my own view in somewhat parallel circumstances some years ago, and the High Commissioner then wrote to the Directors of the Society, asking that such arrangement might be sanctioned. That sanction, however, was withheld, on the ground that such a union of offices was not in accord with the usages of the Society.   I may now say, however, that, as individuals, the Directors are impressed with the great importance of the work, and approve of my undertaking it in present circumstances, although this necessitates my formal severance from the number of the Society's missionaries.

The question referred to by your Lordship as to the action to be taken in Bechuanaland—the powers and duties to be assigned to the Resident Commissioner—are of the greatest importance ; and I shall be happy to wait on your Lordship for their discussion while the High Commissioner is still here.—I am, my Lord, Your Lordship's obedient Servant,

JOHN MACKENZIE.

The following brief note is of some interest at this point :—

11 QUEEN SQUARE,
BLOOMSBURY, 15*th Feb.* 1884.

MY DEAR MR OATES,—In leaving Sir H. Robinson's hotel this morning, I passed President Kruger and Mr du Toit, who were expected.   I had a good look at each in passing.   I hope to be introduced one of these days, for the fighting is over, so far as they are concerned ; and I am quite willing to shake hands.

Dr Jorrissen has gone out in the same ship with my friends the Hepburns.   Hepburn writes me from Madeira that Jorrissen is spreading the story that I have made a bother about the trade route, because I am largely engaged in trade myself ! One of the passengers, a Port Elizabeth merchant, came to Mr Hepburn and laid the matter before him.   Mr Hepburn, of course, was able to reply, " To my certain knowledge Mr Mackenzie has not touched trading even with his little finger."

Some people are unable to believe that a man can act without selfish motives.   They had to cast about for my motives.   Not finding them, they have invented trade.   I am much encouraged with the story.   The cause is feeble which has to resort to such shifts.   However, Hepburn is no doubt right when he says that Jorrissen is bent on mischief in South Africa.—Ever yours sincerely,

JOHN MACKENZIE.

The new Convention was signed on February 27th, 1884, and the news was at once telegraphed by Lord Derby to Cape Town. Mackenzie's appointment was announced at the same time. In England the new departure was condemned by those who desired to " clear out " of Africa ; but by all who had espoused the opposite policy and followed Mackenzie's tireless labours for eighteen months, the saving of Bechuana-land from the Transvaal was regarded as a great triumph, and the appointment of the missionary to rule as a Protector among his own people was welcomed as at once the unsought reward of his unselfish work, and a pledge of the earnestness of the Government. It is now clear that, personalities apart, the weak point in the whole arrangement lay in Derby's dependence upon the co-operation of the Cape Colony, and Robin-son's consequent fear that the British Government would not incur any initial expense in establishing the Pro-tectorate unless the Colony shared in it. Mackenzie, who later was confronted by this, considered it no obstacle to his acceptance of the task, being sure that at last the Colonial Office was entering on a consistent and persistent Imperialist policy in Bechuanaland and beyond, and being sure also of the loyal support of his chief, Sir Hercules Robinson.

Congratulations came to him from all quarters. From private friends, of course, he received many words of affectionate farewell ; for he was a man whom strong men of all kinds learned to love with a strong devotion. The newspapers on the whole spoke heartily and hopefully of the unusual move, and many of the public men with whom his work had brought him into contact wrote or spoke to him warmly and generously of their confident hopes regarding him and his future career in South Africa. The latter class included Mr W. E. Forster, Sir T. F. Buxton, Mr Talbot Baines, and others.

Naturally Mackenzie parted from the London Missionary Society with great reluctance and sorrow. But he was comforted by the broad and generous spirit in which the Directors of the Society treated him in private conference, and by the following minute which they adopted and sent to him. No less grateful to him were the letters which he received from Bechuanaland missionaries, his former fellow-labourers, several of whom now wrote very cordially, and who saw in his appointment the prophecy of better days for those among whom they laboured.

LONDON MISSIONARY SOCIETY

Resolution of the Board of Directors, 19th March 1884

In consenting to the withdrawal of the Rev. John Mackenzie from the connection which he has had with the London Missionary Society for the period of twenty-five years, the Board of Directors feel that it is due both to Mr Mackenzie, himself, and to the Society to place on record the following minute :—

That, whereas serious difficulties have arisen in South Africa, especially in relation to the Bechwana tribes, and that, the interests of good government, the progress of civilisation, and especially the successful continuance of Christian work among the natives, are deeply affected thereby ;

And, whereas, the Rev. John Mackenzie is recognised on all sides as a man who possesses the most intimate acquaintance with the condition of the people, and is well-known to the Boers, and has very great influence with the Bechwana people ;

And, whereas, the Government has requested Mr Mackenzie to accept the post of Resident-Commissioner among the Bechwanas ;

And, whereas, the work to which he is now called, though separating him from the immediate duties of the Christian Missionary, has yet an important bearing upon the successful prosecution of the mission of the Society among the Bechwana tribes ;

Resolved that :—

Although the Board has yielded to what seems to be a

providential indication of the will of God, in the disposal of
the services of its late missionary, it desires to record its
conviction that only in very exceptional circumstances can
the severance of a missionary from his proper duties be anything but a departure from the highest form of Christian
labour; but, at the same time, it would express the sense it
entertains of the high personal character of Mr Mackenzie,
the great value of his work in the past in the Foreign Mission
field, the serious loss to the agency of the Society which his
change of service involves; and, further, it desires to affirm
its unabated confidence in the purity and integrity of Mr
Mackenzie's purposes, and to commend to the loving care of
the Master, whom he has served so long, the life of its late
missionary in the important and difficult duty to which he
has been called.

And the Board would further pray :—

That through the development of a just and humane
policy on the part of the British Government, administered
with the firmness and gentleness which the Commissioner
possesses, there may be inaugurated a future for the Bechwana
people, by which the first beginnings of civilisation and the
early lessons of the Gospel may be carried out in abundant
prosperity, and the production of the highest virtues and the
highest graces of the Christian life.

The departure of Sir Hercules Robinson and that
of John Mackenzie for the Cape was, in each case,
celebrated by a public function. To the former a
banquet was given on March 3rd, at the Empire Club,
and a breakfast was given in honour of Mackenzie,
at the Westminster Palace Hotel by Sir William
M'Arthur. At the banquet, Sir Hercules spoke out
most frankly about the British Policy in Bechuanaland, and especially about the inability of the Cape
Colony to undertake the government of vast native
territories, and the consequent responsibility of the
Imperial Government. With all this the Earl of
Derby expressed his emphatic concurrence. At the
breakfast the most remarkable event was the speech
of the Hon. Evelyn Ashley, the Under Secretary

for the Colonies, who had previously said of every South African proposal, "*non possumus*," and who now uttered sentiments which gave Mackenzie the deepest confidence regarding the future of his own policy.

Among the events which moved him most was the visit which Mackenzie paid to Sir Bartle Frere. He refers to it briefly in " Austral Africa "; but the following extract from a letter to his third son, James Donald Mackenzie, then a student at Edinburgh University, adds some pathetic touches.

DARTMOUTH, 14*th March* 1884.

DEAR JIM,—I ought to tell you of my most interesting and impressive visit to the sick-bed of Sir Bartle Frere. Lady Frere telegraphed on Tuesday that she hoped I would be able to call before sailing, that Sir Bartle had had such pleasure in hearing of my appointment. I had fully intended to go down that very forenoon (Wednesday), so I answered accordingly and went. Had lunch; met a Sir Julius Goldsmith recently from the Congo, and all the Misses Frere. Lady Frere and they were very kind. After lunch went up. Sir Bartle was in bed, slightly improving, but still ill. His eye was bright and his expression, as well as his language, really noble. He spoke as one who stood on the Borderland and who saw both sides—the spirit-world to which he was near and the world in which he had been living. He could not have been more affectionate to me if I had been his son.

After some talk he said, " Well, Mackenzie, you will make a good job of that out there; I know you will. I have no doubt of it. You will get a lot of godly men around you ; see you do that, and work out your own plan, go straight at that, and you have the whole thing in your own hand, or rather you and it are in the hand of God." Many such expressions he used, most affectionate and hopeful. Shook hands; and then, while I stood, seized and held my hand, which was near him. Lady Frere brought him back to the debatable ground of this world by saying, " My dear, but it was only what you wanted to do five years ago." The praise involved did not affect him; he strongly replied, " God's time is the best time." I added by way of strengthening this, "The English public now know better than then what is involved in these South African questions." He agreed warmly to this. His blessing was most devoutly given to me for my full success. Take this dear Jim, in connexion with the breakfast next morning at which there were those who have said that Frere should have been hanged, and I think you will agree with me that God has been helping me in this matter, in bringing together so many of divergent views to unite in favour of this scheme of Territorial Government of Natives which I have been advocating.

.   .   .   .   .   .

On March 14th, 1884, Mackenzie, taking with him his wife and two youngest daughters and also his second son, Dr J. Eddie Mackenzie, sailed from Dartmouth on the *Drummond Castle*, which came to so terrific an end in the year 1896 off the coast of France. At the last he was busy with farewell letters, a number of which were written after going on board. His heart was deeply moved by certain family events which called out letters full of tenderness and sympathy. But other letters dealt with South Africa, and were addressed to those who had aided him. In that which he sent to Dr Dale occur a few words whose spirit pervaded all he said and wrote at that time.

Well, dear friend and helper in this good and, I trust, enduring work, I thank you ; and I trust thanks will be given to you by others when these matters are better understood. Patience and trust in the right! That will be my own motto out there.

We can do with a great deal of praying for. I think I come under two columns or paragraphs, now—missionary and governmental—and need it all.

Good-bye ! Do not lose sight of the subject. Do not think it ought to come right all at once. Be patient also, and hopeful, and when all are so, it will be a happy thing for the workers out there.

As he sat in the train on that 13th of March he was handed a newspaper by a stranger, which turned out to be the *Pall Mall Gazette*. There he found, unmistakably from the pen of his staunch friend and supporter, Mr W. T. Stead, an article entitled " Our First Resident in Bechuanaland." This article was full of Mr Stead's characteristic enthusiasm for his favourite projects. As it contained a description of Mackenzie and his work which is both vivid and impressive, most of it is here inserted.

Our First Resident in Bechuanaland

A sturdy, stalwart, broad-backed, beetle-browed Scotsman, whose sandy hair is beginning to silver with the frost of the second half-century of life, and whose keen blue eyes look out with shrewd penetrating gaze beneath a solid, but somewhat irregular forehead ; that is Mr Mackenzie, formerly of the London Missionary Society, now first British Commissioner for the territory of Bechuanaland. He leaves London this afternoon to unravel the Gordian knot that Boers and filibusters, with the aid of Moshette and Massouw, have been busy tying for the last two years in the country of Mankoroane and Montsioa. This morning, before he left, he was entertained at a quasi-public breakfast by Mr M'Arthur, around whose hospitable board were assembled a representative gathering of politicians, philanthropists, and administrators, to bid God-speed to the new Resident on his departure for his new duties. Seldom has anyone better deserved a hearty recognition of his services than the man who has made the name of Mackenzie worthy to be linked with those of Moffat and Livingstone who preceded him at the mission station which he has exchanged for the Residency of a British Commissioner. The task that is before him is arduous ; the difficulties are all but insurmountable. . . .

England may well trust that stubborn Scotchman with the pacification of Bechuanaland, for he has already given proof of his mettle, and achieved a signal success in a far more hopeless undertaking. . . .

When twelve months ago Mr Mackenzie entered the

field on behalf of his Bechuana clients with unpronounce-
able names, he had everybody against him—the Colonial
Office, the Government, the House of Commons, the press.
The whole nation, so far as it was articulate, was hostile to
his project; and, for the rest, was profoundly indifferent to
such black fellows as Mankoroane and his kinsmen. . . .

In Parliament there was a minority, led by Mr Forster, in
favour of action, but the majority cared nothing for Mankoroane,
and was prepared with philosophical equanimity to witness
the process of natural selection applied in its rudest and
most brutal form to the uninteresting protégés of Moffat.
As for the press, it was indifferent where it was not hostile,
and ill-informed where it was best-intentioned. . . . Nevertheless, this formidable array of hostile forces did not dis-
concert Mr Mackenzie in the least. Apart from the sustaining
influence of what he felt to be a just cause, and his belief in
the overruling Providence, he was buoyed up chiefly by a
conviction in the reasonableness and intelligence of his
fellow-countrymen. "If I can only make them see the
facts," he said, "I do not think there need be any fear
as to the result." And so at missionary meetings, lecture-
rooms, and in public meetings, he set to work to make them
see the facts. . . . Nor did he confine himself to public
speech; his pen was more influential than his tongue. He
had never done writing; and two of his articles in the reviews
enabled him to place his scheme for the future government
of South Africa fully before the public. It was a large
scheme, and an imposing one, and in these days of hand-
to-mouth policies it stood little chance of being listened to,
much less accepted. But it was listened to, and in its
essentials it has already been accepted, and his articles on
the territorial government of South Africa have become the
text-book of British policy in that region. . . . As Indian
Viceroys used to read Mill on the Government of India, so
future South African administrators will have to master the
articles of Mackenzie. . . .

There seemed no limit to his activity. He interviewed
Cabinet Ministers, he buttonholed editors, he haunted the
lobby of the House of Commons. He saw everyone who
had any influence in the matter, and compassed sea and land
if by any means he might make one proselyte. When the
Transvaal delegates came, they imagined that they had only
to come and see, and conquer. If they had come nine

months earlier their anticipations might have been fulfilled. When they arrived, however, it was too late.   Mr Mackenzie had been beforehand with them, and to their unconcealed chagrin, they found that the public would not tolerate their attempt to erect a Boer barrier across the great trade route from the Cape to Central Africa.

Bechuanaland was saved and much more than Bechuanaland. . . . Mr Mackenzie secured the favourable verdict of the Government and of public opinion, not merely for the administration of Bechuanaland, but for the adoption of that far-reaching native policy which he has labelled the territorial system. . . . Without forgetting for a moment the old warning against boasting when donning our armour, we may safely say that we bid Mr Mackenzie God-speed, with every confidence that hereafter he will live in the annals of our empire as the man who, at a grave crisis, saved Africa for England.

CHAPTER XII

AFRICA—JOHN MACKENZIE AS DEPUTY-
COMMISSIONER (1884)

MACKENZIE sailed once more for South Africa, with
high hopes and deep devotion of spirit. No one who
knew him ever suggested that his acceptance of the
Commissionership meant the winning of a personal
ambition. His mind had for many years been set
upon the problem of Britain's place and work in
South Africa. He saw the Boers keeping themselves
poor and lowering their educational, social, and moral
standards steadily by their policy of indefinite expansion. He saw them " eating up " the native territories
and casting whole tribes, who were on the road to
civilisation, back into serfdom and degradation. He
saw the British Government, responsible before God
and man for South Africa, yet shrinking from the
obvious and honourable task of controlling the history
of an empire, irritating instead of appeasing, betraying
the black man and teasing the white man with
changeful policies. Now that with the support of
others he had succeeded in persuading the government to face the whole problem of South Africa in a
new way and with a new spirit, how could he decline,
when he was in turn urged to begin the work ? He
saw with the utmost clearness, as the natural result of
a firm and just and steady Imperial policy, the rapid
elevation of the Transvaal Boer and the black man, as
well as the gradual development and ultimate confederation of all South Africa. It came to him as a
case of inexorable duty as well as a high honour, to
share in working for a hope like that.

The story of Mackenzie's experience as Deputy Commissioner, and the circumstances under which he resigned, together with his own subsequent work for South Africa, are fully told by himself in his large work, " Austral Africa." It will be impossible here to enter into the details as fully as he did. All that his biographer can attempt is to narrate the main events as they appear in the Blue Books, and in his private letters, leaving the reader who desires to study more closely this curious " turn " in South African history, to read it in the careful, elaborate and uncontradicted pages of Mackenzie's own book.

Before he sailed, indeed before Sir Hercules Robinson sailed, Mackenzie received forewarnings of the coming storm. As soon as his appointment was telegraphed to Cape Town it was disapproved by the political leaders who were then dominant in fact though not in name. Among them must not be reckoned Sir Thomas Scanlen and some of his supporters, who represented the " English " section of the Cape Parliament. This party was about to be submerged, however, by the new power of the " Dutch " party, which the Africander Bond had been rapidly enlarging and which it completely controlled. From the latter a message came back to the London papers, announcing that the appointment was generally disapproved, before there was time to make it widely known, or to gather a general opinion even in Cape Town! That was the first stroke in a policy which was carried out with increasing virulence and with decreasing honesty as Mackenzie's work went on. Sir Hercules Robinson hastened to assure him that, as they both knew well " how such thunder was manufactured," he must not be disturbed by the hostile telegram from Cape Town. Mackenzie felt sure of Robinson, and every such word of encouragement, of kindly and friendly consideration made him certain

that the Queen's High Commissioner for South Africa
would stand true to his Deputy Commissioner, whom
he had selected and whose appointment he had urged
so strongly.

When, with his wife, his second son, Dr John Eddie
Mackenzie, and his two youngest daughters, Mackenzie
reached Cape Town, he was very heartily received by
many old friends and acquaintances. But his time
was fully occupied in consultation with the High
Commisioner and Captain Graham Bower, R.N., the
Imperial Secretary, and in active preparations for his
journey to the scene of his own momentous undertaking. The following extract from a letter to his
eldest son gives us his first impressions of the situation at Cape Town :—

CAPE TOWN, *8th April* 1884.

The English colonial politicians have given me a very poor
requital for all that I have said in their behalf. Fearing that
my being a missionary will displease the Dutch-speaking
colonists, they have done their utmost (I include members
of the present ministry) to get me superseded. I got a
bundle of newspapers yesterday from Sir Hercules, containing adverse criticism of Sir Hercules, the Missionary
Mackenzie—especially the scheme of the latter. It was
even mentioned to Mr Scanlen that he should wire to
Lord Derby and get my appointment annulled. Scanlen
had firmness and common sense enough to refuse to do
anything of the sort. I believe the same party are agitating,
that it should be left on record that they objected to my
appointment. Sir H. told me this, but does not think they
will go so far. It means that when Parliament assembles, the
Dutch party may be gratified with the opposition to me which
they hope to show that they have offered. This is really a case
of doing good to a community against its will, the operation meeting only open thanklessness, opposition, despite.
And all this not " on the merits "; but because I have been
a missionary. And this fact is held to be sure to offend the
Boers. Friends tell me the storm is subsiding, and some who
are perhaps too ardent profess to see signs of the wind changing round in the opposite direction. Sir Hercules is clear that

it was worse when he arrived. But good people meet us and
assure us that the respectable class in the Cape Colony is
with us in what we are attempting.

When he arrived at Kimberley, carrying with him
the formal letter of instructions, and a further personal
and lengthy communication from the High Commissioner, his spirits rose. Assured of Robinson's
loyal support, and hoping that the success of his work
would appease the opponents of his appointment, he
was still further encouraged by the spirit of friendly
and sympathetic interest which he found at Kimberley.
This happier frame of mind is reflected in the next
letter to the same son.

KIMBERLEY, 20th April 1884.

MY DEAR WILLIE,—Here we are, all well. The journey
from Cape Town is very rapid, but the coach part of it is
rough also. Your mother was not well after leaving Cape
Town, but she is all right again.

A considerable change has taken place, apparently, in
opinion at the Cape concerning "the New Departure as
to native affairs" as it is called; and confidence in myself
has now been cordially expressed by the *Cape Times* and the
Cape Argus, the latter having had as gracefully as possible to
perform the "Right about face."

Here in Kimberley there has been a constant flow of
visitors, and the greatest interest has been expressed in the
question. I find that my articles have been read, and are
well understood. I was told yesterday, "O, your writings
have been read and studied in Stellaland." Representatives
of the two rival papers here happened to find their way to
the hotel at the same time, and had in company the benefit
of a lengthy exposition of the new policy. They both go in
for it, no doubt, with a sense of professional regret, because
the one won't be able to pitch into the other.

.   .   .   .

This affair, dear Willie, means many a tough battle—
sometimes with those who are working with you. But God
is good and merciful, and will help forward what I believe is
His own blessed work in this distracted land. O for more of
the leavening of high Christian feeling in this new country !

I have had the pleasure of meeting Mr Stewart of the Standard Bank, and Mr Simpson of the Bank of Africa—both Scotchmen and both intimately acquainted with affairs here, travelling very much and knowing all of the best people. They both expressed, in private interviews, their deep interest in my success; and have their eyes open to what it means for the country. I am much cheered by hearing from such a source that the great body of the Dutch-speaking people are thoroughly sound and loyal; and that Republicanism and "Anti-English" feelings are confined to a few. This was most valuable and reliable confirmation of my own view on this vital question. So I am, on the whole, encouraged to fight on; I see for what I am fighting. May it please God to grant me to see some part realized. This week I hope to cross over into Bechuanaland. It is full of complications. It is also well stocked with evil men of our own colour. But I trust in God and in the humanity which still remains in the most of men. The press people here wished me to allow them to say that I should ratify the holdings of the white men. I refused; but pointed to my scheme—narrated my fight for it in London—that instead of clearing the country, the country should be administered; and asked them to form their own inference. I can't get people to see "the other side." If I go committed, the natives would soon hear of it; and the whole thing would be discredited, so far as they are concerned. I see both sides vividly; very awkward, but quite an advantage.

I hear good news from Mr Ashton. My brethren sympathize, and wish me God speed. "I could not have done otherwise." They are also pleased with Lowe's appointment; they think it augurs well. They say the natives are also pleased.

I have been to church since writing as above. Have been asked to preach and consented; so must conclude. This will go to Portobello, but there won't be much delay. Much love to you both, and sympathy deep and real. Your father,   JOHN MACKENZIE.

．　　　．　　　．　　　．　　　．　　　．　　　．

Before the work of Mackenzie as Deputy Commissioner is described some account must be given, even with some repetition, of the situation which he had to face.   History in Bechuanaland had been rapidly made since he left the country in the middle of 1882.   We have seen in a recent chapter how, after the British occupation by Colonel Lanyon and Colonel Warren, the country was abandoned.   Treaties which had been offered by the native chiefs were ignominiously ignored ; obligations which had been undertaken for the time by the Imperial Government were gradually disowned and deserted.   This was defended on the ground that a military occupation for disciplinary purposes could not be construed as involving civil duties, and must not lead to a permanent sovereignty.   It was a bitter day for the native chiefs when the " White Queen's Government " left them ; and it was a bitter experience for some of the British officers to leave the people whom they had helped and protected in the Queen's name knowing, as they did, that disaster would speedily fall upon their territories and their persons.   Lord Kimberley, who was at that time Colonial Secretary, and Sir Hercules Robinson, seem to have believed in the preposterous theory that the Transvaal, Orange Free State, and Imperial Governments could agree upon boundary lines, and would all honourably observe them while, at the same time, the native chiefs outside these boundaries would maintain law and order, and resist the incursions of white marauders.   This plan for solving the South African problem was not only proposed but acted upon by British Statesmen in 1882.

We have already seen that Mankoroane, whose seat of authority was Taungs, while an important chief, was given by the British and Transvaal Governments an exaggerated importance in being recognised as paramount chief.   He very materially aided Colonel Lanyon during the South Bechuanaland disturbances by refusing to join with the rebels and the other chiefs, and by helping to arrest one of the raiders.   In

November 1878 he and his councillors and head-men presented to the British Government through Colonel Warren a remarkable petition in which he prayed the Government of the Queen to take him, his people, and territories under its rule. He only reserved for himself, and that naturally, the right to continue as judge among his own people at Taungs and the surrounding villages; but even to that he added the petition that the Government should decide as to whether he fulfilled this function adequately or not. It need hardly be pointed out that, if this petition had been accepted, a large and valuable territory would have been peacefully and legitimately annexed, and the bitter troubles which afterwards came would have been prevented. It is scarcely credible,' but it is the case, that this offer was not even answered by the British Government! When in the years '81 and '82 marauders from the Transvaal began to overrun Mankoroane's country, when they began to support in actual warfare against him the very chief whom he had arrested in '78 on behalf of and at the instance of Colonel Lanyon, he found himself not only forsaken but hindered by his "august ally, the Government of Queen Victoria." In the first place, the Cape Government had forbidden the sale of ammunition to the Batlaping tribes. When therefore they found themselves attacked by the Boers upon whom no such restriction was placed, that policy had the effect of actual war against the natives. In the next place, it must be remembered that the British Government had at an earlier time absorbed a considerable part of the territory occupied by Mankoroane's people, making them British subjects. It was therefore unlawful and criminal for them to go out and fight with their own chief against his Boer enemies. Surely injustice or blundering could hardly go farther than that. Its natural result was to be found of course in the dismay and distrust of the native tribes, who felt themselves not only ignored and scorned but betrayed by this very Government which they had always regarded as the fountain of justice and security.

Such policy or absence of policy, on the other hand, embittered the inhabitants of the Transvaal, who saw in it a kind of negative assurance that they might do what they liked with Bechuanaland ; the Queen saw no value in it. And yet a third class were affected, for those white people, whether Dutch or English, who lived in northern Cape Colony and Bechuanaland, and who believed that the best thing for the country would have been the establishment of Imperial authority and control, became convinced that no South African could henceforth put any trust in the constancy or wisdom of the Colonial Office.

This was of course a golden opportunity for the Boers within the Transvaal. Their enjoyment of independence after 1881 was seriously marred by a partial recurrence of those conditions whose misery made the annexation of 1877 at once a humiliation and a redemption. Once more the old cure for internal disease was sought, by pushing out the boundaries and taking new and rich farmlands into the republic. Mackenzie was one of the few who saw that this method of cure was aggravating the disease. But it was recognised that in the neighbourhood of British Colonies the annexation of territory must be carried through with at least the outward appearance of legal formality. Formal treaties or contracts were made between groups of Boers and certain native chiefs. These treaties were used as the foundations for new republics, it being understood that as soon as the republics gained formal recognition by the British Government they would be absorbed by the South African Republic.[1]

[1] Niekerk's avowal, C.—4194, p. 11.

There were four native chiefs whose lands lay nearest the Transvaal or partly within it, on the south - western border, and whose names became prominent in these years. They belonged to two sections of the Bechuana race known as the Batlaping and the Barolong. The territories of the latter were the more northerly, Mafeking being their best known centre. The former occupied a large territory within which Vryburg now stands. Each of these sections again was broken up between rival tribes which were often engaged in petty wars with one another ; and the Boers made most skilful use of these local rivalries and fights. Alike among the Barolong and the Batlaping they cleverly named the chief whose territory lay next the Transvaal as the paramount chief of these " nations," as they grandiloquently but confusedly called them. These nominations were made in defiance of the facts, which were notorious throughout Bechuanaland. Having made extravagant promises to each of these so-called paramount chiefs, it was easy to induce them to make the necessary treaties and sign the necessary documents on which the further march of civilisation was to proceed.

For example, let us take the foundation of the republic of Stellaland. The Boers supported Massow of Mamusa against Mankoroane, whose head-town was Taungs. On January 1st, 1882, Massow was induced to sign a proclamation in which he announced his intention of enlisting 300 white men as volunteers to assist him in fighting his rival. He promised each of the volunteers in his service a farm of 3000 morgen, and half of the total booty was to be divided among them. On May 3rd, a further invitation was issued for a hundred additional volunteers. During these and the following months, volunteers were trooping into the country by scores, settling down on all the accessible farms, and even stretching the boundary into the territory of Mankoroane. They quickly formed head-quarters at a place which they named Vryburg. A committee of management of the volunteers was now in existence ; it took the next " legal " step by securing on January 18th, 1883, yet another proclamation from poor Massow, conferring upon them the power of self-government within such part of his territory as was then " inhabited by the white inhabitants, volunteers, and other persons authorised by us thereto." The chairman of the Board of Management was thereafter to be recognised as Administrator of the aforesaid territory. On September 18th, 1883, the " Republic of Stellaland " was formally established, and a government organised. A flag was adopted, which was afterwards described in full by Sir Charles Warren.[1] In one quarter a bird, said to stand for Mankoroane, was represented as caught and held by a white man's hand ; in another there was depicted a fish, the sacred emblem of the Batlaping, pierced through with a sword. Thus, not without prayer and pious exclamations, was the standard consecrated, which committed the new republic to the destruction of the black race. Mackenzie's first task was to destroy this republic and bring the territory under British rule.

. . . . . .

At Kimberley Mackenzie began to encounter practical difficulties. He found that, as soon as it was known that the Imperial Government meant business and that South Bechuanaland was to be kept from the Transvaal, intense activity was created among land-jobbers. These comprised some whom every white man knew to be rascals, and others who stood in good odour in the business world. Some were known, alas ! to be acting as agents for yet others who stood still higher in the social and political circles

[1] C.—4643, p. 201.

of Cape Colony. To all these it seemed nothing less
than disaster to see Mackenzie, the exponent of a fair
and honourable native and land policy, laying his
hands upon the reins of power, in the name of the
Imperial Government. They saw a land commission
to establish English justice between black and white,
between Boer and Britain, entering Bechuanaland.
They saw many fair farms, which had been filched
from native chiefs by lies and fraud, given back.
Some big firms saw the extensive domains which
were coming into their hands by the failure of their
debtors, saved from this sacred destiny. It was a
maddening prospect. But there was one way out ;
and that was annexation to the Cape Colony !
Moreover, to make that more palatable to the British
Government, the Colonial Office must be harassed by
the failure of its Deputy Commissioner. The Parliament at Cape Town could be managed, or events
could be delayed indefinitely, if only a movement for
annexation to the Colony could be set on foot and
the Imperial administration could be discredited. To
secure the latter end it was necessary to do two
things ; first, to hinder Mackenzie's success on the
spot ; and second, to send alarming messages to the
London papers. Mackenzie came to know that one
of the most unprincipled land-jobbers in the country
was in a position to use one of the leading news
agencies. From him and his co-workers went forth
the telegrams which announced in England that
Mackenzie was meeting opposition in Stellaland, that
the Boers were ready to fight, and certain to win ;
and once it was announced, without a fraction of
truth in the statement, that the Deputy Commissioner
had been assaulted and murdered !

The following long letter to Sir Hercules Robinson
describes in a lively manner the strange world of plots
and counterplots in which he found himself, and the

schemes by which British subjects of British blood were trying to prevent Bechuanaland from coming under British authority, for the sake of land!

KIMBERLEY, *April 21st*, 1884.

DEAR SIR HERCULES,—My stay at Kimberley, which is now drawing to a close, has placed me in close contact with the opinion of the leading men of the town and district. The Bechuanaland question is the question here, and the "New Departure" and the "Territorial Government" are in much favour. The hotel has been besieged with visitors every day —some of them fresh from Stellaland—others from Kuruman and different places in Bechuanaland. Many of the latter I see in the street, especially at the early market, which I have visited on purpose.

. . . .

We are in great danger of being thrown into the utmost disrepute, I do not say with philanthropists, but in the House of Commons—in the face of English public opinion—by the state of things with which we have to do. I say this after seeing Hill from Stellaland, and other friends of that side, as well as friends of Donovan. Land, land, land—a wearisome monotone. You have done the Colony a good turn in London, without any thanks. Now your bantling Native Department is hustled out of the way of eager and selfish men who care for you and the Queen whom you serve only for what they can enter in money columns. Mr Hill goes to Stellaland with an annexation petition in his pocket. Mr Donovan advertizes that he has over a hundred farms in Mankoroane's country, which he offers on certain terms ; but application must be made *at once*. Haste on both sides, and at the risk of grave complications, and with the certainty of increasing the difficulties of Her Majesty's Government. The friends of Stellaland disapprove of Donovan ; Donovan on his side so deeply disapproves of the Stellalanders that he wants to fight them, or rather to induce others to do so.

But if Stellaland people get what they want, and Donovan gets what he wants, what remains for the native? Where is our prestige for fair dealing in the eyes of the natives of the interior? Where do we stand in England in the estimation of any class of politicians? You have been opposed in this Native Department from the first by those not far from you in Cape Town. I see their hand in certain telegrams to London—in the Stellaland Mission—in the indecent haste for annexation to the Cape Colony. The whole thing indicates the shallowest ideas of the realities of the situation.

I remember our discussions about a Viceroy as compared with combining the duties of High Commissioner and Governor in one person. I trust that as High Commissioner you will be able to uphold the Native Department which is being created, and not allow colonial politicians to bring it into disrepute almost at its birth; what they need to be taught is simply *patience*; the farms will become saleable; annexation will take place, but not by their eager haste. After seeing more than one person from Stellaland besides Mr Hill, and comparing their statements, I found Hill's to be most opposed to the Imperial Government's plan. A man who professed to have come direct from Niekerk, and who frankly told me when leaving, that he was "off to write to Niekerk" what had transpired at our interview, gave me a much more cheering picture of what awaited me than did Mr Hill. According to Hill, I had no chance whatever, only he kindly said he did not think they would do me any bodily harm. The last words of the other man, professing to be directly acting for Niekerk, were, "Well! shall I say to Niekerk, that you will see him and talk matters over with him?" I answered, "By all means, I not only consent to see Mr Niekerk, but will be glad to do so; and you will please to tell him so." I have no hesitation in saying before entering Stellaland, that just as the telegrams to London were meant to do deadly damage, so was this visit to Stellaland. Both are equally reckless of results; and both with God's help will be equally futile.

What Colonial Ministers should do just now—I am not thinking about this ministry or that—is to come forward like men with a quota from the Colony towards the Territorial Government of Bechuanaland. That is what is expected of them by all classes in England, as you yourself are aware. I believe this will be done by the Cape Colony, whether by Mr Scanlen or not.

Territorial Government would suit the respectable men in Stellaland; it is quite adapted to their case, and their burdens under it would be less than under the Colony. It would not suit the books of impatient traders and specu-lators, *and these are the men we have really to face* in Stella-land and in Mankoroane's country.

What its reception will be, after the petition referred to has been so hurriedly signed, I can't profess to say. Time will tell, if as Hill assures me, they don't shoot me. *If one had only fair play!* In the meantime, in the opinion of some your Deputy cuts a sorry figure going into a country where he has been forestalled by colonial wire-pullers ; but the truth is that this same Colony and its politicians will sink in good men's estimation on account of what has just been done; when people contrast their abstention from saving Bechuanaland to the Colony, when in London they could have done something toward it, with their rushing at it and grabbing it as soon as it had been reserved for an entirely different fate by the Imperial Government.

When he entered the hostile territory, this new and strange Deputy Commissioner invaded it with a mule-waggon, in which rode his wife and two little daughters. His retinue consisted otherwise of his son, the medical officer of the force and private secretary of his father, and some men-servants. There was not a fire-arm in the entire force. It was not, indeed, the usual plan for subduing a young and vigorous republic, for over-awing freebooters and scapegraces as well as deter-mined frontier farmers of bitter spirit, who all hated the idea of becoming English and being ruled by an ex-missionary. It was not the plan which would have occurred to a Captain Bower or won the ap-proval of blustering politicians. But men of another stamp, men like General Gordon, would have seen through it and applauded it as more effective than cavalry and pom-poms. Mackenzie was going back to his own country, which he now knew better even than "bonnie Scotland." He had travelled over all its main roads, knew its towns and their chiefs per-sonally, some of them intimately. He had ridden often across and across it on horseback, alone, by night and day, for one hundred miles or more. By bright moonlight he knew the aspect of its desert stretches and the shadows of its sad, solitary kopjes. At noontide its fierce heat had struck horse and rider with sun stabs from above, and wearied them with the dull waves of fiery air which the hard bare earth threw up. He knew also the white man of the region, as well as the black man and the grey sand. He was not going into the unknown therefore, running into a foolish peril. He knew that the best work would be done by moral influences, and he proposed to use all that were at his disposal. If he had entered alone with one hundred volunteers at his back, his mission would have had a military, coercive character. Entering as he did, he appeared as one who came confidently and peacefully to make his home in his own land. The chiefs who had complained that the White Queen's Government " was always going away " would see that it had come to stay. The Boers and the other whites would see that the new Deputy Commissioner was not only a man of peace, but a man who trusted them. A commander with armed volunteers they would instinctively feel to be against them, but a Commissioner who brought his family among the avowed enemies of the Queen, how was he to be met?

The first point in Bechuanaland to which Mackenzie went was naturally Taungs, where Mankoroane, the chief of that part of South Bechuanaland, lived. He arrived there on Wednesday, April 30th, 1884. His object was to negotiate a treaty with Mankoroane which would place that region completely under the Queen's dominion. For three days the diplomatic battle raged—Mackenzie single-handed against the " strenuous, although covert, opposition of a few white men, who profess to be friends and advisers of Mankoroane."[1]

[1] C.—4194, p. 16.

The Deputy Commissioner did not attempt to brow-
beat them or to drive the chief. He calmly and repeatedly stated the facts connected with his appearance as the representative of the Queen, showed them
the advantage to all concerned of a treaty that would
make a strong and stable government possible, and
gave his reasons for not blindly swallowing all the
land-claims of the white "agent" and his friends.
The white men tried every form of persuasion upon
Mankoroane and his headmen. But so bitter and
angry did their language against Mackenzie become,
that at last the shrewd old native broke out with the
stinging retort, "Why do you object to the messenger
of your own Queen? If I give myself up entirely to
her why are you Englishmen afraid?" Then Mackenzie knew that he had won. Of course there were
white men even at Taungs who had welcomed him
and his administrative plans from the first. They
were glad to see the unscrupulous defeated, and glad
to see a treaty signed by which Mankoroane and his
tribe surrendered jurisdiction within his territories to
the Queen's Government. "The opposition to the
treaty then took up the attitude that they had not
properly understood it ; it was really good, and ought
to be signed at once."[1]

The Deputy Commissioner then faced what was
considered a most critical part of his undertaking,
namely, the visit to Vryburg. It was not without
danger, of course ; but the amount of danger was very
largely dependent, as in all such cases, upon the
personal bearing and methods of the man who
encountered it. Major Stanley Lowe who had been
so long identified with Bechuanaland, and whom
Mackenzie had appointed to the task of raising a
small body of volunteers for service as a border
police, accompanied the party. His presence was

[1] C.—4194, p. 16.

necessary, in order to discover what number of police the situation demanded, and how they could be best disposed over the country. There had come to Taungs a message from the "Administrator" of Stellaland, Mr G. J. Van Niekerk, inviting Mackenzie to go round by his farm on his way to Vryburg, as the "government offices" were at his place. Mackenzie agreed, made the detour, spent a day with the "Administrator," and then went on to Vryburg, where he arrived on Friday, May 9th. The rough and ready frontiersmen had a certain feeling for the fitness of things, and resolved to do all honour to the representative of the Queen. Accordingly, they rode out on horseback to meet the waggons, carrying their gloomy flag with them. After a formal greeting they turned and escorted the Deputy Commissioner into the town. It is significant of the moral effect of Mackenzie's entire method of meeting the situation, that these men sent a messenger in advance of their own cavalcade to say that Mrs Mackenzie must not be alarmed when she saw them approach, as they were bent only on peace. If Mackenzie had ridden with imperial pride, at the head of a hundred volunteers, armed with rifles, there would have been no such kindly message as that, itself a suggester and forerunner of peace. There might have been an ambuscade.

The same afternoon a meeting was convened, at which more than fifty men were present. Mackenzie's first step was to read his commission, and to announce that the Queen's Protectorate had been established in Bechuanaland, *including Stellaland.* This was a complete and overwhelming surprise. It took some days of explanation and rumination for some of the leading and most daring spirits to realise that, in the eyes of the world, no such government as Stellaland existed, and that they were now under Queen Victoria!

For a week Mackenzie remained at this place, spending day after day, in private and personal conferences with the Stellalanders. It is only right to say that he amazed those who watched him sympathetically, with the untiring courtesy and invincible patience of his bearing. He sat for hours in committee meetings, answering questions, listening to protests against the entire procedure. These were not always couched in polite language. Indeed, so strong was the spirit of a certain group, and so vehement their denunciations of the Queen and the country whom Mackenzie represented, and yet so silent and imperturbable was the Deputy Commissioner, that Stanley Lowe rushed out of the place and, after the relief of some indignant expletives, said to his son : "Mackenzie, your father must be more than human to stand all that as he does!" But it was this wise, patient, and frank dealing which gained for him his remarkable victory.

Van Niekerk arrived on the Saturday evening from his farm. All Monday the Volks Committee, a duly elected body and the nucleus of a Raad, through which the affairs of the republic were conducted, discussed the situation. They drew up a list of eleven questions, which they asked Mackenzie to answer before them the same evening. Some of these he dealt with on the spot, some he deferred to the following day. On all subjects he tried to take a position which his auditors would feel to be at once fair and reasonable, both from his and from their own points of view. To the class of original volunteers, he promised that their farms would be given, but if the particular farm now claimed were needed for Governmental purposes, or reserved for the natives, an equivalent farm or a fair price in cash would be given. Regarding all other farm claims, which were numerous, Mackenzie said that a Land Commission would have to be appointed at the earliest possible opportunity to inquire into their history and validity. On the delicate subject of the money obligations of Stellaland he again frankly accepted the situation, but threw responsibility back upon themselves. In accepting their assets he must also accept their debts. But these must be carefully scrutinised, and they must be all paid by the taxation of the farmers themselves, and not out of imperial funds.

The " Administrator " was anxious to be clear regarding the actual relations now established, and the following conversation took place in which the firmness of Mackenzie appears.

THE ADMINISTRATOR. Must I understand that by reading of his Commission, Mr Mackenzie takes over the country as British territory, and as part of Bechuanaland ?

MR MACKENZIE. That is the fact.

THE ADMINISTRATOR. Does Mr Mackenzie, by reading the Commission, mean to imply that the Government of Stellaland ceases to exist ?

MR MACKENZIE. It stands to reason that two governments cannot exist in one country. But, in the spirit in which we have been discussing matters this evening, it is my wish to receive, over the heads of the people here, all that will enable the incoming Government to carry on the government of the country and promote its prosperity.

THE ADMINISTRATOR wishes to know whether Mr Mackenzie intends to assume the reins of government at once.

MR MACKENZIE. The question is already answered in my answer about the proclamation ; Her Majesty's Government cannot both be in and out of the country. With regard to the immediate change of affairs, it is my hope to entrust them into hands which will be suitable and agreeable also, from the people's point of view.

The last words refer to an act by which the Deputy Commissioner sought to win over completely the still hostile minority. Under the power given him by the High Commissioner he nominated, as his Assistant Commissioner for that part of Bechuanaland, whom but G. J. Van Niekerk himself? No one expected this, and it certainly produced much astonishment in Stellaland. Here was a British officer, who showed much firmness in his representation of the Imperial Government, strong determination to have the presence and authority of that government recognised and made effective at once ; and yet he was willing to deal fairly with Dutchmen, and even to use their Administrator as his assistant. The people, except those who already disliked Van Niekerk, were very much pleased. The Volks Committee formally approved of the appointment, *ad interim*, " until such time as it should be decided whether the Colonial Government takes over this territory." ˙ This was the disturbing feature in Mackenzie's work at Vryburg. Under the advice of some English-born colonists at Cape Town and Kimberley, the Stellalanders had petitioned for annexation to the Cape Colony. Men like Niekerk went into this simply to stave off the evil day, and with the real determination to carry out their original intention of uniting with the Transvaal or remaining independent. But so strong was the majority who now favoured Mackenzie's plans that it seemed possible, if Van Niekerk would take the oath of office, to win them all over.

Unfortunately Mackenzie was expected to hasten north, to Montsioa's country, and he was compelled to make a temporary arrangement with the Administrator and the inhabitants of Stellaland. In the meantime, with the assistance of Major Stanley Lowe, peace and order could be maintained for a few weeks till his return.

Mackenzie was himself much surprised at his success. That there were some men unreconciled in Stellaland he well knew. But he received unmistakable proof that the very large majority of the white men—Boers, English, Colonials, and others—believed in him, and were ready to welcome his administration. The men who were engaged at Cape Town in the pleasant task of " tripping him up," as he afterwards put it, denied that he had won over the white population. Of course they could not have admitted that fact and tripped him up at the same time. We shall see later what means they used to destroy his success, and even to conceal the proofs of it when these were at last put into the one indisputable form of a popular vote.

On his way to Montsioa's country the Deputy Commissioner paid a passing visit to Moshette at Kunwana. This was one of the chiefs whom the Boers had used as a cat's paw, and whom they had represented as longing to be under the Transvaal. Mackenzie knew the representation had been false, but looked upon the chief as paying the price of his past misdeeds. Yet it was hard not to sympathise with the wretched man in his chagrin and dismay. The visit to Kunwana was naturally not a cheering one for either party, since it was Mackenzie's duty to announce to Moshette that the rumours he had heard were true ; he was now and henceforth under the Transvaal Government. [1]

Mackenzie arrived at Mafeking on Tuesday, May 20th, 1884, and entered immediately into conference with the heroic old chief Montsioa. Some one ought to write the life of this man, and call his book " The First Hero of Mafeking." He would find in Montsioa's life-long struggle with the Boers for the freedom of his country abundance of stirring adventure. He would find in Montsioa's relations to the British Government much food for humiliating reflection—the black chieftain showing himself so much more noble in

[1] C.—4194, pp. 36, 37.

patience, in his loyal trust, in frank sincerity, than the ever-changeful Government whose protection he believed in and most earnestly sought. Montsioa could not send pithy and humorous telegrams when besieged, but he knew how to send messages of another kind. As far back as May 1883, Mr Nicholas Gey van Pittius had attempted to claim Barolong land outside the Transvaal border. Montsioa based his denial of all claims firmly upon the Pretoria Convention of 1881. In March 1884 he again addressed "the Gentlemen Volunteers, Rooi-Grond," who felt the time had come for surveying and settling his country. Montsioa, the real gentleman throughout these negotiations, says, " I warn you again as a friend that I will not let you do anything of that kind." A month later the same "Gentlemen Volunteers" issued another threat and dated it from " Land Goosen," as they hoped to rename the territory. Montsioa answered curtly, " My friends, I do not know the Land Goosen you write of. My people are living on the lands their fathers have lived on—the lands of the Barolong."

When Mackenzie reached Mafeking the entire population were jubilant. Montsioa at once signed a treaty, in which he gave the British Government jurisdiction within his country and power to raise taxes for the defrayal of expenses. The Boers, led now by Gey van Pittius, had begun to make a little town which they called Rooi Grond, part of which was in the Transvaal and part in Montsioa's territory. These worthless huts were, of course, put there to establish claims, and were not much occupied. Mackenzie rode over to meet with these Boers, but he found them very " shy." They formed an armed and mounted band of about forty men, as reckless characters as could be found in South Africa, men who stooped to do many cruel and murderous acts upon

white men as well as black. With a little company
of half-a-dozen, including his son and the Rev. C. S.
Franklin, a Wesleyan Missionary who later acted as
his secretary, he rode over to the settlement. The
Boer laager was a little way from the water to which
Mackenzie resolved to send his horses to drink. This
left him completely at the mercy of Gey van Pittius.
When the latter sent two men on horseback to inquire
what he wanted, Mackenzie began without loss of
time to read his commission and announcement of the
Queen's Protectorate. "But we were not told to
listen to that," the horsemen said, and rode away as
if from a more material volley, leaving the Deputy
Commissioner to shout the last words after them as
they clattered off.

These desperadoes took advantage of the chance
given them, when all the Barolong men were gathered
in the town to hear and celebrate the making of the
treaty, and swooped down upon some cattle - posts
about fifteen miles north of the town. They captured
booty worth more than £1500, and carried it across
the line into the Transvaal ; there they were at once
safe, for the Barolong would not cross that line even
to recapture their cattle until the White Queen or her
servants should allow them. This incident is mentioned here because it was the occasion for a somewhat adventurous trip which Mackenzie made. He
drove across the border to Zeerust, into the very
district where the cattle had been taken for distribution. Many of the desperadoes were there, and he
saw them. Some of them were men whom he had
known in former days, and they saw him. It was
gratifying to find that a large number of the most
respectable burghers disowned and disliked these
brutal cattle raids ; and yet Mackenzie's complaint to
the magistrate of the district was quite fruitless. It
was all reported at Pretoria, of course, as indeed every

occurrence on that western border was reported continually. But the Transvaal Government sent back word to the Zeerust magistrate that he must take no action.[1]   Thus the poor Barolong found that their first experience of British protection was just this : they must never cross that line for revenge or even for the recovery of their property !

Mackenzie's efforts to reach the Goshen freebooters were all fruitless. These men having no real domicile in Bechuanaland, and making the Transvaal the base of their operations, could not be brought under his official and personal influence, as the Stellalanders had been. They were, besides, almost all men of a wilder and more lawless kind, who were determined to use the roughest means for crushing the indomitable Montsioa and seizing his lands. Shortly after Mackenzie's departure, there was some actual fighting. The Barolong burned the unoccupied huts on their side of the border ; and the Boers at once sent word all over South Africa, that the savages had come upon their homes, with women and children in them, and destroyed them with ruthless cruelty. Reprisals were now felt to be legitimate, and an attack was made by Transvaal citizens, using Transvaal territory as their base, upon territory which had but just been proclaimed as under the protection of the Queen. Of course these men would not have done this, if there had been even fifty British police, under a British officer, on the spot. The Pretoria Government, which knew all and allowed all that went on, would most assuredly have prevented any act which would inevitably and at once have meant a conflict with Great Britain. The day for that had not yet come within sight. But the Pretoria Government knew all the cross winds that were blowing at Cape Town, knew that the Cape ministry were thwarting Mackenzie, preventing the

[1] C.—4194, p. 112.

sending of an efficient police force, scheming for a
Joint-Protectorate of Bechuanaland by Cape Colony
and the Transvaal, and knew that they were safe to
allow these border raids to go on.   In fact, they soon
saw that, afraid as the High Commissioner was of an
open conflict, their best plan was to let the disorder
grow worse, the fierce will of the Goshenites to grow
fiercer.   In the meantime, poor Montsioa saw once
more that the best government he knew of "had
gone away" from his town, leaving him more hated
and less powerful than ever, before his foes.

Mackenzie made the remainder of his tour round
northern and western Bechuanaland more rapidly.
He was detained at one place, where natives had lifted
the cattle of some white people, by the determination to
exert "even-handed justice" upon black as well as
white marauders.   He was determined that no one
should be able to accuse him of showing any partiality
for natives.

At Kuruman he left his wife and daughters,
appointed his son to stem the progress of small-pox,
by making a vaccinating tour through the infested
region, and made his own way back to Taungs.   He
reached that place at the end of June, and at once
was in communication again with the Stellalanders.
A deputation was sent to meet him from the Volks
Committee, the body in whom now supreme power
among the white settlers rested.   Their report to him
was very interesting.   The first fact was that Niekerk
had forsaken them, declining all responsibtility for he
government of the country under Mackenzie.   The
second fact was that the Volks Committee had
assumed full control of the situation, had communicated with Cape Town, and found that the prospects
of annexation to the Colony were so dim and confused
that no action could be taken in relation to them.
The third fact was that they wished Mackenzie at

once to go over the terms of submission to the
Imperial Government, then to go to Vryburg " and
hoist the British flag." " Such," says Mackenzie to
Robinson with emphasis, " such was the request of
Dutch-speaking as well as English-speaking members
of the Deputation." [1] Niekerk was given one more
chance to take the oath of allegiance and accept the
office, which he had formerly agreed to accept.   But
he refused, choosing to remain a Transvaal citizen,
and maintaining his residence within the Transvaal.
Mackenzie was informed by the Stellalanders that at
this very time he was promising to his own party that
the country would be annexed to the Transvaal,
while he professed at Cape Town to be anxious for
annexation to the Colony.

When Mackenzie went to Vryburg, he was received
with much more than the studious courtesy of the
former occasion.   There was some fear of hostile
action from Niekerk, and armed horsemen went out
several hours ride to meet the Deputy Commissioner,
and escort him to the town.   He was conducted to
the court-house, and there it was arranged that a full
meeting of the citizens should be held a week later,
on a Monday.   In the interval, several of the leading
men in the place, including Mr Bodenstein, a brother
of the chairman of the Transvaal Volksraad, went out
in different directions to visit the farmers and state
the facts fully to them, arguing for co-operation with
Mackenzie.   While they were still away Mackenzie
went on with his work, as an Imperial officer in actual
authority.   He found all the officers of the Government ready to be sworn in, and they were sworn in.
Some new appointments were made.   On the day
after his arrival there was a strong desire expressed,
especially by farmers who had come from the Colony,
to hoist the British flag.   But the Deputy Com-

[1] C.—4194, p. 114.

missioner was very careful to avoid any rash step,
which might bring dishonour on that flag ; so he put
the proposal off.   On the following Monday the
public meeting was largely attended.   Three resolutions were proposed and unanimously adopted, in
which the Stellalanders, while still hoping for annexation to Cape Colony, accepted British rule.   In the
midst of these resolutions the following words occur :
" This meeting further desires hereby to record its
welcome to John Mackenzie, Esquire, Her Majesty's
Representative and Deputy Commissioner for Bechuanaland, as the restorer of peace and prosperity to
this country, and call upon all lovers of peace in
Stellaland to co-operate under Her Majesty's rule for
the maintenance of law and order, and the promotion
of the prosperity of the country and its inhabitants."
Perhaps the most significant of the resolutions was
that in which the Stellalanders named G. J. Van
Niekerk and A. J. G. De la Rey, as men who were
inciting " the inhabitants of Stellaland to oppose law
and order in this territory, now under Her Majesty's
rule."   The resolution further stated that these two
men were holding public meetings for these " treason-
able purposes " within the Transvaal, and urged the
High Commissioner to call the attention of the South
African Republic to these " unlawful acts."

Mackenzie's triumph in Stellaland was complete.
Out of the burghers he enrolled a small force of
twenty-five men, for duty in that district ; the anti-
British element was in the minority, and had already
lost moral influence by holding meetings across the
new border in the Transvaal.   So enthusiastic were
the people, that on that second meeting they insisted
on hoisting the British flag.   On hearing that this
might be done, Sir Hercules Robinson telegraphed
in alarm :—

Hoisting the British flag is technically the symbol of

sovereignty ; Bechuanaland is only native territory under
a British Protectorate ; and you are not justified in altering
the status without the express sanction of Her Majesty's
Government.

One can hardly believe that the British High
Commissioner sent that telegram only eighteen years
ago, concerning the territory just north of Kimberley.
Mackenzie's answer by telegram on August 3rd was
as follows :—

> As to the flag, please remember the flag of Stellaland was
> flying when I entered Vryburg. The people themselves went
> and quietly took it down. I declined then to hoist our
> flag until the public meeting had taken place. After the
> first meeting I was importuned to hoist it. I declined till
> the second or adjourned meeting had taken place. After it
> I felt bound to hoist it. They had voluntarily pulled down
> their flag, which had been handed to me. There is such a
> thing as inducing people to distrust you. Had the flag not
> been hoisted after the meeting I should have lost the support
> of the best people here. All the officers have taken the oath.
> We have been exercising sovereignty in Stellaland since we
> first set foot in it. From the first there has been more than
> a Protectorate here.

"There is such a thing as inducing people to distrust you," might be written as a fair judgment upon
most of Great Britain's dealings alike with Boer and
black in South Africa.

We shall soon see how and by whom that flag was
taken down, and the Stellalander was "induced to distrust" once more. On the day on which Mackenzie
sent this telegram about the flag, he had received
Robinson's message of July 30th, inviting him to
"visit Cape Town," and appointing Mr Cecil Rhodes
to take his place. That was the end of John Mackenzie's
service of his Queen as Deputy Commissioner. He was
not unprepared for this event, for even while carrying
on his work as successfully as we have seen, his corre-

spondence with Government House, Cape Town, had shown him that hostile forces were gradually gaining the upper hand there, forces which openly sought his overthrow, but really aimed at other political and personal objects beyond himself. He was in the way of land schemes and Boer schemes. The land schemers were many of them well-known British subjects, but they were willing to work with citizens of the Transvaal to defeat an Imperial officer, and hinder Imperial developments in Bechuanaland. The Boer schemers were well-known at Pretoria and Cape Town to cherish the purpose of extending the South African Republic over the territory now proclaimed as a British Protectorate ; and they saw that if Mackenzie continued in Bechuanaland their dreams must perish. These two sets of men united their influence in Bechuanaland and at Cape Town to "eliminate," as Mr Rhodes openly confessed it, "eliminate the Imperial factor." How they tried this and succeeded, we must now see.

When Mackenzie went north from Cape Town in April, he felt himself in perfect accord with Sir Hercules Robinson regarding the general policy which he was to pursue. It was understood that he would require 200 police to maintain order in Bechuanaland, and Robinson approved the appointment of Major Stanley Lowe to enrol and organise this force. Weeks were allowed to pass during which the enrolment of police went on slowly, being hindered partly by the general uncertainty regarding the real attitude of the respective governments to one another and to Bechuanaland, and partly by obstacles cast in the way of Major Lowe from Cape Town. No real vigorous measures were taken to assist Mackenzie and his chief officer in this work.

In the month of April the letters of Robinson show him cordial to his Deputy Commissioner. He refers to the proposal for the annexation of Bechuanaland to

Cape Colony, and confesses that this may be the best solution of their troubles. He looks forward, however, to Mackenzie's expected visit to Cape Town, upon which they had agreed. This visit was to be made immediately after Mackenzie had completed his first survey of his territory in order to discuss the whole situation and map out the details with his chief. In one of these letters he says, "You may rely, under any circumstances, upon my fullest confidence and support." In May he writes with enthusiasm concerning what he calls Mackenzie's "complete success at Vryburg"; he thinks that Mackenzie "acted wisely in swallowing Mr Niekerk"; likewise was he pleased with the work done at Taungs; Robinson added that he was "sure that Lord Derby and the Colonial Office will be very pleased at the way you have got over the two out of your three difficulties." On May 25, he writes again, saying, that he expected Mackenzie to be at that time "about to start for Cape Town." In this letter the first difficulty is raised regarding the cost of the police force which had been promised to Mackenzie, and without which he would never have undertaken this task.

We estimate that the 50 police you ask for will cost annually about £1200, and the equipment at starting about £5000 more. Have you considered where all this money is to come from, especially if the Stellalanders won't pay for Police, as the papers seem to indicate? However, I shall be able to go into this matter with you soon when you get down here.

On the 16th of June, Robinson is still convinced of Mackenzie's remarkable success.

"I was," he says, "very glad to receive yours of the 31st May from Mafeking, and delighted to find that you got on so much better with the Goshenites than I anticipated. I am pressing the Transvaal Government to come down on that nest of ruffians who have established themselves just within the Transvaal border."

In this letter he further refers to the fact that Mr Niekerk was corresponding with persons at Cape Town, and saying that the Stellalander people were violently opposed to Mackenzie's protectorate or territorial form of government. This leads him to refer to the political situation at Cape Town ;

" My new ministry is not strong, and it is possible there may be another crisis before the next Session. I have not been able to get any decision out of them yet as to what course they will take. . . . They are apparently waiting to get their orders from Mr Hofmeyr, and he is probably waiting for the arrival of the Transvaal delegates here from London."· He repeats his invitation that Mackenzie should stay at Government House on his arrival.

Robinson evidently was being pressed to change his judgment by setting Niekerk's letters and views over against those of Mackenzie's.

At this time Mackenzie, feeling desperate over the absence of police from Bechuanaland, sent several different proposals to Robinson. One of these suggested the formation of a South African volunteer force ; another suggested that Cape Colony, as being the ultimate heirs of Bechuanaland, ought to lend the Imperial Government 100 volunteers for the purpose of settling the country. In connection with these proposals Robinson wrote a letter in the first week of July, which showed a distinct cooling-off in its most curt phraseology and imperative tones ; he lays aside the scheme of a reserve force as impracticable, and then adds the following unexpected words :—

I hope by this time you are on your way back to Montsioa's ; there is nothing whatever to be gained by your visiting Cape Town at present ; and it is desirable that you should be in the neighbourhood of Rooi Grond whilst the free-

booters who are living there just within the Transvaal
border are making attacks upon the protectorate.

The Blue Books show that Mackenzie in a telegram
of this date suggests that there was still much reason
for his visiting Cape Town, and he adds : "There are
too many pressing duties in Bechuanaland for me to
be shut up in Mafeking if it is invested ; your statement about public opinion at the Cape makes me feel
the greater necessity for being there."   To this, on
July 6th the High Commissioner curtly replied :—

I can see nothing to be gained by your coming to Cape
Town at this moment, and I must repeat that whilst the
country is in this its present state you should remain at your
post." [1]

At the same time the High Commissioner gave
Mackenzie authority to raise a force of police and
burghers, to deal with marauders, and said that
Lord Derby had telegraphed the approval of H.M.'s
Government.   The absurdity of this proposal lies on
the face of it ; but Robinson, now blind to the facts of
Mackenzie's position, says, " I am anxious you should
realise that you have to depend on what you can do
locally."

About this time President Kruger and his fellow-
delegates arrived at Cape Town from their European
tour.   Robinson reported to Mackenzie that they
conferred with Mr Hofmeyr, the leader of the Bond,
and with the Ministers, of whom Sir Thomas Upington
was now Prime Minister.   They arrived at the conclusion, the Imperial High Commissioner reports to his
Deputy,

that it was better for the Transvaal to have the Colonies as a
neighbour than the Imperial Government, and that Oom
Paul promised, that if the Colonies would take over the place

[1] C.—4194, pp. 74, 78, 79.

and you were withdrawn, he would use his best exertions to insure the Rooi Gronders dispersing to their homes.

In the letter which gives this information, dated July 18th, the High Commissioner for South Africa goes on at length to describe the pressure which was being brought to bear upon him for the removal of Mackenzie from his office. He piteously complains that he stands absolutely alone in advocating his appointment. "I need scarcely say," he adds, "that this is almost as disappointing and annoying to me as you, but it is a fact, and there is nothing to be gained by shutting our eyes to it."

A definite policy was now agreed upon between Mr Kruger, the Cape Dutch Party, and the Colonial Government, and it centered in one immediate object, namely, the removal of Mackenzie. The next step was naturally left indefinite, Mr Kruger allowing Mr Upington to think that it would be a peaceful annexation of Goshen and Stellaland to the Cape Colony But Mr Kruger went home to Pretoria, and from his place in the Volksraad denounced the very convention under which this annexation was to take place.

In the parliamentary discussion, both Mr Upington and Mr Cecil Rhodes, in advocating the annexation to the Colony, denounced Mackenzie as the one obstacle to a peaceful settlement of Bechuanaland.[1] Mr Rhodes, in this debate, relied for his information upon letters which he quoted, and which he had received from Niekerk!

On July 28th, Robinson wrote another long letter to Mackenzie, concerning the determination of the Cape Ministry to get rid of him. The High Commissioner's supreme interest at this time was divided between, either securing the annexation of Bechuanaland to Cape Colony, or obtaining a money

[1] For report of debate. C.—4194, pp. 85-105.

grant from the Colony towards the expenses of the protectorate. His ministers saw their advantage, and refused to consider either proposal as long as Mackenzie held his post. He says in this letter, " Mr Upington added that the only prospect of settling Bechuanaland was the cordial co-operation between Cape Colony and the Transvaal, in the work. The Transvaal Government, he was aware, would give no real help so long as you are in charge." Sir Hercules strove " to save his face," by proposing that the Colonial Government should nominate some one to act as coadjutor with Mackenzie. This, of course, was also declined. At the same time, he refused to allow Mackenzie any money for his work from the Imperial funds, and warned him further not to think of fighting one half of the Stellalanders with the other half, as Mr Upington, forsooth, had imagined that Mackenzie would do this. Sir Hercules Robinson also referred to the scandalous scenes which had just occurred in the Transvaal Volksraad, where President Kruger, from his place in the House, denounced Robinson and Mackenzie in the same breath, as " liars " and " intriguers," and asserted that, because they had deceived the British public and the British Government, the Transvaal had lost Bechuanaland.

Before this letter was written Mr Rhodes had already left Cape Town for Kimberley. After his arrival there a series of telegrams passed between him and Captain Bower, the Imperial Secretary, which have been published in the Blue Books.[1] It was only when he saw these telegrams in print that Mackenzie discovered the true facts regarding his recall and Mr Rhodes's appointment. They clearly show that when Mr Rhodes left Cape Town there was a general understanding between him and the High Commissioner, and the Imperial Secretary, regarding the immediate

[1] C.—4213, pp. 15 ff.

future. On July 25th, Captain Bower received a
telegram from Mr Rhodes saying that Niekerk and
Co. threatened to use violence against Mackenzie and
his sympathisers. For this information the Imperial
Secretary sent thanks, and asked for more " light on
the situation." On the 29th, Mr Rhodes was asked,
" Can you leave at short notice for Bechuanaland, if
required ? " On the same date Mr Rhodes announced
that there had been a " row at Vryburg, on the attempt
to hoist the British flag." He criticised Mackenzie's
actions and said, " the feeling in Stellaland is only
anti-Mackenzie." Mr Rhodes was only at Kimberley,
and dependent for his information upon rumours and
the evidence of interested parties, but, he added : " I
have gained, I think, a fair knowledge of the situation ;
please reply and tell me position on your side, and
what you wish me to do." Captain Bower replied
that Robinson proposed

to give Mackenzie leave to come down here for purpose of
conferring with him, and to ask you to go to Vryburg and
act for Mackenzie in his absence. Do you think this course
desirable, and do you consent, or do you think that Mackenzie
can be safely left in Stellaland ?

The next day Mr Rhodes flashed back his answer :

I consider Mackenzie's presence at Vryburg likely to
cause disturbance. He is opposed by large party. Am
willing to proceed on understanding if I get matters quiet,
and I think his return likely cause strife ; due weight to be
given to my opinion.

Mr Rhodes was told that the Governor accepted
his offer with thanks, and his commission was telegraphed the same day. On July 31st, Mackenzie,
all unaware of these sinister " wires," sent the announcement of his brilliant success in Stellaland, and of the
passing of the resolutions by the assembled inhabitants,

which we have described above. On this Captain
Bower wired Mr Rhodes :—

Mackenzie telegraphs that things in Stellaland are satisfactory. Either he is living in a fool's paradise, or recent
reports are very misleading.

At the same time Mackenzie was informed of
Robinson's desire that he should go to Cape Town,
and of the appointment of Mr Rhodes to act for him
in his absence. Captain Bower's telegram means
simply that Mackenzie was being recalled, irrespective
of the questions as to whether he had succeeded or
not, as to whether his official report from the scene of
action, or Mr Rhodes's rumours from Kimberley were
to be trusted at Cape Town. The fact stands indisputable, that Robinson's conduct was based first upon the
hostility of his ministers, which *he knew* to be created
by the Transvaal ; and, second, upon rumours which
contradicted the official reports of his Deputy
Commissioner, and which were sent to him by Mr
Rhodes. The telegrams also show that Mr Rhodes,
without being upon the spot or making a judicial inquiry
into these false rumours, advised the removal of an
Imperial officer that he himself might take his
place.

When Mackenzie reached Cape Town he found
himself in the centre of storms. After a few days
he decided to send in his resignation. This step was
taken while he was fully conscious of his own success
in Bechuanaland, but while he was yet unaware of
the telegrams and misrepresentations which have
been sketched above. It was taken because the
Cape Ministry believed they could easily reduce
Bechuanaland to order, and he would not have it
felt that he stood in the way. His motives and
spirit are expressed in the following letter :—

GOVERNMENT HOUSE,
CAPE TOWN, 3rd Aug. 1884.

MY DEAR DR DALE,—Your warm interest in the Bechuanaland question induces me to send you the text of my
letter of resignation, and the documents which the High
Commissioner, at my request, produced on the occasion.

My first impulse was of course not to resign; but in the
circumstances, and wishing myself also to test the sincerity of
the utterances of the Cape Ministry, I sent in the enclosed
letter. They are not touching Bechuanaland a bit more since
I resigned than they were before.

The political situation here in Cape Town is most unhappy
—nay, it is even dangerous; and you know I am no alarmist.
Let me explain what I know of it, of course in strictest
confidence.

In the first place, relations of present ministry and the
High Commissioner are very much strained. I found it so.
I have been, since I arrived here, a go-between as to the
Bechuanaland affair, and there is a slightly better state of
things. But there is no love lost on either side.

On asking Sprigg and Upington why they had not supported Scanlen's undertaking for co-operation with English
Government, they gave first the published reasons—indefinite
responsibility, etc.; but on being pressed, they both said, or,
rather, *shouted*—"We don't believe in the English Government. We are Liberals, both of us, but the Colonial Policy
of the present Government is rotten and detestable. They
would leave us in the lurch on the first convenient opportunity.
We should have to face the opposition of the Dutch here, and
would probably get turned out; but what we are sure of is,
that if we co-operated as you desire us, and sent up officers
now into Bechuanaland to make preparations for annexation,
or lent Cape Mounted Rifles to protect Cape Colonists in
Stellaland who signed the petition for annexation,—there is
nothing clearer to our minds than that in the briefest time we
should find ourselves alone in Bechuanaland, deserted by
the Imperial Government."

You can scarcely imagine the vehemence with which these
things are said. Their minds are exceedingly embittered
against Her Majesty's Government. All the while, as they
declare, their personal sentiments are similar to your own!
His Excellency is good enough to place great confidence

in me, in suggesting that I go and talk with them, and in formally sending me on matters of business; but it is uphill work.

And the worst is not told. These men—our own fellow-countrymen—only hold their present position on sufferance. Mr Hofmeyr and the Dutch party support them, and therefore they stand. They are paying most disastrously dear for this support. It is said everything is submitted to Hofmeyr in secret conclave, and ministers get what are practically orders. Was a country ever in such an unhappy situation? It is explained to me by those who know, that Hofmeyr dared not accept the responsibility of forming a ministry when the Government sent for him to do so. His own followers do not supply material out of which ministers could be made, on account of their sheer ignorance. But in their own opinion they are fully qualified, and would resent being passed over. Therefore the astute Hofmeyr declines the Premiership virtually because he shrinks from appointing English ministers under him, over the heads of his own peculiar people.

I asked His Excellency, as a favour, to wire the last two paragraphs of my letter to the Colonial Office, in order that the peculiar, unusual, I might almost say unique, situation might be understood. He did not consent to this.

The news comes in that Bechuanaland is well-nigh in the hands of the Boers.

Joubert's selection by the Transvaal Government, after his speech and known proclivities, was not polite to the Imperial Government, nor was it in the way of a friendly settlement.

.   .   .   .

Sept. 23.—One thing and another have prevented me from finishing this and sending it off.

My resignation has been accepted, and I am now adrift. I do not know my future. I am deeply interested in this question, and a great deal has to be done here. But how to do it, and also earn daily bread, &c., for myself and family, are questions not yet solved. I have no disinclination, thank God, to resume mission work, but my successors have made, and are making such a frightful mess there, that really it would not be advisable for me to go back to Bechuanaland just now.

I have now left Government House, and have taken rooms

for a short time here.   There will be a public meeting here
to-morrow night.

The action of Germany has acted as a tonic to the sluggish
dullards here.   Four papers here are practically of one opinion :
The Argus, Times, Express, and *Volksblad.*   The *Zuid Afrikaan*
openly advocates freebooting, looting, and serfdom.   It is in
Dutch entirely, otherwise I would send you copies.   The
papers insisted that I must speak at the meeting.   I went to
the preparatory meetings to-day.   I was well received.   But
in the interval some one had expressed a doubt whether it
would be wise that I should speak.   I came in while they
were discussing this.   This gives you an idea of the position
here ; the meeting is to some extent the result of doctrines
which I have been teaching since I came here.   They all say
they would like to hear me ; but what about the Dutch
opposition ?

I said I was no judge whether I should speak or not ; I
dared say there would be enough without me.   When this
would not do, I added, " I suppose you want to know whether
I am going to set you all at loggerheads by what I say.   If
that is the anxiety of those who don't know me, I have the
happiness to relieve it at once ; you may rest quietly in your
minds so far as my speech is concerned."   Such is my standing here to-day.   Queer, isn't it ?   If I can do something
towards healthy speech and clear understanding between
Dutch and English, I shall do something.   I feel my
mind going with this question ; I should like to serve
a high cause in this Colony ; perhaps the way may be
opened up.

In the meantime don't despair.   It is enough to be cast
down ; I do not feel like that.   But despair, and your cause
the right one ?   No, by no means.   Dear Mary, my little
daughter, wrote to me lately, " Papa, I am praying so hard
for you."   I have got the conviction Mary is not alone in
doing this.   Let us wait and work, hoping in God.   Give me
a line.—Ever yours sincerely,

JOHN MACKENZIE.

To Mr Stead he wrote a letter on October 1st, in
which the following paragraphs occur :—

It is no small gratification to me to be able to preach in
Cape Town the doctrines which I preached in England, and

to find that they are cordially accepted. My own reception has been more than I had reason to expect, considering the censure which was heaped upon me. It is only one form of resenting the conduct of their political leaders on the part of this community. They have spoken out for themselves.

The real cause of failure in Bechuanaland is the hostile attitude of the Transvaal. This was pointed out by me repeatedly, with the remark that it was a question for the High Commissioner and the Home Government, and not for me with a few policemen. It will be shown that Sir H. had Lord Derby's express sanction to repel the invasion of Montsioa's country months ago, but did nothing but urge me to go back again personally and try personal persuasion. When I came to Cape Town Sir H. had not done anything with Lord Derby's sanction, but was trying in reality *to throw the onus on the Cape Colony*. I say so, as I was the go-between the parties for weeks; and the negotiations stuck with the blunt question of Upington, "What do you mean then by co-operation? Define what England will do, and what you expect the Cape Colony to do." Sir H. pooh-poohed this then, and did not so define.

Now, dear Mr Stead, don't be angry with me for writing all this. I am in a queer fix. Don't know where to turn, have been really checked and tripped up by knaves or fools or both. What I write is in confidence. But don't trust M—— one bit, nor H——, if you come across them.

LAND Scanlen is nice, and I think trustworthy, but don't betray my confidences to him. The others are his lieutenants.

[In the original letter "Land," written in large letters, fills up the vacant space, as above.]

CHAPTER XIII

AFRICA—THE ROUSING OF THE CAPE COLONY
(1884-1885)

IT will be unnecessary to tell in detail the story of Bechuanaland under Mr Rhodes's Commissionership during the months of August, September, and October 1884. But something must be said in order to explain still later events.

When Mackenzie resigned it was with the feeling, as he said once, shrugging his shoulders, " If these other fellows think they can manage the business, well, let them try it." Mr Cecil Rhodes made the first attempt. He went straight to Vryburg, and sent his first message from there on August 7th. He found what he called the " town section " very favourable to Mackenzie, and confessed that they were very bitter against himself. The reason for this bitterness lay in the fact that he had announced his resolve against Mackenzie's advice, to negotiate with Niekerk. The Vryburg population, since Mackenzie's last visit and the formation of a settled government under him, had viewed with great resentment the recent history of Niekerk's relations to them ; and the idea that the new Deputy Commissioner should deal with Niekerk as in any measure responsible for that portion of British territory, awoke their intense hostility. But Mr Cecil Rhodes persisted in his policy. He left a loyal Stellaland behind him, ready to promote peace and to resist the aggressions of outsiders, and crossed the border to negotiate with an avowed enemy of the Queen for the maintenance of peace in Her Protectorate.

It is impossible for any student of these events to fathom Mr Rhodes's real reasons for this extraordinary step. An approach to a reason is given by him,[1] and is echoed by Captain Bower, in the suggestion that it was necessary to pacify Stellaland in order to use it as a basis for pacifying Goshen. If this was the real purpose it exposes the statesmanship of both these gentlemen to the severest criticism from another point of view.

When Mr Rhodes reached Commando Drift, where Niekerk and his people were assembled, he found them, he said, " exceedingly embittered against Mr Mackenzie, and the section in Vryburg, who had accepted his government." [2] Their bitterness is not in the least unintelligible ; it is only extraordinary that Mr Rhodes should have taken steps to give up the loyalists in Vryburg to its pitiless cruelty. He knew that these people were assembling to reinstate the government which Mackenzie had destroyed ; that is, to treat Stellaland as if it had never been proclaimed a British Protectorate, and as if no British officers had assumed authority within it. And he set himself avowedly to help them.

After some preliminary arrangements Mr Rhodes left for Goshen, summoning Captain Bower from Cape Town to carry on affairs in Stellaland during his absence.

On his way to Goshen, Mr Cecil Rhodes heard that the Transvaal Government, in response to the High Commissioner, had appointed General Piet Joubert as a Special Commissioner, to assist him in pacifying the western border of that country. Mr Rhodes and

[1] C.—4213, p. 41.   [2] C.—4 4213, p. 105.

General Joubert met at Goshen, on the Transvaal side,
and proceeded to negotiate with Van Pittius. Mr
Rhodes received nothing but insult of the most
studied kind, while he was there. The Boers actually
attacked Mafeking, on the night of his arrival at their
camp. Yet he remained within the Transvaal, did
not enter Mafeking, had no dealings with Montsioa,
whom he was sent to protect and deliver,—except
through some messengers who stole up to his waggon
at night,—broke off negotiations when he found that
the Goshenites gave no sign of yielding to his authority,
and that Joubert was either powerless or unwilling to
assist him.

On his leaving, poor Montsioa found himself compelled to agree to a " treaty " of the most unjust kind
—so unjust that Mr Rhodes could not tolerate it.
These events opened his eyes to the fact, as he
reported to Robinson, that the Transvaal was tacitly
allowing these proceedings, and that Joubert was not
in the least anxious to put down the disorder.

Yet Mr Rhodes returned through the Transvaal to
Commando Drift, within the Transvaal, and there
resumed his negotiations with Mr Niekerk, a Transvaal
citizen, regarding the further destiny of the British
Protectorate in South Bechuanaland. He found that
Captain Bower had come to this region, during his
absence in the north. Two steps of great significance
had already been taken by the Captain. In his
anxiety lest the British flag at Vryburg should be
insulted he sent it away to Taungs. The Stellaland
flag, which Mackenzie had received from the hands of
the Stellalanders themselves, and taken to Cape Town,
Captain Bower brought back ; and this he handed over
once more, not to the British in Vryburg, but to Mr
Niekerk in the Transvaal. From Vryburg he sent
messages to Cape Town, which deliberately aimed at

disparaging Mr Mackenzie's work and influence in
that place.

Within a few days four members of the Volks
Committee sent a telegram to Mackenzie, saying that
they deemed it

advisable that you return speedily to Vryburg and the
Bechuanaland. Majority of public approve of your policy.
Rhodes appears only working for Colonial interest, regardless
of position of country. Think you could effect peaceable
settlement. General regret at your absence during present
complications. Rhodes went alone to Niekerk, in Transvaal,
to consult him. Public sentiment here worked upon against
Imperial Government; especially yourself and Vryburg
opinion ignored. Statement made that you do not return.
Please reply.

This message abundantly proves that even after the
visits of both Mr Rhodes and Captain Bower, the inhabitants of British Stellaland felt themselves strong
enough, and united enough, to maintain their allegiance to the Imperial Government. Nevertheless, on
September 8th, at Commando Drift, Mr Rhodes
agreed to terms of peace, dictated to him by Niekerk.
A strange fact is that this agreement was telegraphed
in a mutilated form to Cape Town, and from there
to London, and was approved in London before all its
contents were known.

The very first article stated, "That all transactions entered
into between Mackenzie and the Volks Committee, and the
proclamations issued by him, be cancelled"; that is to say,
the very acts which Mackenzie carried out under his commission, and for which he was sent to Africa by Lord Derby,
were recalled in this manner, and at this time. The second
article stated that "pending negotiations with the Cape
Colony, Stellaland should continue its own government,
recognizing, however, Her Majesty's Protectorate, and subject to the conditions that all executive acts must be taken
in concert and with the consent of the Commissioner for the

Bechuanaland." The third article promised recognition of
the land titles issued by the Government of Stellaland—a
portion of the agreement which no doubt conceals much, and
which gave much trouble later.

The fifth article was, however, the most extraordinary of
all. It postponed the authority of the second article for three
months, which simply meant that the Stellaland Government,
as it was established before Mackenzie reached the country,
was to be restored and maintained with the approval of the
British Government for three months longer.

The logical sequel to these events occurred when, on
September 18th, Niekerk and his party rode suddenly
into Vryburg, taking possession of the town and the
Government offices, and establishing themselves in
power over the territory from which they had departed four months before, and over the inhabitants
who had sworn allegiance to the Queen.

One need not dwell upon the feelings of disgust and
chagrin that seized the loyalist people in Stellaland,
many of whom fled for safety. These feelings spread
gradually over all South Africa, as the full facts of the
case entered the public mind.

·   ·   ·   ·   ·   ·   ·

Mackenzie's resignation, which was telegraphed to
London (August 9th), was not accepted by Lord
Derby until September 18th. During that period
he stayed at Government House, in constant intercourse with Robinson. It is one of the curious facts
which his unselfish spirit brought about, that he was
then actually used by Robinson as a means of communication with the Cape Ministers who had demanded
his recall ; his intercourse with them was frequent and
friendly, just because he determined that his main work
in life was not to promote his own interests or resent
a personal defeat, but to secure the triumph of a
beneficent public policy in South Africa. His spirit

and some of his work are reflected in a long letter to his wife, from which the following extracts are made :—

GOVERNMENT HOUSE,
CAPE TOWN, 21st Aug. 1884.

DEAREST,—You may be sure my time has been very much occupied since I came here. My last letter would show you that I had to do real work for the good of Bechuanaland so far, and to prevent what I believe would have been grave mistakes.

I found, when I came down, this doctrine : " We join and stick to the majority in Stellaland. We doubt if you have the majority ; Rhodes will go and see ; and if not then he will join Niekerk." . . .

In my humble opinion we are assisting as fast as we can in joining Stellaland to the Transvaal, and the only people who realize the situation are Messrs Hofmeyr, Niekerk, De la Rey and that ilk, Sprigg and Upington gracefully following in their train, whether blindly or with their eyes open, who knows? The appointment of Rhodes was a good one, if he had at once gone on to Rooi Grond, as I strongly advised both the High Commissioner and himself. Mr Bower also might have done good at Vryburg by upholding what had been accomplished. Unless we are to suppose that the Transvaal will refuse to restrain its burghers in the Hart River District, Mr Bower's position would have been secure enough at Vryburg. The Transvaal would never have attacked Bower at Vryburg, even with what support I had. If the Transvaal mean to have Bechuanaland we need not meet them half-way and help them to walk over the course.

A few days ago I had an interview with Mr Sprigg and Mr Upington. I have not time to recall all that passed. I stated my views of the situation clearly, and charged them with having thrown away a golden opportunity for securing the co-operation of England with the Cape Colony.

My advice to them was—" Here are a number of men who have signed a requisition to the Cape Colony. There is a dispute among them. The one party annuls the doings of the other. I called them all together, seeking union among them, but one side did not come. That side does not want Imperial Government and does not want Colonial Govern-

ment, although it professes to do so.   It is working for the
Transvaal.   These people threaten those who have accepted
office under the Imperial Government with 'pains and
penalties.'"

"Well, it is the duty of the Imperial Government to
protect them."

"No doubt, but England undertook this in co-operation
with the Cape Colony.   You also have obligations; these
people have asked for annexation ; you have passed a resolution favourable to annexation.   But in the meantime the
country is in danger of passing into the hands of the Transvaal all the same.   Niekerk is working for this ; Joubert will
of course ask for this.   Who works against it ?   The Imperial
Government, if you work with it. . . .   Refrain to act, and I
am afraid Bechuanaland is gone for ever, and becomes part of
the Transvaal ; for I am told the Imperial Government will
not do the work by itself.   Then you are doomed to a second-
rate position.   And why, from your point of view, should you
be excused from anxiety ?   I know about the duties of a
central or supreme power.   But England has a right to
expect your co-operation, and if she had it, she would, along
with you, settle not only this, but every other South African
question."

(Sprigg) "Yes, *say* she would do so ; get us to begin, and
then leave us in the lurch.   She did so before."

" I assure you England would not leave the Cape Colony in
the lurch if she were assisted by the Colony in Bechuanaland.
There are too many reasons pointing the other way.   A
considerable change and improvement took place in people's
views about the Colony when I was at home.   I am afraid
by refusing your co-operation you have dashed all this to the
ground."

"We can't trust the English Government.   If we could
trust them that would be one thing.   We are afraid to trust
them."

"You are wrong in your distrust.   They would act with
you to their last penny.   But if you want to save Bechuanaland for the Cape, send your officer and men at once, having
of course obtained the High Commissioner's sanction."

A great deal more was said, of course.   I made some impression.   They both declared with passion that their wishes
and mine were the same.   I think their distrust of the Home

Government genuine; perhaps mixed a little with spite in the case of Mr Sprigg, at his treatment in the matter of Bechuanaland.

I was so convinced that things were going to be on a wrong track, that I wrote a private memorandum to His Excellency requesting that the Government at Vryburg should be taken up by Capt. Bower, and that he should not merely wait on Niekerk. Sir Hercules was pleased to say that what I then wrote had modified his instructions to Mr Bower.

I trust on every account that these men will have success; but I confess I don't see how it is to come about. The same power that is supreme in Niekerk's and Joubert's Councils is supreme in the Cape Ministry and Parliament; and yet not responsible; for Englishmen have been found who are content to be figureheads to a craft with a Dutch-speaking captain who never appears on deck.

My own resignation is now on its way to London. The telegraphic announcement is already there. Sir H. proposes advance of three months' pay when connection is severed. Sir Hercules declares I am taking it more coolly than he does. He is very kind. There will be a delay of about a week. I intend to visit some friends. Of course there are a few who will be courageous enough to have me. What are we going to do next? How employ the afternoon of life and open a home for our children? May the Guide of our past lives be with us still! Love to the children. Hope Franklin enjoys himself.—Ever,

JOHN MACKENZIE.

As soon as his resignation was accepted, he went into private lodgings. He was deeply disappointed, of course, at the position in which he found himself, but his disappointment was increased when he gradually discovered the forces which had produced this result. Undaunted, however, he set himself to work for the cause which he had at heart, and for which he had given up his earlier career. He found himself very speedily in the midst of warm friends, and their number and their warmth increased as they became familiar with his political teachings and his personal spirit. He was invited to occupy the pulpit of the Congregational Church at Claremont, a suburb of Cape Town. This necessitated only his preaching on Sundays, and left him the entire week for the huge mass of correspondence in which he soon found himself involved.

Just eight days after Mr Rhodes's arrangement with Niekerk, which was dated September 8th, the startling announcement was telegraphed from Pretoria to London that the Transvaal, "being implored by Montsioa, had annexed his territory." Sir Hercules Robinson at once replied "that this was simply the annexation by the Transvaal of about one half of the British Protectorate, and was an open and defiant violation of the Convention." No doubt this matter was very clumsily managed, as a Transvaal official at a later date confessed. President Kruger would have had more chance of success if he had waited somewhat longer. No doubt, also, this act may be called treacherous. But in all fairness to the Transvaal it ought to be recognised that their treachery was the logical outcome of British unfaithfulness to an announced British policy. This may seem a strange assertion, but the facts of the case thoroughly support it. Mackenzie had been sent to proclaim a British Protectorate over Montsioa and Mankoroane ; yet Robinson, who sent him, would give neither money nor men to establish a police force which should make the Protectorate effective. The High Commissioner became involved in discussions, both with his ministers in Cape Town and with his Deputy Commissioner in Bechuanaland, which showed his weakness and unwillingness to act ; every breath of these discussions was as well known in Pretoria as in Cape Town. Further, every grown man in South Africa knew that the Transvaal was the base of operations for the marauders in Stellaland and Goshen, that it was the home of Niekerk and Pittius; everyone knew that the leading newspaper in Pretoria published reports of their acts, that it was as much their official organ as it was the official organ of the Transvaal Government.

Notwithstanding these facts, a high-placed British officer seriously proposed that Bechuanaland should be settled by the co-operation of the Transvaal with Cape Colony! Still further, the Transvaal Government, knowing Mackenzie—his power over the natives as well as over white men, and his strong determination that the Imperial Government should rule in fact as well as in name—demanded his recall through its allies in Cape Town and by direct appeals to the High Commissioner. Not only is he recalled and his resignation accepted; his successor actually goes into Stellaland and, with his eyes open, deliberately hands back the Government of a British Protectorate to Niekerk, a citizen of the Transvaal, and his companions. He moreover, formally renounces all the acts and proclamations of his predecessor. It was surely open to Mr Kruger to ask himself, If Stellaland is thus given back, what can Britain possibly do with and for Montsioa so much further north? The only reason why all this insensate folly and weakness does not excuse the treachery of the Transvaal is that the latter preceded as well as followed those acts. It was not until October 14th that Mr Niekerk took the next step which, if it had been carried through, would have been only the further logical outcome of all that went before: for he drew

up a petition to be signed by the burghers of
Stellaland reciting to himself the failure of the
negotiations for annexation to Cape Colony, and
proposing to him that negotiations be forthwith
opened for annexation to the Transvaal!

In the meantime, in Cape Town and elsewhere
throughout the Colony, the tide of indignation against
the weakness of the Imperial Administration was
steadily rising; it took shape first of all in a great
public meeting held in Exchange Hall, Cape Town,
on September 24th. Mackenzie had been invited
to the preparatory meeting, as he explained to Dr
Dale in the letter quoted above, and was, of course,
invited to be one of the speakers. A most eloquent
and thrilling speech was made by the Hon. J. W.
Leonard, Q.C., in which he defended Mackenzie's
commissionership. When the latter rose to give his
address, he and everyone else were amazed at the
enthusiasm with which the great assembly welcomed
him. He studiously avoided personalities in his
speech, which the *Cape Times* described as "a plain
unvarnished tale, using a simplicity and directness
of speech that was more telling than any laboured
eloquence." He went right at the root of the whole
matter, which was the relation of European races in
South Africa. He denied that there ought to be
any divergence of interest between Dutch and English
in that region. "The real question was, Were they
to go north with the stain of human blood on their
hands or were they to go north as Christians, clean-
handed?" The last part of his speech dealt with
the position of responsibility of the Cape Colony;
he foresaw its great future if the colonists chose the
wise policy; it was for their own interest to see
that the road into the interior was not blocked by
Germans from the West or the Transvaal from the

East ; in order to secure this they must maintain their connection with the Imperial Government.

This meeting awoke enthusiasm all over the Colony ; similar gatherings in the leading towns passed enthusiastic resolutions in favour of a vigorous policy in Bechuanaland. Mackenzie was himself summoned to lecture in many of these places ; wherever he went he maintained the same calm, judicial tone, dealing only with fundamental principles, posing nowhere as a martyr, and parading his wrongs nowhere. His speeches were widely reported, some being reprinted for circulation. Gatherings were held and hostile resolutions were passed by some local branches of the Africander Bond ; but their language served only to emphasise the need for the movement which they tried to check.

In a letter to his friend, Sir Robert Herbert, the Permanent Under Secretary at the Colonial Office, Mackenzie describes one of his lectures :—

I am happy to say that I have so far secured public approval here of the Dutch-speaking students of Stellenbosch, an intensely Dutch place, where the College of the Dutch Church had invited me to lecture to them. I was glad to go. My great object was to cope with the movement which impelled the Ministers. Concealed as it was in the lecture, my object was to *demonstrate the necessity for Warren's going to Bechuanaland in any case.* If he did not go the Transvaal and Cape Colony might find themselves hopelessly at loggerheads, for both wanted the same country, and the method would not work which some had proposed, viz., that the freebooters should choose what government they would come under, for the freebooters were divided on this question. Thus the presence of a third party—a party with force at its command—was absolutely necessary in the interests of peace and a common welfare. I am happy to say this produced a great impression on my audience. I then directed their attention to the advisableness of working for some elementary plan of South African co-operation.

The students cheered my lecture throughout. Dutch-speaking colonists, farmers and others, thought my proposal for a commission under Warren, if adopted, would be the saving of the whole country. When I told them that the lecture would be translated into Dutch as a pamphlet for extensive circulation, they desired that a considerable number should be sent to Stellenbosch.

.   .   .   .   .   .

It was only after I had lived some time in Cape Town, that I came to realize how easily you might have been slipped out of this country by one stroke after another of Dutch "slimness" and cunning, followed by not a very exalted action by English politicians. Mere fighting will not do all that is required.

.   .   .   .   .   .

My friends here tried to persuade me not to resign, but to stand aside and let anyone else try the new policy of siding with Niekerk ; and if it failed, to retain my position. I took the simpler course.

Mackenzie published a letter, signed " Jan Bergenaar," which received very wide attention, and was circulated extensively in pamphlet form.   In this letter he further developed his idea that there ought to be established in South Africa a commission under an Imperial President, on which there should be representatives from every separate South African Government, whose functions, to begin with, should be merely advisory ; and the members' first task would be to investigate and advise upon the Bechuanaland problem.   He proposed that two members should be elected by the Government Ministers of Cape Colony, one by the Free State, one by Natal, one by the Transvaal, and that one should be appointed by the High Commissioner and approved by Chiefs, to represent the native interests.

This proposal was much discussed in connection

with Warren's arrival as Special Commissioner in South Africa, and so favourably was it received by many of the leading men, that it might easily have been carried out had it not been from the beginning disapproved by Sir Hercules Robinson. It would have been a practical step towards that Confederation which in its unpractical forms has been a "will-o'-the-wisp" in South African history. But his immediate purpose was expressed in the words, "What I am working for is to give the Imperial Government something to lean on out here."

To his eldest son he wrote on October 22nd :—

We had a great excitement here this week. The announcement, in the *Pall Mall Gazette*, telegraphed by Reuter, that Sir Charles Warren was to be sent out to "settle" Bechuanaland, gave everybody pleasure here except the evildoers. To myself especially the news was the best I had had for some time. . . . The letters from my Stellaland friends in the *Cape Times* show that really some of those fellows had got to like me middling well, and also that they have some ability. They have not worshipped the rising sun. Government House people tried what they could do with the editor to get him to refuse their communications ; but he has more manly sense of fair play.

I ought to be gratified as well as thankful for the position which I have been able to take up here. The "best people," as the saying goes, are very kind, and ask me to their places, and seem really interested. . . . I am told by reliable authority that my views are making headway among the Dutch people. I expect this week or next to meet the redoubtable Mr Hofmeyr, the most powerful man in South Africa at present ; so some say. It may seem strange that we have not met before. . . . I have wanted to meet him, but did not want to press for it, for really mine is an educative work here. I have been doing that every day. I am sending a copy of my lecture. I am told the Dutch like it ; but it has been misapprehended in some quarters—notably in Natal. . . . I am firing away every Sunday now as a preacher. I think I mentioned that they would like me to make an engagement, for say three months, to supply a little chapel in this neighbourhood—£300 per annum.

Did I mention that they are trying to start a political association here, which shall bind the colonists to England, and really undo the work of the Africander Bond? They showed me a projected prospectus; in fact I have seen more than one, and have myself supplied one. The thing could be done, but some of them are taking the wrong way to do it —bawling out their Englishness and the goodness of England at the top of their voices. . . . Captain Bower is strong for the grandiose style which I was opposing. "I go for the Union Jack—that's my motto." And this is to save South Africa for England at a crisis in our history! I have striven to impress it on them that our hope is in the respectable Dutch people. Some of the English hate me for saying this. They would really like to see them soundly thrashed, and English notions crammed down their throats whether they were willing or not. I said to the Governor and to others —"Your hope is in meeting the Dutch and the Africander Bond on its own ground and fighting it. This you can do, and succeed. By the diffusion of sound and reliable information you can educate your people. If you say this is impossible the game is up. England would not wish to coerce a whole community." The Governor has got into very strained relations with his present ministers, while he keeps up a good deal of intercourse with his late advisers. The Association to which I refer is supported almost entirely by Scanlen's supporters. This is a great mistake; its basis ought to be widened so that the best Dutch could join.

Meanwhile Sir Hercules Robinson was being driven to a firmer position. Towards the end of September he announces to Lord Derby, " That it appears to me that Her Majesty's Government must either abandon the Protectorate or the Convention, or announce to the freebooters of the South African Republic that existing arrangements will be enforced, if necessary, by the adoption of active measures." On October 13th, he is prepared to propose that a force of not less than 1000 or 1200 mounted men should be sent to secure peace, and he proposes that Sir Charles Warren should be appointed in command of the expedition. It was not three months since he had been cross-questioning Mackenzie regarding the expense of sending 200 volunteers to the same territories, because he was sure that the British taxpayers would resent it! The popular indignation over recent events, and Robinson's sudden boldness, made the Cape Ministers, the friends of Mr Hofmeyr, desperate; they now proposed that the High Commissioner should prevent the Imperial Government from acting, and allow them personally to make peace in Goshen. After considerable controversy Robinson agreed, and the Prime Minister, Mr Upington, went north with Mr Gordon Sprigg in the middle of November on their Quixotic enterprise. Their negotiations with Pittius and his freebooters resulted in proposals so shameful, that when they were submitted to Robinson he would do nothing but treat them with contempt. When Messrs Upington and Sprigg passed back through the Colony, they were accorded anything but a favourable reception. On the night of their arrival in Kimberley their effigies were burned in public, and the same thing occurred at Cape Town. A public meeting was also held at the latter place, at which once more, Mackenzie, whose name was not on the programme, was compelled by the gathering to speak. He says of this speech, " I endeavoured in perfect good faith to lay what I regarded as the real question before the enthusiastic meeting, and to withdraw as far as I could popular indignation from the unfortunate ministers themselves." He called for the public support of Sir Charles Warren. " Let him settle the question in all its bearings, as if there had been no Mackenzie, no Rhodes, no Bower." The following sentences are also significant. " When asked after the meeting to join those who were spectators at the effigy burning, I declined to do so; the only personal allusion made (and I must admit that the temptation was great) was, on rising, in a single sentence to recall to mind the words 'injudicious and unpopular,' which the Cape Ministers in an official minute had used of me as an Imperial officer acting beyond the Colony. The striking application of their own words to themselves was clear enough, and caused great amusement to the meeting." [1]

Mackenzie discovered that some of his most important despatches about Bechuanaland had not been printed, and he at once set about copying some of these and sending them to people of influence, both in South Africa and in England. At the same time, he could not live where he did at this time without seeing week by week more deeply into the nature of the opposition to himself and the means which had been employed to unseat him. Some of these discoveries he described at length to several correspondents. One of those to whom he wrote most fully and freely was Dr Dale of Birmingham. Writing to him on November 19th, he names some of the men who worked for his resignation.

Land was at the bottom of that. Had Sir Hercules Robinson stood firm then, things would not have been quite so bad—although Goshen was always beyond the management of a Deputy Commissioner, because it was practically the Transvaal, and this I pointed out as soon as I visited the country.

The Blue-books, if they are all out, will tell the story pretty clearly. I am anxious that you should know the merits of the case. My success in Bechuanaland was real. But I had no support from behind. Sir H. Robinson was favourable himself, but what could he do with his surroundings?

"I never knew, Mackenzie, that missionaries were so detested here, or I should have hesitated to recommend

[1] "Austral Africa," vol. i. pp. 514, 516.

you." "How are they detested, sir?" "Why, I am told they are everywhere looked down on, and you know the opposition you are getting." "They are not looked down on, sir; they are everywhere received into the 'best' colonial families, and belong to them by intermarriage. As to the opposition to me, if you cared to trace it, you would track it home to two sources—prejudice among the Dutch who don't know me, and base selfishness among some of my own fellow countrymen, who know that I am too well qualified for the work given to me to suit their book as land-grabbers."

This took place at my recall. It was in an atmosphere such as that that my "resignation" took place. They will turn against Warren too, for he is a straight Christian man; but they won't be able to raise the same "make-believe" stories about him.

A very amusing thing has happened. Sprigg and Upington have gone to Bechuanaland, where they said some months ago, Mackenzie was the chief, if not the only, cause of the disturbance. They are trotted out to put down this disturbance by Hofmeyr & Co., and when they get to Stellaland they are met with a petition, openly in course of signature, to the High Commissioner, asking that Mackenzie should be sent back to Bechuanaland! What I say about this really wonderful movement is that I have never answered one of these fellows' letters, lest it should be said that I was undermining my successors.

A few weeks later, December 24th, he knows still more, and enters into particulars which even at this date his biographer may not print. After naming the men, their interest in land, their control of the news agency, he describes the tremendous influence which they exercised at Government House. One sentence is of peculiar significance.

"I saw a copy of a letter in which one of the men in this 'swim' writes to another, and asks him why he still trusts in Mackenzie, a political suicide, a broken reed; that is to say, an honest man who is not to be bought."

In a similar strain he writes to Mr Stead on the last day of that year.

Why I have not written to you has been that I have been copying despatches of mine that have not been published. I am sending copies to friends. Mr Chesson has a copy which I have asked him to show you, if you care for it.

The keeping quiet the important statement about land in Mankoroane's is alarming; in fact, unless the thing is hushed up Sir C. Warren must stumble over it and expose a big thing in land, and it was that big thing which kicked me out of office. The Dutch opposition was there, but could not have done it. Why was there English opposition? Land! Or I am a Dutchman also.

In several of these quotations Mackenzie has emphasised the fact that after leaving Stellaland in the hands of his successor, he was most careful to hold no correspondence with his friends there, for the simple reason that he did not wish even to seem to interfere with the success of those who supplanted him. It can be said with all truth that he was willing to put his whole heart into the work of making the administration of Mr Rhodes successful. He spared no pains to advise with the High Commissioner and Captain Bower regarding the right steps to take for the establishment of the Protectorate.

Mackenzie was ever a poor man, and one of the stern facts which faced him at Cape Town was that he must find some means of livelihood before long. He took some share, as we have seen, in an effort to establish an association of the friends of British supremacy in South Africa, and at one time it was proposed that he should become paid secretary of this association, but he avoided this when he discovered that the league was being constructed on too narrow a basis. He had no more sympathy, as he so often said, with the English howlers than with those of Dutch extraction. He could only approve of movements which aimed at the establishment of British authority for the sake of all races in South Africa. He could no more be brought to sympathise with an outcry for mere Anglo-Saxon supremacy than with one for mere Dutch or Kaffir supremacy.

In a letter to his wife he describes yet another proposal which came before him :—

Did I tell you that Rhodes and Bower—through the latter—wanted to interest themselves in my personal affairs, and offered to advance £500, and purchase for me the *Eastern Star* paper in Grahamstown? I respectfully declined. Bower tried my patience to the very utmost limit by assuring me and re-assuring me that he wants to assist me to "get something." He takes up the rôle of special friend.

You will see by the papers that I speak at the Empire League meeting at Wynberg. I went really for Searle's sake, who has been so kind and nice, and who is a sterling man. Well, Bower was good enough in the afternoon, in his office, to go over what he thought I ought to say! I listened patiently—so far as outward mien went—ready to explode in reality. But what capped all was, finding I was so docile, he actually asked me to show him my notes of my speech, that he might make suggestions! He seemed surprised when I said, "Tuts, man; my notes? No, no!"

In the middle of November there arrived a letter from Mr Wardlaw Thompson, Secretary of the London Missionary Society, which gave Mackenzie as much pure pleasure as almost any event in his public life. He describes this to the portion of his family who were in Scotland.

I have had a great pleasure this week, and hasten to make you at home sharers of it, if you have not heard of it. The Directors of the L. M. S. have been good enough to send out a Resolution, which virtually says, "If you want money, draw it at the rate of the married missionary. If you rejoin the Society then your drawings will have been your salary. If you enter government or other work, then you can refund as you are able."

Now, what do you think of the dear old L. M. S. ? I mean to say it is nobly done. I count it one of the honours of my life to reconnect myself in this way. I shall accept of the honour which they do me, but I trust I shall not need to draw money. I feel quite lifted up in my own mind with great thankfulness that the Directors are such broad-minded, thoughtful, Christian gentlemen.

He refers to the same offer in a letter to Dr Dale, from which we have already quoted, and in the same strain of joy and thankfulness :—

I consider that offer one of the greatest honours of my life. I shall never forget it. I hope to be able to do without the actual money, but the *generous friendly offer of* it I mean at once to accept.

Mackenzie, in spite of the fact that he took the duties of life with great seriousness, was not a man who allowed himself to be depressed as long as he saw some definite work to be done. To have a great duty upon him was no burden but an inspiration ; it absorbed him completely, making him at almost each turn in his life a man, for the time being, of one idea. His complete devotion at this period to the service of South Africa sustained him amidst public trials and private anxieties which might have crushed a less faithful man.

To Dale he writes in the month of November :—

As to these (my future plans) I just feel, Dr Dale, that I have put my hand to this plough, and do not want to turn aside while I can do work for the unifying of South Africa under the Crown, for peaceful expansion and for territorial government. Considering everything, Her Majesty's Government may find work for a person like myself. I am still at their service. Of course, I deeply feel that I have been unjustly dealt with. I blame no one. The fact, however, is there. I do not bate a jot in hopefulness.

You ought to have heard the Dutch students cheer my lecture, and cheer me too. The dear old Society is as dear to me as ever; in some sense dearer even. If it were not for the weight of this other business I should just knock at their door as I did some thirty years ago. Of course, I cannot remain long as I am here—staying merely for public reasons. The pot must be kept boiling, and five months' separation from my family is a good while.

To his wife he writes in November :—

When I saw His Excellency yesterday he was more than usually " furthy " and kind. He said Lord Derby had thought of employing me in Zululand, " but really," he added, referring to a recent telegram, " one does not know what to expect, for here, he declares, they are not going to touch Zululand." I did not ask any questions, or refer to the matter again. So you know what I know, that the Colonial Office still think me eligible for their work.

Robinson is not courageous enough. His opinion about me is favourable enough, but he has been brow-beaten by those around him. But cheer up, dearie, the work which I am attempting is a great one ; if I can only do it partially I shall be pleased to see it complete—a united peaceful South Africa under the Queen, with territorial government of native states. . . . May it please Him who has the hearts of all men in His hand so to dispose of events as to bring this speedily about.

CHAPTER XIV

AFRICA—THE WARREN EXPEDITION (1885)

WE come now to an event in South African history which for a time awoke the utmost enthusiasm amongst the vast majority of human beings in that region. It seemed to usher in a new age, and to establish the British Government in new relations with every colony, state, and territory. When Sir Charles Warren arrived at Cape Town, and there mobilised his force of four thousand men, he was welcomed, says Mackenzie, as no other British officer ever had been welcomed in that country.[1]

There was the utmost confidence in the personality of the Special Commissioner, whose long experience of South African affairs and high character made his a name to conjure with among both black and white of all races.

Sir Charles speedily found himself in a hotbed of intrigue. His difficulties we need not here detail, except in so far as they have to do with the life of Mackenzie. Mackenzie recalls with amusement the fact that Sir Hercules Robinson actually requested Warren not to consult Mackenzie regarding the affairs of Bechuanaland. To this, of course, Sir Charles agreed, and he only saw his old friend two or three times for brief interviews in public in Cape Town. Sir Charles Warren called for volunteers, and without difficulty formed a splendid regiment of horsemen to

[1] " Austral Africa," vol.ii. p. 37.

the number of six hundred picked men, and the applicants were so numerous, "that several good regiments could have been enrolled instead of one."[1]

One of the Special Commissioner's first discoveries when he reached Stellaland was of a most disagreeable nature. On the second day after his arrival at Cape Town the High Commissioner and Captain Bower had pressed him to initial a telegram, which they told him would prevent disturbances in Stellaland. He could not, of course, thus early have understood its real purport, but accepted the word of the High Commissioner, and the telegram was sent with his authority. He found afterwards that the effect of it was to confirm Mr Rhodes's agreement with Van Niekerk of September 8th, and thus to confirm all land titles issued by Niekerk without inquiry, as well as to continue the authority of Niekerk in Stellaland. This preposterous arrangement he repudiated as soon as it was discovered, but the repudiation cost him much correspondence and bitter criticism from those who were interested.

Once more the interesting fact is to be recorded, that regarding this very telegram Sir Hercules Robinson had besought Sir Charles Warren not to tell Mackenzie about it.[2]

On January 16, 1885, Mackenzie received a message from Sir Charles Warren inviting him to proceed at once to his headquarters. He arrived at Barkly West in three days, and from that day Mackenzie was a member of the Warren expedition, holding his official position on the Intelligence Department. His services to Sir Charles were varied, numerous, and of vital importance ; the two old friends struck the roots of their friendship still deeper during the ensuing months, occupying, for most of the time, the same

---

[1] "Austral Africa," vol. ii. p. 41.   [2] C.—4432, p. 119.

tent, and consulting together about every important movement of the troops or decision of the Commissioner. When in August 1885, Sir Charles Warren reported to the Home Government regarding the officers who had rendered special services to him, he named Mackenzie at the head of the list. It is a satisfaction to be able to record that he also mentioned in terms of very warm praise two of the men whom Mackenzie had selected as his own assistants in Bechuanaland, namely, Major Stanley Lowe and Mr J. M. Wright of Mafeking.

Concerning Mackenzie, the following is his report :—

1. Reverend J. Mackenzie, whose employment has been specially sanctioned by the Secretary of State, has rendered most important services, and I cannot too strongly express how much I am indebted to him for the assistance he has rendered to Her Majesty's Government. He has acted on several committees of inquiry and investigation with great success ; his assistance to the military tribunal ordered by the Secretary of State has been simply invaluable. There is, I think, no one else in South Africa who could have given the assistance he has given.

The confidence reposed in him by not only the native tribes, but also by the Dutch and English population has been most marked. At the meeting of Fourteen Streams with President Kruger, the presence of Mr Mackenzie was most conducive to the pacific arrangements, and I consider the complete success of the expedition is due in a marked degree to his cordial co-operation and aid.

His complete knowledge of the Sechuana language, and good influence over the native tribes, has enabled me the better to keep the natives and whites at peace pending the land settlement ; and I may further add that I have little doubt that the cordial reception of the protectorate by both the chiefs, Khama and Sechele, is due to the fact that the natives have such great confidence in his good faith.

Reference is made in this report to the meeting at Fourteen Streams where Sir Charles Warren and President Kruger held a conference. The President was obviously alarmed at the strength of the Warren expedition, and manifested his alarm in his eagerness to disown the Goshenites. It must be remembered that these events occurred before the discovery of gold, while the Transvaal was yet poor, and at a time when, in spite of recent pecuniary relief accorded it by Great Britain, the government of the South African Republic was drifting rapidly into poverty and disorganisation. The appearance, therefore, of so formidable a commander, with so powerful and splendidly equipped an army, created alarm in the guilty consciences at Pretoria, and Mr Kruger hastened to Goshen. There he imperatively ordered the Boers to cease from aggressive operations against Montsioa, and then he went down the border to the nearest point at which he could meet with Sir Charles. The discussions between Sir Charles Warren and President Kruger resulted in the assertion and vindication of British supremacy in Bechuanaland; and the effect of this conference, as of the entire expedition, might have been the permanent establishment of that supremacy in a manner that would have prevented the development of Boer ideals regarding a Dutch South Africa.

Both Mackenzie and Mr Rhodes were present at this most interesting interview. The High Commissioner warned Sir Charles Warren against taking Mackenzie, because of the dislike of President Kruger towards him; but Mackenzie records that Mr Kruger treated him with courtesy and consideration. And Sir Charles Warren has put it on record that the presence of the latter was of material value to him and his interests on that occasion. Once more it was demonstrated that the Cape Town cry, that the Dutch hated Mackenzie personally, was entirely base-

less ; opposition to him existed on the part only of
those who saw that his policy must defeat theirs, and
the true friends of Great Britain and British South
Africa ought to have seen this.

The manner in which Imperial interests were treated
at this time is well illustrated by the disagreeable
history of a certain petition which may be here related. The petition has been referred to in one of
Mackenzie's letters already quoted. It was drawn up
by the loyalist Stellalanders as a courageous protest
against the Niekerk-Rhodes agreement and subsequent
regime. On November 5th, 1884, they held a public
meeting at Vryburg, at which it was agreed to obtain
signatures throughout British Stellaland to a statement of their true feelings regarding Mackenzie and
a request for his reappointment. After recalling
the assertion of the Imperial Secretary, Captain
Bower, that he (Mackenzie) " never at any time
possessed the confidence of more than fifty of the
inhabitants of Stellaland, and that only four of
the farmer class accorded him their support," they
affirm that " the majority of the land owners and
inhabitants in Stellaland " had welcomed his arrival,
and " felt sure that the policy which Mr Mackenzie
inaugurated and endeavoured to carry out was the
best for the country." They add the following,
" Your petitioners, placing implicit trust in Mr
Mackenzie's ability to bring about so satisfactory a
state of affairs, are, therefore, still hopeful that it
may please your Excellency to reinstate him in his
former office, and promise in that event to afford
him every material assistance lying in their power
in support of his administration."

The covering letter requests the High Commissioner
to cable this petition to Lord Derby, and states that
" more than one half of the *bona fide* owners of land

in Stellaland 'proper' have signed the same, and
further, that the great majority of the signatures are
of Dutch Africanders of the farmer class." The
letter adds that many more would have signed had
it not been for fear of threats "held out by Niekerk's
party." This petition was returned from Cape Town
by Captain Bower to Mr Rhodes in Stellaland because, he explained, it ought to have been officially
sent through him. Nothing more was done till
February 5th and 6th, 1885, when Mr Rhodes
began an inquiry into the genuineness of the signatures, and cast doubt upon eight. Sir Charles Warren
arrived at Vryburg on February 7th, and was not
informed of the existence of the petition. Months
afterwards he heard of it, when the Stellalanders
themselves went to him to report that they had not
found it in the Blue Books. He at once appointed
three British officers to investigate the history and
value of this petition ; and they proved that only
one signature could be condemned. In his report
on this matter Sir Charles Warren says, "In conclusion, I have pointed out that one of the strongest
proofs of the good feeling towards Mr Mackenzie
is given by the fact that so many months after he
left, and in spite of the coercion of Niekerk and his
faction, so many (94) of the farmers should have
petitioned for his return. . . . I am convinced
that if Mr Mackenzie had had fair play he would
have settled these territories at the time he
came up without a stronger force than two hundred
police."

It would be out of place to make any comment
on these transactions, which Mackenzie himself afterwards described with the utmost self-restraint.

But to return. When Sir Charles Warren began
his journey to Vryburg, Mr Rhodes, with that

petition in his possession, assured the General that
if Mackenzie went into Stellaland with the expedition
he himself would not go. Mackenzie, very sure that
various discoveries were coming, was quite willing
to be absent, and offered to retire. It was arranged
by Sir Charles that he should be sent on a special
mission westwards as far as Kuruman, to gather
information regarding the state of the country and
report. This enabled Mackenzie to enjoy a glimpse
of his wife and two children after a separation of
more than six months. While he was there, busily
at work, a message suddenly arrived summoning him
immediately to Vryburg. It appeared that Niekerk
had actually been arrested, and was about to be
put on his trial for complicity in the murder of a
man named Honey in the year 1883. The murder
had been carried through at Niekerk's instigation,
and under circumstances peculiarly foul and cruel.
As soon as the Cape Town officials heard of this
trial fresh excitement and indignation were aroused.
The representatives of Great Britain did all they
could to prevent the unfolding of this story. Captain
Bower, oblivious to exact dates, sent a message
to the General that Mackenzie had known of
this murder, and had condoned it. It was a fact
that the Captain himself, without knowing the full
truth possibly, had ignored it ; but Sir Charles
Warren could not believe that Mackenzie had taken
any such extraordinary step, and at once sent for
him.

While arrangements for that trial were going on,
Mr Rhodes himself left Stellaland and went to increase the pressure which was being exerted for the
defeat of the Warren expedition from Government
House, Cape Town.

The result of the trial was that only part of the

story became revealed in evidence; the prosecution was stopped, and Niekerk released on technical grounds. These facts are fully detailed by Mackenzie.[1]

During the expedition Mackenzie was appointed to various duties, such as service on special committees, which involved him in a large amount of hard work. The Blue Books contain evidence of the thoroughness with which he carried out the duties assigned to him. He was chairman of the Committee on Native Laws, which comprised, besides himself, six officers of the expedition. This committee conducted investigations and made elaborate reports.

On their way to Mafeking, Mackenzie wrote to his wife a letter which refers to some matters already mentioned, and gives the reader a feeling for the atmosphere in which the members of this Expedition lived.

MARITSANE DRIFT.

We got to this place about three this morning, and had a good sleep after.

Do you know what has happened? Lord Derby has telegraphed out to Sir H. R., who sends it on to Sir C. W., that the latter should not have Mackenzie with him; it might (or would) hinder the settlement!

This came while I was still at Vryburg. Sir C. said, "I'll telegraph to them that I'll settle this in my own way, and by whom I please, or resign." The threat part was dropped, but he telegraphed home in cipher to Lord Derby to say that he considered my presence necessary, and that the greatest misapprehension prevailed concerning me. He then telegraphed to Sir Leicester Smythe, Lieut.-Governor and Commander-in-Chief at the Cape, telling him what had taken place, and declaring that he never knew a case of such persecution as mine was, and could he use his influence in the right direction? This is what he did, after consulting with his officers. I said, on the first flush of the matter,

[1] "Austral Africa," vol. ii. pp. 133-153.

"Let me go, and have done with this." He answered very strongly that he would not hear of it. It then occurred to me that this was really the *first step towards the hasty handing over of the country to the Cape.* They know that I am opposed to this. I wrote privately to that effect to Sir Robert Herbert some time ago; also to others. It is evident the Government are prepared to make a hasty settlement and retire from the country, and leave the same dreadful programme of falsehood, robbery, and blood to be carried on elsewhere. Of course Sir C. W. is opposed to this, but how far his position may come to be that of a man under orders I don't know. I still hope on; with God's help the thing is bound to come right. I saw in a Cape paper—you look and find it too—that the Cape branch of the Africander Bond had resolved at a recent meeting to give special attention to the subject of confederation. This is an immense move in the right direction. This means confederation under the Queen. Not long ago the same people were speaking openly of their own flag, etc., etc. One of them said at that time that this revival of Imperial interest, and the introduction of the Territorial scheme of Government which I proposed, would delay their obtaining a Republic for at least fifty years. Now they seem to have given this idea up and speak of confederation under the Queen. "Alles zal recht Komen"; and the much-maligned Mackenzie will, I humbly trust, have *done something towards it.*

This affair is full of crises. The great one at Goshen is coming. There was one at Vryburg when I got there. The preliminary examination (in the Niekerk murder case) was about to break down, and Warren was going to interfere in virtue of his position, and override the "Civil Court." This would have raised a great cry—Military rule; Despotism, etc. On Monday morning we went down to Vryburg from the camp, the upshot being that Müller, the landrost, said publicly that Ludorf's effort to close the case was "hasty." Then Ludorf himself stood up and declared that "as a man of honour and in the interests of justice" he could not close the case. He knew now what he did not know on Saturday. (This was false.) I had a little to do with the management of this, as I knew the men. It was very amusing to hear how the thing went. Arend (Honey's servant) will be examined when the Court re-opens. His evidence is of the first importance, and will lead to the bringing out of more. The court is composed of Niekerk's own people, and yet something like justice may be expected, with care. The case needs "looking after." There is the utmost consternation in Government House. In point of fact, the court which is trying Niekerk is one sanctioned and upheld by the authority of the High Commissioner and his representatives, Bower and Rhodes. Sir Charles avails himself of the court and jurisdiction which he finds sanctioned in Stellaland and uses it for the trial of Niekerk! The thing reads like the chapter of an exciting novel.

What ought to be done is, to hold the country for a while as a Crown Colony before it is handed over to the Cape Colony. This would be for the good of the natives, for whose sake so much has been done, and it would be an immense blessing to South Africa generally, leading to its speedy consolidation. Everywhere there is a section— sometimes small, but always noisy—who are not loyal to the Queen. Families are sometimes divided. What a mistake to profess to retain the country, and yet throw in no weight on the side of the loyal Dutch colonists.

The expedition reached Mafeking on Friday, March 11th, 1885. The people were naturally over-joyed at the arrival of the long-expected deliverer. The Goshen filibusters wore an entirely different manner. The loud-voiced and more brazen-faced, in fact the guiltier men, had disappeared ; and the remnant were not of the kind to do aught but cringe before the mighty power which now confronted them.

The following extract from a letter to one of his sons throws some more light on these events :—

But one thing Rhodes was clear about. He would not go into Stellaland with Sir Charles, if I went. As he was Deputy Commissioner, and I was nothing particular then, Sir C. agreed to give me work elsewhere in the Kuruman district, which I had pleasure in doing. Sir C. said to me, "This is the best thing that could have happened for you." However, I will admit that altho' my time was well filled up at Kuruman with work, and altho' I had a great deal to hear and see from the loved ones there, yet I was willing enough to respond to the call to come away again and get into the thick of this work and warfare, for it is both combined. Great events had transpired in my absence. Sir Charles informed me that Niekerk was arrested on a charge of complicity in murder, but that Captain Bower had written to say that that was condoned by Mackenzie, as I had known all against Niekerk, and yet had appointed him Assistant Commissioner! Warren said, "I know this is incorrect, but I want you to come at once and say it is not true." When I got to Vryburg I found Rhodes had gone. There had been a big affair, and Warren had given him a considerable piece of his mind, so I was told before I got there.

Niekerk, who is personally a coward—acknowledged on all hands to be so—was induced by Rhodes to cross into Stellaland, and actually presented himself before Sir Charles, and demanded an inquiry and examination into charges which had been preferred against him! This was an astounding step. The *Cape Argus* (Rhodes's paper) pointed out what a fine step he had taken, and mentioned my name as having blackened Niekerk's character. Charges! They came in clouds, and, to crown all, there came the charge of complicity in the murder of a man called James Honey, who had also been a freebooter, but had been of a better stamp than Niekerk & Company. Sir Charles found a court to his hand constructed by Sir H. Robinson and Rhodes. The question of jurisdiction was thus disposed of for him.

Before leaving Vryburg, wondrous cablegrams came from Lord Derby recommending Sir Charles to "separate himself from Mackenzie"—otherwise the settlement would be rendered more difficult! I said I would clear out at once. On no account would I stay on mere permission to stay, after such a cable as that. Sir C. wired straight to London, not thro' Sir Hercules (whom I blame for this), saying that he considered my presence necessary—or some such strong expression. He had made up his mind to threaten resignation in case there had been any uncertainty in the reply. The reply, however, gives him full swing as to having me. This came straight from London. A "Reuter" telegram from Cape Town informs us that there had been a question asked in the House on this subject. I suppose Derby's bowing to

Sir H. Robinson and the Cape ministers had been brought
before the English public.   I am certain they won't stand
it in England.   The reply of Ashley was cool, when you
come to know that a cable had been sent to Sir Charles
on the subject from Downing Street.

There is to be no fighting.   Telegrams will have told
you all about it.   But the freebooters are hopeful that our
stay will only be for a time, and that then they can come
back.

At Mafeking Mackenzie seems to have found more
time for letter-writing.   In addition to those already
quoted two others of special interest may be referred
to.   One was a very long one to his old and most tried
friend, Rev. G. D. Cullen of Edinburgh, to whom he
always opened his heart with peculiar frankness and
confidence.   In this letter he goes over a large part
of the ground already covered in these pages.   It
was here he heard of the birth of his first grand-
daughter, and his big heart naturally overflowed at
this event.

The following letter to his little daughter (Mary)
at Kuruman is worth inserting, as it reveals the way
in which, amid the pressure and distractions of heavy
duties, he could put himself in sympathy with the
interests even of a child :

I have been thinking a great deal about you and Hettie
and Mamma.   Who was born on the 25th of March ?   Was
it not Jeanie ?   I was thinking about it the day before
yesterday, but not for very long.

We have despatch-riders to the nearest telegraph station,
which is twenty miles from here, at a place called Madibe.
They come several times in twenty-four hours, and some
of them usually arrive about twelve at night.   I was not
sleeping very soundly last night.   I heard them arrive and
give in their despatches.   Then they go to their place and
give their horses food, and then, I suppose, go asleep.   A
gentleman in this camp a few days ago sent a message to
a gentleman in London, and an answer has come back.
Isn't that funny ?   So we could speak to Auntie Bessie in

a few hours if we liked to do so; only I have nothing to
say to her in such a hurry.   Of course these messages cost
a great deal of money.   I am sorry to say that my nice,
spirited, and yet comfortable pony died here of horse-sickness.
I have not got another horse yet.   But very few horses have
died as yet.   They have all nose-bags on during the whole
night, and they are not allowed to eat grass till late in the
morning.   But they get oats and other food.   The horses,
however, are fond of the nice grass, and I don't think they
quite understand the secret of sleeping with their noses in
a bag! and then of standing so long before being allowed
to go to the grass.   I daresay they don't think it kind, and
yet it is kind all the while.

They are having grand fun on the top of the rise here
to-day.   There are horse races and mule races, and I don't
know what all.   I am going up after I have quite finished
writing.

It is so nice to think that dear Mamma and you and
Hettie, besides those in Portobello, are always praying for
God's blessing and help to be given to me in the work
which I am trying to do.   Things look very discouraging
sometimes, when people don't do what you would like them
to do; but it is very sweet to look above all men to God
Himself, our merciful Father, and to say to Him, " Thy
will be done."   We wish to do His will here; but the work
before us is not an easy one, especially at present.

Now there is a long letter to your own dear, old-fashioned
little self.   And you go on praying darling, and good news
will come at last.   How are you getting on with lessons?

Without putting off much time Sir Charles pushed
on towards Shoshong where he arrived on Friday,
May 8th, 1885.   Needless to say, it was one of the
supreme moments of Mackenzie's life when he personally and officially accompanied a British Commissioner to the capital of Khame's country.   Once more
he stood looking at the old hills amid which so many
years of his best strength had been spent.   Once
more he met Khame, who welcomed him with the
fervour of an undying friendship.   As usual, the
negotiations at this place were conducted through

Mackenzie, whose peculiar relations to both sides enabled him to deal in private with Khame as his trusted friend and adviser, and at the same time to appear at his court as one of the representatives of the Queen. The peculiar position in which he stood, and his work, are described fully in " Austral Africa," but from another and tenderer point of view in the following letter to his wife :—

We arrived here on Friday. This is Tuesday, yet this is the first scrap I have written in English. I have had a most engrossed and most exciting time of it. Khame's pleasure at seeing me once more, and at such a crisis too, was evidently very sincere ; and on the first interview he said to me in Sechuana, "I shall lean on you as in the olden time ; stop me if I go wrong." There was no need for this, however, as he spoke well both in public and in private, and has won golden opinions from all our party. Even the young officers, who are a little sceptical about hero-making, declare that he is a fine fellow. I have privately drawn up Khame's state- ment for him, and Lloyd has copied it. I daresay this will be suspected by the General, but I am not telling him, lest the knowledge of this should be embarrassing. At anyrate, in the meantime Khame is putting in a map which will show the boundary lines of his country—up to the Zambesi, and which also shows another inner line, which is the country claimed by the Chief for his own use and the use of his people. As to the expenses of the Protectorate, Khame invites the coming of English settlers into the rest of his country ; he says that they ought to be—with his own people —the defenders of the country, and that Khame's contribu- tion to the defence of the country is the large and most valuable territory which he now places in the hands of the Queen. This has all been spoken, and the maps are now being made. I do not know what answer Warren will give to Khame's statement in writing, if he gives any. As the General and I have the same tent he, of course, has seen that I have been doing a deal of writing. We are quite of one opinion on this as on many other points.

I cannot tell you how many enquiries have been made for you, from Ma-Bessie downwards. " Mawillie oa Rae ? " has been the question. Poor Khame ! He declared to me that his prayer had been answered in my coming. The General's speech and Khame's were very good ones this morning. Then others spoke, Gohakgosi, Raditadi, etc. "Their country must not be sold, and strong drink must not come into it. The coming of good English farmers would teach them many things. They were willing to learn, and would welcome such men into their country." This was the drift of the speaking.

We are now with our faces southward, and will probably start to-morrow. As soon as I get within reach of Heliograph I shall send you a scrap, or I may send you one with this.

I have ridden all the way. You need have no anxiety about me. I have lots of bedding now, and indeed have lent Mr Baden-Powell my plaid.

Lloyd preached in English very nicely—all were present. I preached in Sechwana—people crowded both sides of church. If I had not stuck to my text I could not have got on. People very affectionate. The old house is without roof, its timbers having been utilized by Mr Hepburn, which was quite right. Lloyd is building beyond Hepburn's, as it were against the long hill opposite our house, about opposite our old church, of which nothing stands now. Indeed, as to buildings, nothing that I have put up here is now standing. As to the spiritual structure we must leave that to the loving and merciful Master's eye. He knows how little we have done.

The magnificent offer which Khame made to Great Britain, surely one of the most striking events in the whole of British Colonial history, was treated with great coolness in London, and was ultimately laid aside. The Colonial Office came to the conclusion only sixteen years ago, on the dictum largely of Sir Hercules Robinson, that the British people had no interests beyond the Molopo River.

From Shoshong Sir Charles turned his face southwards again. Mackenzie left him at Taungs and proceeded to Kuruman. There he remained a while watching the news of Sir Charles's wonderful progress through the Colony, and ruminating over his own future. He was at once deeply encouraged and much disappointed in the results of the Warren expedition. The whole arrangement of the expedition by Sir Charles was most brilliant. It combined dignity with great military skill and superb political wisdom. Everywhere the General as well as his officers and men had won golden opinions, alike from Boer and British, from black and white. It was an army that any government might have been proud to use for the still further winning of still greater glory. It put South Africa completely at the feet of Queen Victoria. If Sir Charles had been continued in power as Special Commissioner, with a free hand to build up one or two Crown colonies in the heart of Central Africa, we can all see now that the miseries and disgraces of subsequent years would have been prevented. The worst of it is that men like Sir Charles Warren, Mackenzie, and a large number of wise men in South Africa, as well as statesmen of the type of W. E. Forster and Sir Thomas Fowell Buxton and many others in London, understood the facts and told the public the very truth at the time, which all the world sees to-day. Both Sir Charles Warren and Mackenzie had used their utmost endeavours to persuade the Colonial Office that the expedition ought not to be withdrawn until a stable form of government had been established throughout Bechuanaland, and an Imperial Land Commission had completed its work in an imperial spirit.

Yet the Expedition was withdrawn, with the cordial thanks of the British Government, not at the end, but at the very beginning of the real work, which in those days of crisis ought to have been done in South Africa.

Brooding deeply over these things under his old roof at Kuruman, Mackenzie, not without a struggle and profound self-sacrifice, decided that for him the

service of South Africa and his Queen in the world of
political agitation had not been ended.

Writing to his sister-in-law, Miss Douglas, he says :

Sir Charles Warren's time of power in Bechuanaland is
over, and consequently so is mine. Much—very much—
has been accomplished—so as to surprise myself when I
think of it. There is a Crown Colony after all. . . . Now,
I am afraid that when Warren and his expedition leave all
the English people's interest will evaporate also. So I am
really seriously contemplating coming over the water to see
what can be done to keep the matter before the public mind
in its right light.

The expedition has done much. It has pacified the
country and opened up the interior as it never was
before. The Crown Colony and the Land Commission have
been obtained after hard fighting ; but there they are ; even
if the General and I have to clear out—so much has been
accomplished. The General has been badly used by Sir
Hercules, and has written to Government to complain of
serious misrepresentations in last Blue-book. All that is very
distressing, but I trust it will have one good result of showing
people that the High Commissionership is incompatible with
the local politics of the Cape Colony.

You will be glad to learn that Sir C. Warren has written
very kindly about me in his despatches, but I suppose they
will be blocked in giving me any employment while Robinson
is there. Isn't that queer, and he my great friend and
upholder last year ? He has turned on himself. I hold the
same views now as then.

I have written to Wardlaw Thompson and another London
friend with reference to my coming home—especially in connection with securing Khame's country ; and I have asked
Thompson if after consulting they think I should do so, they
are to cable one word, and I shall be making all preparations.
I might do some good, but would be glad of their views, as
I am out here and they are on the spot. Sir Charles and
his staff are anxious I should go. I have put it straight to
Thompson that if I go I must not belong to the class "without any ostensible means of livelihood," and that therefore
they must consider whether the kind of work I am likely to
do is work of which they can approve, and which they can

co-operate with me in doing by enabling me to keep the pot boiling. I have been paid by Sir Charles.

The London Missionary Society wrote to inquire whether he would be willing to go and settle at one of their stations in Matabeleland ; but this he felt himself forced at that time to decline, so deep was his conviction that unless the work which he could do in London were undertaken, almost the entire fruits of his own and Sir Charles Warren's labours would be destroyed. He felt the truth of the words which Mr Theodore Schreiner wrote to him :—

I do trust the Home Government, now that Sir Charles's mission to South Africa has once more made it possible for British supremacy to be a fact in the country, will not let us drift again into the chaotic longings after a Republic, that were the outcome of the indifference and blunders of England with regard to us. With these thoughts it is doubtful whether the sense of loyalty now once more awakened would survive a second extinction.

Mackenzie was much cheered by the extraordinary enthusiasm with which his late General was received throughout the Colony. Sir Charles Warren went from Kimberley through the Eastern Provinces to Port Elizabeth, and was everywhere met with enthusiastic demonstrations. He spoke freely of the future relations of Great Britain to South Africa, and his bold outlines of an Imperial policy were cheered to the echo. He took occasion at every opportunity to review recent history, especially as far as it bore upon the reputation of his friend Mackenzie, and he found that the public mind was well informed regarding the merits of the chief occurrences and controversies.

At Cape Town, in spite of efforts in high places to prevent it, the General's reception exceeded anything that had been seen before.

Mackenzie received letters describing these events

from several of the officers of the expedition, a number of whom had formed an attachment to him which lasted till the end of his life, and which some of them took every suitable occasion to express. Sir Bartle C. Frere, the son of his old friend, wrote to him from Cape Town a letter, from which the following extract may be made :—

I have just come back from witnessing the "Torchlight Procession" in honour of Sir Charles, and hearing his speech to the populace thereafter, during the course of which his warm allusions to yourself elicited six distinct and most hearty rounds of applause, such as I hope made your ears tingle even at the far-off distance of Kuruman. It was very pleasant to hear. Nor, as you are no doubt aware, has there been any but the warmest applause on any of the recent occasions when he has alluded to yourself and your work. As my neighbours at one of the many recent banquets said to me, "They may say what they like about Mackenzie, but there's no doubt that he saved that country!"

From Colonel Terry came similar news :—

You will have seen by the papers the warm welcome given to the General along the route to Cape Town, and here it has—among the vast majority who have joined in it—exceeded all.

Your name was enthusiastically received in Port Elizabeth and here. You may count on the warm support of the Eastern Provinces and of Cape Town, and on a special rally due to the mean attacks of which you have been the subject.

Sir C. W. also gains something in the minds of the people for having stuck to you.

On the 2nd of November Mackenzie arrived once more in Cape Town. He had left his wife and two daughters to keep house with his medical son, who had settled at Kimberley in private practice.

In his first letter to his wife, he speaks of the very great kindness with which all his friends had received him. Several of them, as soon as they knew of his arrival, arranged a private dinner in his honour, and this took place next day at the City Club.

I have just come back from the dinner at the City Club, which a number of gentlemen invited me to. The Hon. R. Southey was in the Chair; Hon. Ebden, Vice-Chair; Lewis, M. L. A. Searle, Wilmore, St Leger, Maclean of Donald Currie & Co., Hamilton Ross, R. M. Ross, Moore, Rev. Sutton Fletcher, Dr Douglas, Dr Ebden, Arderne, Beard, etc., over 20 in all. The thing was got up in a short time—I really don't know by whom. But it was very, very kind. Old Southey spoke so nicely and kindly. I made a few remarks, again identifying myself with them, and telling them a little of what I hoped to do. They were very kind. Then Searle made a nice speech, thanking St Leger for what the *Cape Times* had done. It was quite impromptu, and the meeting took it very well. St Leger replied, and both he and Searle incidentally said the kindest things of me, St Leger declaring that he would back me, altho' all the newspapers in the world went against me. Well, I am pleased and thankful; only it was a wet night, and Mr Arderne ran and borrowed Dr Kitching's coat for me, so I have not caught cold, and you, dearest, can amuse yourself by wondering whether Dr Kitching had more than one coat, or whether he needed this one before I was able to return it.

This is my last note before leaving—only I may add a few lines. The Governor has lost in public opinion here very much. Government House influence was exerted to its utmost bent to frustrate the reception to Warren, but it was impossible. Merriman joined the Committee, but afterwards withdrew, leaving the impression that he had joined it to crush and minimize the whole thing. Hofmeyr is said to be returning with Upington. The Dutch have been grumbling at Hofmeyr's long absence, but he will no doubt pull them all right when he comes back. I have paid my passage. I confess it seems a lonely kind of proceeding, altho' I am going to see my own people on the other side. However, cheer up, dearie, let us wait on God, our Father and Guide. He will guide and uphold us.

In another letter, he once more asks his children for that on which he ever most relied, viz., their prayers on his behalf.

"Pray for me," he says, "that I may be able to do much for this country when I go to England; and that God would put it into their hearts to do the right things, so that there may be peace and good laws and right ways in the country."

He reached London on November 25th, and immediately plunged into war once more in that great battlefield where so many Imperial fights have been lost and won. He little knew when he undertook this task, with a clear perception of the policy he would pursue, and the definite steps in South African development which he would secure, that he would be involved in this warfare well nigh five years, and that during this period of his life he would toil, as few men have ever toiled, with an unselfishness and a devotion to one supreme ideal which would absorb his life, and practically shorten his days.

Before entering on this chapter, we may close by quoting a characteristic post-card which he received from his friend, Mr W. T. Stead, who was then—not languishing—in Holloway gaol.

Well, I am in great spirits, thirsting to interview you. I have made application to have you admitted for one half an hour next week, and we must e'en make the best use of our time.

I am disgusted with Capt. Bower, but I suppose all men were made for some purpose, and now that you and I are together again we must lend a hand to save South Africa once more.

I am very happy, very busy, and watch with some elation the fulfilment of my prophecies.

CHAPTER XV

ENGLAND—"BAFFLED TO FIGHT BETTER"
(1885-1887)

MACKENZIE found the political life of the home country in great tumult over a general election. The Irish Home Rule question occupied the attention of statesmen, journalists, and private citizens, almost to the exclusion of every other interest. The frequent changes of government caused at that period by the Gladstonian policy did only harm to the work of the Colonial Office. Within a dozen years there were no less than six different occupants of the Colonial Secretaryship. Colonel Stanley was in office when Mackenzie landed in England, but was destined soon to give place to Earl Granville; from 1887 Sir Henry Holland (afterwards Lord Knutsford) held the office until 1892.

The following letter to his eldest daughter, written the day after his arrival in London, describes his first day's experiences in his old haunts :—

I reached London yesterday afternoon. Saw Thompson at the Mission House. Looked up at Islington (but missed) the young schoolmaster whom they are sending to Kuruman. Then went to Waterloo Station for my luggage, and brought it to the old place. Only think, B—— out on election work ! People are all daft here, and I suppose you are even worse in the North, where the great wizard has got you all under his spell. At anyrate, everyone will have heard him and seen him, and will thus be able to tell those of a succeeding generation how Mr Gladstone could hold an audience spell-bound.

To-day I went to see Chesson, and missed him. Missed

young missionary again at Mission House. Went to Colonial Institute and found a note of welcome from my friend Oates. Then called for Sir Robert Herbert, Permanent Secretary, Colonial Office. As it was a chance call I felt pleased when told he was in. There was considerable delay, but as one after another of the other assistant secretaries popped in and sat down, I fancied Sir Robert had been letting them know. Mr Bramstone was the first, then Lord Dunraven, then Colonel Stanley's secretary, to say he could not come, as he had an engagement for 4, but would I call to-morrow at that hour?

Well, the interview was to me very gratifying. Sir Robert said straight out before the others, that for his part, he was glad, and yet sorry to see me. He would be much better pleased to know I was in Bechuanaland. We got a map and went over some business. I did not make the interview long. They asked my address for their book, and in every way gave me to understand that I was a welcome visitor.

Sir Robert, when alone, expressed his great regret at the results to myself, and added, " of course we left it in Sir Hercules' hands." I said, " Of course as I resigned, and Sir H. approved, I quite looked for your acquiescence." So I go to see Colonel Stanley to-morrow.

A little later he wrote to his son in Africa, saying :—

I am very busy, but my work, if I can do it, will really be worth accomplishing. May it please God to give me the open support of good and true people in the Colony. However, such may not be His will. Rejected people must always do their duty for those who reject them.

Shortly after his arrival in London, news reached him from Bechuanaland, which confirmed him in the conviction that there was great danger of the immediate return of disorder and disaster in that region. This only made him set his teeth, as it were, to a more determined and a stronger fight. Mr W. E. Forster, his warm friend and supporter of his policy in South Africa, lay on, what proved to be, his death-bed. Mackenzie exchanged messages with him, but the brave statesman's days of active service were over.

His private secretary, Mr Arthur H. Loring, who was deeply interested in South African affairs, took personal pleasure in keeping communications going between the sick man and Mackenzie.

As Mackenzie, during these early weeks of his new life, brooded over his programme, it became clear that there were three great results to be aimed at in regard to the British management of South Africa and its affairs. In the first place, the High Commissionership must be separated from the Governorship of Cape Colony ; in the next place, British authority and government must be effectively extended to the Zambesi ; and in the third place, a reasonable system of territorial government must be established over all those regions that were thickly populated by the native tribes, and where yet there was room for European colonisation.

Incidentally, and as a part of this general programme, Mackenzie was determined to prevent, if he could, the annexation of Bechuanaland to Cape Colony, a step which he knew was seriously contemplated by Cape politicians, and seemed to have the approval of Sir Hercules Robinson. It is hard for us to estimate the courage, not to say, audacity, with which a private individual, without money or political position, set himself deliberately to achieve these ends. Mackenzie himself once said, " People will think my proposal about the Zambesi a sign of madness, but I prophesy that within ten years the thing will be done." Like a half dozen other remarkable prophecies which he ventured on South African affairs, this one also was fulfilled, only in less than half the time he allowed.

How was this work to be done ? The first part of Mackenzie's programme of practical work consisted in the writing of a book. This book took him eighteen months of very hard and continuous labour to complete. He did not enter upon the writing of these two volumes in a spirit of mere self-vindication. The fact that he had been wronged could never have been for him a reason for thrusting himself and his story upon the attention of the public. He resolved to write the history with which he had been concerned, because in that crisis of the relations of Great Britain to South Africa all the main facts and problems of South African history were set in the clearest light. To describe these years and the experiences with which they had been filled, would enable him, historically and pictorially, to make every reader face the heart of the difficulty for himself. First of all, he would show the life of South African natives, and depict their position and prospects under British and Boer predominance respectively. He would be able to describe the political condition of Cape Colony, the parties, the personalities, the strange medley of confused policies, of loyalty and disloyalty, trust and distrust, towards Great Britain which made Cape Town the spot on which the alternative of Boer or British supremacy was to be decided. He could show how the colonists felt towards the mother country when the Colonial Office reduced them to dismay and exasperation. He would also be able to show the readiness of the majority to arise in unbounded enthusiasm when the mother country seemed to have definitely chosen their part. He would also be able to describe the characteristic attitude of the Transvaal Boer. He would show the real grounds and reasons for the hostility of that people towards Great Britain, for their determination to stop the spread of British influence northwards, and even the beginning of the daring purpose to establish throughout South Africa a Dutch Republic. Yet he could show also a willingness of the Dutch to co-operate with the British, and the ease with which a dangerous cleavage between the races could be not merely bridged for a time, but abolished for ever. The practical problem therefore which Mackenzie wished to place before the British public in his book, as in all his writings and speeches, was this : " How deeply do you wish to have a South African empire ?   Are you not now and henceforth inevitably responsible for the future of that entire region ?   If Great Britain is responsible for the future of all South Africa, then the Colonial Office must set itself to plan seriously for the government of the whole ; and the entire organisation of Imperial affairs in South Africa must be directed towards the development of all the races and territories from Cape Town to the Zambesi."

Further, Mackenzie saw with the utmost clearness, as every one does, that the end in view must be the confederation of all the parts in one dominion.   That, he held, ought to be not merely foreseen, still less ought it to be hurried on, but alike with patience and with breadth of vision it ought to be carefully prepared for.   Hence no one existing South African colony or state should be enlarged at the expense of the rest, nor should it be placed in a position of permanent political superiority.   He was able to point to the difficulty caused by the ambition of the Premier Colony in Australia, which for so long hindered confederation on that continent.

In Mackenzie's view there were two main precautions which the Home Government needed to take at once if it would at the same time assert its supremacy and make its assertion effective.

In the first place, the High Commissionership should be an office like that of the Viceroy of India or Governor-General of Canada.   It should be separated from the governorship of any one colony. This separation was advocated, not for the merely negative purpose of preventing complications at Cape

Town but for the far greater positive reasons which
he was able to urge. For in the day when Great
Britain appointed a High Commissioner for South
Africa, gave him a residence and surrounded him
with a court away from Cape Town, her moral
influence and political effectiveness over all South
African races would be multiplied indefinitely.

But, further, Mackenzie saw, as he had for so many
years, that the next step must be the occupation of
all native territories by Imperial officers, who should
be under the direct supervision of the High Commissioner himself. Steadily and quietly these vast
regions would be opened up to European farmers,
miners, and store-keepers, while the native tribes themselves were being wisely led out from their primitive
habits of life into those of a Christian civilisation.

In this manner the two Dutch States, the Orange
Free State and the Transvaal, would become surrounded with new countries, and would find themselves
drawn gradually but irresistibly into the life of a
confederated South Africa.

All this was mapped out in Mackenzie's mind in
the year 1885. Indeed, the main principles had been
grasped by his mind nearly twenty years before that.
Surely this was the project of a true empire builder!
He, however, now showed himself determined to be
no mere dreamer but a practical labourer in this great
undertaking. We can all now see how great was the
outline of South African imperialism which he pro-
mulgated, and how wise were the doctrines on which
it was founded.

It is our task, in this life story of Mackenzie, to
discover the methods by which he sought to put his
scheme before the British mind, and, we shall also be
compelled to see by what classes and individuals the
scheme was approved and aided, and by whom it was
opposed and defeated.

In his work he was most powerfully assisted by the South African Committee, whose secretaries, Mr H. O. Arnold Foster and Mr Arthur H. Loring worked with him most strenuously and loyally. The Committee included such names as Mr W. M. Acworth of the Imperial Federation League, the Hon. Evelyn Ashley, Mr H. A. Bryden, Sir T. Fowell Buxton, Mr Sidney C. Buxton, the Earl of Camperdown, Mr Joseph Chamberlain, Sir William Dunn, Earl (later the Duke) of Fife, Sir Robert Fowler, the late Earl Grey and Mr Albert Grey (the present Earl Grey), Mr Morgan Harvey, and others. This Committee held frequent meetings and issued circulars, planned careful action in the House of Commons, arranged for public meetings, and in every way sought to promote the ends which Mackenzie had in view, and of which they as a whole most heartily approved.

Mackenzie went down to Scotland that Christmas season (1885) and remained there until February. His correspondence grew day by day. Wherever he went prominent men of both political parties found him out, or were sought out by him, for the discussion and promotion of his South African policy. Every man with an African project of any kind, commercial, religious, or political, seemed to think it necessary that he should consult Mackenzie. It would be tedious to enumerate the purposes for which individuals of all sorts sought him out in person or by letter during the next few years, for consultation on African affairs. Willing ever to serve in a good cause, or to prevent mistakes, he found himself in this way involved in correspondence, and even in the labour of investigations, which did not bear upon his own work.

On January 11th, 1886, he spoke at a meeting of the Scottish Geographical Society, at which Mr Joseph Thompson read a paper on "East Central Africa and its Commercial Outlook." He also was consulted by the founders of the British East African Company in Edinburgh and Glasgow. In the end of February he was back again in London, preparing to read a paper on Bechuanaland before the Society of Arts, for which he received the Society's silver medal. He also attended and spoke at a meeting of the Anthropological Institute, where Captain C. R. Conder R. E., read a paper on "The Present Condition of the Bechuanaland, Koranna and Matabele Tribes." Captain Conder wrote to him, expressing his gladness that "we had such a nice little political breeze."

Mackenzie had in January contributed two long and important letters to *The Times* (January 1st and 20th, 1886), which attracted wide attention, and in which he laid down the fundamental principles of his plan of campaign. In an interesting letter to a South African editor he refers to these communications as follows :—

I shall be glad if you can give the whole or part of those letters *in your Dutch columns.* I only want to be understood. I have no fear of the results where I can be heard and my views considered. If my views or my policy were inimical to the Cape Colony the thing would be different; but the fact is, I was alive to the interests of the Cape Colony, as to the North, long before its own political leaders dreamt of the subject.

But there must be no hurried annexation and no hurried confederation, which I fancy some foolish people would wish to make a rush at. Let the Imperial Government administer Bechuanaland for some years, north as well as south Bechuanaland, and *then* let it be considered whether it may not be safely joined to the Cape Colony, or what should be done.

On February 1st he sent to Mr Stead a long letter which contained the following paragraphs :—

Mr Froude's remarks in his new book (*Oceana*) demand special notice. I don't think they will have so much weight as they would have had before the recent education of people concerning South Africa.

Mr Froude writes very much (I have only seen extracts) as he talked to me when I had the pleasure of seeing him some time ago.

I then formed the opinion that Froude was simply "downright angry" with the English in South Africa, as he blamed them for his failure when he went out there on a special mission.

Mr Froude then (privately, of course) admitted to me that the policy I have been advocating would no doubt be the best, but England wouldn't do it, and wouldn't stick to it, and what would be the use of trying? Well, you know a good deal about what happened after that. We have now in our hands, and in our volition (what we had not then) the right to the territory of the interior, and the right to manage immigration into it, and the protection of its native inhabitants. You know how these things have been obtained, and what honour is conferred on England by the trust reposed in her by such chiefs as Khame. There can be no question as to our success on the lines I am advocating, and which hitherto you have assisted me so much to carry. The Crown Colony of Bechuanaland, with the Protectorate to the North, are great facts. Let us turn aside neither to the right hand nor the left, but make our administration in Bechuanaland a wise and real one; let us admit emigrants to Khame's country, and Austral Africa will be by-and-by one of our most "creditable" colonies. Remember they are all Protestants.

The following letter to Dr G. B. Clarke, M.P., has a note of personal interest :—

19th Feb. 1886.

DEAR DR CLARK,—I thank you for your remarks on the Zulu question last night.

I trust we are within sight of a comprehensive and settled scheme of South African policy. I am just about to publish on the question, and hope to give some information on it.

What really blocks the way is the want of an Imperial Head in South Africa. And Sir Hercules Robinson is dead against a disturbance of the present arrangement. His arguments do not hold water, and will be got over, no doubt, but they have weight for a time, as coming from an official in high position, whereas it is really the case that he is practically defending himself as having administered the joint offices in question. When we turn our faces and not our backs to South Africa there will be no difficulty of a serious nature. General Gordon said there was no difficulty.

We have differed, and you wrote against me, as I thought at the time, unfairly, when I was out in Bechuanaland, but none the less I have much pleasure in seeing your remarks made last night.—Believe me, ever yours sincerely,

JOHN MACKENZIE.

To Miss Douglas, April 12th, he writes :—

DEAR SISTER BESSIE,—Seeing that Dr Dale was to speak at Newman Hall's Church I went there yesterday morning. The good pew-opener must needs honour me with a seat well to the front. Dale spotted me after the service, and took me off with him to where he was staying with some friends. We had a long and very interesting talk. He spoke about my letters and what he had done with them, and told me of Mr Chamberlain's "soundness" on the subject to the last. Dr Dale would like a Royal Commission rather than a Committee, and especially objects to Mr Gorst; says he has not much influence, and that he is very partisan. He declares that Chamberlain is the man to take charge of it.

It was as if Dale and I had only parted the day before, he was so kind and really interested.

I had a long chat with Stead afterwards. He would like a Royal Commission rather than a Committee—like Dale in that. He jotted down the subject. He will really help in his own way. He is a capital fellow, and could not be more friendly to me.

This afternoon I went down to the House by appointment, to meet Sir Donald Currie. I wish I could transcribe our talk; I shall not try to-night. By the way we were interrupted—by whom? Dr Clark! I thought he would pass, but no, he came up with a smiling face and we shook hands, and as in duty bound I said, "I suppose I ought to congratulate you on your M.P.-ship." I think he understood exactly what I meant. He was very anxious that I should see him again. I don't suppose he is beyond conversion, even after his low and lost condition on this subject. But I have no time at present.

The drift of Sir Donald Currie's story was impatience with everybody whatever, and especially with Chesson's people; and a full statement of what he himself privately with his personal influence had done for South Africa. . . . At present I have the impression that he wants to unite all the Dutch States with the Colony straight off, and that he thinks he could carry that. I did not ask him too much, but let him talk.

It would be a very serious thing for South Africa if such a union took place at once. It is what we all desire and hope for in the future. It would be a bad job for the natives, with a responsible Government and the Queen at its head, and the majority mostly ignorant Dutchmen, swamping the Englishmen till their voice would not be heard, or at least their votes would count for nothing.

At this time it was proposed that the Government should be persuaded to appoint a Commission or Committee, composed of men of different political sympathies, who should enquire into the whole South African question and report to the House of Commons. Mackenzie's correspondence shows that this proposal was backed up with great earnestness by such men as Mr Chamberlain and Sir John Gorst within the House, as well as by Dr Dale, Mr Stead, Mr Chesson, and many others of the general public. At one time there seemed a good prospect of obtaining this Commission, but the change of government which occurred that summer put a new face on everything, and this hopeful plan collapsed.

In the middle of June, Mackenzie, for the first time, went down to visit his friend, the late Mr John Kirby, a retired sea captain, who lived at Woolstone, near Southampton. Mr Kirby, who had ultimately two sons in Africa, was a most earnest adherent and supporter of Mackenzie's cause. For Mackenzie himself he formed a singularly deep affection, and insisted on contributing personal work, as well as money, to meet some part of the many expenses which Mackenzie incurred in the course of his prolonged agitation. At Mr Kirby's Mackenzie found himself within easy reach of London, and yet in surroundings which enabled him to concentrate his mind upon the task of writing his book.

The following is an extract from a letter written to his son in Kimberley, April 7th 1886 :—

Sir John Gorst has felt moved to take up the South African question. He asked me to come and have a talk on the subject, and I did so. He is to *ask for a Committee.* He put down a few names of those who would be examined. Sir H. Robinson, Warren, myself, Baden-Powell, Ralph Williams (whom he knows), missionaries at home, etc.

I am to see Baden-Powell to-day.

Those were true words that Gladstone used of Forster. He was a noble man. I had quite the idea that he was getting rapidly better, till Saturday when I called. Mr Loring was out. The man-servant, who knew me, said Mr Forster was very unwell, and two doctors were there with him. That would be his seizure from which he never rallied again. So rests a brave and strong spirit after life's battle has been well fought. I shall write for a ticket for the service in Westminster Abbey.

The following extracts are from letters written at this time chiefly to his wife :

11 QUEEN SQUARE, LONDON,
8th April 1886.

This is the evening on which Mr Gladstone is to unfold his Irish Bill. Mr Forster lies cold in his house in Eccleston Square. The service in the Abbey will take place at 12 to-morrow. I have got a ticket from Mr Loring.

I had an interview with Mr Townsend of the *Spectator.* You know they took up the High Commissioner idea after having first objected to it. Had a long talk. Sent him copy of my paper in *Journal of Society of Arts.*

My great object is to avoid personalities, and to supplement the work for South Africa which I was permitted to do here some years ago. The time seems long, darling, for the work is a difficult one to write, and there are these other very important matters cropping up which need to be attended to.

11 QUEEN SQUARE, LONDON,
22nd April 1886.

I dined with Guy Dawnay and his brother, Col. Methuen, and Mr Wodehouse a few evenings ago. Mr Wodehouse is son of late Sir Philip, and takes great interest in Cape affairs. We had a pleasant evening. That is a circle into which Chesson's influence does not extend. Indeed they don't approve of him at all, and I have to stick up for him.

11 QUEEN SQUARE, LONDON,
27th May 1886.

If I succeed in attracting greater attention to the country and get the Protectorate established up to the Zambesi, and the Crown Colony placed on a healthier basis separate from the Colony in the meantime, and if no offer comes to me of work in connection with that, then I shall be more than content to resume my direct work in the Gospel of Christ. But to leave this matter as it is now is not my duty.

WOOLSTONE, SOUTHAMPTON,
23rd June 1886.

I have been here about a week. Mr Kirby is a retired sea captain, and in comfortable circumstances. He has a son in South Africa, in Swaziland. Another in America. His daughter, when a little girl, fell from an old Abbey wall near this place, and was killed on the spot ; and the mother was seized with a stroke of paralysis in consequence, from which she never recovered. He has just the two grown-up sons, and they are both abroad. I knew him a little before I went out last time. He is very kind, and I have greater facility for writing here undisturbed than in London. I don't want to go down to Scotland now if I can help it—till I have settled as to the publication of the book. The enclosed letter will show that I have made a beginning.

.   .   .   .

A friend of mine wrote to me—of course rather a sanguine one, and not Warren or Cullen—asking me if I would not go into Parliament, and saying that there was a way by which

the half of the expense would be paid. Mr Kirby at once
said if I would, he would pay the other half. But my head
is on my shoulders all right, dearie, and I have got to write
this book and see this African business set right, if it be
God's will. And as to money for myself and for those
depending on me—what He giveth I will gather. It is now
late. Good-night.

WOOLSTONE, SOUTHAMPTON,
July 1, 1886.

You don't imagine the work that is before me here. I
only see it in its fulness at times. It is a great work, and
one which will remain. It has no reference—no necessary
reference—to myself, or my own employment in after years.
That I leave in God's hands. I am Jesus Christ's man-
servant. He will not leave me without guidance.

LONDON, July 9, 1886.

That answer to Sir Hercules Robinson on the High
Commissionership comes to be a big thing, reaching to
eighteen pages of foolscap. I have written it three times,
and am just about to send it in. Warren and Baden-Powell
have seen it, and speak highly of it. So does Chesson, who
read it carefully over one afternoon. I may work it into an
article in the *Contemporary*, or perhaps reserve it for the
concluding part of the book.

In early autumn Mackenzie accepted appointment
for deputation work on behalf of the London Missionary Society, and was able also to spend some time
with his eldest daughter on a visit to his friend, Mr
Charles G. Oates of Meanwoodside, for the purpose of
attending the Leeds Festival of Music.

The following extracts from letters to his wife throw
some light upon his work during this period :

OAKLAND, Oct. 7, 1886.

The Bradford people asked me to go back and dine on
their market day at the Liberal Club, and meet a number of
people. I did so, and was considerably encouraged. Public
opinion is not where it was in 1883. The Radicals are now

determined to have a Colonial policy. Some of the old people remain on the old lines. I was planted alongside one of these at dinner, and he went to business at once by asking, Did I think the English Government should protect every Englishman who went beyond our borders, for his own profit? I told him I had acted out my views on that point by refusing to ask for assistance when shut up in Kuruman. But that was not the question. Was Africa to grow by peaceful and orderly means, or by filibustering? The alderman became much more reasonable and friendly, but conversions in cases such as his are hardly to be looked for.

11 QUEEN SQUARE, LONDON,
25th Nov. 1886.

Loring has asked me if I won't undertake to lecture for the Imperial Federation League (paid of course). I said in reply the " burden " on me was that of South Africa. My first work was the book. I hoped to see South African affairs on a better footing.

11 QUEEN SQUARE, LONDON,
2nd Dec. 1886.

When I have anything definite about publishing I shall let you know. Do not be anxious on that score. It is one of the things which have been rolled away from my path, as more than one friend has come forward to say they will bear the risk of publishing the book, in case its subject should be so far forgotten as to be regarded as riskful by the publishers. I am nearly done with the writing now. But the appearance of a long answer from Sir Hercules Robinson to my High Commissionership memo. compels further writing and attention to that part.

I am glad to have written so copiously. I hope to turn it to good account.

11 QUEEN SQUARE, LONDON,
23rd Dec. 1886.

I had no idea it would take so long, altho', of course, I did not really know. I think we may say, " All is well," at the end of the year. We have health ; the children are well and doing well. I do sincerely humble myself for the poor kind of life one lives when engrossed as I have been. I have been like a watch which needs winding, and then goes straight on. The night's rest, the meals, daily work, and *the book*—with some necessary attention to passing events, especially if they relate to South Africa.

I always think your time has been harder than mine. Here in London I do feel lonely. I tire of it very much, but there is nothing for it but to go on.

The new year was brought in, as usual, at Portobello, and the first half of 1887 was again almost completely devoted to the finishing of his book, on which he had been at work since his arrival in England from the Cape.

But Mackenzie found time to carry on correspondence with many people, and his education of the Colonial Office. Early in the year he sent to the Colonial Secretary, Sir Henry Holland (afterwards Lord Knutsford), a communication which led the latter to say that he was "not prepared to recommend the assumption by this country of the great amount of interference in and direct responsibility for the details of extra Colonial affairs in South Africa which your letters appear to advocate." This led Mackenzie to send in the following strongly worded protest :—

PORTOBELLO, SCOTLAND,
5th April 1887.

DEAR SIR HENRY,—I was sorry to receive your official reply to my letter, and after some days consideration I have thought it my duty to lay the following considerations before you privately.

I wish to state to you the opinion, which is based on considerable knowledge, that the position taken up in your letter will be condemned by the conscience and sense of duty of the English public, who engaged in the Bechuanaland Protectorate and insisted on supporting it by the Bechuanaland Expedition. In the estimation of the English public the "direct responsibility" from which you shrink, is already devolved on you by the extension of the Protectorate in 1885. You will allow me to say that I do not think you give full

weight to that very important action taken by the Liberal
Government, especially when coupled with the statement
made by Lord Derby to the effect that a Protectorate really
amounted to annexation (I am quoting this from memory,
but have no doubt of its correctness). These responsibilities
devolve upon you now, and I do not desire to impose on Her
Majesty's Government fresh obligations, but ask you to face
and to discharge those already incurred.

I hold firmly that it is of the very essence of an economical
administration in South Africa that there should be the early
assumption of authority and control of the land settlement in
native territories. Without this you must expend English
money in putting down abuses which my plan would enable
you to prevent.

The Imperial Government occupies a certain position in
South Africa, and has assumed certain responsibilities. I
have suggested a method by which these responsibilities
might be discharged in a way satisfactory to both Colonists
and natives, while it is economical as to Imperial expenditure,
and meets that conscientious sense of duty which the English
public has strongly expressed on the subject. Now the plans
which I propose may or may not be wise, but the shrinking
from responsibility has been the great cause of our trouble in
South Africa, of our low position in the eyes of Colonists,
and of our expenditures of Imperial money. England is
already responsible in such countries as those to which I
have referred, and the attitude of blinking this responsibility
I humbly but earnestly submit is unwise and expensive.

I was grieved to find the word "interference" used in your
letter with reference to proposed Imperial administration of
extra Colonial affairs. It is at least an unhappy expression
to term the performance of such a duty "interference," when
native Chiefs and people beg the Imperial Government as
the Supreme Power to assist them in the administration of
their country, and when loyal and intelligent Colonists
earnestly ask that this course be adopted. Please to remember that the alternative to this "interference," namely,
"letting alone," has landed us again and again in heavy
Imperial expenditure.

In my opinion our success in South Africa depends upon
the discharge, for some time, by the Imperial Government, of
those very duties in native territories which appear to you at
present to deserve the name of "interference." May I take

the liberty to ask you to reconsider the last sentence of your letter and thus avoid, in so many words, abjuring those very duties and responsibilities which the English public certainly desire Her Majesty's Government to perform in South Africa, and which were so fully acknowledged, upheld, and developed by Her Majesty's Liberal Government in 1885.

I make this communication in all friendliness and in strict confidence. The public verdict upon the question at issue will not be difficult to understand when it is given, and I hope in a few weeks to publish a work on the question of our policy in South Africa.

In April of this year (1887), he found himself within sight of the end, and went down to Montrose, the home of his eldest son, to complete his work there. He was thus removed from the distraction of daily correspondence, daily calls, summonses to meetings, and the other innumerable interruptions which interfered with his progress. At Montrose, he remained for nearly four months, and his son had for the first time an opportunity to watch him at close quarters. He was struck with his immense capacity for concentrated hard work. He often rose early, and was standing at his desk before breakfast; and he would work continuously until nine or ten o'clock at night, with intermissions only for meals and a regular walk in the late afternoon. He worked very systematically, gathering his material and arranging it with very great care. His son went over the entire book in manuscript page by page; nearly every paragraph was separately considered, and it was Mackenzie's request that the severest criticism should be applied, not only to the mere matter of expression, but to the spirit and substance of his narratives and arguments. These things he discussed with the utmost simplicity and earnestness, and showed deep anxiety to see the point of every criticism or suggestion before deciding upon it. He took immense pains to make his book a final authority on South African affairs so far as he dealt with them, and to secure accuracy at every point. As many of the chapters necessarily dealt with delicate personal affairs, he determined to make no statement for which he could not refer to an authority. He was thoroughly aware that in writing this kind of book he probably destroyed all chance of any future appointment under Government, but on that, with his characteristic shrug of the shoulders, he said, " I am not in this for that sort of thing, I am only anxious that the facts should be driven home to the English mind, in order that they may do the right thing in and for South Africa." The result of his prolonged labours appeared in the autumn of that year, 1887, under the title " Austral Africa, Losing it or Ruling it : Being Incidents and Experiences in Bechuanaland, Cape Colony, and England." It was a large work in two volumes, extending to more than a thousand pages in all, with a very complete map, many illustrations and photographs. In the preface he states the object that lay before his mind in this and all his labours.

" That object is, on the one hand, to deliver South Africa from the calamities, and England from the expense, heart-rending, and discords, hitherto attending the 'Hammer-and-Tongs Policy' and the equally disastrous policy of 'shirking' ; and on the other hand, to save the empire from having an ill-secured dominion or an ill-disposed because neglected population close to its most important naval station." The entire work is divided into six books. Book I. is entitled, " Illustrations of Native Life and European Expansion," and contains a large amount of information regarding Bechuana tribes, which is available nowhere else. He also describes at length the relation of the British Government to Bechuanaland between 1876 and 1883. Book II. is entitled " The Bechuanaland Protectorate—incidents and adventures among the Freebooters." This is an account in seven chapters of his

own Deputy Commissionership. In Book III., which
he calls "Backing Out," he takes eight chapters to
describe in full detail the history of the machinations
which tripped him up, and resulted in the confusion of
Bechuanaland and the triumph of the Transvaal.
With Book IV. he enters upon the second volume,
and in seven chapters describes "The Bechuanaland
Expedition under Sir Charles Warren." This only
carries the story to Mafeking. In Book V. he
completes the narrative of Sir Charles's work in
Bechuanaland, and unfolds the influences which led to
the premature recall of the Special Commissioner.
Book VI. consists of four chapters, on "The Imperial
Government in South Africa—the Past, the Present,
and the Future." This is a judicial and comprehensive survey of the relation of Great Britain to that
portion of the Empire. After stating the main
features of the past work of England in South Africa,
he goes on to explain the "unrecognised law" which
has ever governed the spread of Europeans in that
region ; he then discusses Cape politics in order to
show at once the natural range of the influence of
that Colony and the limits within which, for its own
sake and for the sake of all South Africa, this influence
should be restricted. He closes his work with a
chapter on "The Sum of the Whole Matter—Imperial
Duties and Imperial Methods." His last pages are
written with the deepest feeling, but in the simplest
and most direct fashion. He describes the future of
South Africa in the light of the policy which he has
advocated. "Like every true vision of the future," he
says, "mine ends in peace, and not in war."
"Assuredly, as England has abolished duelling, and
still retains her honour and her self-respect, so will the
savage arbitrament of war be discredited and disused
the world over, when the thoughts of the victorious
Galilean shall have become the code of the world.

Then the contests of men will consist in the noble emulations of literature, art, commerce, and industry ; in all of which Austral Africa will have its share.   I see these things with the eye of the soul ; they will surely come to pass.   I pray to be permitted to see some of them with the bodily eye also."

CHAPTER XVI

ENGLAND—THE REJECTION OF A PROPHET
(1888-1889)

At the dawn of the year 1888 Mackenzie saw and felt on all sides the influence of his book. Reviews were appearing all over the country week by week, and month by month. Freed from his heavy task, and helped by its results, Mackenzie was now able to undertake the agitation of his cause on a wider scale, and in a greater variety of ways, than had been possible hitherto. The supreme aim before him was, as we have seen, to secure the separation of the offices of High Commissioner for South Africa and Governor of the Cape Colony.

The following extracts from a letter to his wife show the manner in which he resumed the campaign early in the new year :—

11 Queen Square,
London, *14th Jany*. 1888.

As I said, I got here all right on Thursday morning, and found a letter from Mr H. O. Arnold Forster, and a card from Mr Loring, both asking to see me specially, and soon. There was also a note from L. M. S., asking me to give an address to their Young Men's Missionary Band, which meets in the Mission House every month. I corrected the proof, and consented to give this address.

On calling for Loring I found (as H. O. Arnold Forster's letter had told me) that they two were looking forward to meeting Lord Rosebery to-day, and having a talk with him about South Africa, and especially about the High Commissionership. I met Arnold Forster on Friday at his office at Cassels' Place. On both occasions I had a long talk with them, answering all imaginable difficulties, etc., as best I could. They have also got between them the pamphlet which Mr Kirby published, and that last long statement which the Colonial Office did not publish, and other things.

Tuesday evening.—The enclosed letter has been in my pocket for the last two days, waiting for time to put down result of Loring's and Arnold Forster's interview with Lord Rosebery. They were pleased with their visit on the whole, and have sent Lord R. my book, marking certain passages for him to read. He seems to have answered them very guardedly, perhaps sceptically, on some matters; but professed his entire ignorance of the question. The thing is, therefore, still in progress so far as he is concerned; that is all that can be said.

I am dining at Lady Walker's to-morrow, Wednesday. To-day when I came home from my wanderings I found a note from Lady Seafield, brought by her servant, inviting me to dine with them on Friday, and I'm going. Sir C. Warren is to be there, she told me. Really Lady S. is as friendly as friendly could be. I am thankful for it.

I have seen the Amatonga Deputation, but I shall not fill up this page with them. I reserve for it a very striking piece of news which my friend, Sir Charles Mills, the agent of the Cape Colony in England, told me. I let him talk for full half-an-hour or more on his own subjects, and then, on our feet now, I led him on to talk of the High Commissionership. He said first, "They'll never do it." I said, "No, not till they are told by the English people to do it, and then they'll do it sharp." I got him to talk about it, and at last he said, "I wish you all success, Mackenzie. A splendid thing if you can carry it. The Marquis of Lorne should be your first High Commissioner. I may tell you between ourselves that I asked him if he would not go out to South Africa, and he distinctly declined to go out as Governor of the Cape Colony, but said he would go as High Commissioner; and that the Princess would go too." Just think, dearie, what that amounts to in the education of public opinion. No one thought of such a position as the Marquis takes up, some time ago. I do think I may claim something in connection with that. I wrote one memorandum with the express purpose in my own mind of preventing the Marquis from going out as Governor of the Cape, without directly referring to it.

Sir C. Mills told me this with a feeling of disappointment at
his own want of success, but he then brightened up and said,
"If he goes out, and you get a good Governor for the Cape,
then the thing will be done."

Now say that he was saying pleasing things to me, what I
care for is the fact that he asked Lorne, and Lorne refused.
It is a great fact in the history of this movement.

On February 10th he delivered a lecture before the
Kensington Branch of the Imperial Federation League.
The President of the Branch, Sir Rawson Rawson, was
in the chair, and the meeting was very successful.
Mackenzie gave the following breezy description of
it to his wife :—

> 11 QUEEN SQUARE, LONDON,
> *Saturday.*

DEAREST,—The lecture has been delivered, and everybody except myself expressed great pleasure.

There was a good audience for London, especially as it was
a bitterly cold night. The kind of people was what you would
call "superior," you know. There were a good many quite
unknown to me. There were others whose faces I had seen
elsewhere ; and then there were not a few whom I reckon as
personal friends. But to be historical ! I went (dressed) to
the Hall at 5.30 by appointment, to see that everything was
right on the platform. I arranged a music stand for MS.,
and so on. Then went over to Loring's, where I had time
in his study to look over my notes. Dined at 7, Mr and
Mrs O'Brien being the other guests. Mrs O'Brien is one of
the late Mr Forster's (adopted) daughters. Like her sisters,
she is very sweet and nice. After dinner, to the Town Hall.
I spoke from the notes. I could see them fairly well, and
stood after a time with the pointer in my hand, to describe
the map. The lecture was too long, or rather the Chairman
took a longer time than one would have expected, when the
hour to begin with was 8.30. So I had to hasten over the
latter part of the lecture ; when I said I was doing so the
people applauded as if to say, "Go on," but I saw for myself
that the time was getting late.

Sir Rawson Rawson greeted me warmly on my getting on
the platform, and Sir Henry Barkly came forward and shook
hands quite as with an old friend.

I saw Dunn, Rider Haggard, Mrs Reed and young Guy Reed, the brother of Mr Betts, Mr James Buchan, Mr and Mrs Wm. Simpson and party, Colonel Tracy and Miss Tracy, Robertson, Steele (Port Elizabeth); Maynard (your friend), Prebendary Tucker, of Society for Propagation of the Gospel, &c., &c.

Rider Haggard spoke very well—certainly in a most appreciative and complimentary way of myself: I had "saved Bechuanaland and the Bechuanas, and if a man did only that he had done a great work." He started on this track by saying there was one thing which I had omitted, and which looked formidable for a moment. I spoke to him afterwards for a minute, only in whispers, however. I hope to see him by-and-by.

Wm. Dunn spoke, and did so tellingly, as a Cape merchant, as to the value of the policy which I was bringing forward. He referred also to an early acquaintance with me and my young bride so many years ago!

Mr Mackarness, who was once in South Africa, and who writes letters in the *Times* on that subject, spoke. Loring had told me that he was pro-Robinson in his views as to the High Commissioner, so I got Loring to write to him to say that I should be very glad if he came and stated his views without personalities, and left the public to decide. He said in a few words that he wanted to know who was to pay the High Commissioner, where he was to live, and what he was to do. But I really think he had been shaken by the lecture, because he hastened to congratulate me on the lecture as a whole, and on my other writings and efforts in behalf of South Africa, and that he had always much pleasure in reading my communications.

Sir Henry Barkly seconded the vote of thanks to me, which was proposed by the Chairman.

Sir Henry backed me up out and out. He said, in his opinion, my views were thoroughly sound, and such as ought to be adopted. If there had been time he could have illustrated by his own personal experience. As to myself personally, I had had no chance of putting my views into practice, and he hoped that in that extension of our Protectorate which must take place, my services would be brought into requisition. This was meant in great kindness, but I had rather he had not said it.

In replying, I thanked them for their indulgence for such

a length of time.　I said, with, I suppose, a grin on my face, that by far the nicest part of the lecture was that which they had not heard !

Loring was delighted, and so was Mrs L.　She did not know when she had enjoyed a lecture so much.　Mrs O'Brien sent a message by her to say she thanked me for Mrs Forster, for some true things I said about her husband at the outset.

Mr Dunn came up and asked where you were, that he might shake hands with you.　He was disappointed when I told him.

Now if this is not a full and particular account I don't know, and, if I am not a sublimely good person for retailing it all, I wonder who can put in a claim to be good or obedient to orders.

Early in April it was given out that the Government had decided not to establish a High Commissionership, such as Mackenzie and the South African Committee had been attempting to secure ; but this decision, or the attempt to reach it, seems to have been shaken considerably by an important review of " Austral Africa," which appeared in the *Times*, and a very powerful leading article in the same paper, entitled, " Africa after the Scramble." In both of these the *Times* spoke very strongly in favour of Mackenzie's policy.　But at the same time Mackenzie was made aware that the opposition from Cape Town was becoming very bitter.　It threatened to assume the form of a personal controversy when Captain Bower dipped his fingers into it.　This Imperial Secretary of South Africa had written to a well-known English Member of Parliament, assuring him that the separation of the offices would destroy the country, and begging him not to be misled by an enthusiast.　His further characterisation of the enthusiast was such as led Mackenzie to assert that it was " meant to undermine me, and to destroy me."

In the spring of this year Mackenzie first entered

into direct correspondence with Lord Rosebery, and
for a time it seemed as if this leader of Imperial
plans would be induced to master the South African
problem, and become the promoter of Imperialism
there. As the following letters will show, however,
the wide-awake, but cautious Earl, in spite of his
interest in the question, could not be induced to
give it more than casual attention :—

7 WOBURN PLACE,
LONDON, 1st *March* 1888.

I have just come from a long interview with Lord Rosebery
by invitation. Loring went with me, and was present. He,
Loring, was well satisfied with the interview. Lord R. professed
his ignorance, but I found he had got some working knowledge of the subject. We went at it up and down, over
and across, for, I suppose, more than an hour. He spoke
very sensibly, and his objections and questions were such
as one had pleasure in answering. I seemed to satisfy
him on each point, but perhaps that would be too sanguine
a view.

I have been asked to address the Chamber of Commerce
of London. I mentioned this, and he said he thought I
should. Would he attend the meeting, and speak or preside? "Well, no, he had to take his wife to the Continent
soon. He might *attend* it." Loring says this is near enough
in the meantime, and that possibly he will come and speak
when formally asked. So I am going to write to our friend
Dunn, and ask him to introduce me to Mr Tritton, the
present chairman of the Chamber, and have a consultation as
to what should be done.

In the meantime keep a lookout for questions in the
House of Lords as to the High Commissionership. I
expect Lord R. will put one soon. He has already put
one as to the Delagoa Bay railway, which had an important
sentence in it.

Then the Imperial Federation League's political committee at its meeting yesterday has recommended the League
to take up this Austral African question as League business.
This is a most important decision, but it will not be ratified
till a meeting of the General Executive Committee takes
place. It is likely to be carried.

Last night I lectured to a Christian Young Men's Club at Bloomsbury. Had the large map.

7 WOBURN PLACE,
LONDON, 14*th March* 1888.

I have received such a strong, ably written letter, from the editor of the *Grahamstown Journal* this week. It was shown to Lord Rosebery, who read it with great interest. His question as to the duplex offices was in writing, and handed in. Lord Kimberley came to him, and "wired in" on the other side, retaining matters as they are. Lord R. withdrew his question, Kimberley and he being front bench men together on the same side. Lord R. retains his opinion. I wrote him last night, and wait the result. This is strictly private.

A definite attempt was made to secure Lord Rosebery as chairman at the approaching meeting, which led to the following letter from him :—

LANSDOWNE HOUSE, BERKELEY SQUARE,
LONDON, 15*th March* 1888.

DEAR MR MACKENZIE,—Many thanks for your letter, and for the former one which I ought to have acknowledged. Both of them interested me extremely. I incline to think that a question with regard to the Cape would be best asked in the House of Commons.

With regard to the dates you mention, I am afraid none of them would suit me, as I propose going abroad at the end of next week, so that I shall have to read and not listen to your address.—Believe me, yours very truly,

ROSEBERY.

P.S.—I was much interested in the letter Loring showed me, and am grateful to you for allowing me to see it.

One of the most important of all Mackenzie's addresses was that which he delivered on May 14th, 1888, before the London Chamber of Commerce. Mr Chamberlain occupied the chair, and the meeting was both large and very influential. In his opening speech Mr Chamberlain, with his marvellous gift of exposition, set forth the central problem of South African policy. He showed the extreme danger, alike to the Empire and to South Africa, which would result from the policy of neglect.

Now what is the alternative? There is only one alternative, and that is, that we should accept our obligations and responsibilities. We should maintain firmly and resolutely our hold over the territories that we have already acquired, and we should offer freely our Protectorate to those friendly chiefs and people that are stretching out their hands towards us and seeking our protection and our interference.

He shrunk from committing himself regarding the separation of the two great offices ; that, he said,

is a matter which must be left to the responsible officers of the Queen, who have much better opportunities of knowledge than any that I can possess ; but one thing I do say, that if we are once for all to recognize our obligations in regard to this great Continent, we must do so in pursuance of an Imperial policy, and not of a Colonial policy, if in any respect that differs from ours.

The title of Mackenzie's address was "Austral Africa, Extension of British Influence in Trans-Colonial Territories."

He devoted, as usual, the first part of his lecture to a description of the South African Colonies and States.

The second part of the lecture described "Trans-Colonial Native Territories." In the paragraph which dealt with railway communication, he strongly advocated the immediate consideration, both for commercial and political reasons, of " a dominating north-going railway through the Colony of Bechuanaland, so that the trade of the richest country in Austral Africa—a veritable Ophir of the olden time, with its gold and its iron, its cotton and its rice—may be secured for English commerce, and for our fellow subjects in South Africa."

The third portion of the lecture was entitled, " Place and Work of the Imperial Government." After describing some of the influences which had interfered with the development of direct Imperial administration since 1884, he came to make his two great definite proposals, viz., first, "that the Imperial administration should be extended to all Khame's territory, as proposed by Khame himself to Sir Charles Warren, and secondly, the appointment of an Imperial High Commissioner who should be unencumbered with any local office. This, he maintained, would not involve any "interference with the present rights and privileges of the Colonists," nor would it take the form of an "abrupt resolution," but rather of a "necessary growth." The lecturer further discussed the reasons for making this change at that time, and some of the objections which were urged against it.

Mackenzie's address was followed by a public discussion, the first speaker being Sir Charles Warren, who rose to move a vote of thanks to the reader of the paper. He was followed by Sir George Baden-Powell. A discordant note was introduced into the discussion by Sir Henry de Villiers of Cape Colony, whose speech, however, practically admitted the need for the very changes which Mackenzie advocated. This was at once cleverly pointed out by Mr Arnold Forster. Mackenzie's warm friend, Mr Walter Searle, President of the Cape Town Chamber of Commerce, very earnestly advocated the position taken by the lecturer.

The following letter was written by Sir Henry Barkly, formerly High Commissioner for South Africa, and Governor of Cape Colony, who was unable to attend the meeting :—

SOUTH KENSINGTON,
12th May 1888.

DEAR MR MACKENZIE,—I am very sorry not to be able to attend on Monday, and hear your address on "The Extension of British Influence in Trans-Colonial Territories."

Had I done so, and been called on to take part in the subsequent description, I should have urged, as I did at Kensington Town Hall, that it was better, whenever any fresh annexation of native territory took place, that it should be in the first instance under the sole control of an authority directly responsible to the Secretary of State for the Colonies; and, further, that, believing your views as to the arrangements which ought to be made in regard to the introduction of European settlers into such territories, to be the result of much experience and reflection, I was still in hopes that you would some day be afforded a fair opportunity of carrying them into practice, in the course of those extensions of British rule towards the Zambesi, which appear inevitable.—Believe me, Yours very truly,

HENRY BARKLY.

In July news came by cablegram, announcing that a meeting of Government officials had been held at Mafeking, to discuss the project of a Bechuanaland railway. Mackenzie in referring to this, says :—

The movement must be favoured by Sir Hercules Robinson, which is surely good. I fear, however, that he, or rather Bower, has some trick behind, in regard to handing the territory over to the Colony, in connection with this very railway making.

GLASGOW, *Aug. 30th* 1888.

I have been unusually busy, indeed chained to my desk, since I came down. I have just been once to the Exhibition, and have not found time to look up a single Glasgow merchant as yet. My paper for the British Association is ready, but the amount of correspondence just now caused by the tactics adopted at the Cape is very great and very imperative.

You would see the result of the publication of my memo. on the High Commissionership. *Another* despatch from Sir H. Robinson, and a minute from his Ministers' Resolutions, and from the Cape Parliament, deprecating the change which I propose, and which the British public desire.

I enclose the tactical reply to this clever move at the Cape —" a put-up job," as the *Cape Times* calls it. I hope to get this really extensively signed by both parties, and outside Parliament also. If Bechuanaland is made a Crown Colony *really and in good faith*, we shall see the Cape speedily lose all liking for the High Commissionership. What they mean is land ; that must be kept for Imperial needs and Imperial management. When they are assured of this at the Cape the victory will be complete.

11 QUEEN SQUARE,
1st Nov. 1888.

Rhodes and the *Argus* have had a fling at me.—Rhodes in an electioneering speech, and the *Argus* backing him up. Nothing of the slightest importance, and the *Argus* says I am going on slandering the Colony over here. I may send out a few lines, just to tone the matter a little. Not sure yet.

Had a pleasant Sunday at Warlies, Sir Fowell going to collect names for memo. Offers his house for a drawing-room meeting, should that be necessary.

11 QUEEN SQUARE,
4th Nov. 1888.

I have just come from Dr Parker's, where I stayed for communion, which I always enjoy. It is always a time when one can lay one's case before the good Lord as it stands between this time and next communion season. Thank God, there is always something done, something achieved. May He help for the next month.

11 QUEEN SQUARE,
LONDON, *14th Nov.* 1888.

I have been to a meeting of the African Section of the Chamber of Commerce. They have passed a resolution unanimously against annexation of Bechuanaland to the Cape, but it is not valid formally till it has been sanctioned by the General Executive of the Chamber. Then a Deputation will go to Government on the matter. This is so much work done.

In September Mackenzie read a paper before the Geographical Section of the British Association, which held its meeting that year at Bath. He was very well received, as the following extract from a letter to one of his sons will show :—

BATH, *11th Sept.* 1888.

Get a look at the *Times* for Tuesday 11th, and you will see that I have had a very good reception here. The large

Guild Hall was filled, and they were really very kind. It is to appear in abstract in the Royal Geographical Society's paper. Mr Bates, the Secretary, whom I know, was very well pleased with it. Its publication was recommended in a short speech by good and kind Sir Robert Fowler, and also referred to by the Chairman of the Section, Sir C. Wilson. Judge of my great pleasure, in turning away from the recently uncovered Roman Baths yesterday afternoon, to meet dear Mr Neild, who is here, and his family. He simply carried me off bodily, and I spent the afternoon with them, part of it being at a Friend's house in a garden-party. The Friends are delightful people. I admire them very much, and love them.

On November 29th he delivered a lecture at Newcastle, and spent Christmas time at Portobello with his family.

If 1888 was a busy year, 1889 was a year which almost crushed his life. At its beginning he saw the interest of the British public in South African affairs steadily increasing. Wide circles had now been taught, and were inspired with his views, and these circles comprised the most intelligent elements in the community, those who were directly interested in Parliamentary affairs, those whose minds were fast awakening to the splendour of Britain's Imperial relationships and destiny, and those who looked upon South Africa as a field for future commercial enterprise.

Mackenzie felt that his plea for recognising Austral Africa as a great dominion had taken hold of the public imagination. He knew that his arguments from logic and history in favour of an Imperial High Commissionership for all South Africa were unanswerable, and he found men of experience always in his favour. Strong supporters of the Government were on his side. The Chambers of Commerce of the leading cities were on his side. The great majority of the newspapers were on his side. It really looked as if the British Dominion was about to be established in that year of grace, 1889, from Cape Town to the

Zambesi, without noise or war or expenditure of much money, by the final adoption of a great purpose, and the final establishment of a definite policy. If at that time he had seen the announcement that the Government would send out a new High Commissioner for all South Africa and also separate Governors for the Cape Colony and Natal, an Administrator for the Crown Colony of Bechuanaland, and another British representative to guide the development of Matabeleland, this ardent servant of God and his country would have felt that he had accomplished what during these years he had lived for, and that it had been worth while to live for its accomplishment. But "the Assyrian came down," and made havoc of all his hopes.

News reached England that Mr Rudd had visited the capital of Matabeleland, and obtained from the Chief the most remarkable concession known in South African history. Curious stories were afloat regarding the help which he received from important government officials in his efforts to secure the consent of Lobengula to his proposals. In South Africa itself there was an outcry among those newspapers which were yet free to cry out against such events. They argued that as Matabeleland had been declared to be within the sphere of British influence, and as a British representative had already visited it and entered into negotiations with its Chief, this concession, which gave the entire minerals of a vast and rich territory to one man, or a group of men, was a monopoly such as Britain ought to destroy. But protests were too late, and the results of this concession speedily became known.

Feeling that the plot had begun to thicken, Mackenzie made various powerful efforts to persuade the Home Government to take definite action before new influences could be brought to bear upon it. On

February 15th he sent a long letter to Lord Salisbury, making certain proposals regarding South Africa, which seemed to him to concern the Foreign Office as much as the Colonial Office. In this letter he began by describing the critical position of Great Britain in that region. The following significant sentences, the words of a true prophet, occur :—

In South Africa at the present time, the question which is being decided by the persistent efforts of our opponents, and by our own action (and often by our want of action) is— Whether or not South Africa shall be English-speaking and owning the sway of England, or be a Dutch-speaking country, owning virtually the sway of a rival European Power? There are, it is true, a few Dutch-speaking Republicans in South Africa, who bring themselves persistently before the public; but however sincere they may be in their desire to establish a South African Independent Dutch-speaking Republic from the Zambesi to the Cape, the real alternatives are, whether the country shall remain under the influence of England, or come under that of another European Power.

Now, Her Majesty's Government can assist materially in this vital matter at the present time, and that without interfering in any degree with the internal affairs of any Colony or of any self-governing republic.

The first of his numbered paragraphs dealt with the need for developing South Central Africa north of the Cape Colony under a Lieutenant-Governor, " who shall be in direct communication with Her Majesty's Government." He pointed out that Sir Gordon Sprigg had admitted " that this great region could not be successfully governed from Cape Town."

In the second place, this would entail the formation of a more rational plan for the treatment of Bechuanaland than had yet been applied to other regions occupied by native tribes.

And in all this there is no partiality towards the native, only simple justice. The Bechuana chiefs and people, in 1885, expressed their welcome to the Imperial Power, and agreed to hand over the whole unoccupied portions of their country to the Queen. They are prepared, therefore, for the occupation of their country in certain districts by white settlers, only that our recent shilly-shallying on this subject, and our present endeavours to prevent any such settlement have excited suspicion and uneasiness in their minds. They can have no doubt of the coming north of the white men. Our refusal to control their orderly settlement is justly calculated to excite their uneasiness, as they know that the only alternative is brigandage and bloodshed. It is distinctly to this abstention that we owe the Grobelaar incident, which has not yet been settled.

His third paragraph insisted that Great Britain must hold on to Bechuanaland for grave political reasons :—

The Anti-Imperial party at the Cape have been very diligent of late, and they have had the advantage of receiving assistance from unexpected quarters. But, after all, the strength of our position is that we do not interfere with internal Colonial affairs at all, we only *hold on* to those regions where the native inhabitants in the first instance laid us under obligations to them, and where our presence is of great consequence to British commerce and British influence in South Africa.

The refusal of Cape Colony to assist in the building of a railway through Bechuanaland was one of these reasons.

The Colonial railway stopped short for years, scores of miles south of Kimberley. Why? Because Kimberley was and is an English town. It was a commercial sacrifice, but a political pleasure, to keep it out in the desert, and the railway was carried through only in 1884 by the Colonial Government, at the earnest suggestion of the Imperial Government. Since that time Kimberley has supplied a market to the Colonial farmers all along the line, and doubtless they see that they lost severely by not having had the railway at an earlier date. At the same time, Mr Hofmeyr and other Anti-Imperial leaders are dead against railway extension to the British Colony of Bechuanaland, as they were to the British district of the Diamond-fields.

The fourth paragraph suggested a plan by which two results could be obtained. In the first place, Cape Colony would be stimulated to develop its railway system northwards, and, besides, Great Britain would acquire a shorter route into the interior of South Africa. This double result could be obtained if Lord Salisbury would negotiate with Germany for British control of the region lying between Walvisch Bay and South Bechuanaland.

Walvisch Bay is one of the best harbours on all the South African coast. A waggon road, accompanied by well-sinking, from Walvisch Bay to Bechuanaland—followed in the course of time by a railway—would not be difficult of accomplishment, and would be of immense importance to Great Britain, politically and commercially. It would be a set-off to Delagoa Bay in Portuguese hands. The bare possibility of opening such communications would bring the Cape Colony to common sense as to its railway from Kimberley to Bechuanaland. The sharp alternative to their not making this connecting railway to the Bechuanaland border would be the loss to them of the northern trade. I have shown that opposition to Britain can carry some of their leaders a long distance in foolishness and disregard of the material interests of the Cape Colony, but the leverage of a threatened Walvisch Bay route of colonization and commerce into Bechuanaland would cause the Cape Colony railway from Kimberley to the southern border of Bechuanaland to be constructed without delay.

Taking this last mentioned advantage alone, it would warrant Her Majesty's Government doing its utmost to obtain again South West Africa, and so repair an unaccountable and inexcusable blunder of the Imperial Government some years ago.

To his wife he writes as follows :—

LONDON, *Feb.* 22, 1889.

We have had a very important meeting of the South African Committee to-day, Mr Chamberlain in the Chair, Lord Polwarth, Sir C. Warren, and a considerable number of M.P.s were present. Resolved, that a certain number be deputed to meet Lord Knutsford privately and have it out with him, and see what they could get out of him. Were to report to another meeting, and if that is held not to be enough, to fight him. I had a good deal of speaking to-day, as Chamberlain brought it to real, hard, practical work at once, and Sir Fowell Buxton coolly turned to me and asked me what I would say to that. We had a long discussion, and a very interesting one. There was never such a body of influence in favour of my views as at present. The Committee is really an influential one, and we may have some "events" soon.

11 QUEEN SQUARE,
4th March 1889.

The South African Committee had a meeting on Saturday, Mr Chamberlain in the Chair. They reported what had taken place in their interview with Lord Knutsford. I had heard the particulars before from Mr Loring. Considerable progress has been made, but it needs great firmness on our part to prevent the Colonial Office swinging us all around —Chamberlain and all. I was asked to say what I thought of what had been done, and in order to give all present a right conception of the danger I said, looking at Mr Chamberlain, "I am thankful for what has been accomplished, but I really see that, so far, Lord Knutsford has had the best of it." I then proceeded to back this up by showing where he had led them off on side issues. I am to see Mr C. on Wednesday forenoon.

Throughout the spring months of this year the controversy raged fierce in the public press and in political circles regarding the proposed South African Chartered Company. The concession obtained by Mr Rudd in the end of the preceding year had been made the basis for the gigantic scheme of Mr Cecil Rhodes. In this struggle Mackenzie, of course, had a prominent part; and yet he was conscious all the while of fighting a losing battle, for Mr Rhodes made converts from among his own best supporters. They were not in the least conscious of departing from the principles for which they had already worked with him; rather it seemed to many of the best of them that this scheme would go far to realise his own dreams. For how could the proposed opening up of the unoccupied territories of Mashonaland and Matabeleland by means of the enormous capital which it was proposed to employ, do aught but good in establishing Imperial authority in South Africa? Hard-headed, practical Englishmen, to whom the vastness of the commercial proposals appealed, seemed to consider Mackenzie's objections merely academic, and his fears groundless. In brief, as Mackenzie afterwards pointed out, his own years of hard labour in educating the British public regarding South Africa had prepared the way for the Chartered Company.

Mackenzie feared for Bechuanaland, but Mr Rhodes assured Mr Albert Grey that he did not propose to take any part of Bechuanaland. And Mr Causton appeared before a certain philanthropic committee in London to assure them "that the new Company had been formed mainly in the interest of the natives and of missionaries, to prevent unprincipled white men from going in and ruining every one!"

The following remarks of Mr Alfred Milner, now Lord Milner, put the case very clearly from another point of view :—

Whatever may be the personal sentiments of its managers, the force of circumstances will make the Company British. He must be a pessimist indeed who does not see that slowly but surely, and all the more surely because not with such fuss and conspicuousness as to alarm foreign nations, British influence is once more on the ascendant on the East Coast of Africa ; and the stronger we become north of the Zambesi the more essential we are to those who are pushing up to that river from the South. The Cape might be separatist, and South Africa by itself might be separatist, but a South Africa reaching up to the Zambesi, marching into foreign spheres of influence, and needing the protecting arm of Great Britain against Portuguese or German interference with its own development, will lean more and more on us. I think I see the development in Rhodes himself. As a purely

Cape politician he was (is perhaps) Africander. As the author of enterprises which look far beyond the Cape and the Transvaal and reach to the Zambesi, and beyond the Zambesi, he must know (he is much too shrewd not to know) that, without Imperial backing, he is lost.

All that could be said in favour of this policy, Mackenzie felt very deeply; but his opposition was determined upon a knowledge of South African politics, whose real significance it was hard to communicate even to the ablest minds in London. He saw that this movement had arisen amongst men whose statesmanship had already worked confusion in South Africa. Further, they were in sympathy rather with the Dutch than the British spirit in their treatment of native questions. He saw also with great clearness, in spite of the protestations of Mr Rhodes and the confidence of those whom he persuaded— what subsequent events proved to be only too true— that the granting of this Charter would inevitably lead to the absorption of Bechuanaland by Cape Colony and the proposed Company. To Mackenzie's mind, as we have seen from his letters, Bechuanaland was the key to the Imperial position in South Africa. If Great Britain would seize that region, and under direct Imperial control make of it a great Crown Colony, the British position in South Africa would be placed beyond all danger, either from a military or a political point of view.

And last, but not least, Mackenzie held the profound conviction that the future of South Africa would be one thing, if its great native populations were placed under Imperial administration, and another thing if they were left to be controlled solely by the class of Europeans who held sway at that time in her States and Colonies. If the British South Africa Company succeeded in shaping South African politics so that direct Imperial authority over these native regions should be destroyed, the future which he saw was dismal and dark indeed.

As early as July, Mr Albert Grey, now Lord Grey, wrote to Mackenzie to say that after considerable hesitation he had agreed to accept a post on the directorate of the new Chartered Company.

" I should have preferred, with you," he said, " a bolder Imperial policy, but as this is evidently beyond the thoughts and intentions of the present government, and as they have made up their minds to grant Rhodes a charter, it is, I think, desirable that one like myself who is in close sympathy with you and the South African Committee, should be upon the Board. I am very hopeful that the action of this Company may prove instrumental in developing and stimulating in a very great degree Imperial interests in South Africa."

Late in the session of the House of Commons, and at the end of a long sitting, with a minimum of discussion, the momentous step was taken of passing a bill which granted a royal charter to the British South Africa Company. This act empowered the Company to negotiate for and accept from native chiefs in Matabeleland and Mashonaland the right to exercise jurisdiction in those territories.

During the summer of this year (1889) the Government had also sent out a new High Commissioner and Governor of Cape Colony in the person of Sir Henry Loch. Sir Henry Loch was a man of strong character and great experience, as well as firm integrity. One of the shrewdest of South African newspaper editors said of him, that his character was so high that he would probably find it necessary to resign his position before the completion of his term of office ; and this prophecy was fulfilled. But he went out before the charter was given to the British South Africa Company, and began his work at Cape Town before the complications arose which that charter created even there.

After the autumn holidays Mackenzie undertook to write an article on South African affairs, at the request of the editor of *The Contemporary Review*. This article appeared in the November number of that periodical, and extended to twenty-four pages. While it reviewed past history and political events, the most important portion was contained in the last ten pages, where he discussed the granting of the charter to the British South Africa Company ; and this not in any carping spirit, but by way of accounting for the fact that the charter had been given at a time when every one believed chartered companies to be an obsolete method of Imperial administration, and by way of warning the British public that it would be a gross injustice to extend the authority of this Company to Bechuanaland. He also discussed the necessity for the construction of a railway through Bechuanaland. The last section of the article is entitled " Imperial administration prior to local self-government," in which the case for the South African High Commissionership of a true kind was stated with exceptional clearness and vivacity.

During the autumn Mackenzie also undertook a series of deputation services and addresses on behalf of the London Missionary Society. He arranged to give a public address in November at Manchester, upon the "Native Races and Liquor Traffic Commission," and at Liverpool before the Chamber of Commerce. But ere these engagements could be fulfilled, he was stricken suddenly at Berwick-on-Tweed. This occurred on Sunday morning, November 24th, as he was concluding a public service in church. It was towards the end of his sermon that, as he afterwards described it, he suddenly felt as if a thousand needles were being driven rapidly into the back of his neck. The pain was excruciating, but with marvellous self-mastery he brought the sermon quietly to an end, offered prayer, gave out a hymn, and pronounced the benediction. When he reached the vestry he collapsed. The physician who attended him immediately said that the effort he made after the stroke, had worked more mischief than all the preceding anxieties and labours which had brought it on.

Mackenzie had been literally giving his life without grudging and without stint for the good of South Africa. Naturally a man of strong constitution, who had hardly known a day's illness for thirty years, he had brought this upon himself simply by carrying upon his heart the burdens of the races, both black and white, whose struggles he had watched and over whose future he had agonised.

His engagements were all immediately cancelled, and he went down to Portobello, where absolute rest was prescribed for several months. But it was easier for him to rest by doing something. It was a relief to him to be able to write an occasional article for the *Leeds Mercury* or *The Scotsman*; and this he did. As helping to understand the amount of labour which he performed this year, it ought to be recorded that Mackenzie had undertaken the proof reading for a reprint of the Sechuana Bible; and that he had expended much energy and anxious thought over an elaborate correspondence with the Government regarding the rights of the London Missionary Society to the ownership of the fountain at Kuruman in Bechuanaland. This ownership was being contested largely out of hatred of the Society and of some of its promoters; and the victory was won by the Society, which had done so much for South Africa, not without very great exertions and some bitter experiences.

It may also be recorded that several of Mackenzie's South African correspondents called his attention at this time (1889) to the extraordinary manner in which President Kruger had begun to supply the burghers of the Transvaal with guns and ammunition. Men who knew the facts told him of the resolution of the Transvaal Government to see that this distribution of the best weapons was quietly but effectively carried out, and the way in which it was done.

During this year, then, the British Government made its momentous choice, from which many of its subsequent relations to the South African States and Colonies may be traced as with relentless logic down to the year 1899. It decided many things when it resolved to grant a charter to the British South Africa Company, and refused to separate the office of High Commissioner for South Africa from that of Governor of the Cape Colony. To secure this separation and prevent that grant, Mackenzie had in vain employed all the resources of argument and agitation, almost to the breaking of his heart. His prophecy was rejected ; and Great Britain gave South African history over to be directed for well-nigh ten years, by those personalities who received from her hands that charter and those undivided offices. What they made of it we now know. But that prophet described its gloom to an unbelieving people in 1889.

CHAPTER XVII

ENGLAND—THE SAVING OF BECHUANALAND
(1890-1891)

WHEN Mackenzie returned to active work in February 1890, his plan of campaign, along with the ever faithful members of the South African Committee, was to make sure now of the union of North and South Bechuanaland under Imperial administration as a Crown Colony. Much work was also given to prevent the cession of Swaziland to the Transvaal, on conditions which President Kruger was most sedulously urging. It is unnecessary to enter into detail upon the latter question and to describe the kind of pressure which was brought to bear upon the Government to meet President Kruger's wishes.

On February 19th, Mackenzie lectured before the Liverpool Chamber of Commerce, and addressed the Constitutional Club in London in the month of May. In that month also he was invited to take part in a deputation to the King of Belgium, who was on a visit to London. The following extract from a letter of the Rev. J. Grant Mills, Secretary of the Association which sent this deputation to the Belgium King, is of biographical interest. Mr Grant Mills had been negotiating with Count d'Outremont :—

I saw the Count, to whom I repeated the contents of your letter. He then went on to the King and returned with a message, and said that the King would be pleased to receive myself and two others, one of whom was to be yourself, from the Congregational Union. The King specially mentioned you. Count d'Outremont said that the King was specially

anxious to meet experts who knew Africa, and that therefore
His Majesty had expressed a desire that you should come.

Throughout the summer his work continued with
great activity, although there is not much that need
be recorded, since it so much resembles what we have
already described.

On July 15th he writes to one of his sons :—

I am not without some encouragement in my work. You
would see, an order in Council has been published giving
certain powers in North Bechuanaland to the Governor of
Bechuanaland, Sir H. B. Loch, under the foreign Jurisdiction Acts. It was under these Acts that I began operations in 1884. They were found to be quite unsuitable and
inadequate. And yet they will again take up with them
rather than do things in a business way. But it shows they
have seen the necessity of some movement. And the next
thing will be, or ought to be, the establishment of thé
Queen's sovereignty and administration. Then my present
work will be over   May God graciously hasten this.

After the holidays he had various public engagements, amongst which was the delivery of a lecture
before the South Place Ethical Society, one Sunday
morning, on "Systems of Tribal Policy in South
Africa."

About this time Mackenzie performed an act whose
moral value can hardly be ignored. He had seen
announced in the public press a route by which the
pioneer forces of the British South Africa Company
intended to enter Mashonaland. The route chosen
by them was apparently the easiest and most direct,
but it had been marked out by men who, knowing in
general the geography of those regions, must have
known little or nothing of their political situation.
Mackenzie was absolutely convinced that if the
pioneers travelled on that road they would be
massacred by the Matabele. The Company would
be, if not crushed, at least dishonoured at the very
beginning of its history. As he said afterwards, he

could not "bear to think of all those fine young
Englishmen being speared some night" by the
terrible Matabele, whom he knew so well.   Mackenzie
at once saw his duty, and without hesitation did it.
He sat down and wrote to Lord Knutsford, and also
to Lord Salisbury, giving in detail the facts which
convinced him of the extreme danger which would be
incurred by the British South Africa Company if they
journeyed on the route announced in the papers ; and
more than that, he carefully marked out the direction
in which it would be safe for the pioneers to proceed
from Bechuanaland into Mashonaland, naming the
places at which water could be obtained, and the
reasons why Matabele prejudices would not be
insulted, nor their fears be excited if this route
were adopted.   With immense satisfaction he saw
shortly afterwards an announcement in the papers,
that the leaders of the expedition had seen reason
to change their plans, and had resolved upon a new
road into their territory, this being the one which
Mackenzie had marked out for them.

The following letter to the Secretary of the
Company will further illustrate Mackenzie's spirit,
and the attitude which he assumed towards the
Company when once it had been established and
formed part of the life of South Africa.   The letter
makes reference to a further memorandum which he
had recently sent to Lord Salisbury regarding
Walvisch Bay and its importance to Great Britain :—

11 QUEEN SQUARE,
LONDON, 30th Jan. 1891.

The Secretary of the British South Africa Company.

DEAR SIR,—I enclose, for the information of your
Board of Directors, a copy of a memorandum which I recently
sent to Her Majesty's Secretary of State for Foreign Affairs.
I daresay it is within your knowledge that before your

Company obtained its charter I advocated instead Imperial control.

Since the granting of the charter, however, I have conceived it to be my duty to accept the decision of Her Majesty's Government thus practically come to, and to render any assistance in my power to the peaceful opening up of the country by the Company, as, for instance, by suggesting the best route for the Company's pioneers to take in order to enter Mashonaland without fighting.

The enclosed memorandum has reference to the next important question in the development of Mashonaland and neighbouring countries—the question of the best route to England.

Physical geography really answers the question. The Cape Colony railway and the other north-going South African railways will play an important and indispensable part in the development of South Africa, but the route forced on the attention of the pioneers in Mashonaland is one which will minimise the expense and time of transit. The first answer to that is, the route *via* Pungwe River, but the final and permanent answer is a railway across Africa from Walvisch Bay to Pungwe River or Zambesi River. *Via* Walvisch Bay your traveller would have some 2000 miles less to travel than by any other route.—I remain, ever yours sincerely,

JOHN MACKENZIE.

Mr Albert Grey wrote to Mackenzie concerning this letter, and the memorandum to which it referred, as follows :—

The Duke of Fife has been greatly interested by your private letter to me, as well as by your admirable memorandum, which has been copied out and forwarded to every member of our Board. . . . I much look forward to having a talk with you about the various problems for Imperial administration in South Africa, which you have so nearly at heart, and which possess my fullest sympathy.

On February 2nd Mackenzie sent another letter to Lord Knutsford, calling his attention to the memorandum concerning Walvisch Bay, and then dealing very carefully with the problem of Bechuanaland. This he now felt to be the final piece of

work which he had to accomplish—the securing of
an Imperial administration for North Bechuanaland. The heart of his proposal, and his deep
earnestness about it, are revealed in the concluding
paragraphs of his letter :—

11 QUEEN SQUARE,
2nd Feb. 1890.

Everything points to a consolidation of British administration in Bechuanaland for some time to come, and not to the
giving up of our position there.

The expense of this course will not be increased by including North Bechuanaland under British sovereignty, because I
would contemplate obtaining from the Chiefs a cession of
lands unoccupied and unneeded by them, which would be a
source of revenue, and in the course of time, notwithstanding
past failure, I should hope to secure from them direct assistance by some form of tax. Their confidence, which has been
impaired, would, of course, need to be regained, and this
would take time. But there is only one other course, sooner
or later, that of the Hollander Editor of the *Zuid Afrikaan*
newspaper, which he would wish to pass off as the view of the
Colony—to fight them and break them up, and make them
for ever our enemies in their hearts.

Forgive a too long letter. I am sure you will not misunder-
stand it. The responsibility of a very important decision will
largely rest on your Lordship. I have taken the liberty in
these lines to tender advice, which I believe would lead to peaceful development and good understanding between natives and
Europeans of all nationalities. I am thankful that Sir Henry
Loch comes to this country to consult with Her Majesty's
Government, after the personal acquaintance which he has
now made with both South and North Bechuanaland.

This letter to Lord Knutsford was described in the
following way to Mr Chamberlain, to whom he also
announced the fact that he felt his own task of agitation approaching its close.

11 QUEEN SQUARE,
LONDON, 20th Feb. 1891.

DEAR MR CHAMBERLAIN,—I take the liberty to enclose a
copy of a letter which I sent to Lord Knutsford a short time
ago. I was impressed with the very great responsibility which

rested on him at this time, and wrote to him under that feeling. I shall be glad if you will return it after you have had time to look it over.

Lord Knutsford, in reply, said what I had written would secure attention from him and from Sir Henry Loch in their consultations, and afterwards from Her Majesty's Government.

I would not gather from Sir Henry Loch that he was opposed to our views, although, of course, he is duly reserved. I trust you will do what you can in this matter. If you do this, I am sure your judgment and wish would go a great way. There is also another result of your exerting yourself in behalf of a righteous course as to Bechuanaland, and it is this, that if British administration is established in Khame's country, as in South Bechuanaland, I shall regard the work as accomplished which I came over here to help in ; and thus you see, there would be some prospect of my ceasing to trouble you about Bechuanaland.

The Missionary Society for some time past has been urging me to go back to its service again—not in Bechuanaland. I replied then that I would go nowhere till I saw this through, and now I trust it may please God to help the poor duffers of natives in North Bechuanaland, by getting them again to place full confidence in us, to go back to a clearly defined arrangement with Her Majesty's Government, such as that of 1885, and thus secure them their holdings by an Imperial title, which would bring real peace to the country.

I have no reason to suppose that you do wish to be freed from studying the Bechuanaland question ; on the contrary, I think you have a real interest in South African questions, and personally I have much reason to be thankful for your sympathy, advice, and assistance.

I have never before referred to my own affairs, or mixed them up with what I have regarded as my duty to others. I only know that if British administration is extended to North Bechuanaland I shall have brought about what I came over to help in, and be free to look out earnestly and thoughtfully as to what bit of work I can next do before I become an old man.

Mr Chamberlain replied in a reassuring manner in a personal interview, which Mackenzie described to his wife as follows :—

11 QUEEN SQUARE, W.C.,
9th March 1891.

I looked up Mr Chamberlain this morning, and had a short interview. He assures me on the following points :—

1. He is to be consulted by Lord Knutsford before, and not after, they form their policy.

2. No annexation to the Cape Colony. There might be a *rectification of the Northern Border of the Cape Colony.* I said this was nonsense; that meant the annexation of the Bechuanaland Colony to the Cape Colony. No; he did not understand that at all—only a small addition to put right the boundary line. I said that was a mistake, the boundary line was put down by Moysey, an Imperial officer, and afterwards ratified by the Cape Colony.

3. He also assured me that no annexation would take place without consulting the wishes of the natives. My visit was unannounced, but I hope good will come of it.

I ventured to remind him that the special position of honour which he had occupied in recent festivities and hospitalities, owing to his position generally, but specially owing to the interest which he had taken in South African affairs, showed the appreciation of his position which others held. It was for him, therefore, to see that in other ways that position and those views were recognized and deferred to, that he did not make things too cheap.

" When all this Company-mongering is over, the history of the country will show that ours is the true policy to pursue," I assured him. " I want you to be more militant than you have lately been," I added. " I am afraid that steps may be taken which will make all such interference and advice too late."

" I don't know, however, that I want to be more militant at present," he said. " In any case I must think the matter over."

We had some more talk to the same effect. I wish I could make him more earnest about this matter. He is a clever man, and one who would not give up a point if once he gave adhesion to it.

" Oh, Mr Rhodes is more taken up with an Imperial Zollverein than anything else at present."

I replied, " I don't think so at all, but he would be delighted if he could set you all a-thinking about a Zollverein and

Imperial Federation, etc., while he practically advances the Cape Colony northward in South Africa. His object, in short, is to remove the consideration of South African subjects from London to Cape Town. Do you agree to that? Remember it is Africa—a Continent. Surely Britain will not let itself be excluded from presiding over its affairs till it can hand these affairs over to a local Confederation."

"I quite agree that what must be worked for, and what we may expect, is a Confederation."

"If everybody is pleased and willing to transmit the management of the whole thing to the Cape Colony, Cape Town and not London would be the place where a man like myself would have to seek to establish influence and sound opinion."

I left him with the idea that I had made some impression. I should not perhaps have gone, nor should I have spoken so strongly, but for a note from Sir Fowell Buxton, in which he seems to be inclined to give everything up to "local management."

We had a long chat — a serious one — in the smoking-room of No. 11 last night; an American Colonel, an old East Indian, a Liverpool young man, and myself.

"Young Mr Lincoln," the American Minister, called for the American family yesterday. He is not so lankey as the pictures of his father. J. M.

Mr Chamberlain appears to have immediately written to Mackenzie another letter, to which the latter replied as follows :—

LONDON, *March* 11, 1891.

DEAR MR CHAMBERLAIN,—Many thanks for your note, which is reassuring. I cannot but await with great anxiety the outcome of a policy which is touched on, with reference to a country in which I have spent a great part of my life. . . . I cannot forget that the entrance into Bechuanaland by the British Government has been the cause of our revived influence throughout South Africa, just as the holding by the administration of that country now by the British Government will prove itself the key to the complete and lasting establishment of our influence in South Africa generally. This is the crucial step, leading to a future confederation of the various European governments, instead of the haphazard muddle to which the growth of the Cape Colony must lead. I beg your continued interest in a matter which the future will amply show is one of supreme importance.

It soon became apparent that the Government was being gradually driven, by the logic of facts and the urgent appeals of Mackenzie and the various members of the South African Committee, to take some momentous step with regard to North Bechuanaland, for, of all portions of Austral Africa south of the Zambesi, that alone remained without some definite form of civilised government. But as Mackenzie saw the close of his long work approaching, there necessarily arose in his mind the question of his own future. This indeed had already been raised for him by the Directors of the London Missionary Society, who for a number of months had been negotiating with him. Their final proposal was that he should go out in their service to the mission station of Hankey in Cape Colony, about fifty miles west of Port Elizabeth. As all their other important stations were at this time occupied, and they had very urgent reasons for wishing to set a strong man to work at Hankey, this remained as the only definite prospect that they could hold out to him. The following extracts are from a letter to his wife when these negotiations began, and serve to show the spirit in which he faced the task proposed to him.

MANCHESTER, 17th Oct. 1890.

I sent you a copy of the *Weekly Times* with that reference from their Mashonaland correspondent.

I have now received, before leaving London, the formal request of the Directors that I go to Hankey, which I enclose.

It is to start on a new kind of life; new languages, and in a part of the country with which I have had no connection.

The man who goes there can be of no use—or very little use—in general South African affairs. Were I to go there

I should simply give myself to the work there, and to nothing else. It would amount to that.

I don't know how it might turn out, but Thompson's impression decidedly was, that the place would have, in the end, to be disposed of, and the people be left to Colonial life in its general bearings, as has been done on other institutions already. I don't know if he was right in this surmise, but understood from him that this might turn out part of my duties.

So far as my thoughts and sense of personal duty go, they don't lead me to Hankey at all. They have to do with my work elsewhere in South Africa.

I have often said to you that if I had ever so much money I could not have been better placed than I have been over here, to do my work, and that I was where I felt I ought to be in the meantime. I have no such feeling about going to Hankey. I should go there because I was unable to refuse to go at the Society's request, on account of money-obligation to them.

I take it for granted, however, that they will not ask me to go away right off, while the destination of Bechuanaland is undecided, and may be said to be now under consideration, owing to the personal visit of Sir H. Loch to that country. If that is settled, in whatever way, I shall prepare myself to obey the Directors, and go and do my best at Hankey. I have already stated to Mr Thompson's clerk— he was out—that I took it for granted they meant me to remain and see this out after Loch's report.

Also, I asked that I should be completely free from Deputation work, so that I might give my time to the finishing of the Sechuana Scriptures.

This is how the matter stands. I cannot say that I change the whole bent of my life and thought and work, so far done—and more of it being done—to devote myself to the settlement of the affairs of Hankey.

I believe that He whom we serve will guide us at this time. He will open up our way. What I feel is that I must be perfectly open-minded and above board all round, so that there can be no misunderstanding.

If Bechuanaland is settled and disposed of, my sense of obligation to the Society would send me to Hankey, and I am not at all insensible to what might be done there. Not at all. Let us wait on God, and look to Him.

Since the date of this letter, he had learned much more concerning Hankey, and it had begun to occupy a distinct place in his imagination of the future. Nevertheless, it can hardly be said that his heart as yet went out to Hankey with anything of eager anticipation. He was still deeply immersed in the larger problems of Imperialism in South Africa. He everywhere makes it plain in his correspondence that his own desires went out towards some form of administrative work. In the course of his many and earnest discussions with Mr Chamberlain, as well as with Sir Robert Herbert, this subject naturally arose. At last, in the course of an important conversation regarding Bechuanaland and its approaching political settlement, Mackenzie was led to say to Sir Robert Herbert that he was willing to put himself at the service of the Government, if they had any work for him to do. This step Mr Chamberlain very warmly approved. Sir Robert Herbert and Lord Knutsford both received it with apparent cordiality and good-will.

These conversations resulted in his sending to Lord Knutsford the following letter :—

11 QUEEN SQUARE, W.C., LONDON,
21st April 1891.

DEAR LORD KNUTSFORD,—I learn with great pleasure that Her Majesty's Government contemplate an extension of Imperial administration in the Protectorate, and in Khame's country. I think your Lordship is aware that I was so impressed with the necessity for taking this step that I came over to England to do all that a private individual could, to remove misapprehensions and to give correct information concerning a country which had been offered to us on very favourable terms by its native owners.

In view of the step on which Her Majesty's Government has resolved, I am prepared very gladly to resign the work of writing, lecturing, and teaching geography, etc., etc., in which I have been engaged. I feel sure that my humble efforts have not been altogether without result, and that, with the efforts of other and more influential people, public opinion in this country will earnestly support Her Majesty's Government in this movement northward.

The question then arises to me, what to do next? and the answer of my judgment, as well as of my inclination would be to assist (if I might) in carrying out the work of native administration in South Africa, which will now occupy the attention of Her Majesty's Government for some time to come. While fully alive to the difficulties of this work, I should hope to be able to render some assistance in overcoming them, and I cherish the hope and expectation that, with our growing knowledge of the country and the people, and the natives' increasing knowledge of us and your objects, the difficulties of the present would gradually lessen, and in the end disappear.

When I have mentioned this state of mind to friends, it has given them great satisfaction as to the proposed action of Government, and also because, as they are pleased to say, they feel sure that I can be of service out there; and it was Mr Chamberlain that suggested that I should address your Lordship on the subject.

The first important work that arises out of our movement northward, would be to come to a good understanding with the Chiefs of North Bechuanaland with reference to this movement. To be of any real use in North Bechuanaland the Imperial Government must be able to control the settlement of vacant lands. Could this power be again obtained from the Chiefs, as in 1885? Circumstances have no doubt taken place since which render this very difficult. But success is not hopeless, and I am willing to attempt this at the request of Her Majesty's Government. It has been suggested to me that I should mention in what capacity I would propose to attempt this work.

1. Harking back to former experience, one way would be that I should go to North Bechuanaland as I did to South Bechuanaland, as Deputy Commissioner, under the High Commissioner. I think it well to add that, in my judgment, it would be necessary that this Deputy Commissionership should be unconnected officially with the Government of South Bechuanaland. Owing to the past history of the Protectorate, this would be the only practicable, not to say the only pleasant, method for all parties. Of

course I should be anxious to enter the country on the most friendly terms with Sir Sidney Shippard; but I feel sure it would be to the advantage of the service that our work should not be mixed up together.

2. Or, if Her Majesty's Government came to see its way, at some future time, to extend the present colony of Bechuanaland northward, I should be prepared to attempt, as just stated, the initial work in North Bechuanaland, and to take charge of the Native Department, or whatever other office in the enlarged Colony Her Majesty's Government might entrust to me.

3. There is a third capacity in which I am willing to undertake the same immediate work in North Bechuanaland, but in this case it would be to hand it over to others when completed, and to engage in other necessary intermediary or diplomatic work elsewhere, as the High Commissioner and Her Majesty's Government might desire. It will be in the recollection of some that it was contemplated, some years ago, to place on the staff of the High Commissioner a "Native Commissioner" or "Chief Native Commissioner," or "Imperial Native Commissioner," who would be expected to be an authority on native customs and native politics, and who would also be qualified to undertake on behalf of the High Commissioner and Her Majesty's Government the diplomatic work necessarily connected with our position and work in native territories. It will not be disputed that the presence of such an officer would have averted many an untoward and calamitous event. Such work as has now to be done in North Bechuanaland would fall to this officer.

Then, Her Majesty's Government has now before its mind, in Native Territories, certain general objects which a permanent official of this character could do something to further, in a quiet, steady, and persistent way. I need only mention one or two of those general objects which ought never to be lost sight of. Certain steps as to the treatment of land, the result of which would be to win the affections of the people for Her Majesty's administration, and to gradually supersede the communistic relations of the members of a tribe among one another, letting in the fresh, stimulating breath of healthy individualistic competition; and slowly, but surely, and in the general tribal interest, to supersede the power and influence of the Chiefs by an

evidently helpful Queen's Government, and generally, to
lead the various communities forward, cherishing a good
understanding between the old Native element and the
new European settlers in their country, until, in each case,
by God's blessing on our efforts, Imperial administration
could be removed and local self-government advantageously
take its place. I am willing, if called on by Government,
to do my best to discharge the duties of "Chief Native
Commissioner," or "Imperial Native Commissioner." I
should regard the appointment as a high honour, and I
should feel all the stimulus and strength which flow from
the assurance that in this office I had opportunity of serving
my fellow-men, my beloved country, and the common
Father of all.—I remain, dear Lord Knutsford, ever sincerely
yours,   JOHN MACKENZIE.

For nearly three months Mackenzie was kept
waiting for a reply to this application. The reason
for this was that it had to be transmitted to South
Africa for the consideration of Sir Henry Loch,
the High Commissioner and Governor of Cape
Colony.

Lord Knutsford has kindly supplied the present
writer with the following statement of facts. Referring to the letter of application he says :—

Upon receiving this I wrote to Sir Henry Loch, in
which, while enclosing a copy of your father's letter, I
said that there was no doubt of Mr Mackenzie being a
very able man, and Imperialistic in his views, as he had
long been pressing annexation and believed that he could
reconcile the Chiefs to this proceeding ; that I thought he
would be really useful, and that he was the man most
likely to conciliate the Chiefs ; that I personally would be
glad to see him appointed Special Commissioner (perhaps
for one year in the first instance), under Sir Henry Loch's
orders as High Commissioner.

During the delay Mackenzie had been much
encouraged by various interviews at the Colonial
Office, which seemed to indicate that there, at any
rate, his appointment would be received with satis-

faction. He even went the length of describing in a communication to Sir Robert Herbert, on the 10th of May, the plan which should be adopted by a Commissioner appointed to bring North Bechuanaland under Imperial administration. When at last Lord Knutsford announced on July 7th that Sir Henry Loch had decided against the proposal, there could be no doubt of Mackenzie's deep disappointment. Sir Henry Loch said that he had already made other arrangements for the control and administration of the Protectorate, which did not admit of the appointment of any officer to perform the kind of work proposed for Mackenzie. To this Mackenzie replied as follows :—

11 QUEEN SQUARE, W.C.,
10th July 1891.

DEAR LORD KNUTSFORD,—I have to acknowledge your Lordship's kindly expressed note informing me that Sir Henry Loch has made arrangements for the control and administration of the Bechuanaland Protectorate, and does not see his way to avail himself of my services there, and that your Lordship could not press the matter further against his decided opinion.

In reply to this unexpected information, and in so far as the question is a personal one, I shall only say that I bow to your Lordship's decision, for which I have been anxiously waiting for some time : and that I shall never regret having offered my services for a pacific settlement of North Bechuanaland at the present juncture, although those services have been declined. I may be permitted to say also that I have worked for this cause for so many years that I am not afraid that my policy or my motives are misunderstood in Cape Town any more than at the Colonial Office in London : and again, I am quite sure that they have not declined my services on account of my ignorance of Bechuanaland, or my want of acceptability to its people, black as well as white.

Leaving the present aspect of the question, I beg to offer a few remarks on the much graver public aspect. This I can do all the more readily that I have had no private or personal quarrels or animosities in South Africa. The umbrage which

I may have given has been entirely through the public policy which I have advocated, and especially because it is recognized that I had something to do with the revival of Imperial influence in South Africa at a time when it was thought to have been banished and got rid of. I confess I am afraid that that influence, *as a power for good*, is still in great danger of being, in a clever but real way, subverted and banished from South Africa—leaving the Imperial Government with *full responsibility, but stripped of all* power and means of action.

Allow me to recapitulate the heads of the policy to advocate which I have given some years of my life, and which has met with public approval in this country, the intelligent acquiescence of the natives, chiefs, and people, after being fully explained to them, as well as the approbation of the best and most intelligent colonists.

1. I believe I was the first to point out the possibility of the peaceful opening up of native territories under the Imperial Government, accompanied by the recognition of the rights of natives to their holdings, and by intelligent steps taken to secure those lands to their owners under the Imperial Government.

2. There being no General or Central Government in South Africa, and Her Majesty's Government being recognized as practically in this capacity by every State and Colony, it follows that new territories such as Bechuanaland should be administered under Imperial auspices till local self-government became advisable.

3. The third point consists in a recognition of the growth of public opinion here and in South Africa as to South African affairs, which may be shown in this way. Although in 1883 and '84 the growth of the Cape Colony northward was held to be infinitely better than that Bechuanaland should be the scene of outrage and filibustering or should pass over to the Transvaal or Germany, and Britain be effectually shut out of the country; yet, more recently, after the attention of Great Britain and of all South Africa has been directed to these northern countries, it is fully recognized that it is the duty of the Imperial Government, as the Acting General Government of South Africa—and in the interests of the whole country—to consider thoughtfully the disposition of native territories under Imperial protection, so that a Confederation of the European Governments in South

Africa under Great Britain may become practicable in the future; and that therefore both Bechuanaland and Zambesi should be administered as separate colonies or territories until such time as the wishes of their respective inhabitants, and the general interest of South Africa as a whole, made plain what further step should be taken with regard to their future and permanent government.

Now there are doubtless some men in South Africa who would object to all these propositions. They would "hammer" the natives, and rob them of their land, and never recognize their right to own land, or to possess any civil right except to pay a hut-tax. They would "level down" the Cape Colony constitution to the condition of those republics where a man, no matter how good he is, or how much he knows, or how much he has, in character, knowledge, or property, can have no citizen-rights, because he is a native African in his own country of Africa. These people most earnestly desire to see the Imperial Government snubbed and bounced till it retires from all administrative work in new territories: and they do so simply and baldly because the British Government insists that the natives do have rights which a civilized government must recognise. These people do not hide from us that when they succeed in expelling the Imperial Government from responsible administrative work, they intend to introduce, not "slavery," they assure you, but a "domestic institution," some "labour arrangement," in the practice of which Europeans are to march northwards in Africa under the British flag. The one policy is to hold Bechuanaland under the Imperial Government in the assured hope that education, and the introduction of civilized settlers from Britain and from the Cape Colony, will make that country an important factor in "levelling up" the future South African Confederation to the status of the present constitution of the Cape Colony. The other is to drive out the Imperial Government and "level down" the Cape Colony Constitution to the present low status of the Grondwet of the Transvaal.

I know of nothing which illustrates the present South African position so well as the condition of the United States of America before the Civil War. The great question then was, Shall the new territories become Free Soil or Slave States? The corresponding "Southern" view in South Africa at the present time, would expel the Imperial

Government from administration and thus settle the matter in favour of its own views. The best men in South Africa, and I am not now speaking of Dutch or English, earnestly desire the Imperial Government to remain in active administration and responsibility in native territories, so that the "Northern" view and policy may triumph in the future in all South Africa.

I cannot imagine for a moment any hesitation on a question of this nature and magnitude, on the part of your Lordship or Her Majesty's Government, when the real bearings of the question are clearly seen. The one policy is unrighteous, selfish, and destined to be worked out in blood; the other is such as can be laid before South Africa and before the world, and on which the blessing of Heaven can be asked.

The problem in South Africa is not an easy one in any circumstances. What I fear is that Her Majesty's Government is in danger of acquiescing in its own expulsion from active administration in new territories, by a few men in the Cape Colony, before there is a Confederated South African Government to which it could hand over its duties; and I am well aware that no greater calamity could possibly happen to South Africa.

In concluding these remarks on the public bearings of the opposing lines of policy in South Africa to-day, I leave it to Her Majesty's Government to choose which it will follow and uphold. And in this connexion I beg to put it to your Lordship and to Her Majesty's Government to consider well whether the present rejection of a man does not mean, in the present circumstances, the rejection of an indispensable Imperial policy. The individual man cannot help being effaced when he is rejected; but it is quite different with the Imperial Government, whose presence and work are so necessary. I would therefore implore your Lordship, by all that is highest and noblest in our British history and action in the world, to see to it that the Imperial Government is not effaced in Bechuanaland, and that what I would have willingly attempted in North Bechuanaland is really done by some one else.—I remain, dear Lord Knutsford, ever yours sincerely, JOHN MACKENZIE.

To Mr Chamberlain he wrote on the same subject.

11 QUEEN SQUARE, W.C.,
8th July 1891.

I have received the enclosed letter from Lord Knutsford. I also take the liberty to enclose a draft reply, hoping you will do me the favour of looking through it.

I was fully aware that I was proposing to myself no bed of roses in the work which I contemplated. Had the Government desired that work to be done, and supported me along with the High Commissioner, I was prepared to go and do my best, knowing that at such a distance from Cape Town I should have had very little prospect of treading on the toes of any of the Cape Town opponents of Imperial administration in native territories.

But it is better to be told now that there is no room or work for me in North Bechuanaland than to be appointed and then deserted, as was my experience under Sir H. Robinson.

I do not regret having given some years of my life to the work of spreading information about that country and about our duties there. You remember well what it was in 1884, when I was first introduced to you by Dr Dale. Since that time I can conscientiously say I have done what I could for the cause of the weak and the ignorant and for the good of my country.

Allow me to thank you for your kindness and help. The country up to the Zambesi is now in our hands to make or mar.

As soon as Lord Knutsford's letter reached him, Mackenzie walked down to the Mission House and into the office of Mr Wardlaw Thompson and said, " Now, I am ready for Hankey."

Before closing this chapter in his life, it ought to be recalled that among all the labours which we have been describing, Mackenzie had undertaken in the year 1889 to read the proofs of a re-print of the Bible in the language of the Bechuana people. This was undertaken at the request of the British and Foreign Bible Society. The work would have been irksome for any one, but the labour was increased by the fact that, as he went on, he could not help doing a little more than merely compare the former edition with the proof sheets of the new, to secure an exact correspondence of the two. The task was not complete until the end of 1890. The following letter to the late Dr William Wright, the Secretary of the Bible Society, will give some idea of what he had done.

11 QUEEN SQUARE, W.C.,
3rd December 1890.

DEAR DR WRIGHT,—I am glad and thankful to say that yesterday I sent off the last pages of the Sechuana Scriptures : and as the second proofs are only a sheet or two behind, I am quite within sight of the completion of my work.

I should have got through sooner, but that, as you are aware, I had to read 288 pages twice over, owing to the resolution of the Committee to increase the number of copies to be printed. Then I was also laid aside for a time by illness which unfitted me for mental work.

The work itself has been more onerous than might have been expected. I found that in different books of Scripture there were different ways of spelling the same word. I have taken some trouble to bring about uniformity in spelling words, and have at any rate reduced the amount of this dissimilarity.

In reading this I have been able to elide a few mistaken expressions, one or two of an offensive description, which had found their way into use at an early date in the history of the Mission. For instance, the word for "poor" people in those parts of the Bible which were translated at an early date, is "Balala," the name of a single tribe or clan of vassal Bechuanas. The right word "bahumanegi" is found in late books ; I have sought to keep out the word "Balala" altogether, and to use "Bahumanegi" instead. Tlakola = to wipe, specifically as a nurse an infant, had got into Scripture, in the sense of to destroy, or to spoil, although not used in all such cases. I have kept out this word in every case. Sebono is a word *made* from the verb "bona," *to see*, by the early missionaries. It was not in native use, as indicating "vision," "something seen." It was probably not known when this word was made by the missionaries and used by them in public services, that it fatally resembled a nasty word already in too frequent

use in native swearing. Afterwards another word was coined,
"sebona," which had no recommendation. "Sepontsisho,"
a thing caused to be seen, was also afterwards used in
Scripture; and this word I have used throughout for the
other objectionable words.

Then, I have put right some ungrammatical expressions,
and occasionally rearranged an obscure sentence or clause.

I am glad that I have been able to bring this work to
completion, and remain, dear Dr Wright, ever yours
sincerely,   JOHN MACKENZIE.

It is due to Mackenzie and to his Christian faith,
to say in a word that throughout these years of great
toil, of absorbing engagements, and of deep anxiety,
his own religious life was not only maintained, but
deepened. His family letters show abundantly, as
well as those which he wrote to friends of whose
Christian sympathy he was sure, that his earlier habits
of prayer-life remained unimpaired. His separation
from his wife and family, which was only made bear-
able by occasional and temporary re-unions in London
and at Portobello, was turned by him into a means of
divine grace to them. His nine children were made
very sure, by his letters, of his unceasing prayer for
them and watchfulness over their growth. No one
of them took any step in life which did not call out
his fullest sympathy, expressed in the tenderest of
words. He more than once spoke of the absence of
any anxiety regarding them; and he explained this
by his profound faith in the significance of the
baptismal rite. For him that Christian ordinance
was no mere form, or empty ceremonial. It was the
expression and the seal of a covenant between him
and his Lord, in which his Lord bound Himself,
Mackenzie believed, to preside over the growth of
his children and direct them towards the Kingdom of
Life.

As soon as it became known that Mackenzie was
going out again to Africa in the service of the

London Missionary Society, letters poured in upon him from all quarters, especially from those with whom he had been working upon public questions. Nearly all of them expressed great regret that Government had not appointed him to its service in South Africa. The members of the South African Committee immediately attempted to arrange for a public dinner in his honour; but as he was to sail in September, when nearly all his friends were out of town, this was found impossible.

Mr H. O. Arnold Forster wrote to him as follows :—

LONDON, 19/8/91.

DEAR MACKENZIE,—I am greatly obliged to you for your letter received this day.

I heard from Loring that all our hopes of your being able to do the good work in the way we hoped are at an end. I most deeply regret it. I know you will and must feel the disappointment. It seemed as if at last the Government were going to take one wise step, and now from the old quarter comes once more the usual fatal veto.

We certainly do desire to give you some sort of testimony of our regard before you leave, and you will see that the enclosed letter from Lord Grey has reference to a communication from me upon the subject. So many people are out of town that I fear we may meet with some disappointment. But, judging from the letters I have received, it will be from no want of good-will and esteem that any of your many friends will be absent.

I at anyrate shall, I hope, have the good fortune of seeing you, and I beg you will let me know at the earliest opportunity when you expect to be in town.—Yours very truly,   H. O. ARNOLD FORSTER.

As the dinner could not be arranged at that season, the South African Committee resolved to send to South Africa as soon as possible, a gift which Mr Arnold Forster describes in the following letter :—

DEAR MACKENZIE,—Loring and I have been putting our heads together since you left. This is what we have thought of as possible.

1. A despatch box which you may be able to carry about
with you, and which will be identified with your work in our
cause.

2. A really good travelling clock—"compensated," and
not too big.

Perhaps, however, home-counsels may have bettered these
ideas; if so, let me know by return, otherwise I shall go
ahead. Let me know your address in Africa. The things
shall be sent after you with the least possible delay. We also
propose to send you some written record on behalf of the
S. A. Committee, testifying to their deep appreciation
of your work here. Let me add that Loring and I have
been agreeing that you have left us an example of courage,
single-mindedness, and determination to fight for the right,
which will long serve as an encouragement in the days when
guidance and inspiration are so sorely needed. You have
done us both good, and our best return will be to try and
not let your work fall to the ground.—Yours very truly,

H. O. ARNOLD FORSTER.

The presents were sent as described by Mr Arnold
Forster in January 1892, and Mackenzie replied as
follows :—

HANKEY, CAPE COLONY,
20th Feby. 1892.

DEAR MR ARNOLD FORSTER,—I have received your kind
letter, announcing the shipment of the valuable gifts and
keepsakes which my friends of the South African Committee
have been so kind as to send to me, and more recently the
case itself reached this place, containing the despatch box
and the travelling clock. On being unpacked both were
found in entirely good condition, and are as handsome as
they are sure to be useful.

May I ask you to convey my heartfelt thanks to those
friends who have so kindly expressed their favourable estimate
of my share in our work accomplished, and our work attempted and not yet secured, for South Africa.

I would willingly write at length on the very important
questions ever near my heart, and which are no doubt
occupying the Committee's present attention, but I find
myself surrounded here by imperative duties of a very en-
grossing nature, which in the meantime demand my whole
attention. I sincerely hope, however, that the members of

the Committee will redouble their attention to Imperial questions in Southern Africa, for in my opinion present circumstances demand not less, but more watchfulness than before. In my judgment, Great Britain is at the present moment in the utmost danger of losing all practical supremacy and control in the management of Border aud Native affairs in South Africa, while all the time you are given to understand that your influence is increasing. Thus the highest interests of both Colonists and natives—so long secured by the efforts of the Imperial Power—demand the closest vigilance on the part of all lovers of justice and fair dealing. Gratified and cheered by my friends' kindness to me, I remain, dear Mr Forster, ever yours sincerely,

JOHN MACKENZIE.

APPENDIX TO CHAPTER XVII

IN the following letter, whose occasion is explained by itself, Mackenzie gave, as in duty bound, a kind of informal report of the work which he had been doing since 1883, in which he had enjoyed not only the sympathy but the assistance of the London Missionary Society :—

PORTOBELLO, N.B.,
3rd Nov. 1890.

The Rev. R. Wardlaw Thompson,
Foreign Secretary, L. M. S.

DEAR MR THOMPSON,—I have now to reply to the invitation of the Directors to undertake the spiritual charge of the church at Hankey, as one of the missionaries of the Society.

I have endeavoured very earnestly to ascertain the path of duty ; and after prayer and consultation and much anxious thought, have arrived at the conclusions which I shall now lay before you in as few words as possible.

But for one thing, the non-settlement of the Bechuanaland question, I should at once accept of the Society's invitation, and do my best for it at Hankey. It therefore follows that if temporary arrangements can be made by you for carrying on the work at Hankey till such time as the affairs of Bechuanaland are discussed in this country and settled, after the report of Sir Henry Loch on his personal visit to Bechuanaland, I shall be happy to proceed to Hankey and carry out the work of the Society there, in accordance with their present invitation.

In thus subordinating the invitation to engage in work at Hankey to the completion of the work for Bechuanaland, I feel that I shall evoke your sympathy, although it may entail some trouble in making the necessary temporary arrangements.

You will remember that I came over to this country from Africa in the end of 1885 for a specific object, to instruct the public with reference to Bechuanaland and the countries adjoining, so as to lead to an intelligent and righteous policy. My conception of my present work in England has all along been to see all Bechuanaland under the administration of the Queen, and thus secure the rights of all the natives, as well as render impossible the occupation of the freebooter and the filibuster. Besides the *inertia* of ignorance, and the engrossments of the Irish squabble, we had to fight the late High Commissioner, and on account of him, in a secondary way, the present English Government.

I do not think it will be out of place for me to recall some leading events of recent years, in which I have borne part, and in which I have enjoyed the effective co-operation of yourself and of many Directors and supporters of the Society:—

1883-4

The saving of Bechuanaland from the Transvaal, for the Society, for the natives, and for Great Britain.

1884

Rousing the best feeling of Cape Colonists by press and platform as to righteous methods of European expansion; testified to by resolutions at public meetings in chief towns of Colony. It was this sound Colonial feeling, evoked at this time, which induced Mr Gladstone's Government to send out the Bechuanaland Expedition.

1884-5

Establishing British Protectorate in South Bechuanaland as Deputy Commissioner, and also in connexion with Sir

Charles Warren; securing under Sir Charles the peaceful co-operation and goodwill of every chief in Bechuanaland, North and South.

1884-5

Securing a land settlement for South Bechuanaland under Imperial auspices, in direct opposition to the policy of Sir H. Robinson, who advocated that there should be no land settlement till South Bechuanaland was annexed to the Cape Colony. What was gained by this is very clearly indicated by the fact that when Mr Price lately erected a native church at Koning, near Kuruman, a formal protest was sent to him by the European who had claimed Koning before the Imperial Land Court, and who does not hide his belief that he will get redress when the country is annexed to the Cape Colony. I observed also that a petition had been actually lodged already with the Cape Colony Government, against another decision of the Bechuanaland Imperial Land Court, in which that decision had been, as in the case of Koning, in favour of the natives, and against certain European claimants.

1885-90

In England again. By writing "Austral Africa," &c., by addressing the Society of Arts; the British Association; the Geographical Societies of Edinburgh, Manchester, and Newcastle; the Chambers of Commerce of London, Glasgow, Liverpool, and Edinburgh; by contact with men of influence in the political and official world; by formal communications from time to time to the Colonial Office; by these and other means, certain results have been furthered. Among others :—

The policy of Sir H. Robinson of annexing Bechuanaland to the Cape Colony has been defeated once and again.

The annexation of Swaziland to the Transvaal has been defeated, and an Imperial settlement of land and other claims secured for that country.

Public attention in this country directed to the nibbling at the Cape Constitution involved in the Revision of Registration Act, so that those who promoted that retrogressive movement have not gone further, as was said to be their original intention.

Keeping the public thoroughly aware of the immense and vital importance to all South Africa of retaining the British administration of Bechuanaland, thereby lifting gradually South

African policy to the position secured in the Cape Colony by its Constitution. Appreciating these and other arguments, the public censors of Imperial expenditure have not found fault with the Imperial outlay in Bechuanaland; but, on the contrary, public opinion has unanimously demanded a more intelligent attitude than that hitherto assumed by the present Government. It was this public interest in these regions which Mr Rhodes took advantage of on the one hand, while on the other hand the present Government professed to be furthering the highest interests of the countries indicated, in the matter of the Charter of the British South Africa Company.

Restraints were imposed on this Company, and its greater subordination to the Colonial Office secured, in deference to public opinion and pressure. The Company idea was opposed until the Charter was given by the present Government. The position has all along been taken up, that after our contract with the chiefs and people of Bechuanaland in 1885, and their offers to us of territory at that time, it would be unjust, even dishonest, to the British public, to hand over any part of Bechuanaland to a Commercial and Private Company. This position as to Bechuanaland and the Imperial Government has never been controverted. It has been privately assented to by authorities of the Company, and it has been tacitly recognized in semi-official articles on the British South Africa Company.

War and bloodshed in Matabeleland have been, for the time at least, prevented, between the Company and the Matabele. You have seen the map with the route which was suggested by me to Lord Knutsford, and which has been followed without bloodshed. That another route was preferred in certain quarters is certain. And it is equally certain that if an armed European force had attempted to penetrate Matabeleland proper their progress would have been forcibly opposed by the Matabele; and, probably in some "kloof" or other available place of ambush, hundreds, if not thousands, of lives must have been lost in the attempt to force a way to Mashonaland through Matabeleland. Public attention has been directed to the question of the future Confederation of South Africa, especially in connexion with the inadvisableness of adding to the area of the Cape Colony by the annexation of any part of Bechuanaland.

When Mr Rhodes lately spoke of the growth of the Cape

Colony northwards, not one organ of public opinion in this
country approved of it, so far as I am aware.   Even his
friends treated it as a joke, or as a mere sop for the present
gratification of his Africander friends.

These are some of the results of the peculiar work in which
I have been lately engaged, a work, which I venture to say,
is both Christian and Christlike in its grand objects.   I have
not gone into matters of detail; and, indeed, in your case
that would be unnecessary, as many of the movements have
been known to you at the time, and have secured your
sympathy and help.

Now I do feel, without, as I trust, unseemly egotism, that
wide and permanent results have already followed, and are
destined to follow, the above movements, which have already
permanently affected the current of South African history.
In these move.nents I have borne a part; to their promotion
I have given some years of my life; and my friends generally
assure me that without my close personal attention and efforts,
these results would not have been secured.   In this connexion
I desire to express my great obligation to yourself and to other
Directors and members of the Society, who, along with a few
personal friends, have enabled me to carry on this work
hitherto, until, as you will agree with me, the final struggle
and settlement are within sight.

I may be allowed to remark that the work which has
occupied most of my time in England, and in South Africa,
has always been difficult and sometimes trying.   I have shared
my encouragements with my friends; and I don't think I
have troubled them with my disappointments.   My position
has kept myself and more especially those belonging to myself
in more or less anxiety.   But feeling that the work was God's
work imposed on me, I have stuck to it, turning neither to
the right hand nor to the left.   I have had great pleasure in
occasionally engaging in Deputation work, as far as I have
been able.   And I have been reading for the press a reprint
of the Sechuana Scriptures.   Otherwise I have been a man
of one idea, from which nothing has diverted me.   It would
be very easy indeed for me to reckon the books which I have
read during these years, and the holidays which I have taken.

Now, it is evident to me that if we would reap the full
advantage of what we have been doing in the past, we must
not slacken our hand till the final settlement is reached and
British administration is established in all Bechuanaland.

Sir Henry Loch is now in Bechuanaland, and, it appears, thinks even of visiting Matabeleland. His report will soon be before Her Majesty's Government, and the result will probably be a settlement of Bechuanaland up to the Zambesi. If he has to be fought, like Sir H. Robinson and Sir F. de Winton and others, in the interests of righteousness and fair dealing, if he should recommend that South Bechuanaland should be handed over to the Cape Colony, and North Bechuanaland to the Chartered Company as its possession, and that thus the direct Christian influence of Great Britain should be excluded from native policy in the interior of South Africa, I should like to be in the country when the fight takes place. I confess I should not respect myself if I turned away from the Bechuanaland question just now, and left it without that measure of guidance and furtherance which I have been able to bring to bear upon it. No one can exaggerate the issue which the settlement of Bechuanaland will practically go far to decide. What is really at stake is whether "Southerner" or "Northerner" doctrines and tendencies are to prevail in Southern Africa : whether the country is to be split into two camps on the question of colour, or broad justice be done to all, irrespective of race.

The British public is with us, if our views continue to be well explained and kept to the front. I am happy to observe in the last Cape papers, that, notwithstanding all efforts which have been put forth, those inhabitants of Bechuanaland who might be supposed to be most desirous of annexation to the Cape Colony, the farming population (which is chiefly the Dutch-speaking), have recently, by public address to the High Commissioner during his visit to Vryburg, deprecated such annexation. This expression of opinion on their part will give strength to the often expressed opposition of the Bechuanaland natives to Colonial annexation; and if a full expression of opinion to the same effect is given over here, the annexation will not take place; and the whole of Bechuanaland will be administered as a Crown Colony under an improved Constitution, and the peaceful and righteous development of the country secured.

I have endeavoured to make plain to you and to the Directors what stands between me and Hankey at present, but which would not stand between me and it after the Bechuanaland settlement has been made. I have written in entire confidence, as to tried and dear friends, to whom I

have been known for over thirty years ; and know my letter
will be received in the spirit in which it is written.   I don't
think you will judge me to have decided wrongly when you
consider the present imminent position of the Bechuanaland
Question.

When that truly important matter for all South Africa is
settled, if you have, in the meantime, succeeded in making
temporary arrangements, then for Hankey !—With very high
regards, believe me, ever yours sincerely,

JOHN MACKENZIE.

CHAPTER XVIII

AFRICA—MANY-SIDED WORK AT HANKEY (1891-1898)

HANKEY is the name given in honour of a former Governor of Cape Colony to a settlement about fifty miles west of Port Elizabeth. It is situated in a very beautiful valley, formed by the Gamtoos River, which falls into the sea, about twenty miles south. This was one of a number of estates which were acquired by the London Missionary Society early in the century under the sanction of Government. Originally the Hankey estate consisted of more than 4000 acres, which were purchased in the year 1822 for £2500. The theory of such a settlement in South Africa was this—that if the Society owned large enough tracts of ground in suitable districts and gathered upon it those natives who were willing to break away from tribal government and to place themselves under Christian instruction, strong centres of civilisation and religion would be established. The missionaries found very early that combined superintendence of industrial and social development, where they did not possess magisterial authority, weakened instead of strengthening their moral influence over the people. The theory, therefore, did not work out well in practice, and the Society ultimately parted with all its settlements. The process of resigning these was by no means easy. It required repeated dealings with the Home Government, and finally with the Cape Parliament; and it required also prolonged and often most irritating negotiations and transactions with the native residents themselves.

In the year 1876 an Act of the Colonial Parliament was passed, enabling the Society to transfer its land on certain conditions to the natives, and also to European purchasers. As a result of this final Parliamentary action, all the remaining stations were got rid of by the Society, excepting only Hankey. Here the same difficulties which obtained elsewhere seemed to concentrate themselves with peculiar intensity. Few Europeans were found willing to purchase land for the purpose of settling upon it. The natives who had been the tenants of the Society, accustomed to indulgent treatment in reference to rents and other responsibilities, did not relish the sterner demand which came upon them when they agreed to make periodical payments, with a view to ownership. The result was that large numbers, after many years, were found to have paid neither capital nor interest, and, of course, had escaped the payment of rent. It was necessary, therefore, for the Society to resume occupancy, and exercise both its rights and responsibilities once more.

The Hankey settlement is peculiarly isolated. Its only market is Port Elizabeth, which cannot be reached except by traversing a very rough and hard road ; this always requires two days, the night being spent at an inn about half way. Yet the soil is very fruitful, and in good seasons the people make an abundant living in the easiest manner. There has, therefore, been no stimulus to social or individual ambition, and the population fell long ago into ill repute throughout that district, and even beyond it, for laziness, quarrelsomeness, and incapacity.

When Mackenzie arrived he found that the affairs of the village were supervised by a Board of Management. There was no provision nearer than the town of Humansdorp for the religious instruction or care of Europeans. The coloured church had been declared by the London Missionary Society to be an inde-

pendent church, over which he could assume pastoral
care only after receiving and accepting a " call." The
Society had for a number of years employed Mr J.
S. Hultzer as their general and business manager,
whose duty it was to collect the rents and superintend
the estates. The Society had also employed for some
time a Mr Spindler, a civil engineer, for the purpose of
investigating plans of irrigation and carrying them
out. In no direction did Mackenzie find that affairs
were going on with even reasonable smoothness or
prosperity. There was a tangle in the relation of the
administrative powers to all the rest. There was a tangle
in the property relations and rights of the Society ; a
tangle in the industrial conditions, responsibilities and
rights, both of the white and coloured farmers, as well as
the tenants of the Society. There was a tangle in church
affairs, and a tangle in the educational work of the
community. His parish, as a spiritual teacher and
pastor, extended beyond the village of Hankey to
several out-stations, where he was expected to superintend the work of native preachers, ordained and
unordained.

The task of Mackenzie at Hankey was the straighten-
ing out of all these tangled relations. He was simply
sent out to put Hankey right from top to bottom. It
was understood when he was appointed, and when
others remonstrated against his appointment to a
sphere so obscure, and toil so thankless, that it might
be accomplished in three years. No one knows how
soon Mackenzie saw that the task was no three years'
task, but the work of a life-time. He gave himself to
it, not indeed without the exercise of conscious self-
control, but with profound peace of mind in the
consciousness of doing his duty. When the doors to
further employment under Government were closed,
and the London Missionary Society had this one door
only to open for him, he accepted this, as his letters

abundantly show, with perfect simplicity of motive and humbleness of heart, as the work which his Master now laid upon him. When he found himself at Hankey, and the whole sordid facts stared him in the face, no mortal heard him grumble. He did not look over his shoulder, nor hesitate in any one step. He had come to give himself to Hankey and for Hankey, as he gave himself long ago to and for Shoshong and Kuruman, and as in later years he had given himself to and for South Africa as a whole. The earthly sweep of his task seemed narrow, but the sense of responsibility and the spirit of devotion were the same—only deeper and richer. For during these last years, when he worked as hard as in the days of his prime, and when his strength was gradually being undermined, his friends noticed a certain ripening of the spiritual man, of which we shall speak later.

One of the chief difficulties to which Mackenzie had looked forward when he accepted his new appointment, consisted in the fact that he must learn to preach in the Dutch language. It is true that he had for many years used the colloquial "Taal" Dutch of South Africa ; but its ungrammatical lingo he had not mastered, and what he knew of it afforded him very little help for a thorough learning of pure Dutch. It has been the custom of Dutch-speaking South Africans, both European and coloured, to conduct all their public religious worship and to do all their preaching and speaking in high Dutch ; hence Mackenzie, at fifty-six years of age, had to face the task of learning a new language. Even before he left England he set himself with his own grim determination to do this as thoroughly as possible. He at once procured the necessary books, grammar, dictionary, etc. He also purchased religious works in Dutch, and was especially careful to procure a Dutch translation of Spurgeon's sermons, in order, as he said, that he might become familiar at once with the religious idioms and vocabulary of that language. The first result of his characteristic determined diligence was this, that having arrived at Hankey on Tuesday, October 7th, he at once obtained the help of Mr J. S. Hultzer to go over the material for his Sunday service, to criticise his sermon as to its language and structure, and did actually on the first Sunday after his arrival conduct the whole service and preach the sermon in the Dutch language!

Mackenzie with his wife and two daughters speedily made themselves at home in Hankey. They were, on their arrival, pleased to receive a hearty welcome, with a formal address from the Europeans. Amongst these, as they afterwards found, there had been many bickerings and contentions; but they came in as strangers, and refused to hear of or to recognise any such past events, resolved from the first to treat them as indeed past and done with.

Mackenzie shut himself into the valley of Hankey as completely as if he had never covered all South Africa with his interest and service; as if he had not haunted the lobby of the House of Commons for days and months and years; as if great statesmen and public men were unknown to him. He shut himself into this little valley, refusing for many weeks to read newspapers which would divert him from his present duty, or to be drawn into any important discussion which might still connect him with public life, and distract him from Hankey. To the laborious task of preparing his weekly sermon in Dutch, and another in English—for he instituted a regular English service every Sunday besides all other addresses and speeches incidental to the pastorate—he added that of immediately confronting and thoroughly studying the administrative, industrial, and social affairs of the community. For many months he wrote a long letter every fortnight to the Rev. Wardlaw Thompson, the foreign secretary of the London Missionary Society. These letters bear witness to the minuteness with which he studied every fact connected with Hankey.

Before the end of 1891 he began to make practical proposals. In the beginning of 1892 he was able to report that he had obtained from the Board of Management a resolution which gave him, in the name of the Society, certain powers without which he felt that an improvement of the conditions could not be secured.

On January 13th, 1892, he writes :—

By this post you will get a copy of the agreement which I have succeeded in making with the Hankey Board of Managers, which brings to an end the protracted deadlock which has prevailed here as between the Society and the Board.

In a letter he says :—

It is, from my point of view, the best bit of business the Society has done here for some time. Such an agreement represents a state of mind, and that state of mind would seem to be rather a novelty here in Hankey. It will be my part to make it permanent, so as to carry us through the equally delicate matters connected with the enlargement of the irrigable area at Rooi Vlakte.

The essence of this arrangement consisted in the assumption by the Missionary Society—which meant by Mackenzie—of the management of the Klein River, which formed an important feature in the further development of the estates at Hankey. The Board agreed to pay to the Society £50 per annum "to assist it in the water management."

Throughout these early letters Mackenzie enters with the utmost minuteness into questions concerning the irrigation of various portions of the estates, and the engineering work necessary to accomplish that. He had to carry through negotiations for the acquirement of new ground, in order to obtain control of certain waters ; and having obtained it, he had to build furrows, deepen and strengthen a dam, besides negotiating for the repair of a famous tunnel which had been cut through the mountains, to bring the water of the Gamtoos within reach of certain portions of the valley.

Naturally it would be impossible to record here the details of these investigations, and the labours which they involved; and for many personal reasons it would be inappropriate to refer more definitely to the many negotiations with individuals in Hankey and elsewhere which his letters described. Suffice it to say, that this series of letters of itself represents an amount of work which most of us would have considered sufficient to occupy a man's whole time and thought.

It may not be unsuitable to give the following as one or two specimens of the kind of letters of which so many passed between Hankey and London for several years:

HANKEY, 13*th April* 1892.

DEAR MR THOMPSON,—I failed to send off by last post a letter on some of the matters which have recently engaged my attention here, and so it goes to-day. Although one of great interest, especially to one who knows Hankey and its people as you do, I feel sure you will think with me that the enclosed agreement with Mr Young is of the utmost importance, both to Hankey and to the London Missionary Society.

Upon receipt of your letter, I began to approach Mr Young as to the use of the fine natural reservoir of Apple Drift. After a severe and protracted bargain-making struggle, we have come to terms as to Apple Drift, and the right to raise it and send back the water; also as to the portion of land on this side of the river as far up as the Falls, near the corner of the road where it turns in the direction of Mr J. S. Young's house. I felt that without the land on this side of the river the arrangement would not be satisfactory. I had included the lower gardens of Mr Young, opposite Apple Drift, but his ideas were so great that I dropped them, reserving, however, the right to purchase any part which might

be submerged by the raising of our present Hankey dam, at
a certain rate per acre, or by exchange of land.   I need not
further define or describe what you know, and what is fully
shown in the agreement and in the sketch.   Mr Spindler,
some time ago, standing near our dam, said, " Procure Apple
Drift and raise this dam ten feet, and you can place Hankey
and Newlands also beyond all want as to supply of water."
At once, however, as soon as the purchase was made, he
came to me, taking it for granted, as it were, that we were
to put up a very great embankment—at least twenty-five feet
high !   Then we could do so and so.

Now I am for nothing of this extensive sort.   We have
now a splendid natural dam at Apple Drift.   I propose to
add to it an earth or clay dam, in short, go on with what
nature has been doing, and then lead out from Apple Drift
to our present Hankey furrow.   This taps a water supply
hitherto untouched.

Then I would raise our present dam and put it in thorough
order and keep it as a reservoir of reserve water for a time of
drought.

If it were thought worth while, another dam or reservoir
could afterwards be made where Mr Spindler intended to
have his dam, or at other convenient spot on the river course,
raising every dam so as to connect with Hankey furrow.

In short, from Apple Drift downwards, there could be and
doubtless will be a series of dams or reservoirs for the storage
of water ; while out of Apple Drift itself is carried on the
usual work of irrigation.   We can work ahead and know we
are going right, and then we must advance slowly.   The
outlay connected with this purchase, beyond the price
mentioned in the enclosed agreement, will be confined to a
furrow from Apple Drift to our present Hankey furrow ; and
the enclosing of the piece of land which Mr Young requested, and which will be as advantageous to one side as
the other.

I need not tell you what this bargain really means.   It
means the irrigation of Newlands, as far as our land goes, I
believe ; and it means the irrigation of Thorndale as it has
not been irrigated before, at anyrate, in dry years.

Mr Hultzer thinks it would pay if you cabled your consent,
as natives wish to live in Newlands this season.   Mr Spindler,
it seems, said to Mr Hultzer, "This lightens my Gamtoos
scheme wonderfully."

The word *consent* would be enough in your cable, and certainly you will never have consented to anything of equal importance to the Hankey of the future.—Believe me, ever yours sincerely,   JOHN MACKENZIE.

HANKEY, *April 27th*, 1892.

DEAR MR THOMPSON,—Hankey has just been visited by an unusual downpour of rain. The Klein River is "down" in great force, and the little Bingo, which you remember just beyond the village on your way to Mr Young's, has come down in a volume quite unknown to anyone in Hankey. It has caused the death of one of the people, a man, and an excellent swimmer, who must have attempted to cross it on his way home, as being only the Bingo. His body was recovered this morning in the bed of the Klein River below the bridge. The bridge, of course, is temporarily a bridge no more, but a log of wood floating in the Klein River, moored to a tree by a chain.

The Bingo rose to such a height as to carry clean away the wooden aqueduct by which the water furrow for our gardens and lands is brought along. This was seen by some of the people, who acted well and rescued the component parts of the wooden furrow or aqueduct. They are now lying on the bank on this side, not much injured, only battered here and there.

This accident has precipitated what must have taken place soon—the taking down of these wooden troughs in order to enlarge them so as to let an increased flow of water come down, and also to raise them, so as to make of more use the dam at the corner of my garden. At the present level of the big furrow it soon holds as much as the level of the furrow permits. Now we want more water in this distributing dam, and in order to get it, it must be fed by a furrow at a higher level. We have, Mr Spindler informs me, a fall of nearly six feet between our present dam and this distributing dam. Two feet would be enough, so we can raise our furrow, and thus place at the people's disposal a large supply of water, at the bare cost of the enlargement and strengthening of the wooden aqueduct now out of order at anyrate, and the adding to the inner side of the village furrow a sufficient embankment to bring down the quantity of water which we want.

Instead of putting in those light wooden poles in the bed

of the Bingo, and to be again at the mercy of its torrent, I
propose, by the advice of all the great authorities here, to
get, if possible, three ship's beams which would be long
enough to reach from one bank to the other. They are
usually to be had at Port Elizabeth on reasonable terms,
being from wrecks. So we are writing by this post to try
and secure them and the necessary timber to enlarge the
water-shoot.

Sunday before last I was to have been up the Gamtoos
River, but our deacon Solomon Felix, sent a note to recommend that I postpone my visit till last Sunday, in order to
give more people notice. I did so, and went up last Saturday, accompanied by Mr Ingram. I was advised to write to
Mr Gert Kok, a farmer at Quagg, who has the best place for
holding a service. I did so, and was well received and
entertained by him. The place is used by him as a store,
but in a few minutes, by willing hands, it is changed into a
place of worship, and on this occasion Mr Kok's sister
speedily covered with cloth the packing-case which served as
a pulpit. I believe the place holds some 200, and it was
quite full. A third of the number, perhaps, were Europeans.
The morning and afternoon services were in Dutch, so that
all could understand. After the morning service we had a
meeting of the members of the native church, at which the
names of two deacons were approved of for their district.
The Europeans are, of course, chiefly members of the
Humansdorp Dutch Reformed Church, and I understand
the Rev. Mr Groenewald, their pastor, occasionally visits
Quagg and holds services in this large room. I found they
had no appliances for an evening meeting, which I should
have been glad to hold in English. So Mr Ingram and I
resolved to come home, as the clouds were threatening up
the Gamtoos. It was well we did, or otherwise we should
still have been on the wrong side of the river.

Next Sunday, according to a promise of long standing, I
am going to Kreisfontein, that is, if the Gamtoos River kindly
falls and permits me to cross. I shall then be in a position
to enquire into the matters of the loan and the bond held by
Mr Dahl, concerning which I have received, in a letter from
Mr Mudie, a copy of the Directors' resolutions, and your
accompanying remarks. You may trust to me to do my best
in the matter.—With kindest regards, yours sincerely,

JOHN MACKENZIE.

The following letter refers to one of the few occasions when Mackenzie gave himself a "day off" for sight-seeing and recreation :—

HANKEY, 25*th May* 1892.

MY DEAR MR OATES,—I have only time to say to-day that I shall do my best for Mr —— ; and I think he will get on well if he adapts himself to the circumstances which I described to you.

. . . .

We are jogging on here, making some progress, I trust. We had a day's outing yesterday, and went to the top of the hill in our neighbourhood, from which we could get a grand view of the Gamtoos River, above and below Hankey. From a point still higher (which some of us visited a week ago) we could see the ocean dashing against the coast to our south— not more than some 12 or 14 miles as the crow flies. But yesterday we went for the view of the winding Gamtoos, and not for the far-off view.

The road was frightful. Some of our party went in an ox-waggon. Mrs Mackenzie and one of the girls went in our Cape cart. But no conveyance would be easy on such a road. We got home, however, without any accident, and I rather pleased with the doings of the two horses which had to pull the cart.

There is said to be a Bushman's cave in our neighbourhood, with drawings—almost unknown. Indeed it may be mythical. We must first explore and ascertain facts before we organise a party.

But time has come, and I must close. We all join in kind regards.—Ever yours sincerely,   JOHN MACKENZIE.

During the year 1892, he had the pleasure of receiving as an assistant and pupil, Mr G. Cullen H. Reed, a son of the late Rev. Andrew Reed, B.A., London, and a grandson of Mackenzie's old and most valued friend, the Rev. G. D. Cullen, M.A., of Edinburgh. Mr Reed, who had had a training as an engineer, proved himself of the greatest value to Mackenzie, both as an adviser and a practical assistant in the work which had to be carried through ; for after Mr Spindler left Hankey, there fell to Mackenzie's hands once more, as a necessary task, the superintendence of practical building and engineering work.

When Mr Reed left, in the beginning of the next year, Mackenzie wrote, saying :—

We are all sorry to part from Mr Reed. I shall miss him most. He was truly my right hand man, and I don't know how much he saved me in every way he could.

Just before Mr Reed left, Mackenzie had written as follows :—

Jany. 29, 1893.—Mr Reed is likely to leave us soon now. I have taken all the services to-day, and I daresay I shall find it pretty stiff.

It can only be considered as a calamity to Mackenzie's own life, as well as to the efficiency of his work, that no successor to Mr Reed was found and sent out at this time.

One of Mackenzie's chief aims in regard to Hankey was to secure its connection with Port Elizabeth by a railway. He knew that in days to come Cape Town must itself be connected with Port Elizabeth by a much shorter route than that which at present goes around through De Aar. If he could hasten the building of even part of this railway he would help to bring that consummation nearer, and at the same time take the longest step towards the industrial development of Hankey and other similar spots on the southern coast. To further this aim he stirred up a strong local agitation, corresponded personally with the Government officers at Cape Town, and even went, accompanied by Mr Hultzer, as a deputation, to wait upon the Department and urge their plea.

He assisted in drawing up the petition from the railway committee at Hankey to Sir James Sievewright, Commissioner of Crown Lands and Public Works.

The most obvious argument was based, of course, upon the prosperity of the people, the increase of the products from that district, and the promise of greater development if the railway communication were granted to them ; but a still stronger argument based this appeal to the Government upon the fact that the Department of Public Works proposed to enter upon expensive irrigation schemes in other districts of the Colony. These schemes could only be made remunerative to the Government of the Colony if they were made tributary to its railway system. If, therefore, the Government would be forced to build railways for the districts which were yet to be irrigated, at its own expense, how much more should this be done for a district like Hankey, where local enterprise and industry had really created an extensive irrigation system and produced a condition of affairs deserving not only of praise, but of practical encouragement.

It was with great delight that Mackenzie heard, after long consideration and discussion, that a survey of the district was being undertaken, although the actual building of the railway must be postponed. He had to be content with some minor improvements in the way of better district roads, and some valuable bridge building.

Another discussion which Mackenzie had with the Government may be described here, for the light it throws upon yet another side of his own varied activities in Hankey. The nearest doctor, when the Mackenzies arrived there, lived twenty miles away ; and many hardships were endured around them in consequence of this.

A movement in 1896, for the appointment by Government of a district surgeon at Hankey, led to the following letter :—

HANKEY, 26th May 1896.

Dr Turner, etc., etc.,
Board of Health, Cape Town.

SIR,—I beg to bring under your notice the neglected condition of this district as to medical advice and attendance. I may mention that a petition from the people of the district was sent to Government some time ago on the subject, and that more recently I directed the present Colonial Secretary's attention to it.

At the last census there were over 1200 people in Hankey and neighbourhood. Both sides of the Gamtoos River—above us and below us—support a large population.

There is at present only one district surgeon, who resides at the village of Humansdorp.

Our request is that a second district surgeon should be appointed for a subdivision of Humansdorp district, who should reside in Hankey, and who should have charge of the Eastern part of this wide district.

I have carried our request beyond this, and represented to Government that, instead of being left as we are at present, there should not only be a district surgeon here, but that a Government assistant dispensary should also be opened at this central place for the benefit of the poor among both white and coloured people.

Although we are fifty miles from Port Elizabeth, the coloured people of Hankey are very closely connected with that town, as servants, etc. It is natural that when they become ill there they should come home; but once here they are beyond the reach of such medical attendance as they can pay for. I need hardly say that it is a very serious thing for people with diseases contracted in a seaport remaining without suitable medical attendance.

Then, with reference to the registration of deaths, the alleged cause of death among this very considerable population is at present only the guess of unskilled people.

To myself this subject has also a personal reference, which I must not omit.

When a missionary in Bechuanaland I was for many years accustomed to attend medically, not only my own family, but European traders and hunters, as well as the natives in whose country I was living. When I came to Hankey in 1891 nothing was further from my mind than that I should be called upon to prescribe for ailing people. But I soon found it was otherwise. Both white and coloured people begged my assistance, and I had not the heart to refuse. I could not but see that when the travelling expenses were added to a doctor's bill, it would be beyond the means of those people—of many of the white people as well as of the coloured people.

Dr Beckett, who was in poor health at the time, settled in Hankey last year. Of course, when he arrived I ceased entirely to have anything to do with medicine, taking everybody over to the doctor's house.

We first petitioned for Government assistance while Dr Beckett was living here. When no favourable reply came to our request Dr Beckett removed from Hankey. Matters here have reverted to their former most unsatisfactory condition. I am attending people and administering medicine every day, not only spending a considerable portion of my time and not a small amount of my own money on medicine but liable to be told, and I suppose to be told correctly, that I am breaking the law of the Colony.

Now I am entirely unwilling to go on with this, and I feel sure the Cape Colony Government is in a position to do better than this for the people of this district.

I am told that in other parts of the Colony similar subdivisions of districts have taken place. I am told also that special arrangements have been made elsewhere for the assistance of really poor people to procure medicine and medical attendance. I beg to call your special attention to our case, and hope you will be able to assist us. I should have addressed you earlier, but was ignorant of the scope of your duties.

The case, as I have said, is in the Colonial Secretary's hands. As he is a medical man himself I am counting upon the sympathy of Dr Te Water, and feel sure that on full enquiry both you and he will be convinced that the small extra outlay in granting our request will be more than repaid by the improved and satisfactory condition of the district from a medical point of view.—I have the honour to remain, your obedient servant, JOHN MACKENZIE.

The following extract from a letter written by one who had a good opportunity of watching Mackenzie at work in this little community for a while, gives a vivid account of the manner of his procedure :—

He can wait, and if you cannot do that here, you are not good for much. The things he has had to stand, the bickerings, trials, small intrigues, and insults, are incredible. They would have sent some other man mad in a month. And what has come of it all? He has the rudder in his hand,

and he practically steers everything. And the funny thing is, that all the steering is done through the people themselves, through advice, hints, new ideas sown amongst them. In all public meetings, board meetings, etc., Mr Mackenzie is present, although he does not always take the chair. He conducts the meetings all the same. He sits at the top of the hall, amongst the people, and sets one idea starting in one direction, and another in another, then caps them with his own speech, and so carries the affair on. It is a perfect study to an onlooker. And what is the result of it all? Why, the place is changed. Hankey is getting known. Farmers who never looked at each other before are now on visiting, and in some cases, intimate terms.

Throughout these varied activities Mackenzie's interest in his purely religious work never flagged. He would sit for hours in the evening with a group of native deacons, working over the minutest details connected with the pastoral supervision of his wide parish. His preaching, of which we shall speak again later, was always very practical and intensely earnest. It seems to have reached its highest mark on communion Sundays. In preparation for the celebration of the Lord's Supper, and at the Table itself, whose significance he ever revered most humbly and most deeply, his manner became peculiarly tender and his voice thrilled with emotion. And Mackenzie had the joy of seeing the fruits of his labours as a preacher of the Gospel. Not only was the religious life of some of the Europeans visibly and avowedly deepened; he also received considerable additions of the coloured people into membership of the church from time to time. He was not one, however, who at any period of his missionary career felt it right to speak of the numbers whom he had led to Christ.

He made frequent visits to the out-stations and distant parts of the district under his care. On some of these occasions his services were conducted in peculiar places and under trying circumstances. The following descriptions of two or three incidents by one of his daughters, Mrs E. D. Sheilds, help us to realise more vividly the actual work :

THORNHILL

One Sunday my father and I spent at Thornhill.

During the week the news had passed from farm to farm that on Sunday "Meinheer" would preach. By courtesy of the blacksmith these services were held in the smithy, a long plank building with iron roof and two doors opposite each other.

We walked up from the inn about a mile distant, enjoying as we went the luxuriance of the vegetation and the green-ness of the grass after the recent rains. As we came near to the smithy, clouds of dust were issuing from the doors, for the native deacon was sweeping it out. Accustomed to the irregularity caused by differences in time, we spread a plaid in the shade of a tree and rested. In time the natives assembled and sat on seats formed by planks resting at each end on naves of wheels. When we entered we found about thirty natives, labourers from adjoining farms. At the back of the smithy stood a Cape cart in course of being mended.

Two chairs were placed near the anvil with their backs towards the empty furnace and in full light of the two doors. A table was in front of the chair used by my father. The other chair, as I had declined it, was occupied by the deacon.

The small congregation was composed of people of all ages, women carrying babies, old men, youths, and large boys with that almost preternatural solemnity with which black boys are gifted.

The service was simple, and the address in Dutch listened to with deep attention. I remember that the preacher was trying to impress on their minds a sense of the reality of the spiritual life. He said to them "When you look at me, what do you see? Do you think you see me? You see my body but me you cannot see. My body is my home while I am on the earth. When we die, we leave the empty shell behind, we do not die."

Thus in simple words he raised their minds to the contemplation of the life beyond this and of the hopes of the Christian.

KLEINFONTEIN FUNERAL

At Kleinfontein, about six miles from Hankey, a sad accident had happened. A farmer's son had been gored to death by a buck which he had wounded a few minutes before.

It was summertime and very hot; yet because the road to the place was too bad for a Cape cart my father decided to ride. Accompanied by Mr Ingram and Mr George Crawford, we had a ride over the hills in the burning sun.

At last we came to the edge of a cliff, and away down in the valley below us lay the white farmhouse and its out-buildings. On the sward around the house were the waggons, carts and horses of those attending the funeral. In order to reach the house we had to dismount and lead the horses down a steep decline, almost too rough and steep for us to walk down ourselves; at the bottom we remounted and crossed a rocky stream.

It is extremely difficult for me to realize that at that time my father was fifty-eight years of age. Now I can see that for a man of his age this kind of travelling was much too trying.

In front of the house, in the shade of a tree, the funeral service was held. When amid deep silence the beautiful voice had spoken words of comfort and hope, the sad procession was formed. The coffin was carried by the dead youth's "mates," as the Dutch would put it, up a narrow red path and laid in a grave on the hillside in view of the house. The burial service was read and the customary handfuls of earth were thrown in, rushes were strewed on the coffin, and we returned to the homestead.

After an interval in which coffee and cake were handed round, there was a general "inspanning" of horses and oxen and a saddling up of riding horses. We rode home through the valleys—for there were more than one—in the evening sunshine, having to cross the same stream half-a-dozen times, as the road wound downwards with the river.

FINGO CHURCH

It was summertime. The sun had set, illuminating with golden light the fertile valley, the red kranzes, and the distant mountains. In the village the usual evening occupations were being concluded. The natives who had cows or goats had milked them, and put them in the kraals made of thorn bushes or of aloe hedge. At last the many sounds of village life gave place to a quiet which was broken only now and then by sounds of laughter or of talking, and here and there the lights of the cottages shone out.

We also had had our cows milked and led into the cow-shed. The horses came up from their evening drink at the stream. My father, walking or standing in the large yard with one of his daughters or a grandchild with him, looked with critical eye at the animals, patted and spoke to one or other of them, and made some remark to the native boy about them. Then we had our evening meal, the hour of which followed in primitive fashion the coming on of darkness. This evening we were slightly earlier than usual, as my father had to go over to a meeting in the Fingo Church.

The native minister, whose name is Nathaniel Matodlana, had on different occasions had troublous times in his church. Many a time he came over and held long talks with my father, receiving the help he sought. On this occasion he had asked my father to go over and listen to the discussion of some irritating question by the native deacons and advise with them.

I went to keep my father company. We had to drive in the starlight, through the river and up the steep hill to the Fingo village where the white church shone through the dark. We entered the church and waited for a time till the deacons dropped in, dressed in their Sunday clothes.

The discussion was carried on in two languages, Dutch and Kaffir. Those of the deacons who could only speak Kaffir fluently were interpreted by their minister into Dutch. Now and then my father would put a question to him in English, which he also knew well.

One after another the disputants rose and spoke, vehemently or not as the case might be, but all lengthily and some with a certain rough oratory. Time passed, and my father sat almost silent while the case was being argued out. Now and then he rose and brought them back to the point at issue, perhaps making clear to them the position they had reached and giving them a lead in the right direction. As time wore on lines of physical tiredness showed themselves on his face, but no sign of haste or wish to curtail matters was visible.

I had been watching the scene from a side bench, with the eye of one gazing on a picture of the struggle between good and evil, between light and darkness. The full light of the one hanging lamp shone on the grand head, the hair nearly white, the noble brow and the strong, patient, tired face. Before him, the first row in full light, the second row half in the shadow, were the dark faces of eight or nine men, with evil passions struggling for mastery.

At last, after a discussion of nearly three hours' duration, they were addressed by " Meinheer," whom they all honoured. The case was summed up by him, his conclusions based on reasons made clear to them. Then came the fresh cool air, the drive home, the splashing of the water, as the eager horses trotted into the river.

While Mackenzie was thus engaged in the industrial and spiritual development of the community, he was also deeply interested in, as well as responsible for the educational work. The district school, which was annually visited by a Government inspector, and which earned a Government grant, was watched over by him with very great care, especially as his own daughters became teachers in it. He had not been in Hankey long before extensive educational plans began to germinate in his mind. If Hankey was to become a rich, fruit-farming district, connected by railway with Port Elizabeth, and later with Cape Town, why should it not also become a great educational centre, the Lovedale of that portion of the Colony? The Society owned a rich estate, which could be made in many ways to subserve such an enterprise. In his imagination he saw arising there a school for the general education and manual training of coloured boys and girls ; who should be sent out thoroughly fitted for an active and earnest life as school-workers, and whose exertions should help to stir ambitions in the sluggish hearts of other members of their race. He saw also an advanced school for the training of native preachers, a theological institution that should provide trained men for the ordained ministry among the coloured churches.

In the last year of his life he was working upon this project for a school, and carried on constant correspondence concerning it, not only with the Directors of the Society in London, but with his old friend Mr Henry Beard of Cape Town. From a very interesting account of his relations with Mackenzie and estimate of his life-work and character, kindly supplied by Mr Beard, the following paragraphs may be selected as relevant here :—

Of these results in reference to the temporalities at Hankey, a London merchant of large business experience, who visited Hankey in 1897, in the interests of the London Missionary Society, wrote to me in the following words : "John Mackenzie is doing well; he is consolidating the estate and when he leaves, I am confident it will be more valuable than ever it was." To his friends it must be one of the perplexing instances of the fact that God's "thoughts are not our thoughts," to find that he was not permitted to carry out these projects, to the conception and advocacy of which he had given so much time and thought, during the later years of his administration of Hankey Mission Station. He cleared the ground and laid the foundations, and "another buildeth thereon."

The nature of the projects alluded to and the considerations by which they were supported, are strikingly illustrative of the character of one who was eminently a practical man of shrewd common sense, and yet was always moving on the plane of the higher life and with a simple directness pursuing the highest ends. Mr Mackenzie was of opinion that the estate could be profitably devoted to fruit-growing. He looked for this to be carried out by means of a commercial association in the hands of business men, who would work the industry on lines that would yield a moderate return on the capital, but who would not be indifferent to the interests of the labourers, whose advantage was Mr Mackenzie's primary aim.   In a memorandum on the whole subject, he made suggestions as to two modes of dealing with the matter from the business point of view, but he added, " You will not expect me to go into the strain of a company floater "—a bit of quiet humour, very characteristic.   For to anyone who knew him, nothing could be more amusing than this ironical suggestion of John Mackenzie as a company promoter.   He was content, having pointed out the way in such matters, to leave the carrying out to others, while he busied himself with other aspects of the project, the higher interests which it was to subserve.   Still, while turning his attention more to the details of those higher interests, he looked to the fruit-growing scheme as one not simply to bring regular wages to his people, but to " introduce fresh ideas and liberal thoughts."   Another of his proposals was for the establishment at Hankey of a school of higher grade than the mission school, for the children of the better class in the coloured churches throughout the colony, with manual training for both girls and boys.   In connection with this, he proposed to have a class for Evangelists, eventually from those who had attended the school, who would be qualified for their work by a course of sound Biblical instruction, supplemented by Evangelistic work in the neighbourhood. While submitting his schemes to the London Missionary Society and his friends, he proceeded to have the bricks made for the four to six cottages which were to be provided for the Evangelists.   He reported that these bricks were made as payment of what otherwise would be bad debts, and that if his proposals are not accepted, which he cannot anticipate, the bricks can be sold—a worthy example of Scottish prudence in pushing a forward policy.   This project of religious education he urged upon the Missionary Society, as a fitting development and coping-stone of all its earlier work in the Colony, from which it is finally withdrawing. In the same memorandum he detailed the wants of the Dutch-speaking and the Fingo coloured people, and proposed to provide adequately for the pastoral care of both, and even of European residents, as a part of the whole scheme and in connection with the foregoing.   There is the impress of the man of broad views throughout the entire document and its proposals.

The Institution of Hankey is to be for the enrichment

of South Africa, because it would come to be a centre of more valuable influence in a country which is undoubtedly so much in need of it. The presence of missionaries coming direct from England is to be desired, not only for the sake of the churches that they serve, but because it has a beneficial effect on colonial society, when "there is a strong tendency in the Cape Colony to level downwards towards the Transvaal policy!"

While it is true, as we have seen, that Mackenzie was able to watch some of the best blessings flowing from his labours in Hankey, it ought to be said that he was not one of those who cherish an impatient eagerness for a visible and personal triumph, or even for palpable and measurable "results." Two extracts bearing on this very point may be given here from letters to his dear friend, Mr Charles G. Oates :—

HANKEY, 13*th Dec.* 1895.

Allow me, dear friend, to send you very warm greetings at the close of the year, and best wishes for 1896 and for all your future. It has occurred to me to mention to you what I have often taken to heart as a lesson : that *results* are in the hands of God. It is for us to do our work faithfully —that is our part. When we come short in that, as alas! we do, we must be humbled and sorry ; but as to the results, they are not our department—they are in God's hands.

June 25, 1897.

There is one thought in connection with this that I want to mention to you, if I have not done so before, and it is this. I think you did all your share of what might have been a most gratifying success. The actual outcome does not change what you did ; that lies with others ; and part of it with Him who is over us all, and whose orderings, however mysterious and at times disappointing, are yet the expression of a Father's wisdom and love. A succession of bad seasons, and the approach of an insidious disease, combined to make commercial success impossible to poor —— ——. From all I can gather, however, he himself seems to have become more spiritually minded during his last illness.

During the Hankey years, Mackenzie's domestic
life had some elements of joy and some of sorrow
which he had hardly tasted before. He now had
a home for his daughters, to which also two of his
sons were able to make occasional visits, and in
which he had the peculiar and tender delight of
sometimes seeing little grandchildren running about.
He, of course, won their hearts as completely as they
won his.   In January 1895, he, for the first time,
gave away one of his daughters in marriage, when
Jane Alice became the wife of James Campbell
Rodger, now of Bulawayo, Rhodesia.   He passed
through a very strange and painful experience, however, when he received a succession of announcements
from Scotland within a few weeks or months of each
other, of the deaths of his own brother and his four
sisters.   To this he refers in a letter which he wrote
to Mr Charles Oates, regarding the death of his remaining brother, Mr W. E. Oates :—

HANKEY, CAPE COLONY,
5th May 1896.

MY DEAR FRIEND,—Your letter with the very sad news
from Madeira has just come to hand; and I have the
opportunity of at once acknowledging it.   I have also
received the *Suffolk and Essex Free Press*, which contains
some mention of your brother as known to his neighbours.
. . . I send you this note at once, to be, as it were, a grasp
of the hand, at this time of great sorrow which has come to
you.   Mrs Mackenzie and I deeply sympathise with your
sister-in-law in her deep affliction, and my heart is sore for
the dear children who lose so tender and loving a father.

Do not lose heart in your loneliness—grasp the pilgrim-
staff more firmly.   Each one of us must work out his day
resolutely and with his very best efforts.   The Master has
still something for us to do.   Others drop from our side;
we work and wait his call.   I think I mentioned to you
that soon after I came here my only brother and four
sisters—all of them older than myself—followed one another
within a short time to the grave.   It made a deep and, I

trust, abiding impression on my mind, as the solitary remaining one of the family. But some time after, in writing to a young friend about this, I remarked that, notwithstanding what had happened, I might live to be as old as Old Parr. Each one is immortal till his work is done.—We join in sincerest sympathy, and I remain ever yours sincerely,

JOHN MACKENZIE.

CHAPTER XIX

AFRICA—LAST CONTRIBUTIONS TO IMPERIAL POLITICS (1892-1898)

WHEN Mackenzie went to Hankey, he knew that his political history was practically at an end, that from that spot he could never continuously influence public opinion, either at home or in South Africa. And indeed, as we have seen, the work which he had undertaken was so extensive and so absorbing that for many months he hardly allowed himself to read the newspapers, or to think of the outside world. But as affairs at Hankey came gradually under control, his mind could not but return to the wider interests with which he had been so closely identified. From the year 1892 his correspondence in various directions shows how closely he watched political events, and how earnestly he tried, in what ways were possible to him, to reach the minds of those who wielded power in London or at Cape Town.

In 1895 he welcomed Mr Chamberlain to the Colonial Office with peculiar delight and expectancy. At this time he wrote to his third son, now a barrister at Kimberley, as follows :—

HANKEY, *2nd July* 1895.

MY DEAR JIM,—It is a wonderful change from Lord Ripon to Mr Chamberlain at the Colonial Office. Annexation is not now quite where it would have been, or might have been in Ripon's hands.

Of course, it will depend on what has been done by the late ministry.

So far as I am personally concerned, there is no first-class statesman who has so identified himself with my views as Mr Chamberlain has done. It so happens that a letter of mine to him is now on the ocean, referring to annexation especially, and saying what I think should be done. This was, of course, to enable him effectually to oppose the expulsion of the Imperial Government from active affairs in South Africa; for that is what Mr Rhodes really means— the Cape Colony to get one slice, and the Chartered Company the other slice, of old Bechuanaland.

It may all happen yet; but it is not quite so likely now. We are all in God's hands. I hear from Bechuanaland that people—white people—informed Reuter, Cape Town, that a petition (or petitions) was in circulation against annexation. Reuter did not publish the information; but he published the views of a Mr Theal who is up there, and wired them over the Colony. This gentleman is, I believe, a land surveyor, and has a right to his view, which is for annexation.

Shortly after Mr Chamberlain's appointment, two remarkable events occurred, which focussed attention upon the new Secretary. The first was the re-appointment of Sir Hercules Robinson (later Lord Rosmead), as High Commissioner for South Africa and Governor of Cape Colony. There can be no doubt that this most unexpected step was taken at the instance of Mr Rhodes, and that its fruit was seen in a few months' time, when the Jameson Raid occurred.

The other event was the visit to England of three Bechuanaland chiefs, of whom, of course, the best known and most powerful was Khame. They went to England expressly to protest against the proposal that North Bechuanaland should be handed over by the Imperial Government to the Chartered Company.

It is aside from our story to narrate the interesting and impressive progress which Khame made through England and Scotland, and the agreement at which

Mr Chamberlain arrived, by which a strip of Khame's territory on his eastern border—which was not to exceed, at its widest, ten miles—was handed over to the Company for the purpose of building a railway to Bulawayo. It was in connection with the proposed annexation of North Bechuanaland, which Khame's visit defeated, that Mackenzie wrote the following important letter to Mr Chamberlain :—

HANKEY, CAPE COLONY,
24th July 1895.

DEAR MR CHAMBERLAIN,—I regard it as remarkable that I should have felt moved to write to you as I did some weeks ago on South African affairs. I had been silent for years. But the time to speak out and prevent weak people from doing wrong, partly from ignorance, partly from weakness, seemed to have come. Little did I think that my letter would find you in charge of the Colonial Department. Of course, so far as pushing one's views is concerned, I have been personally out of it since 1891. But the views remain ; they are those of all leading minds. The wonder is, however, that Mr Rhodes has not sooner had his way, so persistent are his people and so heedless as to their statements. You will be confronted with the question of the disposal of Bechuanaland, the Protectorate, and Khame's country.

As to the Crown Colony, you have it quite in your choice to hold it in Imperial hands, although the Cape Parliament has agreed to take it over. You will thank them for that kind offer, but it is one of those points on which you would wish to have more light, before taking so important a step.

The opposition in Bechuanaland to the annexation to the Cape Colony is too serious for Her Majesty's Government to proceed hastily with that measure. As to the Protectorate and Khame's country, the whole of that territory has, in your view, occupied the same position since 1885, in connection with Her Majesty's Government. The Chief Khame was taken specially under Her Majesty's Protection ; and the Earl of Derby, the then Secretary of State, specially requested that the chief should then be acquainted with that fact, and

that the Protection should be a real one. This was done,
Sir C. Warren visiting Khame personally.[1] Thus in 1885
we took under our protection a chief whose territory extended
northward to the River Zambesi.

Nothing that map-makers could afterwards do in London, in
the way of colouring maps, could interfere with this historical
establishment of an Imperial Protectorate over Khame in
1885.

Mr Rhodes ought to be well content with the territories of
Lobengula, Mashonaland and Matabeleland, which his
Company has secured by conquest, a conquest in which
he was very materially assisted by the Imperial Government.
He may have indisputable titles to a great many things north
of the Zambesi; I don't know. But he has no title at all, and
practically not a leg to stand on, in Bechuanaland Protectorate or Khame's country. I consider that the thing is unheard
of, that an Imperial Protectorate, against the wishes of all its
people, should be handed over by the Imperial Government
to a commercial company. Why, even the Cape Parliament
speakers in the recent debate called this a hole-and-corner
proceeding. At present the Imperial Government is synonymous with weakness and unreliableness. It is openly reviled
out here by such men as Mr Rhodes. I should dearly like to
see this all changed. It would be easy to make the Imperial
Government well-liked by both natives and Dutch-speaking
people if our Government were in charge of such a country as
we are now speaking of. The natives would get justice and
would have confidence, the unoccupied tracts of country
would be opened up and used by settlers. The Government
of this Colony would soon come to take up a position of
influence in South Africa, and a distinct advance would be
given to a future confederation of South Africa. I need not
say, what I have often said before, that this is without doubt
the natural destiny of the country; but that nothing tends to
hinder this more than the present movements of Mr Rhodes
and his policy, and that of Sir H. Robinson, of always
aggrandizing the Cape Colony. The other countries won't be
sat upon, they will not consent, they have finally refused to
be swallowed up by the Cape Colony. I beg to tender my
sincere congratulations to you on filling the office, which I
remember you once told me it would be your desire to fill, if

---

[1] See "Austral Africa," ii., 209, 210.   Blue Book, C. 4432, p. 48.

ever you came to be offered a seat in a Cabinet. I trust you will leave your mark in Downing Street, and especially influence its officials as Englishmen, to be ashamed of being outdone and superseded by the officials of a Chartered Company—Englishmen like themselves, and, like themselves, responsible to the British House of Commons.—Ever yours,   JOHN MACKENZIE.

Concerning the Jameson Raid itself, Mackenzie remained almost entirely silent. Like all lovers of South Africa, he felt the shock to the depths of his soul. He refers to Mr Chamberlain's attitude in passing allusions, and speaks most highly of his firmness, dignity, and courage. But the revelations which occurred from month to month, and culminated in the disclosures before the Committee of the House of Commons, never received any sustained criticism, as far as can be found, from his pen.

At the close of the year 1895, he was asked by the editor of *The Contemporary Review* to write an article, which he did, upon the British South African Company, with special reference to its conduct of the first war, and its native policy in Matabeleland and Mashonaland.

This article appeared in *The Contemporary Review* for March 1896, and it attracted a great deal of attention, both in England and in Cape Colony. Having gained direct information from many sources, and possessing a close personal knowledge, not only of the country of which he spoke, but of the customs and prejudices of the native races, he was able to estimate the conduct of the Company with peculiar authority. He says that he had been silent regarding the Company, avoiding all criticism of a public character, for seven years; but that he felt the time had now come for passing judgment upon the manner in which it had fulfilled the task assumed by it and laid upon it by the Imperial Government. He found that his own predictions had been abundantly fulfilled, and his worst fears realised. The Company's affairs were conducted by men who did not possess the imperial spirit, nor acted towards subject races as British Imperial officers are universally expected to act.

In the first section of his article Mackenzie described the earlier methods of the Company in opening up Mashonaland for its European settlers. It did not appear that even in relation to the white men who entered under its ægis, the Company's policy was broad-minded and successful. Before long these white men found that the conditions of life were harder and the prospects of profitable gold-mining were poorer than they had been led to expect. The Company was unable to open up its mines in Mashonaland so as to make profitable returns. On the other hand, the Company found itself in a country where the native population was ready to give it a warm welcome. Industrious workers in iron and cotton who had been long oppressed by the cruel Matabele were led to expect that the Company, representing England, would bring peace and justice with it to their land. It was through the position of protector of the Mashonas that the Company was first brought into conflict with the Matabele. The Matabele resented the Company's interference with their custom of massacring the Mashonas, and turned upon their white protectors. The result was the invasion of Matabeleland by the Company, with the aid of Imperial forces operating from the south-west. The Matabele were mowed down by the Maxim guns, and at last, finding themselves unable to come to close quarters with their enemy, gave up in despair, and fled. This victory gave the Company for the first time the sovereignty of the whole country. This was a splendid opportunity for "establishing their claim to supersede the Imperial Government." Alas, the Company's administrators struck out a native policy " entirely at variance with what is generally known as British native policy." Mackenzie says : " It is capable of proof that the Company's management of native affairs has been a complete failure." This strong indictment he argues with abundance of evidence from actual events, which he cites through five pages of the article. The most foolish feature in the administration of the Company was its enrolment and drill of six or seven hundred young Matabele soldiers to act as native police, and the removal southward before the Jameson Raid " of so many white men with guns and ammunition—all of which eventually fell into the hands of President Kruger." · The darkest spot in their policy was, to Mackenzie's mind, their method of compelling the natives to work in the service of the Company. Their effort " to re-establish forced labour in South Africa as a permanent institution " was, he maintains, without reason, there being no ground for the complaint that there was a scarcity of labour.

Regarding the relation of the Company to Cape Colony, Mackenzie had some things to say which involved continual reference to the personality of Mr Rhodes ; for the link of connection between the two was to be found in the fact that he was at that time both manager of the Chartered Company and Prime Minister of the Cape Colony. He had some more strong things to say regarding the claim that Mr Rhodes " had been allaying race feeling in the Cape Colony." The process of amalgamation of the races he showed to have been going on steadily and naturally without any assistance from any one individual human being, and he believed that the process would go on faster if men would cease to discuss it as if racial hatred were increasing instead of disappearing. Mr

Rhodes as a Cape politician had won the admiration
" of two opposing parties in the Cape Colony for
opposite reasons." There was a section of patriotic
Englishmen who believed in his Imperialism, while on
the other hand the Africander Bond " admired and
loved Mr Rhodes because he was so un-English in
his views." " As a politician the late Premier's votes
have always been with the Bond ; sometimes, as on
the Excise question, he has been the only Englishman
voting with them."

The next section discusses the relation of the
Company to the South African Republics, in which
the writer says that it is viewed by them " with the
utmost aversion." He pointed out with great vigour
that the policy of the Chartered Company had actually
led both natives and Dutch Republicans " to call for
the Imperial Government to step in instead of the
Company, and resume the position which it should
never have abdicated." Mackenzie had no doubt that
the policy of the Company, as disclosed by its entire
dealings with the natives, the Colonists, and Republicans, and as fully revealed in the Jameson Raid,
" was to place the Transvaal, and afterwards South
Africa, under the Chartered Company." The Raid
failed, because " the root-idea—the commercial company idea—on which the attempted revolution was
based, was a false one." It " was founded on the idea
that money could do everything." What Mackenzie
described as the conspicuous failure of the Chartered
Company in South Africa, led to the problem of its
future ; and on this point he believed that nothing less
was possible than rescinding the Company's Charter.
This of course would bear merely upon the functions
of Government, leaving the entire and vast work of
developing the rich and extensive gold mines of
Mashonaland and Matabeleland as the sole responsibility of the Company. " In the meantime," he adds,

" the duty and privilege of Britain is in 1897 what it was in 1889—only much emphasised by the history of the intervening years—to administer the affairs of the country in its present stage of development, and to place that administration under the supreme control of those who should not be mixed up with other South African affairs."

It may be added that this article, which very soon passed out of print, not only made a very strong impression upon its readers, but has never received, so far as the present writer knows, an authoritative reply to its deadly criticisms. The following letter refers to it :—

HANKEY, 8th January 1896.

MY DEAR MR OATES,— . . . I have sent home an article on " The Chartered Company in South Africa : A Review and Criticism," which I hope may appear in the *Contemporary* in February.

I have had special and reliable information from Matabeleland, and the facts will, I think, astonish the ordinary English reader. Having the telegraphic wire in their own hands, and having also some English papers ever ready to back them up, the Company has got to occupy a position to which it would appear it has not the slightest title, judging from what it has actually done.

Its native policy has been a complete failure, and a disgrace to Great Britain.

It was almost inconceivable that the long oppressed Mashonas should have sided with their oppressors, the Matabele, rather than with the white men, who, it was supposed, were their friends and protectors. I was for weeks here, refusing to believe that the Mashonas had also risen, till at last the evidence was undeniable.

While our general native policy was such that the Mashonas preferred to fight along with the Matabele rather than assist the white man, in Matabeleland the Company undoubtedly established *forced* labour as a permanent institution. Incredible, you say ; nevertheless the fact. The Company has lowered us far below the Transvaal Boers as to the treatment of the natives.

In short, if Old England stands where she stood as to fair dealing and righteousness, it is impossible that this charter of the Company can be renewed.   Of course that would not interfere with the Company's gold mines, or with their railways, so absolutely indispensable to the profitable working of the mines.

I do not know whether you have noticed it—that the leading men in the Cape Colony have objected to the past methods, while the Transvaal and the Free State have unexpectedly called on the Imperial Government to assume the authority delegated to the Company.   It would certainly give England a position of vantage, so far as those States are concerned, if she assumed the government in the northern country at the call and suggestion of those who are supposed to be so much opposed to our government.—With kindest regards, I am, ever yours sincerely,   JOHN MACKENZIE.

In 1896 Mackenzie's mind was kept brooding over the problem presented by the Transvaal.   The Jameson Raid drew the attention of all thoughtful men to study the conditions in the South African Republic which made such an event possible.   However guilty Mr Rhodes and Dr Jameson had been, it was quite evident that their plan was suggested by the state of affairs at Johannesburg ; and Johannesburg was not composed of a class of people likely to be embroiled in political insurrections either for the sake of amusement or because they were anxious to be " in politics." Quite evidently the leaders of such a community would naturally wish to be let alone to pursue their business ambitions, and would rebel simply when business was being rendered impossible.   Mackenzie, having given much attention to the situation, resolved to embody his conclusions in a letter addressed directly to President Kruger.   As this letter, which he dated from Hankey on June 18, 1896, grew under his hand, he resolved to make it an open letter, written in the first place in Dutch and sent to the leading Dutch papers, but forwarded also in an English form to the English papers.   We have no assurance, of course, that it was ever read to President Kruger, who for some years had made himself dependent almost entirely upon the aid of a private secretary and reader. It is not at all probable that the President's advisers would consider this clear, strong, earnest letter such an one as should reach Mr Kruger's ears.

The letter is constructed on lines which a true South African would recognise at once as being appropriate to a Dutchman's habits of mind and prejudices. As he would be, so it is, frankly religious, basing some of its most powerful pleas upon the principles of righteousness and the sense of responsibility to God. After an introductory paragraph, Mackenzie recalled a former occasion on which he and the President had met ; then he passed to one of his fundamental positions. The Transvaal had indeed been first invaded by the " Voortrekkers," who were farmers, and who there found a land prepared for them. But the country to which they went was a country prepared by the Almighty, not only for the farmer, but for the gold-seeker and the gold-miner. To this idea he returns several times, driving it home in such fashion as to reach the conscience of any open-minded Dutchman. In a later paragraph he says :—

As a matter of fact the Republic is to-day the country of the gold-miner just as it is the country of the farmer, and it is unjust as well as impolitic not to admit this fact in a practical way. The present condition as to population has not been brought about by any human policy or planning ; it has happened in the providence of God ; and it has therefore occurred for the ultimate good of all the inhabitants.

He recognises that President Kruger has, " in God's providence," been called to a very hard task. " David's call from the sheep-cote was not so sudden as the call to Your Honour to rule over this influx of popula-

tion." This influx had found the farmers unready to
meet the new conditions.

With great delicacy Mackenzie attempts to lay the
responsibility for the failure, not upon President
Kruger personally, but upon the unwillingness of his
" farmer Raad " to grant equality to the new people
because they were miners. Then he shows that these
gold-miners came from the best countries in the world,
and were men of education and character, and strikes
hard upon one delicate spot when he asks, " When
did the custom begin, to make a difference among
white men, and to say that some were citizens and
others were not ? " This policy was not only contrary to South African tradition ; it was contrary to
the principles of a republic, " The people of a republic are the real governors of the land." An appeal
was made to the experience of California, and Australia, and New Zealand to prove that it was possible
for farmers and miners to work together prosperously
in the same country ; it could not be to the miners'
advantage to do any harm to the land they lived in
and from which they gained their wealth. Broadly
he says, " The action of the farmers is to blame for
the present unhappy, un-Christian, and dangerous
state of things." Thus he comes upon the use by the
South African Republic of the term " Uitlander " to
describe all new white residents ; and he puts his
finger on another of the sensitive spots in the Transvaal body politic, when he urges that the President is
not consistent in the use of the term, for there are
some new residents strictly " Uitlanders " whom he
receives to full favour, and whom he uses to the detri-
ment of the rest of the " Uitlanders."

It is said, and Your Honour will be able to judge of the
truth of the statement, that the gold-miner is one of those
parties, and the speculative "Uitlander," who lives off the
gold-mining industry is the other. It is freely declared that

Your Honour's Government has been more or less used by the speculative class of "Uitlanders" to enrich themselves at the expense of the real producers of the wealth of the country.

Such an accusation, he urges, could only be silenced by a policy of justice to the miners. He proceeds in succeeding paragraphs to warn President Kruger that there is no possibility of European intervention in the interests of the South African Republic.

They (European Powers) all know that the Republic is, by its own agreement, under the suzerainty of Great Britain. As Great Britain has no mind to retire from that suzerainty, it follows that any competing agreement between the Republic and any other European Power—if such a thing existed—would be regarded by Britain as a hostile action both on Your Honour's part and on the part of the European Power in question.

War would not remove his troubles, but rather create conditions under which they would re-awaken ; and those who brought the war on would carry the responsibility of a shameful undertaking ; " blood would be shed, antipathies roused, the Merciful Saviour of all men—miners as well as farmers— deeply offended, and the beneficial result of it all— nothing, absolutely nothing."

There can be no doubt of the sincere efforts of Her Majesty's Government to allay such warlike feeling, and to lead towards the peaceful settlement of all difficulties. It will be for Your Honour and for your Raad to cherish equal self-restraint, and to lead the minds of the farmer population in the way of peace.

In dealing with recent events, he deeply regrets " the recent invasion of the Republic by the officers and men of the British South African Company." But such events were not in times past unfamiliar to President Kruger. He reminds President Kruger that he himself once " took the field at the head of one

armed section of the burghers against another armed
section of the farmers"; and that he had again been
concerned in 1879 in the movement against the annexation by Great Britain.   In each of these instances he
and his companions felt their cause to be good, and
their warfare righteous ; so felt the miners about their
intended insurrection.   He must not, therefore, mix up
the miners, who only sought to have their grievances
removed, and their political claims recognised, " with
the perfectly unjustifiable actions of the officers of the
Chartered Company."   For Mackenzie, the grim prospects which he describes in a later paragraph, arose
from the fact that President Kruger admitted no
responsibility for the conditions which prompted the
miners to their desperate movement.

" There is no promise of redress of grievances, no regret
expressed, that under Your Honour's Government a body
of intelligent men should have been driven to try an armed
demonstration after every constitutional method had failed."
His present advisers were, he said, " enemies of peace and
goodwill in South Africa."   " The miners are not even like
the mercantile class, members of which often leave the
Republic when their children grow up. . . . The miners are
like the farmers—they have come to stay."

The President ought to face his Raad with a
settled policy in his mind, " of welding together the
two classes of your people by gradual and well
thought out measures."   If they refused, he had
constitutional means for dissolving the Raad and
making an appeal to the burghers, demanding that
if he were to continue their President, they must
change their policy towards the miners ; and this
appeal, Mackenzie would, with all confidence, address
to their Christian conscience.   This conclusion, he
urged, would " be the crowning achievement " in Mr
Kruger's career, by which he would lay " the foundations of a united community at peace within itself,

and in harmony with the general aims and aspirations of the rest of South Africa."

This letter, which appeared in the *Cape Times*, July 20, 1896, was reprinted in pamphlet form, and was read all over South Africa. It is, in the opinion of the present writer, one of the best pieces of work which Mackenzie ever did as regards the mere matters of style, and of consecutive and convincing argument. It is a model at once of frankness and courtesy, of insight into the mind addressed, and into the best means for persuading it.

In 1897, his correspondence shows that Mackenzie was watching very closely, and with much anxiety, the course of events in the Cape Colony, as well as in the Transvaal. He was indignant at the deliberateness with which party leaders emphasised the influence of race upon political life in the Colony. To this he refers very indignantly in a letter to his friend, Mr Henry Beard of Cape Town.

In this letter he uses the expression, "Stick to opinions only," an idea and an injunction which he repeatedly insisted upon. He held that as long as men discussed South African industrial and social problems as race-problems, they strengthened the Africander Bond, and rooted it more deeply in the affections of its own supporters ; but the moment that fair-minded, clear-headed, justice-loving men began to discuss *opinions*, to advocate broad policies on their merits, and in doing this to ignore racial distinctions, that moment they began to sow discord amongst the members of the various races themselves. Mackenzie spoke from experience. In a discussion of practical policies on grounds of justice, in a discussion of political opinions in the light of the future of South Africa as a whole, Mackenzie had found it easy to divide not only Englishmen but even Dutchmen also, against one another, and so to make possible the rearrangement of party affiliations, not on racial, but on purely political lines.

HANKEY, *May 9th,* '97.

DEAR MR BEARD,—I have to acknowledge the receipt of a copy of the Bazaar Book, which is really very well got up. I have not had time to read the stories yet, but have no doubt they will be good, in such surroundings.

Well! you have been in deep water—or is it a strong storm of wind?—since I left you. You have got a certificate of character from Mr Garrett that you ought to be in the Cape Parliament—that is something, even although he adds, " but not for Cape Town." Why is there no one to tell this young man that there are *limitations* to most men's eye-sight. His sight is probably not always good, for he can see no difference, or he will see no difference, between Mr Rhodes and the Imperial Government. He does a great dis-service to his own country and his own Imperial Government by constantly making it and Mr Rhodes convertible terms. That sort of thing can hardly be done unconsciously. Is it possible that it can be done in perfect sincerity?

I am heartily sorry for Merriman. What a pity he should go so far merely to obtain political advantage. By the way, why did the *Cape Times* say it was a division on race lines? It did not seem to me to be so.

Mr Innes spoke and acted like a man. Let him stand to that; let him wait till people come to him and say to him, " Lead us; we know our views and we know yours; be our leader." What has been done so long by one minority after another has been too degrading—practically to approach the Bond and beg to be employed by them in the job of governing the Cape Colony. Ignore the Bond's stronghold—that of race. Stick to opinions only. On these lines I feel sure you will yet see a strong party, with Mr Innes at its head. If Mr Rhodes again pushes to the front, it will be a bad thing for you all, and for the Colony. He has as yet no opinions; he knows only one process—which is something else than politics.—With kind regards to all at Highwick, I am ever yours sincerely, JOHN MACKENZIE.

In this year, also, Mackenzie began to correspond with one whom he had welcomed most warmly to the

Colony as its new Governor, Sir Alfred Milner. His personal acquaintance with Mr Milner had begun in 1882, when the latter was a journalist in London. It increased to a friendship through much correspondence in later years, when Mr Milner was private secretary to Mr Goschen. In those years he had prophesied a great future for "young Milner," as he sometimes called him, and noted with satisfaction his promotion to work in Egypt. Lord Milner's letters to Mackenzie, after his arrival in South Africa, are both numerous and very cordial. Once only was Mackenzie able to meet the Governor personally. That was on the occasion of a journey which Lord Milner made from Port Elizabeth along the coast westwards. Mackenzie joined his party near Humansdorp, and rode in the "cart" with him to that village. There he took part in the welcome which was enthusiastically accorded by the entire countryside to the new and popular representative of the Queen.

In 1897 there occurred one of the most shameful of all transactions in all South Africa—the war between the Cape Colony and certain districts of South Bechuanaland. After a protracted struggle, in which the Colonial Government is accused of having displayed cruelty as well as incapacity, the terrible story was closed by the forcible deportation of large numbers of the Bechuanaland people to be placed on the farms of Boers, in Cape Colony, as unpaid and compulsory servants of those farmers. This was done, not only by way of reprisal, but nominally for the good of these people, and as an indemnity for the expense of the war. Even Sir Gordon Sprigg advocated this policy, denying that it partook of slavery, and insisting that it was devised and carried out in a philanthropic spirit.

Mackenzie had throughout these events remained silent, like Achilles, but with better reason, nursing a deep grief in his heart. When urged to speak he declined. When asked by his fellow-missionaries in Bechuanaland why he was silent, he was able to explain that he did not feel that any speech of his at this time could do any good. The time for speaking was years before ; then he had stood alone, unsupported, and even opposed by some of the very men who now called for his voice. He had then declared what would happen if South Bechuanaland were annexed to the Colony, and nothing in subsequent events had astonished him, except the measure of the folly and the injustice. But he did write, at the conclusion of the whole affair, the following important letter to his old colleague and friend, Mr J. S. Moffatt, to whose hands it now fell to help with the educational and religious instruction of the unhappy exiles from Bechuanaland.

HANKEY, CAPE COLONY,
29th Oct. 1897.

MY DEAR MR MOFFAT,—I am much obliged to you for sending me the copies of the *Times* and other papers with Langberg and other up-country news.

I am glad that you and those working with you are going to test the legality of what the Government has done. I noticed that that was Mr Chamberlain's answer to the Aborigines Protection Society.—Everything is in the hands of a British Colony; if there is anything wrong, let it come out before the law courts of the Colony.

I am in the position of having foreseen this, and of having laboured for years (and for a long time not unsuccessfully) to prevent that country from coming into the hands of the Colony. I still think it was a profound mistake to have joined on South Bechuanaland to the Cape Colony; it increases the difficulties of those who keep before them a South African Confederation. So-called leaders have misled the Cape Colony with the dream that the Colony would yet be practically synonymous with South Africa. This appeal to selfishness has become, or is becoming, too absurd for belief. In the meantime the annexation of *Bechuanaland was simply rushed*. " Make haste ; annex at once—there is a large party against it." That was the advice of the Dictator to the Cape Town Parliament, and his advice was taken. That advice was not in the interests of the Cape Colony, which already as a Government has too much territory. It was not in the interests of Bechuanaland, to cease being a Territory under the direct control of the Central Government in order to become a distant part of the huge Cape Colony.

The best thing that could be done now in the real interests of the Cape Colony—in the interests of all the people of Bechuanaland, and especially as looking forward to the future Confederation which many good men believe is still before us—is for the Cape Colony to give back South Bechuanaland to the Imperial Government, to be prepared for self-government under its auspices and to be managed in conjunction with North Bechuanaland. We should then have two Provinces in the North—Rhodesia and Bechuanaland—the Zambesi being the northern boundary of both. *Imperial administration can never retire from Rhodesia now, till the country is self-governing.* So should it be with reference to the Central Country of Bechuanaland—from the German line on the West to Rhodesia on the East, and from Zambesi on the North to what was the northern boundary of the Cape Colony before the recent mischievous annexation.

It is time for real leaders to lead the Cape Colony, and to show them that the extension of the range of the administration of the Colony is now a disadvantage, and no longer an advantage in the eyes of all who keep steadily in view the happy future of a great because United South Africa. The country is growing, and is sure to grow. It is for wise men to plan that it may grow proportionately and usefully. No one wishes to interfere with the self-government of the peoples out here. The time will come when the northern countries will be able to manage their own affairs. The Imperial Government should then retire; but not till then.

I am fully persuaded that this is the view of the intelligent Cape Colonist. He may go north personally; more likely his children will go north. But he is distinctly of opinion that the Colonial Government at Cape Town should not take in hand with the management of territories so far away as Bechuanaland or Rhodesia. He is determined to enjoy all the advantages of a British subject in any or all the British colonies and countries throughout South Africa;

but he holds it to be unwise for a single Colonial Government to attempt to govern everywhere.

I was thankful to observe that a committee of ladies had
been formed in connection with the Bechuanaland prisoners ;
and I trust that their number will come to include leading
members of all Christian churches.   We all need high ideals
kept before us.   Who is to place them and keep them there
but the ministers of Christ, and those Christian ladies who
from the earliest days of Christianity were ever near to Christ
and to His Cross ?

I think it is difficult to say how you are to feed and clothe
those whose food has been destroyed or used up in the late
protracted disturbance.   Feed them you must, as a Christian
Government : enslave them you may not.   As it seems to
me, you cannot punish those whom you have not tried.   A
state of war was never proclaimed : the right of a trial therefore remained to all.   But from a plain Christian man's
standpoint, who wishes the best to be done in present
circumstances, if the contracts were altered and made for
only two years, we should be nearer to the conviction that
the Government were not enslaving, but only providing food
and clothing for the destitute survivors of Langberg.   If our
Government did that—changed the engagements to two
years ; and if they approached the Imperial Government
with the request that they would resume the administration
of Bechuanaland, having the future of South Africa in view,
I think the whole Colony would say that they had got well
out of what has been a conspicuously bad business.   I may
explain that I have been away from home lately, and not so
attentive to the newspapers as I ought to be.   Thus I did not
know of the meeting recently held in Cape Town on this
question till after it was over.   Were I to classify myself as
to Colonial politics, I should like to belong to the Progressive
Party, and I have sympathy with all Progressive men, without
reference to their descent.   The settlement of the present
question, in my humble opinion, lies now in the changing of
the contract to two years, and the giving up of Bechuanaland
to the Imperial Government, that it may in the future become
a province in the South Africa of our children, if not of our
own time.

I had not intended to write on this matter.   My advice
had been disregarded.   Men had not then found out whither
their dictator was leading them.   I write now, because there

are people in the Colony who wish to know my views concerning a country which I first entered in the end of 1858. It now belongs to Progressive men throughout the Colony to decide for a sound policy with reference to the North. Have all the advantages of it, but leave its vexations and its government in the hands of the Central or Imperial Government, until it can govern itself locally.

I am free to admit that in giving this advice years ago, I was following the example of the United States of America— holding the young Territory under the Central Government at Washington until such time as the "Territory" had legally qualified itself to enter the number of the "States," and govern itself.—I am, ever yours sincerely,

JOHN MACKENZIE.

About this time Mackenzie was cheered by receiving two requests from England, which showed that he was not altogether forgotten in the homeland. One was another urgent call from the editor of *The Contemporary Review* for an article on Bechuanaland, and the other was a request from Dr MacLeod, the editor of *Good Words*, for three articles on South Africa. The latter he entitled "Glances at South Africa," and they appeared in the July, August, and September numbers of that magazine, in the year 1898, with a number of illustrations and photographs.

The Contemporary Review article appeared in February 1898. It occupied sixteen pages, almost all of which were given to the recent disturbances in Bechuanaland.

His narrative shows that he deeply suspected treachery of a very disagreeable kind behind the initial steps of that disturbance in 1897. The incapacity of the Colonial policy was abundantly proved, and the deliberate slowness with which the necessary steps were taken for arresting murderers was thrown into prominence. Then he set forth the manner in which, when the disaffected natives from the east of the country took refuge among the

Langberg hills in the west, no effort was made to discriminate between the intruders and the real inhabitants of that region—"on the whole a quiet and well-conducted people."

We are told, for instance, that on more than one occasion Luka Jantye, the Chief, took great trouble to put himself right with our people. It was stated that he offered "himself and his allegiance and service, and that practically these were distrusted and rejected." This Luka was himself killed under circumstances of peculiar atrocity. "I decline to write the details," Mackenzie says of the sanguinary story. "Thank God, there cannot be many people who would or could do such things, except as a duty."

Then he deals with the confiscation of lands, a proceeding which in a new country almost invariably implies some measure of underhand work. Mackenzie stigmatises the motives which led to this procedure with considerable vigour. The indenture of the starving Bechuanas to Colonial families for five years is likewise described in appropriate terms. Finally on this subject he says:—

I do not press this matter further and inquire who personally was to blame for it—incompetence or worse, is written on the whole transaction. At whose special door this charge lies I care not to enquire. My strictures are not written from the point of view of a political opponent to the present Colonial Government.

This leads him, in two concluding paragraphs, to describe, and once more to condemn the annexation of Bechuanaland to the Cape Colony. He sees in all the steps which led up to it the hand of the Chartered Company, and the ambition of "this big amalgamating power to be supreme in the whole of South Africa."

CHAPTER XX

AFRICA—PREACHER AND COUNSELLOR
(1891-1898)

WHEN Mackenzie landed at Cape Town in 1891, he found himself in the midst of the annual meetings of the Congregational Union of South Africa. He received a very warm welcome, and from that day was one of the most earnest and sympathetic members of the Union. He attended its meetings every year, except one, until the end of his life. He was placed on many of its most important committees, and in connection with them did the same faithful and patient work which he gave to every undertaking. He was appointed to a large number of special committees which had the disagreeable task of investigating cases of difficulty, such as settling church quarrels, preventing litigation over church property, etc. The testimony is uniform and unanimous that his work on these occasions, which for obvious reasons cannot be more minutely described, was of the utmost value.

In an obituary notice which appeared in a Year-book of the Congregational Union after his death, it is said :

As a spiritual adviser he was at his best. With what wonderful patience he would listen to native disputes, and sift out all their tiresome details, until the whole case was clear to him, and then with what a wealth of sanctified common-sense, diffusive charity, and persuasive wisdom he would express and apply his judgment !

On the same feature of his work and the spirit in which he performed it, Mr Beard in his memorandum has written as follows :—

516

It was in dealing with elements like these in the small South African Congregational Union that some of the finest qualities of John Mackenzie were displayed, winning the respect and affection of his co-workers. It may have seemed to others a small sphere for one who had been occupying the position of the previous years; perhaps at times, it may have seemed so to himself. But there was no sign of it in the readiness with which he threw himself into every subject, and the interest he manifested in every question bearing upon the welfare of the churches and the promotion of their work.

On one occasion, when a large "Coloured Church" had been seriously divided, and feeling had run high between certain ministers and their adherents, Mr Mackenzie was sent on a deputation to visit it. In a private letter giving a full explanation of the faithful way in which the deputation had dealt with the various individuals, Mr Mackenzie wrote as follows :—

"As to the people I have not time to write details. But on the last Sunday evening, before a very large congregation, I indulged in some very plain speaking, tempered by the heavenly teaching of our Lord, as to forgiveness, washing His disciples' feet, etc., and towards the close asked all those who desired to agree with our decision and to cherish those Christian feelings to stand up, while I engaged in a short special prayer. Practically the whole congregation stood up : and there was great joy expressed at the close of the meeting. The quarrel is over."

Those who knew Mr Mackenzie and his calm and dignified yet earnest manner of address, can well picture the impressive scene on that Sunday evening, in that large congregation of impulsive, eager, and unlettered African Christians.

In the year 1893 he acted as Chairman of the Union, and delivered the annual address on September 25th, at Queenstown. He took as his subject, "The Christian Outlook in the Cape Colony," and his address, which fills twenty-two pages of the Year-book of the Congregation Union, covers a great deal of ground.

He began with the Congregational view of the Christian church. While explaining its relation to, as well as its difference from, other sections of

Christendom, he especially emphasised the gradual
approximation to one another, in their practical
methods, of Presbyterian and Congregational churches
in South Africa ; and with great delight he pointed
to the co-operation of these two denominations in the
past. He insisted that the methods of church
government must " be capable of adaptation to the
diversified and changing conditions of mankind in all
parts of the country."

Having thus laid down his religious and spiritual
principles, he went on to apply them to the concrete
circumstances in South Africa. He reviewed the
internal work of the churches, and the need of the
highest morality and the intensest spirituality.

Some of our pastors and office-bearers may stop from
fighting with " wild beasts," so to speak, the strong lower
passions of their flocks; the disgusting customs of a
heathenism still clinging to the minds of the people. Be
encouraged, brethren, in your most difficult but most
necessary work. Whatever you do, do not lower the
standard of what Christ requires. . . . Christian brethren,
the most hopeful thought to my mind in connection with the
future of the country is this—that wherever a Christian
church exists, we have an agency for making and keeping
men and women pure, truthful, honest, and godly.

The condition of colonisation was briefly discussed,
and a large space was devoted to the problem of
strong drink in South Africa, especially in Cape
Colony.

Our appeal to our fellow-Christians throughout the
Colony, and our own efforts as a Union must first be
directed to the reduction of the number of licensed places in
our villages, and to the withdrawal of all canteen licences
throughout the Colony. The government of the Free State
has excelled the government of this Colony in the matter of
restriction placed upon the sale of strong drink.

Under the heading of " The Question of Colour,"
Mackenzie placed great emphasis upon the fact that

in the Congregational Union men of different races met on an equality and with great freedom.

It is a thrilling and soul uplifting thought, the confluence of the older Christian communions with the newly opened up rill of South African Christianity. . . . We are of many races and classes, but if we have put off the old man and have put on the new, then among us there is neither Greek nor Jew, circumcision nor uncircumcision, barbarian, Scythian, bond nor free, but Christ is all and in all. . . . Whether in religion or in politics, the man who proposes to assemble and organize his own race or his own colour only, has practically forsaken the region of argument and discussion, and trusts to his power to coerce his opponents by the mere weight of number, and in the end by mere brute force. . . . Let no one ever seek to organize the members of this Union on race lines. Let us avoid it as we would a bitter sin.

Then he discussed also at considerable length " The Location Act and Stock Stealing," where he dealt with one of the most constant causes of dispeace and disorder in many districts of Cape Colony. He condemned all proceedings by the government which would deal with the natives *en masse*, as if they were all given to stock-thieving. He urged missionaries who laboured in such districts to give constant and broad-minded teaching to the native people regarding this crime. He denied the common assertion that it was part of their nature to steal, and in doing so, cited the history of the border raids in the south of Scotland, in which his own ancestors, no doubt, were concerned.

Of course it was long ago—so long ago that we do not feel much disgraced by the fact. Indeed, with us romance and poetry have thrown their glamour over these old-world doings; but there is no doubt that when the lady of the house on the border line between England and Scotland placed on an empty covered dish, to be opened by her lord before his family, a significant pair of spurs—it was in our estimation as colonists, an unblushing incentive to stock-lifting. Her ladyship's larder was empty, and the border had to be crossed to obtain supplies.

He would therefore have the colonists regard stock-thieving as at once a relic of barbarism, destined to pass away, and a crime which must be stamped out by firm, but discriminating justice.

Then he discussed, under a number of brief paragraphs, misunderstandings which were likely to rise among them as Christian men of different races in a new country. He noted that the utmost confusion prevailed amongst those who discussed what they called "The Native Question." Within the church he would expect mutual sympathy and help amongst all true believers of every race.

But with reference to what I may call general society, what are my social rights? Simply to let alone. I have no social right which society declines to give to me. If people do not want my society they find no difficulty in letting me know it. Have they wronged me by so doing? By no means. Let me go among those who are more likely to care for me. Society sanctions the intercourse of those who approve of one another.

Towards the end the following sentences occur :—

Does it not appear from what I have said that there is hope in the future before us all in our South African life, without expecting anything unreasonable from one another? The church door is open; the court room is open; the doors of our friends' houses are open; and there is fair pay for fair work. Let us thank God, and live our life, and do our work, with joy and gladness, with earnestness and deep humility. No one can think worse of us than we do of ourselves when we are alone with our Saviour.

His last words in this Chairman's address were :—

God grant that this Union may long show how all races of South Africa may live together and work together for God and their fellow men.

Mackenzie's last attendance at the Union meetings took place when they gathered in September 1898,

at Uitenhage.   His brethren all remarked the evident
decline of physical strength which they saw in him,
while yet he took a full part in the work and deliberations of the Assembly.   On a Friday afternoon, September 23rd, Mackenzie introduced the
subject of " Church work and progress."   Several of
those who heard this address have referred to it in
correspondence since that day, and all bear witness
that he spoke with such intensity and earnestness
as to produce an unusual impression upon his
audience.   So remarkable indeed was the emotion
which his bearing and his message quickened, that
the Assembly agreed at once to cease from further
discussion of the subject, and spend the remainder
of the time in prayer.

He made a half-playful address on another occasion,
of a social character, in response to the toast, " New
men and old days," in which again he seems to
have touched a tender chord, mingling what was
playful with what was pathetic in the few sentences
which he uttered.

At the communion service, where Christians of
different denominations and races met, he spoke on
the 21st chapter of John, urging the communicants
to control the impulsive, active Peter within their
hearts, and to give precedence to the loving, intuitive
John.   "We felt," it is added by one friend, "that
he was simply rendering the order of his own experience, and that in him Peter, the leader of men,
had learned to acknowledge the greater nearness to
Christ of John, the divine."   This correspondent, the
Rev. J. Frederick Philip, after quoting a few lines
from Matthew Arnold's " Rugby Chapel," says that
there are many passages in that poem " which might
have been written not only for the children of John
Mackenzie, but for us, who look to him as a spiritual
father."

While Mackenzie was thus deeply involved in industrial and social and denominational schemes he was, it must be remembered, hard at work as pastor and preacher. His command of the Dutch language became more and more extensive, so as to receive the praise even of those who heard him in large Dutch-speaking churches at other places.

Mackenzie spared no labour upon his work as a preacher; his files of manuscript sermons, which he kept in the same methodical way in which he preserved all of his manuscripts and correspondence, show that he spent much time and thought upon them. They are in the main, of course, simple, earnest discourses adapted to the needs of a rural population. Many of them are written out in full, covering ten to thirty pages of manuscript; others are preserved only in brief jottings. The course of thought in the majority of his sermons shows that he was in deep earnest about the central features of man's religious and moral life. To him it was clear that a man's relations to God are supreme and fundamental, and on these he spoke with intense solemnity. But for him, as for all true teachers of the Gospel, the religious life must find expression in a man's human relationships, in human conduct; the eternal appears under the conditions of time and amid the changes of a finite experience. Mackenzie's sermons were therefore directed no less to the practical problems of everyday life than to the deep questions of our relation to the living God through Jesus Christ. Under this head he placed the consideration of the larger national and political questions. He did not shrink from discussing these. He could not speak, for instance, on the text " Love your enemies " without applying it skilfully, but with great boldness, to the attitude of the various races in South Africa towards one another. Nor could he preach as he

did at various places on the passage (Matt. xx.
20-29) where two brothers appeal to Christ for
positions of prominence in His Kingdom, without
coming to consider the principles of human government, and the manner in which the spirit of the
Son of Man is to be realised in the political world.
Nor could he deal again with the parable of the
fig-tree, without pointing out its lessons for the
national conscience as well as the solemn and urgent
appeals which could be obviously based upon it in
addressing the will of individual men. It seems
fitting to give here two or three brief extracts from
some of these sermons to illustrate his spirit and
manner.

The first one is taken from the sermon on Matt.
v. 43-45, entitled " Love your enemies." When he
preached this at Caledon Square Church, Cape Town,
on April 18th, 1897, he added the following passage,
which was written and delivered because he found
the atmosphere of Cape Colony growing thick with
suspicion, recrimination, and all the conditions that
make for war :—

Brethren ! So far I have addressed to you remarks which
I recently made to a small European congregation in a
secluded church in this colony.

Speaking here from this pulpit to-night, I wish to add a
few remarks on the subject of our text.

I am addressing many who are the humble followers of
Jesus Christ : men and women who call Him sincerely Lord
and Master. Allow me to say to you this evening, with deep
conviction, that the peace and prosperity of this country are
in your hands. Who is the enemy of South Africa ? The
man who tries to separate Christian people on account of
their race or descent. Brethren ! these men are our
enemies. We say earnestly, Whom God in His providence
hath joined together in this land, let no man, and no
party, and no newspaper, try to put asunder ! Christian
people ! (I would my voice could resound through the
whole of South Africa)—be not silent at this juncture.

That whole matter is really in your hands. Look not on your own things but also on the things of others. Through you let the Spirit of Christ kill the spirit of hatred and selfishness, which leads to war through all the land. English-speaking people! be Christians first; loyal, true servants of Jesus. Dutch-speaking people! brothers in faith and hope! fellow-workers in bringing about the establishment of the glorious Kingdom of our common Lord! be Christians first: loyal and true servants of Jesus. Christians! unfold fearlessly the Banner of Christ our Lord. Let us all assemble under its ample folds. Demand it of all the rulers and governments in South Africa that the wild-beast age of mankind in this fair land shall pass away, and that the real and practical reign of Christ Jesus shall be established in our midst.

Brethren, shall we kneel and offer the same prayers—shall we approach the same sacred communion and openly declare our deep love and true devotion to one Saviour and Master, and then go out and speak words of malice and hatred against one another, and urge on one another by bitter words to hotter anger and vengeance? I say, Let not this be! May God Himself forbid!

I call upon the Christians of South Africa in this time of need, by the humble exercise of a true Christian spirit in their daily life—Receive one another, bear with one another, have sympathy with one another, as the good Lord has so lovingly and patiently borne with you.

Blessed are the peacemakers here in South Africa as everywhere, for they shall be called the children of God.

The Parable of the Fig-Tree

(Luke xiii. 6-10)

Dear brethren, we have spoken from illustrations in the history of the past, which show that there comes a time of judgment even in the dealings of the God of mercy. The Babylonish captivity, and the destruction of Jerusalem, and the scattering of the Jewish people are striking illustrations of this truth.

But what was true in the time of Isaiah and in the time of our Lord is equally true in our own day.

I am persuaded that the doctrine of our text is true of the nations of to-day, as well as of God's ancient people. It is at present high-tide, so to speak, as to the prosperity of the British Empire. Those whose ancestors were rude barbarians when the words of our text were spoken by Christ have risen to an unprecedented height among the nations of the earth. But should our people fall away from righteousness, should they become self-seeking and self-indulgent, should God be forgotten or dethroned, in our aims and our plans as a people, then, without doubt, the word will go forth, "I have sought fruit on this tree and find none: I have sought spiritual life, and find only coarse materialism: I have sought humble faith and obedience to Him whose power has raised them so high, and I find only self-laudation, contained in empty and boastful affirmations about western civilisation: I have sought a nation to serve Me in My Gospel, a nation to carry the evangel to the ends of the earth, but where I have found fleets of war-vessels and fleets to carry merchandise, I see only one or two vessels made to carry My evangelists: I have sought a people to exemplify the teaching of My Son in their social and national life, and behold, I find a people given to revelling and drunkenness and immorality, among whom the greatest moral guilt goes unpunished, because it has become sanctioned by long practice and usage. Brethren, it is not our western civilization that will save us as a people, any more than Greece or Rome was saved by civilization. We stand not in the forefront of the nations to-day through our army or our navy or our modern weapons of warfare. We stand where we do through our character as a Christian nation—a people on whom evidently the blessing of God has long rested. Thank God for the Christianity which still animates the British people. Thank God for what measure of sound character, true faith, and sincere devotion, are to be found among our people. Should these be found among our own people, should these grow and abound, then the blessing of Heaven will continue to rest on us as a nation. But should the great Gardener seek this heavenly fruit among us, and seek it in vain, then no weapons of defence can save us, for we shall ourselves have decayed and become effete; and the word shall go forth, "Why cumbereth it the ground? Cut it down." Therefore he is the truest patriot who seeks to raise the character of his people;

for the true greatness of a nation—that which will give permanence to a people—consists in the virtue and purity, the honesty and truthfulness, and the spiritual ideals of the great body of the people.

But once more, our text carries a message not only to nations, but to individuals. We are individually represented by this fig-tree. The Divine voice is heard saying, " I have come for so long seeking fruit in this life, and find none. Why cumbereth it the ground? Why suffer it longer to cast around it a baleful, selfish, worldly influence? Cut it down!"

But, brethren, we have an Advocate at God's right hand, who intercedes for us. We have also a Divine Spirit standing at the door of our hearts and knocking for admission. "Let him alone, while I still knock at his heart and beg him to yield himself to My guidance, while I win him by love and patience, while I warn him by fearful lessons in events around him. Let him alone a year longer that he may bear the fruit of repentance, humble faith, and Christian life; and then if that fruit is not apparent, thou shalt cut him down."

How solemn, brethren, that while we are living in thoughtlessness—taking the days as they come—the eye of our God is examining our life and our character, seeking heavenly fruit, unmistakable tokens in our character and life that we are the children of God through faith in Jesus Christ! How solemn that in the Council of the Godhead it should be said by the Voice of Righteousness—For years have I sought fruit here and find none: why cumbers he the earth longer? And the same Divine Voice in another tone, the tone of Mercy replies, Spare him a little longer: he will see My Cross: he will realize My love for him. And again another note of mercy, Spare him a little longer: if he will only willingly admit Me and yield to Me, his scarlet guilt shall become white as snow: I will create within him a clean heart and renew a right spirit within him.

Brethren, listen to the Heavenly Voices speaking round us and about us. Where is the Heavenly fruit in our lives? If we are only willing and believing, Divine aid will do the rest. Thank God that there is this Divine Mercy. But remember! our text this afternoon points to a life tragedy: to the fatal time when a deaf ear and a closed heart shall have brought *doom* on themselves. "If it bear fruit, well: if not, after that then thou shalt cut it down."

The following selection will be found very interesting, because it contains several echoes across the years from those early "jottings," of which examples have been printed above. It seems also to express sincerely, and even bluntly, the principles on which Mackenzie had very earnestly endeavoured to live, and which inspired him for every change of work, for every ardour of self-sacrifice :—

HUMAN AMBITION AND CHRISTIAN DISTINCTION

(Matt. xx. 20-29)

.   .   .   .

III. *Christian Distinction.*—Our Lord pursued the subject thrust upon His notice to its legitimate end. James and John would be "great"; they would be "first" in His Kingdom. They were willing, as far as they knew, to share with Him the fortunes of that Kingdom. It therefore became their Guide and Teacher, for their benefit, and to the benefit of the rest of His disciples, as well as for the edifying of His Church in all ages, to explain what was Christian Distinction, and how it could be attained.

Yet once more, therefore, the true Messiah announces that His Kingdom shall be the antithesis of the kingdoms of the earth. He describes what has been common to kings' courts and to the courts of First Consuls or of Presidents—the eager pursuing of personal claims ; the partizanships ; the elbowing others out of your way; the walking roughshod over a man who is down, leaving to those who are called fools the work of raising him up and setting him on his feet again. These things have been, and alas, still are ; and they will be, till Christianity shall have filled men's hearts, and then the antithesis of our Lord's lesson will have ceased. The kingdoms of the world shall have become the kingdoms of God and of His Christ.

But if not by self-reliantly pressing their individual claims and pushing others out of the way, how is distinction to be achieved in the new Kingdom of the Messiah? Is everything on a dull, monotonous level, or is there a real province for emulation and ambition among the servants of Christ ; and if so, what is that province? And what are the rules which apply to Christian ambition?

The love of distinction, the desire to emulate, is not by any means crushed by the religion of Christ. Rather is it directly encouraged and guided, as witness the directions given in our text. They might aspire to be "chief"; they might covet to be "first" in rank; and their Master graciously gives them plain directions as to how this is to be secured.

The Patriarch is Head of the Eastern Church, the Holy Father or Pope is Head of the Western. The Primate of England is Head of the Episcopal Church of that country, and so in Scotland and Ireland. The Moderator of a Presbyterian Church is its Head for the time. So among the Wesleyans is the President of the Conference for the time being. So among the Congregationalists and Baptists, the Chairman of the Union for the year. If you look at any book of reference you will find that these are the acknowledged Heads of Churches; and these books will tell you how to address these dignitaries, so as to express that conventional reverence for their office, which in the beginning must have been evoked and must have been earned by the holders of these offices. If I look at my book of reference then I can have no doubt as to who is the chief or head in these Christian communities. But if I turn to my New Testament and take this text for my guide, these dignitaries may or may not retain a chief place in Christ's Church. If they do, it will be as workers, and not for any other reason. The text is clear. "It shall not be so among you. Whosoever would be great among you shall be your servant, and whosoever would be first among you shall be your bond servant or slave; even as the Son of Man came not to be ministered, but to minister."

Here, then, we have pointed out to us the true scope for Christian ambition, with specific directions as to the manner in which it can be followed successfully. As we might have expected, true greatness in Christ's service is within the reach of all His followers, within the reach of the poor as well as of the rich. To be a Christian at all, means that you are striving to please God in your daily life; that you are enthusiastically loyal to Christ your Lord and Master; that you avail yourself of the help of God's good Spirit so freely offered to us all; that you consecrate life, social position, education, yourself, in short—all that you have and are, to Christ your Lord, placing yourself on His altar as a living sacrifice, which is a most reasonable thing for each and all to do. To go a step further than this, and to seek Christian *distinction*, is to excel in the eye of Christ, to surpass others in working, in serving, in slaving for Christ. The eye of the Lord passes by the men who in His Church forget this lesson, although they may be esteemed great among men, as Samuel allowed to pass by one after another of the likely sons of Jesse. The eye of the Master passes by one after the other till it rests on the humblest, most self-forgetful, most diligent Christian. He' is the chief, he is the first in rank, in the eye of our Lord.

And his place and his reward are assured; no one can dispossess him of them. Here surely is strong consolation to every Christian heart sincerely seeking the Master's approval. This choice joy, this crown of human life, is placed within the reach of all. And no one can defraud the most distinguished in the Master's eye of his merited reward. It is his, and it shall be given to him by the Master Himself. Take heart, therefore, Christian soldier, your Captain's eye is never off you; He knows your every step. Have they elbowed you aside because you are old or ill? Have they brushed past you, and all but trodden you down in their hasteful, selfish rush? Heed it not. One eye is ever on you. You can always come into contact with the Master Himself, whom you love and serve.

But remember and please to be quite clear about this; that true Christian distinction is to be earned by work only. You can't meditate yourself into this chief place; nor can you get it by mere asking. It will not be bestowed on the man whose highest Christian effort is to keep a diary, in which he narrates what it occurs to him to put down at the end of the day. It is sweet and helpful to meditate; it is good—especially at certain times—to keep jottings of your thoughts and your experiences; but neither your diary nor your meditations will secure for you a chief place in the eye of the Master. If you would excel you must do it by working for Christ; you must be like Him who was not ministered to, but who ministered constantly to others, giving them even His very life.

Here, then, brethren, a glorious prospect opens before you. You have seen the platform of social or human ambition, on which the Saviour does not frown, but only declares it to be inadequate. We have attempted to describe the higher

Christian platform of life and action, conjoining the present with the future, time and eternity, the light of Christ's character and teaching lighting up our view of things. From that high platform of Christian devotion we come to answer the further and still higher question, as to distinction in the service of Christ; and we have heard the wonderful and sublime answer of Christ. Distinction can be earned by work done for Christ, even by the cup of cold water, if you can do nothing else. Distinction can be earned by work only, and once earned, no one whatever can defraud you of your reward. The surprised disciple may exclaim, Lord, when saw we Thee hungry and gave Thee food? But He will answer as He did.

Brethren, I know that your heart burns within you with the generous glow of a self-forgetful Christian devotion. You would work for Christ; you would serve Him; you would willingly slave for Him. And you are ready to ask me, What are we to do? Does your mind hasten towards some strange scene, some distant clime, as if there you would serve your Lord and earn His approval?

It may not be necessary for you to leave the scene of your present pursuits; it may be necessary only to let in on your daily habits and thoughts the higher teaching of this morning's lesson. Thus a new spirit can elevate your present daily life. The work done can be done for Christ. What are you to do? A friend can advise, a pastor can teach and guide, but Christ Himself can inspire. How can I know what you can do for Christ? How can I measure your service to Him? That may not be dictated by me. That may not be set you as a task by any man. That is a question which your love and devotion to Him alone can answer. How your life-service shall be rendered can be settled only on your knees, can be decided only in sight of the Cross and in view of Eternity. What I say is this, When on your knees, when in view of that Cross, and of the vast cycles of our eternity, *then be ambitious*, then consider how to secure Christian distinction. You know now how to obtain it. Let us serve for it; let us slave for it. The laurels of mere temporal ambition do always wither; but the crown which shall reward your Christian ambition shall adorn your brow for ever and ever.

CHAPTER XXI

THE RIPENED LIFE AND THE SICKLE
(1898, 1899)

WE have already seen that Mackenzie's friends noted during the years 1897 and 1898 a remarkable mellowing of his character. It is now our duty, as we approach the end of his life's story, to speak more definitely on that topic. It may not be too much to say that the entire course of his words and work from the time of his youthful jottings to his last labours in Hankey have shown that Mackenzie's nature united certain apparently inconsistent qualities. He was a man of great strength of will with a capacity for what we must call " driving through " duties and difficulties ; but with this there was united an abundant emotionalism which made him full of sympathy for the position and feelings of others. His vigour was therefore united with tenderness, his fearless judgment was only tamed, and yet was actually controlled, by those deep springs of affection within him. The preceding chapters have already shown how wide were his practical interests as he looked out upon the problems of the human world around him. From the beginning to the end he had within him the passion of the evangelist ; at no time would he confess that he subordinated his desire for bringing men to God to any other conception of duty. It was in the interests of this task that he was drawn into political life, and from political labours he returned at the end to this. And yet, he was able at no period of his life to give himself solely to evangelistic

efforts.   He had a sincere and earnest interest in all
sides of the life and work of every community he
touched.   Whether at Shoshong or Kuruman or
Hankey he ever had his eye upon pastoral as well
as evangelistic duties, upon educational as well as
pastoral, upon industrial as well as educational, upon
political as well as industrial.   With Mackenzie to
think was to act.   He was not one of those who
could see something that ought to be done and leave
others to discover it ; what ought to be done he must
try to get done as soon and as well as circumstances
and his own powers of persuasion and work could do it.

As we have seen, the period of life which he spent
at Hankey embraced all these separate interests, and
none was wholly neglected by him.   That, however,
which appeared most clearly to all observers was not
so much the measure of success which he attained,
as the development of his own spirit.   He quite
evidently impressed all who came in contact with
him, as a man who lived for the sole purpose of
doing good ; his self-sacrificing labours in all directions were aimed at nothing less than conveying
some definite boon to some individual or class.   And
this benevolence of spirit was recognised as being
based upon his religious consciousness ; he was no
philanthropist of the shallower type, doing the best
for men out of mere pity for their temporary or
physical disabilities ; he viewed them and all their
burdens of disease and sorrow, of ignorance and strife,
in the light of the eternal, and he strove to deliver
them from these because he walked with God.   There
ran ever through his life the continuous reference of
all things and all duties to the name and will of God.
This did not appear, indeed, in set phrases, for no man
could be so religious and yet employ so little of the
conventional verbiage of religion as he.   But men
knew that his religion, his dependence in all and

through all upon God his Father and Saviour, was
for Mackenzie the deepest and the highest fact in his
life, and the root of all that he did and hoped to be.
The powers of the world to come had truly entered
into his experience in those far-off years of youth, and
through all the intervening decades the grasp upon
his nature had become more firm, subduing the entire
manhood to their sway.

Before we come to tell the story of his last illness,
it may be well to illustrate as briefly and simply as
possible the truth of this estimate of Mackenzie's
ripened Christian spirit.

There is no direction in which a man is more
severely tested than in his attitude towards opponents
in public life.   The command of Jesus that men should
love their enemies is not easy to obey ; still less
that which he seems to have described as the supreme
manifestation of such love, namely, sincere prayer for
those that are deliberately and malignantly hostile.
Here was one of those features in Mackenzie's conduct
which most impressed those who watched him in his
public work.   The following paragraphs by Mr Henry
Beard of Cape Town, a most careful and affectionate
observer, will confirm these words :

A marked feature in the succeeding years was the fair
and generous way in which he spoke of such political
opponents.   This may be exemplified from the pages of
" Austral Africa," but it was still more significant to notice
the same in private conversation and correspondence.   The
tendency of political life everywhere, but especially in a
Colony, is to see in all self-interested motives and to dwell
on the personal aspect.   This was a man who was too large-
minded to yield to such a tendency.   Habitually seeking
not his own, he thought on a higher plane, and could not
condescend to personal resentment where momentous interests were in question.   But there was a remarkable
tenacity of purpose, which no opposition or unfavourable
circumstances could damp.   Most men, after defeat such as

he suffered when he resigned office in Bechuanaland, hopeless of turning the tide, would have returned to their former work, if, like him, they esteemed it highly. He, apparently roused the more by successful opposition, addressed himself to the task of turning the official mind and awakening and directing the public interest. In this to a certain extent he succeeded.

It was no less striking to see the same man, when he found how other questions were crowding out the consideration of South African problems from the public mind in Great Britain, quietly resuming his missionary work, still of the same steady mind, watching the course of events, and still seeking by occasional articles in English periodicals to influence public thought in favour of that comprehensive policy, which he deemed so vital to future right relations between the Mother country and the two European races and the Natives in South Africa; or, anon, appealing to the reasonableness and better feelings of the Dutch whom he esteemed, as in his letter to President Kruger of June 1896. Manifesting no resentment, the man who, for a while, had played so prominent a part in connection with statesmen and soldiers and the large affairs of public life, turned back again to the simple and obscure duties of the missionary life as he found them at the old colonial mission station of Hankey. There, the same clear judgment and the mingled firmness and kindness which had been applied to subjects of national import and government of territories was employed, with no less interest and self-devotion, to settle the details of village allotments, the landlord's rule and improvements, the affairs of the mission school, or the irrigation scheme. Nor, so far as a friend could detect, was there any trace of unworthy disappointment, or discontent, in that large mind and heart. At Hankey he showed the same qualities of a leader of men as in Bechuanaland. He soon gained the regard of the neighbouring farmers, to whom his name, at first, must have been synonymous with the opponent of their race.

Nothing brought a keener pain to Mackenzie's heart than the suggestion that he felt enmity towards any man. When he read in a newspaper one day a reference to "Mackenzie and Rhodes" as great public foes, he turned with deep feeling to his wife

and deplored such assertions, adding words which from his lips could not mean anything less than all that is most sacred and sincere. He said that there was no one beyond his immediate family circle for whom he prayed more constantly and more sincerely than Mr Rhodes. Whether a man who stands outside of the Christian experience can feel the true meaning of this word of Mackenzie's or not, those who have entered into that life of prayer as an actual weapon and who have tried to use it for the blessing of an opponent, can appreciate what that utterance implies. That kind of prayer can only be preceded by a personal struggle and personal victory over self.

The affectionateness, the sympathy of Mackenzie's nature shows itself most clearly in relationships, and in the presence of events, which make it hard to find and publish illustrations.

Fortunately one of his daughters, who left her home at Hankey for a period of study in Germany, under conditions of health which made the separation a great trial to herself and her parents, is willing to have the following extracts from her father's letters printed, simply that he may be better known to the readers of these pages.

HANKEY, *April* '97.

I think it would be good for you and it would be delightful for us if you came south any time next week. I have no copy of the *Contemporary*. I don't suppose there will be one obtainable in Kimberley. It will be most serviceable if Mr Ropes reprints the article in one sheet as an *Advertiser* supplement. See the *Spectator*. It has a swinging review of the article for which I am very thankful. Try to see the *Speaker* also. I have not seen it. Mr Percy Bunting of the *Contemporary*, writes me that the article is attracting great attention at home, and that he (Bunting) has offered the (Chartered) Company space in the *Contemporary* for a reply. He expresses an opinion as to the probability of this taking place, which it would be hazardous to quote ; he might be mistaken. I am delighted about the reprint in this country, because my great object is to unite all progressive men in this country in the hearty recognition of the Imperial Government in Native Territories, till these are fit for responsible government.

HANKEY, 3rd Nov. '97.

You are in good hands. Your Heavenly Father's arms are underneath and around you. There has been no day that we have not thought about you, ay and prayed about you, for the two things with us are really one. . . . The post brings us the news of Lord Rosmead's death. I am afraid I shall be compelled to refer to what I regard as some serious mistakes in his past career as High Commissioner. It makes me sad to think of his decease. We were so closely connected in 1883, 84, 85.

The Governor (Lord Milner) has gone north, saying everywhere the same healthy sound things. He bids fair to become popular with everybody.

HANKEY, 22nd Dec. '97.

Perhaps I had better tell you my present circumstances that we may be in sympathy while you read. The cart is to start early to-morrow morning to bring in John and family from Uitenhague. Everybody is writing elsewhere, and I am in the old place that you know. . . . May the good Lord, whose you are and whom you desire to serve, be ever with you all the New Year; wherever you are. A special blessing on you, dear, I humbly ask from the Lord, our Father. Pray for us too, dear lassie, and so bind ourselves to one another by this strongest bond.

When we discussed your going to Leipzig we concluded that it would be the most complete change ; that you had commenced with a certain teacher, and that there would be few if any distractions from your studies as a student in Germany. I don't know how all this will appear to you in London. I only recall what you said and felt here ; to me it is an open question and must be judged by you to the best of your ability.

I have just written a note to John with greetings to the bairns, and to say that there are a few apricots in the garden. There is a specially good crop of them this year. Do

you remember the white gardener who was with ——?
He is now with us.   He can't speak English.   He has not
the right number of teeth for clear enunciation.   His
thoughts are of less practical value to us than, perhaps,
their own merits demand.   You have to manage matters
by direct questions.   He is capital for looking after the
fruit in the garden ; and the servant girls got a "wakener"
also from him, despite his deficiency as to teeth.   He may
be said to have shown what he had of teeth to them.

HANKEY (*undated*).

Some of your remarks touch me keenly.   You went with
an object.   Go forward and follow it out in God's name,
and trusting to His strength.   As your day so shall your
strength be.   God will be sufficient for you every day.
There may be no great overplus of strength, but you will
always be more than conqueror against everything that
opposes you.   Make up your mind to ignore it.   God will
make you able to ignore it.   Fill your mind with something
else, something that will not annoy or worry you, but fill
you and satisfy you.   I hope you follow my meaning.   It
is quite clear to myself : and *I have trod the road myself.*
So cheer up ! you can do all things through Christ
strengthening you.   Lean on that and fear nothing.—Your
father.

HANKEY, 1*st March* '98.

We are all well here, and all full of confidence that you
are also, and going to be, well—a joy to yourself and
satisfaction before your God and Father : and a joy to us
all who belong to you.

HANKEY, 13*th April* 1898.

I was so glad that you were feeling so fit and even
joyous with reference to the work before you and generally
with reference to your future.

" That's my brave lassie ! " says one thought.   " That's
my humble trustful daughter in the Lord," says my whole
soul.   I have no fear whatever, my dear, concerning your
affairs.   The good Lord will uphold you and see you
through every maze and over every difficulty.   Live near
to Him, confide in Him, and He will not disappoint you.

HANKEY (*undated*).

. . . I am reminded of post time, so good-night, dearie, over the land and over the ocean in the directest way— by way of the throne and the Heart of God our Father. A blessing abide on you all the days and every day !

HANKEY, 25*th May* 1898.

That was a delicious letter which you sent to me. I am thankful for it. It has been quite a joy to me. It will surprise you more and more how very successful we people can be in shutting out our beloved Father from the world of our hearts and thoughts. How glorious is even a glimpse of communion with Him ! For is he not Love, Beauty, Light, Mercy, and always our Strength ? We can do all things through Jesus Christ. May all your days be bright, my dear lassie, Divine strength encircling you. . . . They are beginning to talk learnedly about the great benefit of a journey to Kimberley. Of course Het is going—that is long settled. Then your mother would undoubtedly be much better of a visit to Kimberley. But it would appear, also, according to John, that there are special indications that I should perform this tour. I am going to write to old Mr Philip of Graaf Reinet. If he can come down and take my place here, then we'll a' gang thegither; but if he cannot do so, then I shall stay where I am—which is not at all a bad place !

. . . So cheer up, dearie, we are hand-clasping across the sea. Paper is done. Very much love.

HANKEY, 15*th June* '98.

Can you find any means of getting more of human companionship—some one to supply Mary's place, as far as possible ? Look around you and see. It would be nice for you to share rooms with a girl of the right sort. God grant that you may find her. . . . In the meantime, you are plodding away—determined not to be discouraged or driven back. Stronger is He who is with you than all that can be against you. It is, I am sure, a matter which prayer and faith in the nearness of Christ can conquer. Trust in Him with all your heart and He will bring you through. But nice human intercourse makes your life easier. If you can only secure it, do not let the question of money keep you apart from good companionship. It will be such a help to you in every way. And may God bless and guide you, my dear girl.

. . . To-morrow is going to be a "great occasion"—a "pink and white tea." Proceeds for a new harmonium for the church. Are you all attention? Perhaps some one will be able to describe it to you. I believe my pink tie is prepared. You can easily guess by whose deft fingers. The white will be supplied I hope by the shirt part. With love.

THORNHILL, *26th June* '98.

I have been thinking of you and your friends on your pedestrian tour. I feel sure you will have enjoyed it very much. And I trust it will do you very much good. I am very much pleased to hear that you are purposing to have Miss M. to share your rooms. It will render you much happier to be in companionship. I came in here yesterday afternoon. Conducted services last night in Dutch ; church full. To-night public meeting ; to-morrow go into "the Bay." There was some talk about our going north also ; but I do not see my way at this time. Very, very much love, my dearie. Rest in the Lord ; He will bring it to pass.

HANKEY (*undated*).

Jeanie and I came back last night from Humansdorp. We were there one night. Jee at the Bakers', and I at the Magistrate's, in their new house. The occasion was the opening of the new Public School, which has been named the Milner Institute. The "function" was on Monday at 11 o'clock. There was a great turn out of Beauty and Fashion : you can take your choice as to under which head you will put Jee and myself. . . .

HANKEY, CAPE COLONY,
19th Oct. 1898.

Do you know where I am sitting this evening? Well, I'll tell you. I am sitting, as it might be, at the foot of the bed in the end room, next the—hm—the henhouse! I am sitting in the corner nearly opposite the window of the old bedroom, which is now a glass door from the Bay! So that you do not need to go further when you come, if you wish to see me, than to stop at the pipe where we water our flowers, because my door is there, or very near to it. I am sitting looking towards the window which was, of the little study. It is now nearly overgrown with ivy outside. But much nearer to me as I sit, there is another window driven into the wall next to the yard, not far from the end of the oven!

. . . It is very nice to hear of your pegging away at your studies, and it is also to be noticed that occasionally and lately, there has been some mention made, vague, undated, of your return to this fair land. I did not fail to note what was said.

HANKEY, 2nd Nov. 1898.

I have been longing to write to you for some time; so here goes. Not that I have much to say that is worth writing. Only I should just like to send a wee note. I have been delighted with your letters lately.

This is just a word of greeting, a good cheer to you. Do not be alarmed at all by what may be written about your father. He has not been very well. People can't be always quite well. But you can see for yourself that I am all right.

They have not sent out the assistant whom they promised me, but I am aware that it is difficult sometimes to find the kind of man wanted. I have no doubt Mr Thompson will be doing his best. . . . I think I shall hand this on to the young people to finish. With love always, your father.

HANKEY, 30th Nov. 1898.

Your mother is going to write this letter to you, but I thought I would just begin it for her. That is our way of doing things, you know—for instance, our way of cooking a dinner; your mother does it, only I look in to see that it is all right. So now I am going to bed, and she is to write our letter to you, my very dear lassie.

Towards the end of 1897, Mackenzie's health became very unsatisfactory; a slight twist which he gave to one knee resulted in symptoms of a most unfavourable kind. But he persisted in work, walking up and down the steep hills of Hankey, carrying on his business negotiations and his pastoral duties as diligently as ever. When Mr Wardlaw Thompson, the foreign secretary of the London Society, visited Hankey in March 1898, he was struck with the great change in Mackenzie's appearance; his hair had whitened rapidly, and his movements gave unmistakable signs of weakness. It had been long before felt that Mackenzie ought to have an assistant at Hankey, and this was urged upon Mr Thompson with great emphasis at this time; his own judgment clearly approved of that step, although obstacles arose to prevent the Directors from taking it.

In the month of April following, Mackenzie's mind was full of the approaching marriage of his third daughter, Elizabeth Douglas, to Mr Edward Sheilds of Kimberley. This event, which affected him very deeply, took place on the anniversary of his own wedding day, April 27th, 1898. He invited his friend, the Rev. William Dower of Port Elizabeth, to come and assist him. On the evening of the 26th, while the house was full of guests and gaiety, he took Mr Dower into the garden to arrange with him for the service on the morrow. When asked by him to take the main part and tie the knot Mr Dower demurred urging that Mackenzie should himself perform that sacred duty. But the latter, sitting down on a rustic seat, and making his friend sit beside him, held out his hand, and, pointing to the swellings on his fingers, said, "You know, Dower, that I have had some experience with medicine and have become familiar with some facts. Now you see these fingers? I know that when *that* is there it means that there is something (pointing to his heart) very seriously wrong in here. Accordingly," he continued, "I know that I ought not to undertake that part of the service which I might be unable to carry through to-morrow, and so I will just begin it and you will do the rest." To this, of course, there could be no answer, and his sorrowing friend braced himself for what was now for him a service of peculiar pathos and significance.

Two or three months later, Mackenzie found him-

self involved in heavier burdens than ever. Mr
J. S. Hultzer, who had for years acted as business
agent for the Society at Hankey, resigned his position, to engage in the publication of a newspaper at
Humansdorp. While Mr Hultzer agreed to conduct
necessary official duties from Humansdorp until a
successor was appointed, his removal nevertheless
entailed much additional care upon Mackenzie. The
latter was deeply interested in Mr Hultzer and his
new project, and he agreed to write an editorial
article every week for that paper. This usually
absorbed Mackenzie's time on Wednesday evenings.
Late on that afternoon the mail arrived from Port
Elizabeth, bringing him his home and colonial newspapers, as well as correspondence ; and he spent long
hours in studying the political situation before proceeding to discuss it in his next article, which he
wrote the same evening.

A collapse came on October 22nd, 1898, when
another " stroke " fell upon him, once more depriving
him of power over his limbs and for a little while
even of the power of speech. The latter he quickly
regained, the former returning more slowly. His
alarmed household at once telegraphed to his former
assistant, and dear friend, the Rev. Cullen Reed, now
a missionary in Matabeleland, who very promptly
responded, and reached Hankey in the month of
November. His presence there was an immense
relief to Mackenzie, as it enabled him to go away
for change and rest. The demands upon him may
be illustrated by the fact that only a fortnight after
his stroke he felt compelled to attend a meeting of
Hankey tenants and landowners, to plan for the
irrigation of a piece of land whose crops were
threatened with destruction ! In December, Mackenzie
and his wife left for Kimberley, where they stayed
with their son, Dr J. Eddie Mackenzie. Here he

received every attention, and was closely watched by more than one physician. Some progress was made, but many of his friends saw that improvement could only be slight and temporary. Letters began to pour in from all quarters, expressing sympathy with him, and many of these touched him deeply. He avoided political discussion as much as possible, refraining from reading the newspapers, and giving himself up to light literature, short walks, and quiet conversation with his family. He could not do more than write a few words to his children on other continents and in South Africa. The end was hastened by a rash deed which came from his parental love. His son, Mr J. D. Mackenzie, was engaged on an important case before one of the judges in Kimberley, and Mackenzie determined to go down to the court. He went out towards noon of a very hot day, became interested in the case, and sat for two or three hours following it closely. Then he walked all the way home, missing the carriage which his medical son brought to take him home. Almost immediately the final stroke fell. His strong constitution fought hard for some days, but the end came rapidly. He knew what the result must be ; yet, with what was no doubt his characteristic considerateness for others, he avoided all reference to it, meeting his death as he had met all the tasks of life, with unflinching courage, indomitable faith, and unwearied sympathy for those around him. On the 23rd of March 1899, the toiler fell on sleep and rested from his labours. He was buried in the cemetery at Kimberley two days later. The funeral was largely attended by the citizens of Kimberley, of all shades of opinion.

A memorial service was held in the Scottish Church at Kimberley on the Sunday following, March 26th, when a careful and generous estimate of Mackenzie's life was delivered by the Rev. Henry Richards, the minister of the church.

During those days, telegrams came in large numbers from all the Colony and from almost every continent ; tributes of admiration for his character and work appeared in all the English-speaking newspapers in South Africa, and in nearly every daily newspaper throughout Great Britain. Many of these obituary notices ran to considerable length, and were evidently written by men who had watched his career, and had formed a high opinion of his services to mankind and to the British Empire. Private letters were sent from all kinds of people, from Khame and from the High Commissioner, from fellow-workers in Church and State, from poor parishioners in Hankey, and from young men whom he had guided to the best life.

As soon as was possible many political associations and public bodies in South Africa passed resolutions concerning Mackenzie's services to the country and expressing sympathy with his widow and family.

For all who were connected in any way with Mackenzie, it has seemed a most strange fact that within eight months after his death his beloved South Africa was plunged into the shame and horror of the great war ; truly he was taken from the evil to come. About a year before, a friend asked him at Hankey whether he thought a war between the British and the Transvaal would be likely to occur. He stopped suddenly, stamped his stick emphatically upon the ground, with a gesture some of his friends remember, and said, " That would be an unspeakable disgrace." It would be surpassing all the responsibilities of a biographer to attempt to form a judgment of what Mackenzie would have said about the war if he had been alive and full of health and strength. It is safe to say that he would have thrown all his energies into the task of saving South Africa from such disaster ;

how he would have attempted it no one may try to estimate. It is sufficient to know that his heart would have brooded with an infinite sorrow, not only over the evil and indefensible policy of the Republics, but over all the blunders in the past relations of Great Britain to South Africa which at long last made this war appear all but inevitable. In public as in private life it is uncourteous to say, " I told you so." But it may not be ungracious for a biographer to say to those official guides of British South African policy who, ten and twenty years ago, were leading their country into this disaster, " He told you so." And not he alone, be it remembered. Mackenzie's was never a solitary voice, even when he spoke on behalf of the true Imperialism in the development of South African territories. He always had the joy and confidence which arose from knowing that strong minds agreed with his, and that men of wider political experience and higher official authority, both in South Africa and in Great Britain, believed in the principles which he expounded and in the policy for which he so passionately pled.

It is strange to look over Mackenzie's life and realise at once the variety of his achievements, and the curious fate that has fallen upon much of his work on its outward and earthly side. Khame's people were led, nearly twenty years ago, away from Shoshong to found a new capital at Palapye. Over at Shoshong itself the old mission station is abandoned, and its many buildings, on which several missionaries spent so much labour, have crumbled into ruins. Kuruman has fallen from being one of the capitals of Bechuana life to the position of a remote and uninfluential village ; and the educational institutions, which Mackenzie hoped to see expanding into great centres of influence over all the land, have dwindled into insignificance. When he engaged in the task of saving the interior of South Africa for the British Empire, he did work which indeed remains ; but he saw the honour and pleasure of realising it, snatched from his hands and transferred to those very men who had not aided but hindered its inception. When he had carried on his long years of toil in London and throughout England for the creation of a true Imperialism, the awakening of a sense of responsibility amongst Englishmen and Scotsmen for the whole of South Africa, he again saw the ideas which he had sown broadcast reaped as a rich harvest by those whose spirit was opposed to his own, and whose theory of Imperialism he considered untrue and unpractical. And, again, when he forsook this wider sphere of activity and went to the little corner at Hankey, it was to build up new hopes and to lay foundations of new schemes ; yet when well within sight of realising some of these, he was once more removed, his work put into the hands of others and the schemes which he planned left for them to fulfil.

But he would be short-sighted indeed and ignorant of the Christian valuation of life and a life's work, who would pronounce this varied career anything less than nobly successful. There is another side. To have moulded the life of a whole tribe directly and through its great chief, as Mackenzie moulded the Bamangwato ; to have exercised the wide educational and spiritual influence over all Bechuanaland which he did from Kuruman ; to have been the man who first forced Great Britain to face her God-given task of controlling the destinies of the entire region from the Cape to the Zambesi ; to have set forth from platform and pulpit, in magazine and volume, in newspaper and blue-book, the true principles of British policy in relation to all the races of that vast region ; to have gone back and done his best for one community, small though it was, in Hankey, while yet helping as he did to inspire the religious enthusiasm of the members of his own denomination throughout the country; with all and through all these great tasks to have maintained his own inner life of fellowship with God, unhindered unstained; and finally, under this influence to have ripened into a noble, beautiful character whom so many loved, and from whom so many lives received their purest impulses, their strongest faith—surely this deserves to have spoken over all its pages from first to last, even from the lips of man, that " kindly judgment " which he hoped to hear (and hears, we trust) from the lips of his Master, " Well done ! "

APPENDIX I

WRITINGS OF JOHN MACKENZIE

1. BOOKS

1. Ten Years North of the Orange River. A Story of Everyday Life and Work among the South African Tribes. From 1859 to 1869. Edinburgh: Edmonston & Douglas. 1871.

2. Day Dawn in Dark Places. London: Cassell & Company. 1883.

3. Austral Africa: Losing it or Ruling it. Being Incidents and Experiences in Bechuanaland, Cape Colony, and England. 2 volumes. London: Sampson Low, Marston, Searle & Rivington. 1887.

2. PAMPHLETS

1. London Missionary Society. Statement made by the Rev. J. Mackenzie, of Bechuanaland, at a Meeting held at Westminster Palace Hotel, July 25, 1882. London: Printed by Yates, Alexander, & Shepheard. 1882. Pp. 8.

2. Bechuanaland, the Transvaal, and England. A Statement and a Plea. London: Printed by Yates, Alexander & Shepheard. 1883. Pp. 14.

3. The Transvaal and the Bechuanas. Report of Public Meeting in Edinburgh. Edinburgh: Printed by Lorimer & Gillies. 1884.

4. The London Missionary Society in South Africa: A Retrospective Sketch. London: Published by the London Missionary Society. 1888. Pp. 21.

5. Austral Africa: Extension of British Influence in Trans-Colonial Territories. Proceedings at a Meeting of the London Chamber of Commerce. Assembled on the 14th May 1888 to hear an Address from Mr John Mackenzie. The Right Hon. J. Chamberlain, M.P., in the Chair. London: P. S. King & Son. 1888.

6. Austral Africa: Extension of British Influence in Trans-Colonial Territories (with Map). [Reprinted from "The Journal of the Manchester Geographical Society."] Pp. 31.

7. Bechuanaland and the Land of Ophir: A Paper read to the British Association at Bath in September 1888. From the "Proceedings of the Royal Geographical Society." November 1888. Pp. 10.

8. Condition of Bechuanaland. Statement of Facts. 1882-1890. London: Alexander & Shepheard.

9. The Christian Outlook in the Cape Colony: Being the Chairman's Address to the Congregational Union of South Africa. Port Elizabeth: Printed by H. C. Gray & Co. 1893. Pp. 22.

10. The Farmers and the Miners of the South African Republic. A Friendly Letter to President Kruger. [Reprinted from *Cape Times*, July 20, 1896.] Pp. 6 (double columns).

3. MAGAZINE ARTICLES

NINETEENTH CENTURY

South Africa and England. May 1883.

CONTEMPORARY REVIEW

England and South Africa. January 1884.

The Expansion of South Africa. November 1889.

The Chartered Company in South Africa. March 1897.

Bechuanaland. February 1898.

GOOD WORDS

Glances at South Africa. July, August, and September 1898.

IMPERIAL FEDERATION

Imperial Government in South Africa.   July 1888.

JOURNAL OF THE SOCIETY OF ARTS

Bechuanaland and Austral Africa.   March 1886

4. NEWSPAPER ARTICLES

Many Articles appeared either as Editorials or " From a Correspondent " in—

The Diamond Fields Advertiser.   1877-1882.

The Scotsman.   1883-1890.

The Leeds Mercury.   1884-1891.

And less frequently in other periodicals in Great Britain and South Africa.

5. MISSIONARY REPORTS

Extracts from Letters or special Articles appeared from time to time between 1859 and 1898 in—

The Chronicle of the London Missionary Society.

6. MEMORANDA AND LETTERS

Addressed either to the Foreign Office or the Colonial Office were printed in the Parliamentary Blue-Books between 1878 and 1891.   A complete list cannot be obtained.   It would be lengthy, and would include some elaborate communications.

INDEX

AFRICA, 13, 31, 36

"Afrikander Bond," 281, 287, 313, 363, 366, 382, 508 (its strong-hold)

Alexander, Rev. Dr Lindsay, 38, 261

America, United States of, 295

Annexation, what is it? 223, 224, 243, 244, 276

Arnold Forster, Mr H. O., 401, 416, 417, 460, 461

Ashley, Hon. Evelyn, 292, 293, 306, 385, 401

Ashton, Rev. William, 46, 185, 187, 188, 316

Austral Africa, 413-415, 420

BABOONS, strange habits of, 97

Baden Powell, Sir George, 388, 406, 408, 424

Baines, Mr Talbot, 304

Bamangwato (see also *Shoshong* and *Khame*), 68, 72, 75, 79-84, 96, 99, 100, 107-117, 178

Barkly, Sir Henry, 291, 292, 293, 294, 418, 419, 424, 425

Barkly West, 189

Beard, Mr Henry, 393, 489, 508, 509, 516, 533

Beaufort West, 49, 51, 53

Bechuanaland, 199-202 (disturbances in), 206, 239 (under British officers), 242, 245, 249 ff. (deserted), 275, 283, 317-320 (history, 1882-1884), 397, 425, 430, 431, 433, 434, 443, 444, 446, 447, 448, 463, 464, 467, 495, 496, 497, 510 (Cape Colony at war in), 514, 515

Bechuana People, their progress in civilization, 205, 221-223, 229, 230; their wrongs, 205, 206, 228

Bedford, 20, 21, 36

Belgium, King of, 439

Bible, revision of Sechuana, 437, 457-459, 466

Bodenstein, Mr, 337

Boers, two classes of, 270

Bower, Captain (now Sir) Graham R.N., consults with Mackenzie, 314; telegraphs Mr Rhodes about Mackenzie, 346, 347; a suggestion of, 353; removes British flag from Stellaland, 354; restores Stellaland flag to Niekerk, 354; "might have done good," 357; instructions modified, 359; his political "style," 366; and High Commissioner, 370; would help Mackenzie, 371; and Stellaland petition, 378, 379; becomes personal, 420

British Association, 426

British Empire, 525

British Government and Sand River Convention, 204; how forced north of Vaal River, 204; and border tribes, 207; and paramountcy of chiefs, 209; appealed to, 213; duty to Bechuanaland, 223, 224; proposed administration by, 229-230; responsibility for Bechuanaland, 239-241; invited by tribes, 241; "provisional" acceptance, 242, 249; a kingdom despised by, 249; deserts the Bechuans, 250, 251; the real question for, 253, 254; its border policy, 275; zigzag ways, 275; and supremacy, 276; its gifts to the Transvaal, 286; and Colonial co-operation, 289, 299; deserts Bechuanaland, 317; embitters Transvaal, 319; opposed by British subjects, 322; treats offer of territory coolly, 388; recalls Warren Expedition too soon, 389; its real question, 399; and Bechuanaland, 402; its responsibilities in South Africa, 411; and supremacy, 429; and a

553

for Bechuanas, 254 ; describes his Kuruman plan, 254 ; view of Transvaal responsibility for disturbances, 255, 256 ; leaves for England and meets Sir H. Robinson, 256 ; letters and documents, 228-231, 233-234, 234-238, 241, 243-246, 247-249, 250, 254-255, 255-256

Chapter X.—Arrival in England, 257 ; the public attitude towards South Africa, 257-258 ; his first public address, 258-259 ; re-union with children, 259, 260 ; Elgin once more, 260 ; ordination of his son, 260 ; on deputation work, 261 ; writes to Gladstone, 261 ; letter to W. Dale, 262-264 ; work in London, 264 ; among the editors, 265 ; on Mr Morley's and Mr Courtney's attitudes, 266-267 ; "as the Choctaws," 266 ; at the Colonial Office, 268 ; attitude to Transvaal, 269 ; varied efforts, 269-270 ; Christmas holiday, 271 ; the arguments he met, 271 ; appeal from Mankoroane, 272 ; writes a pamphlet, 272 ; encouraged by Lord Derby, 273 ; celebrates silver wedding, 273 ; article in *Nineteenth Century*, 274-277 ; on "clear-out" policy, 277 ; letters and documents, etc., 259, 262-264, 266, 270, 272, 273, 274-278

Chapter XI.—Writes "Day Dawn in Dark Places," 279 ; preparing for Transvaal delegates, 279, 280 ; his alarm at their proposals, 281 ; explains their real aim to be supremacy, 281-283 ; their attitude to missions, 283 ; gains support of *Pall Mall Gazette* and *Spectator*, 284 ; exposes Mr Kruger's "history," 284 ; his share in the Conference, 286 ; proposes plan for governing Bechuanaland, 289 ; is encouraged by Lord Derby, 290 ; addresses meeting at Mansion House, 291 ; describes it, 292 ; describes interview with Lord Derby and Mr Ashley, 293 ; opinion of Frere, 294 ;

speeches at Edinburgh, 295 ; article in *Contemporary Review*, 295-296 ; his policy supported by Sir H. Barkly and Sir Bartle Frere, 297 ; hesitatingly accepted by Lord Derby, 297, 300 ; opposes cession of territory to overburdened Transvaal Government, 299 ; is offered Deputy-Commissionership, 300 ; his letters of acceptance, 301-303 ; his motives attacked, 303 ; congratulations, 304 ; cordial minute of London Missionary Society, 305, 306 ; farewell breakfast, 306 ; visits Frere on his deathbed, 307, 308 ; sails for the Cape, 308 ; appearance and work described by Mr Stead, 309-311 ; letters and articles, 281-283, 285, 290, 292-294, 295-297, 301, 303, 305-306, 307-308

Chapter XII.—His spirit in new enterprise, 312 ; reception of his appointment at Cape Town, 313 ; describes it, 314 ; reception at Kimberley, 315 ; "sees both sides," 316 ; Transvaal expansion weakens the Transvaal, 319 ; meets difficulties among British at Kimberley, 321, 322 ; describes land-hunger as his chief obstacle, 323 ; and the intrigues of opponents, 324, 325 ; how he invaded a hostile republic, 325, 326 ; successful negotiations with Mankoroane, 326 ; reception at Vryburg, 328 ; announces Protectorate, 328 ; his negotiations with Stellalanders, 329 ; appoints Van Niekerk as Assistant-Commissioner, 331 ; his success, 331 ; arrives at Mafeking, 332 ; meets the Boer filibusters, 333 ; dangerous trip to Zeerust, 334 ; completes tour, 336 ; reaches Kuruman, 336 ; Taungs, 336 ; friendly welcome at Vryburg, 337 ; "the restorer of peace," 338 ; Boers hoist British flag, 338 ; summoned to Cape Town, 339 ; his recall and its promoters, 340 ; went north with confidence of Robinson,